HUMANITARIANS AT WAR

THE RED CROSS IN THE SHADOW OF THE HOLOCAUST

GERALD STEINACHER

OXFORD

UNIVERSITY PRESS

OXFORD
UNIVERSITY PRESS

Great Clarendon Street, Oxford, OX2 6DP,
United Kingdom

Oxford University Press is a department of the University of Oxford.
It furthers the University's objective of excellence in research, scholarship,
and education by publishing worldwide. Oxford is a registered trade mark of
Oxford University Press in the UK and in certain other countries

First Edition published in 2017

Impression: 1

Published in the United States of America by Oxford University Press
198 Madison Avenue, New York, NY 10016, United States of America

British Library Cataloguing in Publication Data

Data available

Library of Congress Control Number: 2016945572

ISBN 978–0–19–870493–5

Printed in Great Britain by
Clays Ltd, St Ives plc

Preface

This book looks at the events of the Holocaust and the impact in the immediate postwar years for the humanitarians of the Red Cross. It is not so much a book about the Red Cross in the Second World War and its humanitarian work for prisoners of war (POW), which the Swiss-based International Committee of the Red Cross (ICRC) considered its main responsibility and where it achieved much. Readers may read the first chapter for a short overview of this topic and consult the rich bibliography for further reading. This book was written for an interested and educated British, US, and Canadian audience, but not necessarily historians. The book therefore also includes many references to the history of the American Red Cross, US, and British policies towards Switzerland and the ICRC. Given that there are very few recent studies in English about the ICRC and the Holocaust, the author has invested much effort to translate and therefore integrate a wide number of literature and research findings from German, Italian, and French-language publications.

Humanitarians at War is not a super-detailed institutional history but a new interpretation of the critical role of the Swiss organization—tightly intertwined with the creation of the little-understood Geneva Conventions—in creating an international dialogue about the rules of war in the twentieth century, the treatment of both combatant and civilians prisoners, the limits and possibilities of 'neutral' status during wartime, and the possibilities of transnational/international organizations in publicizing, ignoring, or stemming genocide. This book is written for anyone interested in the history of Europe, the Holocaust, and Jewish history, as well as human rights, humanitarian aid, and humanitarian-aid organizations.

'Promise me. Promise me you will never be just a bystander.'

Lou Leviticus (alias Rudi Van Der Roest),
Holocaust survivor 1931–2015

Contents

List of Illustrations

Cast of Characters

Folke Bernadotte, Swedish diplomat and nobleman. President of the Swedish Red Cross; rescued thousands of Scandinavian and Jewish concentration camp inmates in the waning days of the Third Reich; leading Red Cross humanitarian and United Nations Peace Mediator to Jerusalem, where he was murdered in 1948.

Friedrich Born, delegate of the International Committee of the Red Cross (ICRC) in Budapest. Thanks to his personal commitment and, together with other neutral diplomats and philanthropists, he helped to save thousands of lives.

Carl Jacob Burckhardt, Swiss historian and diplomat. From 1937 to 1939 High Commissioner of the League of Nations in the Free City of Danzig/Gdańsk. Vice-president of the ICRC, from 1945 to 1948 officially its president. From 1945 to 1949 he served as Swiss ambassador in Paris.

Albert E. Clattenburg Jr, US State Department official and diplomat. Expert on prisoner of war (POW) questions and international law inside the State Department; head of US delegation to the Geneva meeting in 1947; 1948 diplomat at the American Embassy Lisbon.

Adolf Eichmann, SS officer and Holocaust perpetrator. Escaped 1950 to Argentina; 1961 trial in Jerusalem.

Suzanne Ferrière, member of the ICRC, deputy director of the International Migration Service.

Roger Gallopin, Swiss lawyer and ICRC official. Director of the ICRC's division for POWs, internees, and civilians.

Edouard de Haller, Swiss diplomat. Honorary board member of the ICRC; 1942–1948 Swiss delegate for international aid initiatives; Swiss delegate at the Stockholm conference 1948.

Leland Harrison, US diplomat. 1937–1947 ambassador to Switzerland.

Heinrich Himmler, German officer and political activist. Close collaborator of Adolf Hitler, as chief of the SS one of the top Nazi criminals.

Max Huber, Swiss lawyer and Judge of the Permanent Court of International Justice. Served as the Court's President from 1925 to 1927; President of the ICRC in Geneva from 1928 to 1944 (from 1945 to 1947 president ad interim).

George C. Marshall, US politician and general. Promoter of the Marshall Plan for European recovery; US Secretary of State in 1947–1948; in 1949 served a short term as president of the American Red Cross; 1950 Secretary of Defense.

Saly Mayer, Swiss Jewish leader and representative of the American Jewish Joint Distribution Committee in Switzerland. Worked very closely with the ICRC on relief for Jewish victims.

Basil O'Connor, US Lawyer, philanthropist and close confidant of US president Franklin Delano Roosevelt. From 1944 to 1949 head of the American Red Cross and from 1945 to 1950 Chairman of the League of Red Cross Societies (the umbrella organization for national Red Cross societies).

John W. Pehle, assistant to the Secretary of the Treasury; 1944–1945 director of the War Refugee Board (WRB).

Wallenberg Raoul, Swedish businessman and humanitarian. Saved thousands of Jews from certain death during rescue operations in Budapest 1944–1945; in 1945 he was taken by the Soviets and probably died after a few years in captivity.

Gerhart Riegner, German representative of the World Jewish Congress in neutral Switzerland. Author of the 1942 Riegner telegram that provided reliable information about the Nazi plan to systematically murder all European Jews.

Eleanor Roosevelt, US diplomat and human rights activist. As First Lady she was very active with the American Red Cross during the Second World War; in 1945 appointed as US delegate to the United Nations General Assembly promoting the Human Rights agenda.

Heinrich Rothmund, Swiss government official, longtime head of the aliens branch of the police immigration authorities. Favoured a tough stance on Jewish refugees coming to Switzerland; from 1945 to 1947 Swiss delegate of the Intergovernmental Committee on Refugees (IGCR).

Paul Ruegger, Swiss diplomat. Ambassador to Fascist Italy until 1942; from 1944 to 1948 Swiss ambassador in London; 1948–1955 president of the ICRC. Under his presidency the reform of the Geneva Conventions was completed and the position of the ICRC much strengthened.

Johannes (Jean-Etienne de) von Schwarzenberg, Austrian diplomat. 1940–1945 worked for the ICRC in Geneva and eventually in charge of aid initiatives for Jewish victims of the Nazi regime; after the war Austrian ambassador in Italy.

Ernst von Weizsäcker, German diplomat and ambassador. Leading official in the Nazi German Foreign Office; 1943–1945 German ambassador to the Holy See, one of the prominent defendants in the subsequent Nuremberg war crimes trials.

Introduction

When future historians are able to analyse the circumstances which made possible the annihilation of one-third of the Jewish people—the bulk of European Jewry—as well as the barbarous slaughter of untold masses of other civilizations during the Second World War, there is one set of problems which will give them the greatest difficulty: Where was the enlightened, civilized world, particularly the humane, neutral influences, while all this was going on? Where above all, was the International Red Cross Committee [ICRC]? For the ICRC has a specific obligation, owing its essential character as laid down in its statutes, to safeguard the hard-won principles of civilized conduct in war-time.

These sentences were written and published by a Jewish survivor of the Holocaust in May 1945, just weeks after the liberation. These questions formulated by him 'for future historians' are at the core of this book. What did one of the oldest and most prominent humanitarian organizations do during the Shoah? What were the consequences for its (in)actions during the genocide? What would happen to the hard-won rules of warfare and protection of civilians? Who would safeguard them in the future now that the Red Cross had failed so tragically? Did nineteenth-century humanitarianism still have a future after Auschwitz and if so, who should carry on the torch? *Humanitarians at War* addresses all these questions.

Purpose of this Study

In this book I examine the challenges faced by the Swiss-based International Committee of the Red Cross (ICRC) during the crucial years of 1944–1950 and the organization's handling of these challenges. I find that a series of crises—financial, leadership, and reputational—severely damaged and shook the organization's foundation. At this time, the future of this important humanitarian organization did not look bright.

Humanitarians at War shows that the ICRC's actions and attitudes after 1945 were in reaction to the challenges presented by both the Holocaust and the new postwar international order. These challenges included: (1) the competition between Switzerland and Sweden in the humanitarian arena, (2) the revelation of the ICRC's failure to aid victims during the Holocaust, and (3) the ICRC's attempts to regain its humanitarian reputation.

First, the ICRC was affected by the competition between neutral countries, especially Sweden and Switzerland, in the humanitarian arena. During the Second World War the Swedish and Swiss governments were accused of not remaining neutral, but rather openly supporting Nazi Germany. After D-Day and with an Allied victory in sight, these governments' reaction was to quickly redirect their policies. In order to improve their standing in the world, they had to change their policies and humanitarian aid was one way to achieve this.

Since by 1944 most European Jews under Nazi domination had already been murdered, Swiss and Swedish humanitarians and their governments focused their rescue efforts on Hungarian Jews, the last remaining national Jewish community now facing deportation and annihilation. Carl J. Burckhardt, since January of 1945 president of the ICRC, understood the message. The ICRC seized this moment under pressure from Washington, which made it very clear that the US government would not tolerate the ICRC's lack of action and hiding behind legal constraints.

This humanitarian competition between Sweden and Switzerland, between the Swedish Red Cross and the Swiss-based ICRC, also turned into a race between two ambitious men: Burckhardt and Count Folke Bernadotte, the president of the Swedish Red Cross. At the end of this humanitarian competition, Swedish successes overshadowed the Swiss, and the Swedish Red Cross gained enormous respect, admiration, and moral standing. Therefore, Sweden emerged from the Second World War with a much better reputation than Switzerland, at least in the eyes of the victorious Allies. Sweden was ultimately seen as the good neutral, while Switzerland was painted as the duplicitous and opportunistic one—with long-lasting consequences.

As the ICRC urgently needed to improve its image, it attempted to do so through new aid initiatives for civilian post-1945 refugees—something it had tragically failed at during the war. The ICRC decided to help German expellees and other uprooted refugees unrecognized by the Allies. With tenuous legal authority and limited experience in issuing refugee papers, the ICRC began issuing its own travel documents to (ethnic) German displaced persons in February 1945. Soon, thousands of former Nazi collaborators and SS men from all over Europe, including known Holocaust perpetrators such as Adolf Eichmann, availed themselves of these documents. Various government agencies, especially the US State Department, secretly pressured ICRC leaders to rectify the situation, warning that the reputation of their organization could be compromised. Given that the ICRC was already under heavy attack for not doing more to help Jewish concentration-camp inmates and refugees during the war, this was a potentially explosive issue that posed a serious dilemma: should the ICRC stop helping all refugees simply because a few 'bad apples' had cropped up among them?

Second, in the immediate postwar period the Swiss-based ICRC faced a series of crises. Switzerland's role and the shortcomings of the ICRC during the Holocaust had damaged its credibility. The damage was significant enough for Sweden's National Red Cross Society to call for the ICRC and Switzerland to be replaced as the guardians and promoters of the Geneva Conventions (international rules of warfare) and Red Cross ideals. What if the Red Cross headquarters had been in Sweden? Would they have done more and earlier? After all, Sweden had helped rescue almost all Danish Jews in October 1943 during a dashing rescue operation. The ICRC found itself in a major existential crisis and came close to losing its unique status. Folke Bernadotte soon became a star in the humanitarian arena between 1945 and 1948. He was all over the media, helping in Greece, Hungary, Germany, and finally in Israel/Palestine. His opinion carried weight, especially with the Americans, but even the Soviets respected him. Bernadotte's proposals to internationalize the ICRC or to change its role found widespread support with other national Red Cross Societies. Would Sweden take the lead and would the Geneva Conventions as a result turn into the Stockholm Conventions? This possibility alone was a national humiliation for Switzerland and its self-perception.

But the crisis of the ICRC was also a crisis of humanitarianism. It was a crisis of nineteenth-century humanitarian ideas. It brought to the forefront the question of whether Red Cross founder Henry Dunant's ideas still have a place on a twentieth-century battlefield. Given the world's recent experience with genocide and atomic weapons (Hiroshima and Nagasaki), the

Geneva Conventions seemed hopelessly outdated. Even the president of the American Red Cross was doubtful, and Bernadotte soon looked into new ventures under the flag of the United Nations (UN). He was to become the first UN peace mediator in Palestine/Israel, where he was murdered in 1948.

Ultimately a number of factors came together to resolve this crisis. Central to the survival and viability of the ICRC was the successful reform process of the new Geneva Conventions. The ICRC with its expertise and experts took the lead in this effort even before the war in Europe ended. The successful reform process of the Geneva Convention proved vital, not just for the ICRC's survival, but for the future of humanitarianism as well.

The State of Research

Existing research convincingly documents the failures of the ICRC during the Second World War, including its silence on the Holocaust explored in works by Jean-Claude Favez, Arieh Ben-Tov, Paul Stauffer, and others. In contrast, there are very few publications in English about the organization's fate and activities in the immediate postwar years. My research contributes to the academic literature on the factors that shaped the new standards of international human rights and humanitarian standards in the immediate postwar years, namely 1945–1950.[1] The Nuremberg principles of 1945, the Genocide Convention in 1948, and the Universal Declaration of Human Rights in 1948 are often considered the result of lessons learned from the Second World War and the Holocaust, as 'firewalls against barbarism' (Michael Ignatieff). This is also true for the New Geneva Conventions of 1949. However, my research suggests that this exceptional innovation in humanitarian law was also an important part of the ICRC's (and the Swiss government's) overall strategy to strengthen and legitimize its (humanitarian) standing in the world. This book, however, is not a step-by-step account of the making of the Geneva Convention, but about internal international Red Cross power struggles and humanitarian politics.

My research also informs our understanding of what motivates the policies of humanitarian organizations. I show that these organizations are often driven by self-interest and that their policies are at least in part shaped by power struggles and fights for influence. As such, my findings will have relevance to questions of how international aid organizations have responded (and may respond in the future) in times of war and genocide, and how and why their policies have evolved as a result.

Sources and Methods

The book's narrative is heavily based on archival sources. In addition to the files of the International Tracing Service and the ICRC in Geneva as well as the Swiss Federal Archives, I undertook extensive archival research, especially in US and Israeli archives. Of particular use were the records of the American Red Cross and the State Department at the US National Archives. In addition, the rich archival holdings at the United States Holocaust Memorial Museum and at the International Institute for Holocaust Studies at Yad Vashem/Jerusalem provide the backbone of this project. Of particular use were the 60,000 microfilmed pages from the ICRC archives relating to concentration camps, Jewish victims, and postwar refugee policy. Concerning the wartime years, the records of the American Jewish Joint Distribution Committee were a very valuable source. Archives in Yad Vashem and at the Central Zionist Archives in Jerusalem gave me a better understanding of the work of the World Jewish Congress and its relationship with the ICRC. I also made good use of the personal records of ICRC presidents Paul Ruegger, Carl J. Burckhardt, and Max Huber conserved in Zurich and in Basel. This book provides new insights into their decision-making, especially into Ruegger's presidency, which has hitherto been under-researched. The correspondence between the Swiss government and the Red Cross presidency was very useful, as were the files relating to the history of Swiss refugee policy, conserved at the Federal Archives in Bern.

This book is in many ways a history from above, looking at the leadership of the ICRC and its decision-making. This also holds true for Folke Bernadotte of Sweden and Basil O'Connor from the US, two of the other major players in the humanitarian world after 1945. Given the many US archival sources reaching from the American Red Cross to the State Department, the book has a strong US perspective. I also looked at central figures in the history of the American Red Cross ranging through the Clara Barton papers at the Library of Congress to George C. Marshall's papers in Lexington (VA). The role of the American Red Cross in all these discussions and events from the Second World War during the Geneva Conference of 1949 is clearly outlined. Much space is devoted to the president of the

American Red Cross, Basil O'Connor, on whom no authoritative biography exists to this day. There is also no study about the relations between the American Red Cross (AMRC) and the ICRC. Also, relatively little is known about the interaction between the US government and the AMRC. This book helps to fill this gap. The Swiss sources, not least those relating to the Swiss government and ICRC officials are, by contrast, much richer. I tried to make the sources communicate with each other as much as possible to give the reader a unique insight, which the political and humanitarian actors at the time did often not have. Therefore, I also systematically analysed the *New York Times* and *Wall Street Journal* between 1944 and 1950 as well as Swiss newspapers of the time. I tried to include the Swedish side as much as possible through secondary literature, Swedish newspapers, oral history interviews, and other Swedish sources, the publications of the Commission on Jewish Assets in Sweden at the time of the Second World War (1999) and through contacts with individual experts on Swedish history.

This research question grew out of my last book *Nazis on the Run*, where I dedicated one chapter to the history of the ICRC and its travel papers based on new research results. After this project I became ever more interested in the history of the ICRC. Soon I wanted to learn more about the history of the Red Cross and its role during the Holocaust. In an earlier study *Rotes Kreuz und Hakenkreuz*, I looked almost exclusively at the wartime activities of the ICRC by summarizing the existing research and relying on mostly German language publications. It helped me (and I hope a wider, non-academic audience) get a good overview of the secondary literature on Red Cross aid for Holocaust victims. In contrast to my previous works, *Humanitarians at War* takes a completely new approach. Based on primary sources it focuses mainly on the *aftermath* of the Holocaust and the consequences of wartime experiences for the new world order both in and outside the Red Cross family.

In 2009 I taught a course at the University of Lucerne in Switzerland on the 'Red Cross and the Swastika: The Red Cross, Switzerland and National Socialism', which was well attended. This was the first time that I had a chance to address a wide range of issues related to the Second World War, the ICRC and Switzerland. The work with my students, their feedback and questions, but also the advice of fellow Swiss colleagues such as Aram Mattioli encouraged me to work on this new book project. At this time I also started to study an abundance of secondary sources about Switzerland as well as the ICRC, and I consulted a number of archives. I stayed at the former training centre and boarding school for nurses, 'Theodosianum' in Limmattal, just outside Zurich, whose library had many popular and some rare books about Red Cross work, which I read with great interest. In 2014 the building of the nurse's training school was torn down. The place where this research project first took shape therefore no longer exists. History moves on and my research focus has widened. Since then many questions kept me restless, researching and searching for answers. This book is the attempt to answer some of them.

In the following pages, I will show how the ICRC was able to survive a major financial, leadership, authority, and institutional crisis, and ultimately shift its role. Because it was able to do so, it remains one of the oldest humanitarian organizations still in operation. Humanitarian intervention can take place only after careful deliberations, which must take into account numerous competing interests. My study underscores the importance of knowing the history of humanitarian organizations and the politics behind their decisions in the face of war crimes and unfolding genocides. This topic is vital for understanding global politics in the twenty-first century.

I

The Birth of an Idea

The Red Cross is one of the largest humanitarian organizations in the world today. It is omnipresent and at the same time little understood. Its ubiquitous namesake emblem, visible on ambulances and hospitals around the world, is commonly associated with war relief and aid efforts in disasters. But how did it all begin?

The Red Cross was a product of nineteenth-century humanitarianism. It was originally conceived as a way of humanizing war by helping reduce the suffering of soldiers. But its mission eventually grew to include a concern for the suffering of civilians in both war and peace, and the provision of disaster relief. The greatest achievement of the Red Cross was the Geneva Conventions, regulating the rules of warfare and therefore laying the basis for international humanitarian law. The Red Cross and the Geneva Conventions proved very successful during the First World War in protecting prisoners of war and wounded soldiers. But the genocides and civil wars of the early twentieth century tested their capabilities and exposed the limits of the humanitarian organization. The Red Cross' failure to address the Holocaust has been widely documented and studied. But the debate within the organization brought about by this failure and the consequences of managing that crisis are less known. To understand them, one needs to take a look further back in history to the foundation of the Red Cross, the early challenges it faced, and the way it changed in response. In this chapter I trace the organization's humble beginnings in its Swiss homeland.

The Founding of the Red Cross

The idea of the Red Cross was conceived on the battlefields of Europe. In 1859 Henry Dunant, a Swiss businessman from Geneva, witnessed the fierce battle between Austrian and Sardinian–French troops near the town of Solferino, just south of Lake Garda in northern Italy. When the slaughter ended, soldiers of the French and Austrian emperors and their allies were left on the battlefield dying and alone. Only a few military medical personnel remained to help the wounded, not uncommon during wars of the time. Some of the local population, especially clergy and women, came to the soldiers' aid and set up improvised field hospitals. Deeply disturbed by what he saw, Dunant put his business obligations aside and joined them, organizing the provision of medical services at the Solferino battlefield. With 40,000 men dead or dying, neither he nor the other volunteers could do much to reduce the suffering.

Figure 1.1. Swiss businessman Henry Dunant from Geneva, founder of the Red Cross movement.

Dunant's life-changing experience in Italy culminated in an important realization: there seemed to be a need for a permanent humanitarian organization that would care for wounded soldiers with better planning and more resources. His 1862 book, *A Memory of Solferino*, chronicled what happened on the battlefield and quickly became a bestseller, effectively popularizing Dunant's humanitarian agenda. The battle of Solferino would turn out to be a watershed moment for modern humanitarianism.[1]

On his return to Geneva in 1863, Dunant, along with four fellow citizens who shared his ideas, founded a new private association that was to put his agenda into action. With this the world's oldest extant secular international humanitarian organization came into existence. The association was later to become the International Committee of the Red Cross (ICRC). Its symbol, a stark red cross on a white background, was chosen soon after its founding. Reversing the Swiss national flag, a white cross on a red background, the association's symbol was a tribute to the founders' nation. From the outset the ICRC was a private association operating under Swiss law. Its decision-making committee was eventually expanded to a maximum of twenty-five members, men and women, but always Swiss nationals. While the composition of the ICRC's helm has never been international, its activities have always reached far beyond Swiss borders.

Zeitgeist of Humanitarianism

The foundation of the Red Cross was part of a wider nineteenth-century humanitarian movement in Europe and the Americas. The movement derived its name from the Latin word *humanitas*, meaning kindness, and took on the broad mission of promoting human welfare. Humanitarians were often active in charitable and relief organizations, including such groups as the Quakers, the Salvation Army, and the Red Cross. The zeitgeist of the time was particularly receptive to humanitarian agendas. Social, political, legal, and health reform movements were gaining traction. There was a rising popular support for a number of previously controversial ideas: suffrage, prison reform, poverty amelioration, sanitation initiatives, religious tolerance, wider education, abolition of slavery, and the banning of torture and public executions, among others.[2]

The humanitarian mission of reducing human suffering and bettering humanity was to be applied to war as well. Chivalry and certain agreed customs of war between 'civilized' Europeans were now to distinguish organized killing from 'savage barbarian' violence. At the basis of this idea lay a certain optimism about spreading European civilization all over the globe, therefore making wars less brutal.[3]

Events during the Crimean War (1853–1856) further illustrate this point. In the Crimean War, the Russian Empire fought over influence in the Holy Land against a coalition of France, Britain, the Ottoman Empire, and Sardinia. Russia wanted the Orthodox Church to control the holy sites of Christianity, while France backed the Catholic Church's claims. During the war a number of battles were waged and thousands of soldiers were wounded. As in the battle at Solferino, these soldiers received poor medical care, if any. After British social reformer Florence Nightingale got news of the lack of care for the wounded soldiers, she led a group of nurses to the conflict area. On witnessing the unsanitary conditions in a field hospital in Istanbul she reached out to the British public and found widespread support for her cause. A new hospital was set up and the mortality rate of the wounded was drastically reduced. Inspired by what she was able to achieve during the Crimean War, once back home in England Nightingale professionalized the nursing system and introduced basic hygiene standards (for example, hand washing with soap) to prevent infections.

As was the case with most humanitarian initiatives of the nineteenth century, the Red Cross movement drew heavily on the Judeo-Christian idea of *caritas*, the importance of performing works of mercy and charity.[4] This is reflected in the movement's original Latin motto, *inter arma caritas* (in war, mercy). There can be no doubt that the source of this inspiration was Dunant's evangelical Christian background. Furthermore, many of the ICRC's early pioneering members were motivated by the New Testament parable of the Good Samaritan and held in high regard the principle of 'impartial assistance to anyone who is suffering, whether friend or foe'.[5] The idea of assisting *all* suffering people without taking nationality into account was central to the movement, as this statement from a Red Cross publication suggests: 'I am blind to the uniform you wear, and see only your wound, that I may tend it. I am deaf to the language you speak, and hear only your cry, that I may bring you comfort. I know not who you are; I only know your distress.'[6] But impartiality proved difficult for the Red Cross to maintain. Independence and neutrality, two other core principles of the movement, were at times pushed aside as well, especially during wartime, as we will see later in this book.[7]

Dunant's success in growing his humanitarian ideas from a notion conceived on the battlefields of Solferino into an international movement was no small achievement for a private citizen. But he aspired for more and soon became involved in various other humanitarian and philanthropic projects. These endeavours consumed his time and attention, which led him to neglect his business commitments and eventually file for bankruptcy. Ironically, the bankruptcy scandal turned Dunant into an outcast in Geneva high society and he was forced out from his own creation, the ICRC. It was not until the final years of his life that he was rescued from obscurity and honoured with the 1901 Nobel Peace Prize.[8]

The award brought to the forefront a fundamental conflict at the core of the Red Cross' mission. Should it help spread peace around the globe, or should it limit its activities to humanizing war?

Geneva Conventions

After the founding meeting of the Red Cross in Geneva in 1863, the Swiss government called for a diplomatic conference to give the newly founded organization's ideas the binding form of a treaty. While Red Cross officials could propose and draft new rules, they had no power to implement them on a global scale. It was up to national governments to turn these rules into international law, which they did at a two-week meeting in Geneva in August 1864. The treaty, now commonly known as the First Geneva Convention, was signed by twelve European states of the time: Baden, Belgium, Denmark, France, Hesse, Italy, Netherlands, Portugal, Prussia, Spain, Switzerland, and Wuerttemberg.

This First Geneva Convention aimed at the 'Amelioration of the Condition of the Wounded in Armies in the Field'. The signatory nations agreed to respect the neutrality of medical personnel, ambulances and hospitals, which were to be clearly marked with the protection emblem of a red cross on a white background. The protection extended to both medical personnel that were members of armed forces, as well as civilian medical volunteers. The civilian volunteers were organized into national humanitarian aid societies, which were connected through the ICRC in Geneva.

With only ten articles, the First Geneva Convention was rather short, but nonetheless it was sufficient to outline a basic framework of humanitarian law under the oversight of the Red Cross.[9] The conference in 1864 was followed by a second one in 1868, which added provisions for the wounded and ship-wrecked naval personnel at sea. Other conventions followed, as we will see.

While the First Geneva Conventions have gained prominence for helping usher in an age of humanitarian law, it is important to acknowledge that it was not the first nor the only effort along these lines. While the ICRC was working on the First Geneva Convention, on the other side of the Atlantic similar ideas were shaping the laws of war as well. During the American Civil War the German-American legal scholar Franz Lieber was asked to formulate a code of conduct for the Union armies. Now that fighting was to be with Southern gentlemen, and no longer with Native Americans or Mexicans, there was a sudden impetus to define what constituted proper treatment of POWs. Captured Confederate soldiers were not to be killed or tortured, but instead treated humanely. The Lieber Code inspired European lawmakers on the rules of warfare, which resulted in the Hague Treaties of 1899 and 1907. The Hague Treaties together with the Geneva Conventions played an important role in the ICRC's work, especially during the First World War.

First Experiences with Wars in Europe

The German-Danish war of 1864 was the first armed conflict after the ratification of the First Geneva Convention. Prussia claimed Schleswig-Holstein, a predominantly German-speaking area under Danish rule, and a confrontation followed. For the first time ICRC delegates were sent to a conflict to observe the warring parties' compliance with the Convention. The delegates carried letters of recommendation from the Swiss government and were recognizable by their Red Cross armbands. Their mission was to serve as neutral intermediaries between belligerents. The conflict was also the first test run for the Prussian Red Cross founded in 1864, which dispatched volunteer doctors and nurses to the war zones. Although the ICRC and Prussian Red Cross made efforts to follow through on their mission, their success was limited—they were still young organizations with no established recognition among the generals on the battlefield.

With the German-Danish war of 1864 being of relatively small scale and short length, the first real test of the ICRC was the Franco-Prussian War of 1870–1871. This conflict between the two Continental European military superpowers of the time, the Kingdom of Prussia and the French Empire, meant a clash of mass armies and modern weaponry. At the outset of the fighting both countries attempted to adhere to the Geneva Conventions, but this proved difficult since the specifics of the Conventions were still not well known among the combatants on the ground. The ICRC tried to organize a field ambulance service, gather information about those missing or killed, and arrange correspondence between POWs and their families. But as a result of communication problems, rapid army advances and chaotic retreats, the organization was able to accomplish very little. However, the end of the Franco-Prussian War of 1870–1871 saw the ICRC expand its field of operations.

Both the German-Danish war of 1864 and the Franco-Prussian War of 1870–1871 exposed the challenges that the ICRC and Red Cross societies would have to face again and again when attempting to adhere to impartiality and neutrality, two of the organizations' core principles. During these wars, the ICRC and Red Cross societies were confronted with the suspicion of the warring states. Red Cross volunteers were suspected of being spies or sending war materials to the enemy under the organization's cover. This made it difficult to ensure the cooperation of the opposing armies, for instance in gaining access to places under siege or crossing military frontiers. What exacerbated the problem during these early wars was that the red cross, the organization's protection symbol, was at times abused by the military, using it to protect military vehicles or to transport weapons and ammunition.

Even though many accused the ICRC and Red Cross societies of violating their principles of neutrality and impartiality, being perceived as upholding them posed challenges as well. It significantly impeded the organization's attempts to secure funding and a network of advocates. The late nineteenth century was a time when nationalism was very strong, so impartial aid for friend and foe alike was seen as unpatriotic, dangerous and simply wrong.

It is important to recognize that the charge of abandoning impartiality and neutrality was not levied equally against the ICRC and the national Red Cross societies—outsiders made a clear distinction between the two. Early on in their history, the national societies conducted activities on a small scale and helped mostly their own fellow nationals, which is why they were often thought to be promoting national interests. In contrast, the ICRC benefited from its association with the Swiss government, which was known for its long-standing neutrality. As a result, the ICRC in Geneva, as opposed to the various national Red Cross societies, was more often accepted as a neutral intermediary by warring parties and its services were more often expected to be impartial. But maintaining a reputation for impartiality and neutrality challenged the ICRC again and again over its long history. As we will see in this book, the challenge was particularly difficult to overcome when the organization's home nation was fighting for survival. With Switzerland under the threat of attack, many expected the full support and involvement of its own ICRC rather than a refusal to take sides.

Expansion and Nationalization of the Movement

The first national Red Cross societies were private organizations formed by philanthropic minded citizens. But in the age of nation-state building and nationalism this quickly changed, as the example of Italy shows. The Italian Red Cross society was founded against the background of the creation of the Italian nation state in the 1860s. Established in Milan in 1864, the society was soon taken under the wing of the newly created Italy. With that, it ceased being a private organization and instead became a government agency expected to be an auxiliary of the nation's armed forces in times of need. The Italian model was soon adopted by other nations and most national Red Cross societies became closely linked with their respective governments.[10]

The European Red Cross movement inspired similar ambitious projects across the Atlantic. The beginnings of humanitarian relief work in the US date back to the Civil War, 1861–1865. But it was after a trip to Switzerland, that the American humanitarian Clara Barton and a circle of her acquaintances founded the American Red Cross in 1881. The organization's initial focus was on peacetime relief work.[11] This was a departure from the original Red Cross idea of aiding war victims and caused tensions between Washington and Geneva. But Barton succeeded in her campaign to bring her native country into the Geneva Conventions and the United States ratified the treaty in 1882. Just as in Europe, the American government soon began to exert its influence over Barton's private initiative. The charter of 1905 provided that six members of the organization's Central Committee, including the Chairman, be appointed by the President of the United States. The President often chose members of the U.S. government and military as his appointees, and the American Red Cross often served as an auxiliary medical service in wartime.

Some ICRC officials initially assumed that only Western societies would be able to fully understand and adhere to its standards of 'civilized' warfare.[12] But with the Ottoman Empire and Japan applying for admission in 1868 and 1887 respectively, the core ideas of the ICRC spread beyond the Western world.[13] With this expansion came the addition of new symbols to the organization's now widely recognized red cross. The red crescent was uni-laterally introduced by the Ottoman Empire on the basis that a cross might offend the sensitivities of Muslims. Similarly, the red cross was later replaced by a red star of David in Israel. Although the ICRC originally insisted on retaining the red cross symbol and emphasized that it was never meant as an allusion to the Christians' cross, nevertheless the Christian origins of the movement were indisputable, so alternative symbols are nowadays used in some non-Christian societies.

As of 2015, there are 189 national Red Cross, Red Crescent, and Red Star of David societies. These national societies work together and cooperate with the ICRC in many ways, although they remain legally independent organizations. The American Red Cross, for example, is an organization governed by U.S. law with its own goals, rules, traditions, and staff. Although the international Red Cross family is held together by its common princi-ples, conferences, and joint agreements, there is a clear distinction between the national societies and the ICRC.[14] First and foremost, the ICRC is the only one that enjoys a special international status enshrined in the Geneva Conventions as detailed later in this chapter. Second, the ICRC has the task of supervising the implementation of the movement's core principles. It traditionally held the right to recognize new national societies and welcome them into the international Red Cross movement. Finally, the ICRC has the responsibility to protect its symbols—red cross and red crescent alike—against abuses and attacks by warring parties.[15]

Towards the First World War

The period leading to the First World War saw the ICRC tested by two armed conflicts. The Boer wars (1899–1902) in South Africa, between Dutch settlers (Boers) and British forces, were one of the first major conflicts of the 20th century. The Boers used guerilla warfare against the superior British armies. In response, the British set up concentration camps, where an estimated 25,000 civilians, mostly Boer women and children, were killed by hunger and disease. Given the distance from Geneva and all the logistical challenges this created, as well as the unconventional warfare used in the conflict, the ICRC could do very little to help.

Another conflict that left the organization powerless to intervene was the Russo-Japanese war of 1904. The ICRC called on the Russian and Japanese governments to respect the 1864 Geneva Convention and sent funds to aid organizations in the conflict region.[16] But once again distance posed a serious challenge to the organization's ability to carry out initiatives on the battlefield.

The impotence of the ICRC in the Boer Wars and the Russo-Japanese war is in stark contrast to the organization's successes during the First World War. That conflict, more than any other, pushed the Red Cross onto the center stage of global politics and gave the organization its defining worldwide role. Despite the still wide use of cavalry, the First World War was a war of modern weapons and as a result a war of mass killings. Machine gun fire could wipe out hundreds of soldiers in just a few minutes. The use of air force and long-range cannons made the distinction between front and hinterland less clear. Blockades and counter-blockades attempted to starve the civilian enemy population into surrender and brought the war's destruction to common people. In sum, the First World War was unlike any conflict previously seen.

It might therefore seem surprising that the ICRC was able to meet the challenge of the war and come out of it more respected and stronger than ever before. Until the outbreak of the First World War, the ICRC was still a small Geneva-centered organization with limited administrative staff. But this changed quickly and within a year its staff grew to 1,200 volunteers. During the war the ICRC became a central global hub for sending food parcels to POWs, tracing soldiers who were missing in action, and coordinating the work of ICRC delegations around the world on an unprecedented scale. The ICRC made POW camp visits by delegates a high priority and made sure that POWs were treated humanely. It collected information about the whereabouts of POWs and passed it on to the next of kin. The ICRC also began to raise concerns about the treatment of civilians and asked that the same protections granted to POWs be extended to enemy civilians in internment camps.

With its response to the demands of the First World War, the ICRC proved its value as a humanitarian organization. Its mission rested on a solid foundation of humanitarian ideals and with the approval of and agreement with the Geneva Conventions, the ICRC's work was grounded in international law and received financing from the Swiss government, the national Red Cross societies, and other donations. For its accomplishments during the First World War, the Committee was awarded the 1917 Nobel Peace Prize.

Despite its many humanitarian successes during the First World War, the ICRC struggled with itself when addressing war crimes and atrocities. As a bad sign of things to come, the First World War highlighted the conflict of interest for those with both an ICRC membership and a Swiss government position. As discussed earlier, the ICRC had a history of selecting its members from the ranks of the Swiss government, so being a member of the Committee while holding a government office was not uncommon. And in February of 1918, this proved to be a problem. At that time the ICRC issued an appeal to the warring powers to stop the use of poison gas, which killed indiscriminately. This appeal is remarkable in and of itself, since it marked a change from the ICRC's traditionally more discreet approach to pursuing its humanitarian agenda. However, two Committee members refused to sign the appeal because they were Swiss government officials at the time. In their view, Swiss neutrality prevented them from supporting the ICRC appeal. Despite the obvious conflict of interest, the practice of allowing Swiss government officials to be members of the ICRC continued—with serious consequences for both the organization and the victims of war, as we will see in later chapters of this book.[17]

Interwar Period

At the end of the First World War the world was faced with a devastating refugee crisis. During the war and in its aftermath three major Empires collapsed: Russia, Austria–Hungary, and the Ottoman Empire. Russia was thrown into a bloody civil war starting in 1917. Small nation-states were born under chaotic circumstances and began to force out their ethnic minorities. The survivors of the Armenian genocide fled to Syria, Bulgaria, Soviet Armenia, and other countries. In 1923 ethnic Greeks were forced out of their ancient home regions in the new Turkish state, while ethnic Turks had to leave Greece. Communist leaders in Russia stripped opponents of the new regime of their citizenship and often forced them into exile. In sum, many anti-fascists, anti-communists, and members of religious or ethnic minorities found themselves stateless in a world of nation-states. With so many refugees on the move, the First World War introduced a new era of humanitarianism.[18]

Some of the early international humanitarian efforts to aid refugees were overseen by the League of Nations, an organization founded with the goal of guaranteeing peace and international order. In 1921, the first Office of the High Commissioner for Refugees was founded. Before too long, several other institutions began to offer help to specific victim groups. Prominent among them was the Nansen International Office for Refugees (1931–1938). Named after the internationally renowned Norwegian explorer Fridtjof Nansen, the organization introduced a novel idea: the Nansen Certificate. Also known as the 'Nansen passport' for refugees, it allowed a refugee to travel and cross borders legally.

The ICRC was heavily involved in international efforts to provide refugee aid and introduced its first travel documents in 1918/19. It also helped with the distribution and administration of Nansen Certificates.[19] It also began work on extending existing international humanitarian law to cover refugees. The issue of better protection for refugees was at the center of discussions at the 10th International Red Cross Conference in 1921. At this conference the government signatories of the Geneva Conventions were asked to consider a new treaty that would codify refugee protection and the ICRC started drafting the treaty. This marked the beginning of the ICRC's continued efforts to protect the interests of refugees, which played an important part in the organization's indiscriminate handling of uprooted people after 1945 and contributed to criticisms of the ICRC, as we will see later.

The League of Red Cross Societies

The ICRC's respected international standing after the First World War drew attention and sparked competition from the USA. During the war, the USA experienced a humanitarian awakening of its own and its national Red Cross society began to pursue the ambitious goal of 'making the world safe'[20] by expanding its work outside its homeland's borders. The intention of the American Red Cross was to take the lead in the international humanitarian movement and it saw the League of Red Cross Societies as a way to do so.

Founded in 1919 in Paris the League of Red Cross Societies aspired to serve as a forum for national Red Cross Societies. The League was the brain-child of U.S. banker Henry P. Davison, the chairman of the American Red Cross War Council. By creating it, Davison hoped to challenge the ICRC's leadership role in the Red Cross family.[21] He imagined an American-led Red Cross movement that would become active in providing all forms of wartime and peacetime emergency relief to soldiers and civilians. Davison was very close to President Woodrow Wilson and knew that he could rely on the President's support to fulfill his humanitarian ambitions.

Tensions between the ICRC and the League proved unavoidable. At the time of the League's founding, only the victors of the First World War and their allies were allowed to join. The national Red Cross Societies of the Central Powers and of Soviet Russia were initially excluded, which the ICRC was eager to point out violated the humanitarian principles of neutrality and inde-pendence. But the two organizations overcame these initial tensions and even-tually hammered out a compromise.[22] The work of the ICRC would henceforth be mostly limited to times of war, while the League, as an active worldwide umbrella association, would focus on helping civilian victims of disasters.

The connections among the national Red Cross societies and the rela-tionship between them and the ICRC were formalized in a statute passed in 1928, which confirmed the ICRC's seperate and independent status. The international Red Cross movement now accordingly consisted of the ICRC, the League of National Red Cross Societies, and the national Red Cross societies. The platform for discussions of the movement became the International Red Cross Conference, which ordinarily met every four years. The RC conference itself was a deliberative body lacking the author-ity to command, similar to the UN general assembly after 1945.[23] The ICRC had to accept the existence of the League whether it liked it or not, but the rivalry between the two organizations never completely ceased and often made their relations less than harmonious.

The Geneva Convention of 1929

A major change in humanitarian law took place in 1929 with the adoption of rules governing the humane treatment of POWs.[24] During the First World

War the ICRC did already care for and protect POWs, but it was the Geneva Convention of July 1929 that created the legal basis for this protection. The treaty, signed during the Convention by fifty-three states, was prepared by the ICRC and the national Red Cross societies. Although The Hague Conventions of 1907 contained some provisions for the protection of POWs, the Geneva treaty was broader and more detailed. The treaty also singled out the ICRC and granted it special powers and responsibilities in the context of POWs. The ICRC was to supervise the application of the Geneva Convention of 1929 by visiting the wounded, sick and imprisoned soldiers.

Neutral countries like Switzerland acted as a protecting power. A 'protecting power' in the world of diplomacy refers to a third party acting as an intermediary on behalf of two states in conflict. The ICRC would work alongside the protecting power, but was itself (legally) not a protecting power.

It is important to note that while the Geneva Convention of 1929 moved international humanitarian law forward by codifying protections for POWs, it stopped short of extending similar protections to captured or wounded civilians.[25] But this legal limitation did not always stop the ICRC's activities. As a private association, the ICRC often used its 'right of initiative' to intervene in humanitarian emergencies, even in cases not explicitly covered by the Geneva Conventions.[26] After all, the international Red Cross movement often shaped emerging law instead of relying on existing law.[27] As presidents of the ICRC repeatedly stated, interventions to stem human suffering in wartime came first, ahead of the interests of states and national governments.[28] Thus, the ICRC often undertook humanitarian actions not because these were supported by international law, but because they promoted the Red Cross ideals and fitted with the ICRC's traditional humanitarian role. In fact, following the First World War the ICRC became very concerned with the fate of civilians trapped in enemy territory. The organization attempted to address the status and protection of these civilians during the 15th International Red Cross Conference in Tokyo in 1934. A draft treaty was agreed upon, but the Second World War (WWII) broke out before the treaty could be ratified.[29]

Testing the Limits of the ICRC Leading up to the Second World War

The 1920s saw civil wars and political unrest, which led to a dramatic increase in the number of political prisoners in many countries around the world. The ICRC and national Red Cross societies saw their right and obligation to intervene on behalf of internees in the Soviet Union, Italy, Austria, and Germany among others. But any intervention was limited by the fact that actions within these countries could only be effective by cooperation with the countries' national Red Cross societies. Of course, if a society was not able to help, it could request support from the ICRC and the Red Cross family. But the fact that the ICRC could only step in if asked to do so was to have disastrous consequences in the future.

According to the Swiss historian Jean-Claude Favez, the ICRC's experience in Fascist Italy was an ominous foretaste of its later dealings with Nazi Germany.[30] In 1922 Benito Mussolini, a journalist and leader of the Italian Fascist party, was named prime minister of Italy. Italy was to become the first European country to turn into a right-wing dictatorship, characterized by racism and aggressive ethno-nationalism. The regime's political enemies were either forced into exile, murdered or sent to internment camps on remote islands (*confino*). While care for political prisoners in Italy was seen as part of the Red Cross agenda, it proved difficult to provide aid. The country's national society, closely aligned with the Italian government, did not challenge Mussolini's ideology and seemed uninterested in the plight of internees. The ICRC was cautious to intervene for fear that any cooperation with Mussolini's government could be exploited as a propaganda tool by the regime. When the ICRC eventually asked the Italian Red Cross to visit political prisoners and their families and provide relief, Mussolini immediately granted the request. The Italian Red Cross was allowed to visit political prisoners and their families on some islands and would report back to the ICRC in Geneva. Mussolini's eagerness to engage with the ICRC reinforced the organization's initial suspicions and caused its then president Max Huber to avoid direct intervention for political prisoners in Italy. Huber could not prevent the Italian Red Cross from falling in line with Mussolini's politics, but he could still try to keep the neutrality and moral authority of the ICRC intact. To find out whether he could accomplish this while still helping political prisoners in Italy, he formed an ICRC Commission tasked with finding avenues for humanitarian intervention on behalf of internees. But the minutes of the Commission's meetings testify to its hesitation more than to its will to act. After 1933, when the Nazi government rose to power in Germany, the Commission's attention shifted to the situation there, with Hitler now following in Mussolini's footsteps.

The Spanish Civil War of 1936-1939 further tested the unity of the Red Cross family. In 1936 Fascist forces under the leadership of General Franco started a rebellion to overthrow the democratically elected left-wing government in Madrid. Mussolini and Hitler sent troops to support Franco's Fascist cause. They were met by anti-fascist fighters from all over Europe and the Americas—Ernest Hemingway among them—who volunteered to aid the Spanish Republic. The Soviet Union and Mexico sent money and war material to boost the left-wing forces. The fighting grew into a civil war, where different fractions (and their foreign allies) controlled different parts of Spain and its colonies at different points in time.

The Spanish Civil War of 1936–1939 was unusual in that it was not fought between two nations and their armies, but was instead a war that divided the citizens of a single country. The Geneva Convention of 1929 was not designed for such a scenario. Nonetheless, the ICRC started a number of aid initiatives and some of its officials were at times quite successful in reducing the suffering in the conflict. Given the lack of a legal basis for the ICRC's interventions, the organization's accomplishments during the war were quite remarkable.[31]

While the ICRC did its best to uphold the Red Cross movement's humanitarian ideals, the involvement of the Italian Red Cross openly defied the movement's core principles of neutrality and impartiality. When asked to step in and provide aid, the Italian Red Cross sided with Franco's Fascist forces rather than offering its services to both sides in the conflict. This was not surprising, since the Italian Red Cross was in line with Mussolini's regime and acted as an auxiliary medical corps for the dictator's army. But the experience underscored the fact that *caritas* was not always *inter arma*, in the words of one historian.[32]

The ICRC's handling of the Italian war against Ethiopia in 1935-1936 also highlighted the organization's limits. The invading fascist forces committed many war crimes, including launching poison gas attacks (banned by the Geneva Protocol of 1925), bombing civilian targets and even Red Cross hospitals, and executing unarmed POWs. But these violations of humanitarian law elicited little response by the ICRC.[33] From the viewpoint of many European leaders, humanitarian rules were made for wars between 'civilised' nations, and not for wars against 'barbarian' ones, which they perceived Ethiopia to be. This widespread view made it possible for ICRC officials to downplay fascist war crimes. What probably also contributed to the ICRC's silence was that many of its eighteen members were close to conservative or right-wing parties and sympathized with the Mussolini regime. They were convinced that Fascism could be used to stop the advance of communism.[34]

In sum, the period leading up to WWII tested the limits of the Red Cross movement's capabilities and commitment by forcing it to deal with the plight of political prisoners, and to address the suffering brought about by wars in Spain and Ethiopia. The ICRC and national Red Cross societies' conduct through these crises foreshadowed their handling of their humanitarian mandate after Nazi Germany attacked Poland in 1939. If the ICRC was reluctant or unable to help civilian political prisoners in Fascist Italy, would it have the strength or conviction to intervene when the Nazi government began to persecute, imprison and eventually murder a large number of its own citizens? The Geneva Conventions could not be applied to these 'internal affairs of a country,' since they had never defined a clear right of humanitarian protection for groups persecuted by their own government.[35] If national Red Cross societies had become extensions of their home nations' governments and, as in the case of the Italian Red Cross, had openly sided with abusive dictatorships, would the German Red Cross remain impartial and neutral? And finally, if the ICRC remained silent when a powerful European government was committing war crimes on a massive scale, as was the case in Ethiopia, would the ICRC speak out when an ostensibly 'civilised' Western nation such as Germany began to commit acts of unthinkable cruelty against its own citizens as well as against those of other European nations? The answers to these questions were to reveal one of the profound failures of humanitarianism during the Second World War.

2

The Silence on the Holocaust

The International Committee of the Red Cross (ICRC) inhabited a complicated place in the international community during the Second World War, one subject to many internal and external pressures. The organization's wartime story and choices must be understood in this context. While the ICRC's own history, understanding of humanitarianism, and organizational structure certainly shaped its actions, the delicate political position it occupied by operating in a small neutral country also impacted on the decisions of its leaders. The three ICRC presidents who served during the Second World War era had their own unique temperaments and ambitions, which had implications for the organization's engagement or lack of it on behalf of civilian victims of the war. Whatever the reasons for the ICRC's failure to assist civilian victims, particularly Jews, until late in the war, the consequences were dire for millions of Europeans and called into question the organization's mission and fundamental mandate. The ICRC's failure in 1942 to make a public appeal to Germany to stop its violations of humanitarian principles and the agency's tardy assistance in late 1944 to the Hungarian Jews who remained alive had lasting repercussions. In the short term, it also led many in the international community to ask whether the Red Cross movement would not be better served if placed in Swedish hands after the war.

The Power of Personality

Three personalities shaped the ICRC in the years from 1928 to 1955. The first was Max Huber, the organization's president from 1928 to 1944. Carl Jacob Burckhardt, who was Huber's right-hand man and successor, served as president from 1945 until 1948. The third was Paul Ruegger, who had been involved in ICRC activities years before he took over the leadership in 1948 after Burckhardt's official resignation. All three men played a significant role in shaping the international Red Cross's response to the Second World War and the Holocaust.

Max Huber, born in 1874, a lawyer by profession and a devout Christian, came from a well-respected Lutheran family in Zurich. He served as chairman on the board of two large companies and had many business interests in Germany and Italy.[1] A professor of constitutional and international law at the University of Zurich, he was widely published and chaired the permanent Court of International Justice in The Hague between 1924 and 1927.[2] From 1930 to 1938 he also served as president of the Nansen International Office for Refugees.

Huber's personal motivation for serving as president of the ICRC stemmed from dual convictions: his faith in the rule of law and adherence to Christian mercy and compassion. His was a 'humanitarianism based on

Figure 2.1. Long-time president of the ICRC Judge Max Huber in the 1930s.

faith'.[3] The title of Huber's 1943 book in German, *The Good Samaritan: Reflections about the Gospel of Jesus and Red Cross Work*, signalled his understanding of his role quite plainly.[4] Huber saw the ICRC as a moral authority based on Christian values. The work of the ICRC rests—in addition to the principle of reciprocity enshrined in the conventions—on the moral authority and reputation of the Red Cross. In a 1944 Swiss publication about the Red Cross, the institution is hailed as the 'moral conscience of humanity'.[5] Huber's biographer writes: 'The Red Cross presidency leaves the man who is in charge a relatively small space in which to manoeuver. But if he is prudent and watchful at the same time in order to make the best of the possibilities, he enjoys a unique moral standing and thus the chance to protect humanity as otherwise perhaps only the Pope could.'[6] One of Huber's successors called him 'the great spiritual leader of the Red Cross movement in most difficult times'.[7] This he was certainly not. The elderly Huber (he was in his late 60s at this time) was a very cautious person. He avoided making big decisions and seemed, at times, completely overwhelmed by the challenges presented by totalitarian regimes, genocide, and total war.[8] He was often ill during the war years, repeatedly leaving decision-making to his vice president, Carl Jacob Burckhardt.[9] Huber often portrayed the ICRC as apolitical, not acknowledging the inevitable encroachment of politics on most humanitarian projects.[10]

Huber's alter ego and successor, Carl Jacob Burckhardt (not to be confused with Jacob Burckhardt, the Renaissance historian), saw the ever-present hand of politics more clearly. A very ambitious man, he viewed the ICRC as a stepping stone that could ultimately help advance his diplomatic career.[11] Acting as a kind of 'foreign minister' (Paul Stauffer) of the ICRC, Burckhardt operated on two levels, one of which was official Red Cross business and the other, secret diplomacy.[12] He had already attained some international recognition as a biographer and author. But it was his function as High Commissioner of the League of Nations in the Free State of Danzig that first catapulted him into the spotlight of international politics. As a result of Germany's defeat in the First World War the Eastern German town of Danzig was cut off from the Reich and turned into an independent entity under the authority of the League of Nations. Representatives of various countries were appointed by the League to function as commissioner. Burckhardt served as commissioner between 1937 and 1939, at a time of increasing tension between Nazi authorities and the Polish government over the future of the city. Burckhardt was considered 'the only Swiss personality known and recognized in all of Europe in these immensely eventful war years'.[13] As a career diplomat with his own personal agenda, he wanted to influence the course of events in Europe. As a historian, he did not want to limit himself to writing about history, but sought to *make* history. Burckhardt gained academic fame as a historian for his volumes about the seventeenth-century French statesman Cardinal Richelieu. Like Richelieu, the great diplomat trying to achieve a balance of power in Europe under French leadership, Burckhardt wanted to serve the balance of the great European powers in his own age. For Burckhardt, Germany and France were the two columns on which European culture rested. He naturally therefore showed himself very concerned about tensions between these two nations. Burckhardt the historian also identified great men as the driving forces of history. The afterword of the 1935 German edition of his Richelieu biography showcased this admiration for outstanding leaders and their deeds, for example in his description of Richelieu as 'one of the great leaders of more recent history'. In this context violence appears as a necessary evil and reforms often come with violence as a side-effect. Or at least this is an impression one can easily get from reading Burckhardt: 'Like all great rulers and creators in world history Cardinal Richelieu was also a great destroyer.'[14]

Due to Huber's ill health, Burckhardt had taken over most ICRC business by the autumn of 1942. He had very little interest in purely humanitarian work and, in contrast to his predecessor, did not portray himself as someone following in the footsteps of the biblical Samaritan.[15] The ICRC interested Burckhardt because it was one of the very few Swiss institutions with an international scope. Furthermore, Burckhardt, the product of one of Basel's elite families, identified the Soviet regime as the main enemy of Europe and Western civilization in general.[16] The idea of using the ICRC as a tool to fight the advance of communism appears at least to have been an undercurrent in his decision-making and reasoning.

Burckhardt's dealings with Nazi Germany reveal his anti-communist stance, but also his interests in helping maintain Switzerland's independence. Burckhardt found clear words to condemn National Socialism as an 'extreme form' of fascism, really a 'weard mix of confused ideological concepts', a 'false doctrine' (*Irrlehre*) as he stated many years later after the war.[17] Although he disliked Hitler—the parvenu from the Austrian provinces—and other 'primitive' Nazis, he always saw Germany as an important and powerful bulwark against the communist threat in the East.[18] Burckhardt therefore had few reservations about attempting to reach practical compromises with

Figure 2.2. Carl J. Burckhardt visiting the German battleship *Schleswig-Holstein* in his function as High Commissioner of the League of Nations in Danzig/Gdańsk, August 1939.

the Nazi regime. In 1936 he attended the Olympic Games in Berlin and was an invited guest at the annual Nazi Party rally a year later in Nuremberg. He inspected German concentration camps in the 1930s and officially lauded the commandant of Dachau for his discipline and decency.[19] Moreover, in a letter to Hitler in 1936, he praised 'the Faustian achievement of the Autobahn and the Labour Service' and the 'joyful spirit of cooperation, which manifests itself everywhere'.[20] During his time as high commissioner in Danzig, Burckhardt moved very cautiously, anxious not to upset the German leadership. This stance paid off. Minister of Propaganda Joseph Goebbels complimented Burckhardt when he wrote in his diary, 'This man could be useful one day. It is a pity that we don't have diplomats like him.'[21]

Burckhardt was no great admirer of Hitler, but no particular friend of the Jews either. This was already evident before the war when he remarked, to a friend in a private letter written in 1933, that 'there is a certain aspect of Judaism that a healthy Volk has to fight'.[22] His antisemitic pronouncements continued long after the war had ended. In 1959, for instance, he was still asserting in an early draft version of his memoirs that the Jews had declared a fight to the death against fascism and therefore it had been the Jews who had wanted the Second World War.[23] Antisemitism of various kinds and degrees was very widespread at the time even in well-educated circles in Europe and the United States. Yet Burckhardt's own negative stereotypes and prejudices against Jews never culminated in demands for violence and ultimately genocide of the type found in Nazi ideology. At the end of the day, antisemitism on its own does not sufficiently explain Burckhardt's indifference to the fate of Europe's Jews, an indifference which is, however, clear and which inevitably impacted on the ICRC's wartime priorities.[24] While Burckhardt was interested in maintaining good relations with Nazi Germany, his eventual successor, Ruegger, cultivated ties with fascist Italy. While his mentor Huber was a man of unbending principles, Ruegger proved more flexible in serving both the ICRC and his country.

Paul Ruegger's background had prepared him for an international role. He was born in 1897 in the Swiss town of Lucerne, but he spent his childhood with his family in the waning years of the Austro-Hungarian Empire. Later he moved back to Switzerland and completed his studies, writing a law dissertation under Max Huber.[25] Ruegger was a conservative Catholic who had very good contacts in the Vatican, especially with Secretary of State Cardinal Luigi Maglione.[26] After filling a number of other posts, including one at the International Court of Justice in The Hague he was eventually appointed Swiss ambassador to Benito Mussolini's Italy in 1935.[27]

Ruegger loved Italian culture and the Italian language. He married an Italian baroness and promoted Italian-Swiss friendship (*amicizia italo-svizzera*) wherever possible. Together with his superior, Minister Giuseppe Motta, he strove to please the Italian king and Mussolini alike. In line with Motta, Ruegger downplayed the crimes committed by Mussolini's forces in Ethiopia and, after the introduction of Italy's anti-Jewish laws in 1938, he began proposing bureaucratic barriers to keep Jewish refugees from its southern neighbour out of Switzerland.[28] As historian Dominique-D. Junod has pointed out, 'Nothing in Ruegger's proposal indicated that the minister of Switzerland in Rome [Ruegger] gave a thought to the very cruel plight of the innocent people his plan would affect.'[29]

In 1942 this suddenly changed. Italian Foreign Minister Gian Galeazzo Ciano threatened to declare Ruegger a persona non grata, although the exact reasons have never been uncovered.[30] Ruegger was suddenly ordered back to Switzerland, and after a short term of service with the ICRC (he would return to head the organization in 1948), he became Swiss ambassador to London in 1944. There he worked to repair Switzerland's somewhat tarnished image with the British. Although the British had previously opposed Burckhardt's nomination for the post as he was seen as too pro-German, Ruegger proved more acceptable.[31] London diplomatic circles were not particularly pleased with the new man's close ties to Italian government officials and court circles, but Ruegger skilfully presented Switzerland's humanitarian traditions in the best light possible. British historian Neville Wylie has summed up his talents trenchantly: 'More than most Swiss, Ruegger was able to wear both "crosses" (the Swiss cross and the Red Cross) on his lapel simultaneously.'[32] As Wylie points out, from the very start Ruegger succeeded in positioning himself as Britain's intermediary between the Swiss government in Bern *and* the ICRC in Geneva. Ruegger had already shown adeptness in avoiding any confrontations with Switzerland's aggressive fascist neighbours, which was completely in line with Swiss government policy and with the ICRC leadership as well.

A Delicate Balance: The ICRC between Switzerland and the Third Reich

With the expulsion of Soviet diplomats in 1918, the Swiss government had made its anti-communist stance clear very early. During the chaotic years of the Russian Revolution, ICRC delegations defended the interests of Swiss citizens and Swiss property in war-torn Russia. It acted not as a neutral and independent organization, but as the quasi-diplomatic arm of Switzerland. No wonder that the Soviets early on made no real distinction between the Swiss government and the ICRC. And relations between Bern and Moscow remained icy. Yet Swiss diplomacy remained on good terms with fascist Italy and Francisco Franco's Spain. Giuseppe Motta, director of the Political Department of the Swiss Foreign Office between 1920 and 1940, was, as we have seen, deeply pro-Italian and a fervent anti-communist.[33] In 1934 he opposed the Soviet Union's bid to become a member of the League of Nations, although during Italy's war of aggression against Ethiopia in 1935–1936, the Swiss government did take part in the (rather weak) international sanctions levelled against fascist Italy. The Swiss government was, therefore, not always willing to accede to Mussolini's wishes. Motta, however, was very pro-Italian and worked against the sanctions imposed by the international community. On his suggestion, Switzerland was among the first countries to recognize the annexation of Ethiopia by fascist Italy.[34] Thus the Swiss government seemed to have chosen camps in the interwar years.[35] Its relationship to Nazi Germany must be seen against this background. This notwithstanding, Hitler's aggressive foreign policy and annexation of neighbouring countries such as Austria made many Swiss uneasy, concerned about their own continued independence. Switzerland was not a strong military power and was certainly no match for Hitler's war machine. It was after all a small country of about 4.5 million people compared with an estimated 67 million in Nazi Germany (as of 1933). Yet it remains unclear whether Switzerland was ever high on Hitler's wish list of territorial acquisitions. Wylie, for instance, argues that it is unlikely that the Germans ever seriously planned to attack Switzerland.[36] After an Axis victory however it is very likely that Switzerland would have been divided up between Fascist Italy and Nazi Germany. Despite all the support the Swiss gave the Axis, Hitler and Mussolini still had complaints against them. Switzerland provided a forum for resistance fighters and plotters against the fascist regimes. Many prominent political dissidents and a good number of German and Austrian Jews found a safe haven there as well. There was no shortage of German complaints about the Swiss not collaborating enough. At the same time, the Swiss spent the war trying not to give Germany any grounds for invasion and yielded to many German demands, both real and perceived, in order to achieve this end.

The Swiss government's policy towards Jewish refugees from Hitler's Germany is telling in this regard. After the Nazi takeover in 1933, thousands of Jews and political opponents of the Hitler regime fled Germany, but lacked secure, long-term options. After years of economic depression, even countries that had once welcomed immigrants such as the United States became very restrictive in their immigration policies. An international refugee conference convened in 1938 in Evian, on the French side of Lake Geneva, but ended with few concrete results, only underlining that refugees from Nazi Germany were hardly welcome anywhere.[37] Chaim Weizmann, who would later become Israel's first president, remarked bitterly that the world was divided into two camps: those who wanted to get rid of the Jews and those who refused to give them refuge.[38] Historian Deborah Lipstadt has passed a similar verdict on this state of affairs:

> America as well as other Allied nations, neutral nations, the Vatican and international agencies such as the International Red Cross—accorded the rescue of the Jews a low priority at best. There is an increasing body of evidence which documents that at times, the Allies—State Department and Foreign Office

officials in particular—not only failed to pursue rescue opportunities but actually worked to frustrate and prevent the possibility of rescue.[39]

Even with anti-Jewish measures intensifying in Germany in the late 1930s, the ICRC merely stated it was neither able to nor empowered to assist, and suggested that international refugee organizations take up the burden. There is no evidence that the organization pressured Swiss government officials to loosen the country's own very strict refugee policy, implemented after the Nazi takeover of power in Germany in 1933.[40] Despite the fact that Switzerland had a small Jewish community of 18,000 to 20,000,[41] foreign Jews were especially unwelcome, and they were often denied status as 'political refugees' and the chance for temporary asylum. With Hitler in charge in Germany, the Swiss Federal Department of Justice and Police demanded that 'undesirable elements (Jews, political extremists, suspected spies) are to be kept out' of Switzerland.[42] Switzerland admitted about 30,000 Jewish refugees, but probably rejected as least as many at their border.[43] When Germany annexed Austria in March 1938 (the so-called Anschluss), the Swiss were alarmed, fearing the same fate might lie in store for them as well.

After March 1938 Austrian Jews, the majority residing in Vienna, faced harsh new prohibitions and discrimination, becoming targets not only of public humiliation but of brutal violence. As a result, the World Jewish Congress (WJC) urgently asked the ICRC for support and intervention.[44] Adolf Eichmann, Himmler's adviser on Jewish matters, came to Vienna in the wake of the Anschluss in order to organize the expropriation of as many Jews as possible and force them out of the country. In this initial phase, Eichmann's solution to what was called 'the Jewish Question' was pushing for mass Jewish emigration abroad. Indeed, in the first few days after the Anschluss, some 3,000 to 4,000 Austrian Jews fled overnight across the border into Switzerland.[45] The notion that Switzerland might be overwhelmed by 'foreign elements' worried the head of the Swiss Police, Heinrich Rothmund, and his superiors.[46] Swiss authorities soon concocted a plan to 'defend' the country from Jewish refugees. Two weeks after the Anschluss in March 1938 the Swiss government introduced visa requirements for all Austrian citizens. But Austrian Jews, their home country now being annexed, would soon hold German passports. Up to that point, Switzerland had not required a visa from German citizens entering the country. Now, in order to continue visa-free travel for 'Aryan' Germans to Switzerland, a solution had to be found. As a result, the German government marked the passports of 'non-Aryan' Reich Germans henceforth with a red 'J' stamp (for 'Jew'). German Jews were now also required to apply for visas in order to enter Switzerland. In exchange, the passports of Swiss Jews would also be marked with a 'J' (*Jude*) stamp. Rothmund did not wish to publicize the details of this agreement with Berlin and worried that the international community might accuse Switzerland of being too friendly with Nazi Germany. Rothmund was also eager to make clear that Switzerland had its own ways to deal with the 'Jewish'. He rejected the brutality shown by the Nazis and pleaded for more 'civilized' methods. Switzerland was also eager to point out its own independence and distinctness from Germany. While Rothmund wanted to keep Jewish refugees out, he did not want to be seen as a puppet of the Germans.[47]

Jews were only granted temporary asylum, and the few who were lucky enough to be admitted had to leave Switzerland as soon as possible. Eastern European Jews in particular were considered by Rothmund as impossible candidates for assimilation into Swiss society. Switzerland was also not willing to carry the financial burden for these temporary and unwelcome guests. The costs for the refugees had to be paid for by the Swiss Jewish community.[48] Jewish activist Gerhart Riegner, himself a refugee from Nazi Germany stranded in Switzerland, called this Swiss version of discrimination preventive antisemitism ('*vorbeugender Antisemitismus*'): 'They did not have to fire Jews from leading positions in Swiss politics, the Swiss press and the Swiss economy, because they never allowed them to get there in the first place.'[49] Rothmund and others wanted to make sure that Switzerland was not run by Jews. The new measures now put into practice, therefore, were to prevent the 'Judaization of Switzerland' ('*Verjudung der Schweiz*'), as Rothmund put it in an official letter to his superior in 1938.[50] The borders were to be sealed as much as possible and Switzerland should be particularly unwelcoming to Jewish refugees. A Swiss official at the German border was lectured by his superiors that 'the job of our agency is not to make sure that the Jews are doing well'.[51]

Historians Monika Imboden and Brigitte Lustenberger do not mince words regarding the Swiss decision-making at the time: 'The introduction of the J-stamp, initiated by Switzerland, is one of the shameful blemishes in Swiss refugee policy.'[52] Ultimately, many private Swiss individuals and government officials tried to help Jews, both unofficially and officially. These included Paul Grüninger, the border police chief of St Gallen, who helped many Austrian and German Jews cross the border into Switzerland illegally.

He was dismissed in 1939 and convicted for abuse of power and falsifying documents. Only in 1995 did the Swiss courts finally annul the verdict against him.[53]

In 1939 the German term 'Blitzkrieg' was quickly introduced into the English language. It referred to short wars in which the aggressor advanced swiftly, with the help of coordinated and intensive armoured and aerial power. It was first applied in Poland, where modern German military technology smashed the Polish cavalry following the German invasion in September 1939 which started the Second World War. Poland was defeated and completely occupied in just twenty-seven days. In spring 1940, Denmark, Norway, Holland, and Belgium surrendered in a matter of days. France surrendered after one month. Only Great Britain remained to fight against Nazi Germany and its allies in 1940/41. At that time Switzerland was completely surrounded by the victorious Axis Powers. In the summer of 1942 the Swiss government decided to restrict refugee laws even further. Citing short food supplies, limited housing, and internal and external security issues, a presidential order established that 'refugees who have fled purely on racial grounds, e.g., Jews, cannot be considered political refugees'.[54] The Swiss government kept the national Swiss Red Cross on a short leash, but tolerated small-scale humanitarian operations. A private Swiss initiative for child relief together with the Swiss Red Cross formed a Coalition for Relief to Child War Victims. In the summer of 1942, after the deportation of their parents, thousands of Jewish children were left on their own in Nazi-controlled France. The Child Relief executive board was deeply alarmed and wanted to get these children to safety in Switzerland. Edouard De Haller, the Swiss official in charge of international aid work, belittled these efforts, commenting that:

> The members of the executive board have clearly not escaped the wave of naive generosity that is sweeping our country at present. They simply want to ‹save› the children at all costs, i.e., to save them from [the threat of] deportation which they will face when they reach the age of 16, or earlier should the age-limit be reduced.[55]

Although xenophobic and nationalistic attitudes were often common among Swiss police and Foreign Office officials, they were not necessarily antisemitic. Many officials were willing to help a certain number of German and Austrian Jews as long as they thought that such actions would not endanger Swiss independence.[56] However, antisemitism was certainly a factor, as illustrated in the case of police chief Rothmund. Ultimately, Swiss government officials kept only a small number of Jewish refugees in Switzerland. They even hesitated to grant permission in the summer of 1945 to an initiative that sought to take in 350 child Holocaust survivors from Buchenwald concentration camp for a short period, largely because a permanent host country for the children had not yet been found—the government was afraid that the children would not leave again. For this reason, Eduard de Haller sought assurances from officials of international aid organizations in London that they would later 'liberate us from these children'.[57]

How far some Swiss leaders were initially willing to go in order to please Nazi Germany is obvious in the case of the so-called Swiss military medical mission. This was an initiative by high-ranking Swiss military leaders, with the blessing of the Swiss government and technically under the umbrella of the Swiss national Red Cross. In 1941–1942, groups of doctors and nurses from the Swiss army were sent to the Eastern Front in order to support the German war effort against the Soviets.[58] The doctors were subject to German military law and were not allowed to care for wounded Soviet soldiers or Russian civilians.[59] Swiss historian Werner Rings sees the Swiss medical mission to the Wehrmacht on the Eastern Front as less motivated by humanitarian concerns than by the Swiss army's opposition to Bolshevism. The intent of this mission was clear: such an act of good will would improve relations between Switzerland and the Third Reich, illustrating how Switzerland was at times willing to please Hitler in order to avoid German anger preventively.[60] Swiss Jews active in rescue efforts harboured few illusions about the motive behind the mission: 'It was intended to mollify German anger at the Swiss', Riegner remembered.[61] The Swiss never provided a comparable de facto state-sponsored medical mission to any of the Allied armies, leaving little doubt that the mission on behalf of Germany was not a neutral gesture.[62] But individual Swiss citizens went even further in their support for the Nazi cause. At least 755 Swiss enrolled voluntarily in the Waffen SS, Heinrich Himmler's fighting force, during the war.[63] Switzerland was also an important market for art looted by the Nazis, with a number of Swiss art dealers eager to enrich themselves. They helped to facilitate the selling and the hushing up of the provenance of such stolen art works.[64]

After the outbreak of the Second World War in Europe in 1939 and the German Blitzkrieg, Switzerland was on its own. By 1940 it was completely surrounded by Axis powers, who could have cut off the country's main food supplies at any time. With a policy of flexibly adapting its 'neutrality' to prevailing circumstances, the small country tried to preserve its remaining freedom and independence from the mighty Third Reich. The political scientist David Forsythe has explained this process of accommodation, writing that 'Swiss policy during this period was to tilt toward the Nazis through such matters as cooperative banking, so as to guarantee Swiss independence and forestall any thoughts in Berlin about an invasion of Switzerland'.[65] Switzerland was also careful not to upset Nazi Germany with its foreign and domestic policies, especially regarding Jewish refugees.[66]

After Stalingrad and D–Day, with an Allied victory in sight, the Swiss gradually liberalized their refugee policies and became willing to provide a safe haven for more victims. An example of this is the generous acceptance of 20,000 Italian soldiers crossing into Switzerland in September 1943, when the German Wehrmacht occupied most of its former Ally's territory. These Italians, like other military personnel crossing or deserting into Switzerland, were treated as internees and held in special camps. With them came also many Jews and civilians. Although some of them were rejected at the border, most were admitted. The total number of refugees and internees in Switzerland eventually rose to 320,000. Switzerland therefore accepted more refugees than most other countries. But these numbers were mostly made up of non-Jewish refugees.[67] At the same time it opened its borders to more refugees, Switzerland began cooling its once-warm relationship with Nazi Germany. At the end of March 1945, the Swiss Police Department issued an order that Gestapo, SS, and Nazi officials should be denied entrance at the border. Now the Nazis rather than the Jews were unwelcome in the Alpine republic. The Swiss again proved to be very flexible in their refugee policies.[68]

Inside Nazi Germany

Cries for help for concentration camp inmates came soon after Hitler's appointment as Chancellor. A Jewish refugee in April 1933 wrote to the ICRC in a dramatic letter about the brutality in such camps: 'I beg you again in the name of the prisoners – Help! Help!'[69] The writer referred to Dachau near Munich, the first regular concentration camp set up by the Nazis. A major obstacle for the ICRC was legal in nature. As pointed out earlier, the 1929 Geneva Convention protected soldiers, not civilians. As a result, and according to international law, the treatment and welfare of German Jews detained in camps in Germany in the Nazi era were considered to be the internal affairs of that country. Moreover, the ICRC continued to understand its main mission as caring for wounded or imprisoned soldiers. It thus had few legal tools with which to help Jews and other victims of persecution in concentration camps.

Soon after the Nazis came to power in Germany, Huber, the long-time president of the ICRC and an experienced lawyer and devoted Christian, decided that his organization should provide aid to detention and concentration camp inmates in Germany.[70] But what could be done and how could it be done? Huber agreed as early as September 1933 that 'the intervention of the ICRC in Germany in favour of political prisoners is a very delicate question'. At the same time, he was happy that Burckhardt showed an interest in this problem and was willing to take steps. A case should be prepared and discussed with the German Red Cross.[71] The president of the Swedish Red Cross also addressed the issue of Nazi concentration camps with the ICRC and the German Red Cross president. Prince Carl of Sweden pointed to the decision made by the Red Cross family that they had an obligation to care for political prisoners. After stressing the deep friendship between Sweden and Germany he stated that he was acting in 'the interest of Germany and the humanitarian cause'.[72]

The German Red Cross responded that it took an interest in concentration camp inmates and could visit the camps anytime. The situation there was good, housing and food was satisfactory, sports activities and well-equipped hospitals were provided. The German Red Cross official then even went so far as to write that the living standard in the camps were higher than most of the inmates were generally used too. The Germans then invited the Swedish Red Cross president to visit German concentration camps and to convince himself about the good conditions there.[73] Huber was forwarded this letter by his Swedish colleague. It must have aroused his suspicion since the parallels with Mussolini's invitation were obvious. He certainly considered a possible Nazi propaganda coup, but he had to save face. If Sweden was about to inspect Nazi camps, the ICRC should do so too. The visit of an ICRC delegation to a number of concentration camps was now seriously considered. The German Red Cross president let Huber know that they had already asked for permission from the German government and had 'found willing agreement'.[74] Max Huber was probably more concerned than delighted to receive the news. The Nazis were obviously eager to get the ICRC 'inspecting' their camps. The German Red Cross made no secret of the fact that Burckhardt was their man of choice: 'It can certainly be expected that Professor Burckhardt will lead the [ICRC] delegation'.[75] Caution was the order of the day during a September 1935 meeting discussing the next steps. Based on his recent experiences with German officials, Burckhardt said to his ICRC colleagues that it is 'dangerous to occupy oneself' with the concentration camps and therefore extremely important to act with discretion. The ICRC visit would certainly be used by the Nazis to show how marvellous everything was, Burckhardt explained to his ICRC colleagues. Of course, he knew what was really going on there and said that he had just recently been made aware of murders in camps. Burckhardt showed himself concerned about the dangers of abuse of the planned inspections—and the potential propaganda value for the Nazis. But the ICRC intervention might also help to improve the situation of the inmates. In contrast to wartime, the argument of reciprocity would not work in the case of concentration camps. Burckhardt asked his ICRC colleagues to carefully balance these pros and cons. Other speakers at the meeting stressed that the visit would probably not change the situation, even though the Nazis cared very much about world opinion, in particular in the views of the United States and Great Britain. The two women in the meeting, Suzanne Ferrière and Renée-Marguerite Frick-Cramer, stated that the ICRC should at least do everything to give news to the families of the inmates.[76] As we saw earlier, Burckhardt's visit took place and his report contained only a mild critique. His main criticism was that political prisoners and criminals were not separated. SS officer Reinhard Heydrich, soon to be one of the main organizers of the Holocaust, reacted to Burckhardt's critique in a short letter, where he showed himself listening, but not greatly impressed: 'From a national socialist point of view political criminals are on the same level as professional criminals; this is also evident from the new penal code.' 'Heil Hitler!'[77]

The ICRC quickly realized that very little could be done for political prisoners in Nazi hands, particularly since the national Red Cross Society in Germany had opted to fall in line with the regime—a process known as *Gleichschaltung*—rather than face being shut down. In many ways the ICRC depended on the cooperation of the German Red Cross to achieve its mission there. The German Red Cross was deeply Nazified and obstructed many attempts of the ICRC to help concentration camp inmates. German Red Cross official Walther Georg Hartmann, the most important contact between Geneva and Berlin, was often praised as being one of the few

Figure 2.3. Germany 1945(?): Carl J. Burckhardt of the International Committee of the Red Cross (right), visiting a camp for POWs.

remaining humanitarians in the leadership of his organization. Yet even he had been a member of the Nazi Party since 1933. Nazi Party files describe him as a 'political leader' of the Nazi-aligned association of the German Red Cross and a member in various sub-organizations of the party.[78] These affiliations, interestingly, did not hinder his postwar career for long. In 1950 Hartmann became the secretary general of the refounded Red Cross in democratic West Germany.[79] This may have been due to his relatively moderate position; Hartmann does not appear to have been a fanatical Party man, nor was he directly responsible for war crimes. His superior however certainly was. In 1937 SS-General Dr Ernst Robert Grawitz was appointed leader of the German Red Cross. Grawitz, a fanatical Nazi and close follower of SS leader Heinrich Himmler, was himself deeply implicated in the euthanasia murders of handicapped people and medical 'experiments' in concentration camps. Men such as Grawitz in the German organization's leadership made sure that the actions of his Red Cross colleagues were in line with the policies of the Nazi leadership. The German Red Cross had for all practical purposes lost its independence and neutrality and turned into a National Socialist medical service unit supporting Hitler's Wehrmacht.[80]

These facts were certainly not kept a secret or hidden from the public. The widely distributed Meyers encyclopedia wrote in 1942 under 'German Red Cross': 'by the Reich law of December 9, 1937 pertaining to the DRK [German Red Cross], the organization was completely restructured as a united national corporation under the patronage of Adolf Hitler'. Included in its duties were medical service for the army and air-raid protection, care for POWs and those injured by war, and other services 'depending on the requirements of the Reich, the Nazi party and the Wehrmacht'.[81]

Red Cross nurses were expected to support the German total war effort not only by caring for wounded soldiers; they were also expected to contribute to the final victory by strengthening the men's fighting spirit through active participation in mass rallies and other events in support of the regime. Like the common soldiers in Hitler's army, Red Cross nurses and doctors swore a personal oath of allegiance to the Führer.[82]

Once recognized by the ICRC, the national Red Cross societies became completely independent of the ICRC. As a result, the ICRC never had much say in the societies' operations and management and was powerless to intervene in this instance as well. Thus, the ICRC in Geneva did nothing when in 1936 German Jews were shut out of the ranks of the German Red Cross Society. This was a clear breach of the basic principles of the Red Cross movement, but the ICRC did not protest. ICRC headquarters in Geneva responded to a German Jew in 1933, who asked for support in this context: 'In our opinion it is not correct to claim that you could not turn to the German Red Cross because as a Jew you would get no reply from them. I think you have to admit that it would be more correct to follow our advice and to try there first, before you make such kinds of claims and allegations.'[83] The ICRC went on to say that questions of membership were an internal matter of the national Red Cross and Geneva therefore had no right to interfere. With the pogrom of 1938, the so-called Kristallnacht, thousands of Jews were arrested and imprisoned in concentration camps. This was the beginning of a new chapter of persecution, because until then it was mostly political opponents of the Nazis who had been locked up. The open physical mass violence during and following Kristallnacht took most German and Austrian Jews completely by surprise. Humanizing the conditions in Nazi camps now became even more difficult.

Furthermore, the German Red Cross repeatedly told the ICRC not to intervene on behalf of German Jews because such requests would be ignored.[84] The Nazi government's stated view was that its treatment of 'enemies of the state' was an internal domestic matter. Within weeks of the German invasion of Poland in September 1939, the ICRC in Geneva asked the Nazi authorities if they still favoured Jewish emigration. The SS leadership responded affirmatively, but made it clear that Jewish organizations in Germany were not allowed to contact the ICRC directly, and for that reason, the organization should not waste its time and energies on the problem. The ICRC agreed.[85] In the summer of 1941 Hartmann, the German Red Cross official, also made it very clear to Geneva that enquiries from relatives forwarded by the ICRC about concentration camp inmates would no longer be answered for the duration of the war.[86] Huber eventually withdrew to the modest stance in which 'to recognize the limits of humanitarian aid is the condition for its survival'.[87] Historian Monty Penkower has concluded, 'The ICRC insisted that it could not challenge the Nazi onslaught against European Jewry. First, the German authorities considered their treatment of its Jewish population an internal matter. Second, the protection of even "civilian internees" had not yet received sanction in a separate [Geneva] convention'.[88]

Not Speaking Out: The ICRC's 'Most Shameful Moment'

In retrospect, the year 1942 proved to be a critical one in the ICRC's policy towards civilian victims of the Nazi regime and European Jews in particular. The ICRC leadership learned early on of Nazi plans to murder European Jews. Burckhardt, the ambitious diplomat, historian, and ICRC vice president, who was perhaps the most influential official of the ICRC even before he became its president in January 1945, had early knowledge of the 'Final Solution'. Burckhardt maintained close contacts with German diplomats and officials, as well as with members of refugee circles, Christian humanitarian groups, and the leaders of Jewish organizations. One of those was Gerhart Riegner, the representative of the World Jewish Congress (WJC) in Switzerland, who was also in Geneva during the war. Burckhardt knew from his contacts with German government officials that from late 1941 the Nazi leadership had decided to systematically murder all European Jews. There was, however, no written order from Hitler for the genocide, possibly because that was not necessary. With Hitler's takeover of power German Jews faced discrimination, forced emigration, and eventually widespread acts of violence during the 1938 Kristallnacht pogrom. But it was not until the outbreak of the war that the Nazis and their allies launched a systematic mass murder campaign. In the wake of the invading German Wehrmacht in Poland 1939, Nazi killing squads murdered thousands of Jews and members of the Polish 'intelligentsia', among them Catholic priests. With the invasion of the Soviet Union in June 1941, Hitler and his associates launched a war of annihilation with the systematic extermination of millions of Jews, Slavs, and other targeted groups. In the war in the East, there would be no more respect for international law and no restraints. At a conference in a villa at the Wannsee lake outside Berlin, Nazi officials under the leadership of SS General Reinhard Heydrich coordinated the logistics for the systematic and industrialized murder of millions.[89] This was in January 1942. Riegner had been informed in July 1942 about the planned mass murder of all European Jews, possibly through gassing. Riegner met Burckhardt a few times over the summer of 1942 and informed him about the Nazi extermination plan.[90] In August 1942 Riegner sent a telegram through the British and US consulate to the president of the World Jewish Congress in New York, information that was passed on to Allied governments. But the US government was cautious, withholding the information until its accuracy could be verified. Among the people approached by US State Department officials was Burckhardt. On 7 November 1942, Burckhardt told the US consul in Geneva, Paul C. Squire, that Hitler had issued an order in 1941 to make Europe 'free of Jews' ('*judenfrei*'). Burckhardt did not use words such as 'murder' or 'extermination', but seems to have just repeated back the language of his two well-informed German sources. However, he made it clear that *judenfrei* could only mean the murder of the Jewish population, as they had nowhere else to go. On 17 November 1942, when Burckhardt met with Riegner, the ICRC diplomat left no doubt that he already knew what was happening. Burckhardt told Riegner about the 'order of Hitler, to exterminate the Jews of Europe by the end of the year' ('Befehl Hitlers, die Juden bis zum Ende des Jahres in Europa auszurotten').[91]

Burckhardt's information was probably not decisive, but together with a number of other sources it helped form a picture of Nazi Germany's intentions to murder all European Jews.[92] The US State Department now saw no reason to withhold the information any longer. On 17 December 1942 the United States, Great Britain, and ten other Allied governments publicly denounced Germany's plan to murder the Jews of Europe. The Allies also warned the perpetrators that they would be held responsible.[93]

Knowledge about Nazi atrocities did not, however, translate into action. The ICRC's leaders discussed the conditions of concentration camp inmates and possible aid work for this group of victims. As pressure from various international and Jewish aid organizations increased, the ICRC felt the need to address the brutality of the war, particularly the massive bombing of civilian targets, cities, and the deportation and mass murder of civilians. The draft appeal's wording remained vague and failed to name the perpetrators. Nevertheless, it could be read as a reference both to the Nazi regime's atrocities against Jews and Slavic populations and to the Allied bombing of civilian targets. The draft appeal emphasized, among other violations, the special fate of the victims of deportations. It declared, 'Certain categories of civilians belonging to various nationalities are being deprived of their liberty for reasons connected with the state of war, and are being deported. Or they have been taken hostage and risk being put to death for acts of which they are usually not the perpetrators.'[94] The ICRC called upon the governments at war to at least grant POW status to civilians in concentration camps. Acknowledging its own principles, ICRC leaders concluded they could no longer stand by and avoid taking a moral stand. By the summer of 1942 the majority inside the organization's leadership was ready and willing to do something. One possibility was to issue a public declaration protesting the increasing violation of humanitarian norms. The four women on the twenty-three-person committee were particularly vocal in their support for action: Suzanne Ferrière, Marguerite Frick-Cramer, Lucie Odier, and Renée Bordier.

The news from Geneva about a possible ICRC declaration on the violations of humanitarian law by Germany alarmed certain Swiss officials in the capital, Bern. Edouard de Haller and Philipp Etter were Swiss government officials and also members of the ICRC committee. They had Swiss national interests in mind and were concerned about these developments. Anxiety had reached a high pitch since the Anschluss between Germany and Austria in 1938. The central government in Bern was careful not challenge the ICRC's de jure and de facto independence in any obvious or direct way. In the eyes of Max Huber, the ICRC was 'an international institution, completely free of national interests', as he stressed in a public talk in 1944.[95] But Swiss government officials nevertheless tried to influence any possible ICRC declarations regarding Germany, not wanting to antagonize their neighbour. In truth, the ICRC was itself not always 'immune to the siren call of Swiss nationalism'.[96] Burckhardt did not question this common interest; in fact, he believed the

ICRC was the one Swiss-based institution that could allow Switzerland to play a leading role in the realm of international diplomacy.[97]

The relationship between the Swiss government and the ICRC was sometimes competitive and sometimes cooperative, and Geneva did not usually simply give in to the wishes of Bern. However, the line between the two was never particularly sharp. The Independent Commission of Experts Switzerland–Second World War (also known as the Bergier Commission after its chair, the Swiss historian Jean-François Bergier) has concluded that although the ICRC was officially independent, its policies and its decision-making were 'strongly influenced' by the Swiss government.[98]

The Swiss government had representatives in the committee and helped finance the organization's operations. It was common for Swiss diplomats, lawyers, and officials to serve terms on the ICRC in the course of their professional careers. ICRC President Burckhardt even served as the Swiss ambassador in Paris between 1945 and 1948 while at least formally still heading the Red Cross. His successor, Ruegger, had also been an ambassador before becoming ICRC president. Philipp Etter, a member of the Swiss government and in 1942 the Swiss federal president, was simultaneously a member of the ICRC. Giuseppe Motta sat on the Swiss Federal Council and headed the foreign affairs bureau while serving on the ICRC.

This sometimes close and cosy relationship between the ICRC and the Swiss government would come to shape and contribute to the most consequential failure of the ICRC during the war. Tellingly, it was Swiss President Etter who intervened in the critical 14 October 1942 ICRC debate about issuing a declaration of protest. Etter rarely found time to attend meetings of the ICRC, but he made sure to be in Geneva for the meeting on 14 October.[99] At this meeting, he made clear what kind of outcome the Swiss government wanted to see. Max Huber was absent due to ill-health and Committee member Edouard Chapuisat chaired the two-hour meeting in Geneva's Hotel Métropole. Huber stated in advance that he would support the decision of the majority. His position of discretion was well known both in and outside the committee.

With Huber absent, it was now very much up to Burckhardt to take the lead. Along with other Red Cross leaders, Burckhardt warned that the organization's 1942 draft declaration was too anti-German and that it could sabotage the ICRC's ability to aid POWs in Germany. This argument has often been repeated in defence of the International Red Cross's inaction on behalf of Holocaust victims during the war. It is important to recognize, however, that protection of and aid to POWs was based not only on the Geneva Conventions but also the principle of reciprocity. Nazi Germany took an active interest in the well-being of its POWs in British and American captivity.[100] Would the Axis powers have retaliated against Allied POWs because of an appeal concerning imprisoned civilians in German hands? The so-called 'shackling crisis' seemed to have confirmed these fears.[101] In August 1942, 5,000 Canadians and 1,000 British forces crossed the English Channel and landed on the French shores of Dieppe. Canadian commandos handcuffed German soldiers on the beach during the raid, allegedly to prevent them from committing sabotage. The German government responded by shackling some 4,500 British and Canadian POWs. In addition, the Nazi German government threatened to disregard the Geneva Conventions in their treatment of the captured soldiers. The possibility of Germany completely abandoning the Geneva Conventions greatly worried Burckhardt and may well have played a part in making the 14 October public statement more restrained.[102] Burckhardt believed little would change with an official protest against the systematic murder of Jews and other civilians. On the contrary it could even make things worse, at least for POWs. According to Riegner, Burckhardt stated that the ICRC 'had just barely managed to manouver through the dangerous cliffs of a German denunciation of the Geneva Conventions'.[103]

The ICRC ultimately gave the planned declaration of protest a 'first class funeral', as government representatives cynically put it afterwards. At the end of the meeting it was decided to intervene in grave cases directly and discreetly with the governments concerned. Whatever the ultimate reasons and interests of the key players, their decision remains controversial. The Swiss historian Jean-Claude Favez has underlined the fact that the minutes from the meeting reveal the 'deft way in which the proposal was shelved'.[104] Burckhardt did not share his detailed knowledge of the 'Final Solution' with his fellow ICRC colleagues such as Huber before or during this meeting. Had he done so, a protest might have been more likely. Years later, Riegner was still puzzled by this lack of communication: 'It seems strange that Burckhardt should never have spoken to his International Committee of the Red Cross colleagues of the information on the "Final Solution" he had obtained from German sources.'[105] But Burckhardt's position was in line with his opposition to any form of public protest; he preferred quiet diplomacy instead.[106] Moreover, he probably knew about the Riegner telegram and the plans for an international appeal. In his 7 November 1941 meeting with the US diplomat Paul Squire, however, Burckhardt claimed all the credit for similar initiatives inside the ICRC for himself. Squire reported back to Washington:

> Dr. Burckhardt. who deals with External Affairs in the International Committee of the Red Cross, informed me that it was his plan to direct a public appeal throughout the world on the question of the Jews and hostages and that the matter was discussed at a full meeting (about 24 present) of the International Committee on October 14, 1942. It was decided, however, that such an appeal (1) would serve no purpose, rendering the situation even more difficult and (2) would jeopardise all the work undertaken for the prisoners of war and civilian internees [excluded in this category were most political prisoners and deportees] – the real task of the Red Cross.[107]

Burckhardt obviously twisted the real course of events and his own convictions when talking to the US diplomat.

Madame Frick-Cramer stated that now that the committee had decided against a public statement, it should intensify its direct interventions with governments. She was particularly referring to the mass deportations and Nazi camps. Suzanne Ferrière, head of the migration service, was also eager to help and would turn out to be particularly active and engaged in the coming years. There was clearly already at this time some uneasiness in the air about the decision that had been made. Several of the defeated pro-appeal members of the ICRC were also concerned with the possible long-term consequences of the ICRC not speaking out. 'With great prescience, several Assembly members [...] speaking in advance of President [Philipp] Etter at the 14 October meeting, said that if the ICRC did not issue the public statement under consideration, its future work would be tainted.'[108] Nothing less than the reputation of the humanitarian organization's moral authority was at stake. In the words of the latter-day British human rights activist Caroline Moorehead, 'In failing to take "a strong moral line" [...], they failed not only the Jews, but themselves.'[109] Yves Sandoz, a current member of the ICRC, struggles with an explanation: 'The main reason was likely linked to the fact that the Committee felt such public appeals would have no tangible impact, except to endanger the ICRC's ongoing activities and those it might be able to carry out at a later stage of the war.'[110] Around the same time in 1942, Burckhardt realized that its dependency on the Swiss government would harm the international standing of the ICRC. He complained about the rivalry between the ICRC and the Swiss government in a letter to a member of the Swiss parliament at this time. According to Burckhardt, the Swiss authorities were competing with the ICRC in many humanitarian areas, for instance the exchange of wounded POWs. Burckhardt then went on to say that in the war all nations have 'noticed with concern that the Committee has drifted into an unwanted dependency on Bern'.[111] The ICRC was expected to work with the Swiss government for the common goal of national defence, despite the clear separation that theoretically existed between the state and this international organization.[112] As historian Caroline Moorehead has observed, 'In the late 1940s, the International Committee was widely perceived to be in Berne's pocket and when Berne was discredited so was the Committee.'[113] Burckhardt was well aware that the dependence on Bern could backfire on the ICRC's international standing. And he even afffirmed that its moral authority could be damaged by such a state of affairs, saying in 1942 that: 'The moral authority that the ICRC still enjoyed at the Peace Conference in 1918 cannot [be] regained anymore, once it is lost.'[114]

There can be little doubt that the ICRC violated its own principles at this time, especially its principles of independence and neutrality. Max Huber himself time and again had stressed the importance of neutrality and impartiality as central principles for the organization:

> For the ICRC, whose most important mission in war time is providing help for the victims of war as a neutral intermediary between the war parties, *impartiality* is the real vital principle. Its impartial mission can only be fulfilled based on strict political *neutrality*, on full independence of any national, supranational, political, social, or religious organization. Impartiality means the readiness to serve all [victims] equally.[115]

Despite Huber's impassioned defence of neutrality and impartiality, Jean-Claude Favez makes very clear the consequences of the ICRC's inaction: 'The importance the ICRC attached to its credibility took it paradoxically down a road that led to a loss of credibility and therefore of authority within the Red Cross movement and in the wider world.'[116] Thus for some the decision of 14 October 1942 would become the ICRC's 'most shameful moment' in the Second World War.[117] Although the Red Cross achieved much in helping the plight of POW's, especially in Western Europe, its role in the context of the Holocaust still casts long shadows and 'has haunted it ever since'.[118] It was only in the 1990s that the ICRC publicly admitted that its silence on the Shoah was a 'moral defeat'. In the words of Peter Maurer, ICRC president since 2012: '[The ICRC] failed as a humanitarian organization because it had lost its moral compass.'[119]

3
Intervention and Opportunism

The International Committee of the Red Cross (ICRC) obviously faced external pressure from the Swiss government, but internal considerations also spoke against a daring and comprehensive programme of aid to Hitler's victims. Yet after 1942 the ICRC tried to move past its failure to make a public declaration protesting against Nazi crimes and humanitarian violations. It slowly began to show more interest in the fate of European Jews and other civilian victims of Hitler's regime. The impetus for the ICRC's heightened interest in offering more decisive aid came not only from its own ranks. The changing tide of the war in favour of the Allies and the pressure of Jewish aid organizations inside and outside of Switzerland also provoked a response. The organization embarked on a two-pronged strategy. First, it began intervening in countries that were allies or satellites of Nazi Germany on behalf of civilian concentration camp prisoners— including Jews. Second, it started sending food parcels to concentration camps such as Dachau, Oranienburg-Sachsenhausen, Ravensbrueck, and Buchenwald. Although the Red Cross's relief work for imprisoned civilians was very much limited within Germany, the ICRC was soon active in Nazi allied and satellite states, especially Hungary.[1] Then, in the final stages of the war, other neutral nations, above all Sweden, began to compete with the Swiss in the humanitarian sphere.

Rescue Efforts for Camp Prisoners

As we saw in Chapter 2, help for concentration camp inmates and particularly Jews seemed almost impossible in the first three years of the war. The Nazi authorities and the German Red Cross were not cooperating, especially when Jews were concerned. A letter from the ICRC to the headquarters of the American Red Cross from early 1943 summarized the ongoing deadlock well:

> The International Committee of the Red Cross have always been concerned with the welfare of civilian prisoners in concentration camps, maintaining that they could not pass over this category of internees, since they are enemy nationals in the hands of a belligerent. Hitherto, however, and despite all our efforts, the German Authorities have not allowed the International Committee to assist these prisoners, on the grounds that they were arrested for motives of public safety or for having committed crime.[2]

But the ICRC and others kept trying. The ICRC's aid relief work for civilians was often carried out under the umbrella of a body called the Joint Relief Commission (JRC). Since the summer of 1941, ICRC president Carl Jacob Burckhardt, who was always more pragmatic and hands-on than his predecessor, Max Huber, had worked on creating a JRC that could coordinate the aid work of the League of Red Cross Societies and the ICRC. Its creation meant overcoming the long-standing tensions between the League and the ICRC that had existed since the creation of the League in 1919.[3] Officially and publicly, of course, both organizations praised their positive, cooperative relations. The JRC would play a significant role in helping the international Red Cross to achieve the second prong of its strategy, sending food aid to camp prisoners. Given that the idea of a public protest had been abandoned by the ICRC, Gerhart Riegner and Paul Guggenheim from the World Jewish Congress (WJC) demanded at least more practical aid for Jewish camp inmates. In May 1943 they demanded that food parcels should be sent to these victims, as was already common practice for POWs. Guggenheim stated that after this war the world would sternly ask if his organization and the ICRC had done enough. Guggenheim went on to say that as things stood at that stage, he was doubtful that one could answer that question positively.[4]

Jean (Johannes) Schwarzenberg, an Austrian nobleman with Swiss citizenship, worked at the division for civilian internees at the ICRC headquarters, and from 1942 onwards was responsible for bringing relief to concentration camp prisoners.[5] The ICRC faced no small challenge in organizing a campaign to provide food for camp inmates. In principle, the Nazis did allow shipment of parcels to concentration camps, but only if they were addressed to specific individuals. This was of little use, since the Nazi government typically did not give out information about the location of most concentration camp inmates and deportees.[6] Therefore Schwarzenberg's food parcel programme started on a very small scale. He had a list of only fifty names of Norwegian concentration camp prisoners. The first test run in June of 1943 was relatively successful, and thirty signed package receipts made their way back to Geneva. By mid-November 1943, 882 packages had been sent to Germany, most to Dutch and Norwegian inmates, thirty-one to Jews (their nationality left undefined). The ICRC took this as sufficient proof that the aid had reached the intended internees and called the pro-gramme a great success. Based on this limited positive experience, the ICRC even asked the American Red Cross to support lifting the Allied blockade so that the programme could continue and expand, but this request met with little success.

At the end of 1943 individual concentration camp commanders gave permission for collective deliveries of parcels for certain groups of inmates, mostly along national lines. In May 1943 the ICRC could report that some food parcels had reached ghettos in Poland and the Theresienstadt ghetto in occupied Czechoslovakia. The Jewish Elders in the ghettos had signed the receipts, which the ICRC saw as an indication that packages had reached the groups intended.[7] In the spring of 1944 the parcel service to camp civilians was extended, and the status of Schwarzenberg's office raised, but resources and personnel were still scarce for his special aid divi-sion. Aid for Jews remained limited, and mainly rested on the food parcel program to a number of camps and ghettos. But crucially all depended on the goodwill of the Nazi authorities. In June 1943 the ICRC delegate in Berlin proposed to extend the parcel scheme to camps such as Auschwitz-Birkenau, only to be rejected by Walther Hartmann from the German Red Cross. Hartmann claimed that the Jews were employed exclusively in labour camps in the East and that food and medication there was reportedly abun-dant. Therefore, Hartmann wrote, shipments of supplies to these camps were in principle not necessary.[8] This brusque answer from Berlin shattered hopes in Geneva.

The Allied blockade was another obstacle for this kind of relief aid. At first some food could be bought from South America, Hungary, Turkey, and Sweden, but with the war expanding and becoming more intense this became more and more difficult.[9] The Allies were willing to let the Swedish Red Cross and the ICRC provide aid to the starving Greek population under Nazi occupation, despite the blockade policy. However, the same consideration was not extended to Jews in concentration camps and ghettos in the rest of German-occupied Europe.[10]

But there were small successes too. Since the receipts often included the name of the recipient along with names of other prisoners in the same camp, the ICRC was able by March of 1945 to combine this information with that from other sources to compile a list of nearly 56,000 people and their locations. The organization thus did slowly emerge as an important conduit for bringing some limited aid to Jews in Nazi-occupied Europe. Starting in 1944, large quantities of food parcels were sent to concentration camps and ghettos, often financed by Jewish organizations and delivered through the ICRC.[11] In the autumn of 1944 the US government allowed 260,000 American Red Cross parcels to pass the blockade. The ICRC was mainly a trustee for financial and material aid provided by other organizations and governments. While the camps in the East, especially the death factories such as Auschwitz-Birkenau, Treblinka, and Sobibor, remained out of reach,[12] thousands of food parcels did eventually reach Jews in camps, particularly in the last months of the war. Given the massive scale of suffering that had occurred in Nazi camps and ghettos, this ICRC effort may seem like a trivial contribution, far too little, far too late. However, the concentration camp food parcels programme could be seen as a 'weapon of last resort' for the ICRC, and it played a very important role in the ICRC's postwar account of its activities during the Holocaust.[13]

The ICRC worked together with a large number of other Jewish and humanitarian organizations, including the Quakers and the Young Men's Christian Association (YMCA). But the ICRC's help for Jewish victims was largely financed by Jewish organizations working in Europe. Schwarzenberg made very clear that most of this relief work under the flag of the ICRC was financed with 'Jewish money' ('*jüdischem Geld*').[14] According to ICRC sources it received 22 million Swiss francs from Jewish organizations.[15]

Saly Mayer and Gerhart Riegner were among the main Jewish contacts for the ICRC in Switzerland. Mayer was president of the Association of Jewish Communities in Switzerland and later also a representative of the American Jewish Joint Distribution Committee (JDC) or 'Joint'.[16] The JDC had been founded on the eve of the First World War in New York and was active in a wide range of rescue activities for Jewish victims. It helped with emigration, was sending food parcels, opening shelters and soup kitchens (not at least for displaced persons), helped to finance the efforts of government agencies, and in some cases even provided ransom money in order to save Jews.[17] As we have seen, Riegner was a German Jew who found refuge in Switzerland and served as a representative of the WJC based in New York.

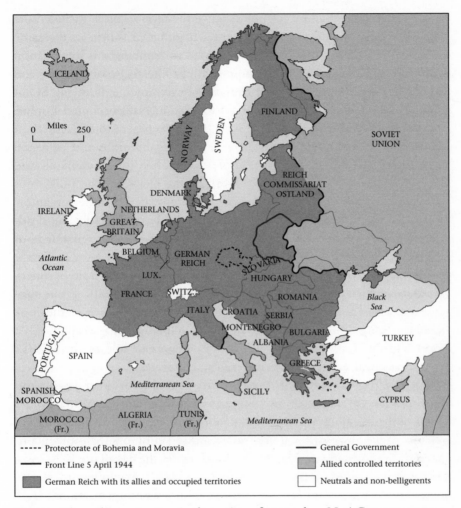

Map 1. The military situation in the spring of 1944 when Nazi German troops invaded Hungary

The WJC, founded in the 1930s, was an international organization of Jewish associations, which fought antisemitism and often lobbied for a range of causes. The ICRC worked with both men and the institutions they represented on a regular basis. But Red Cross representatives appear to have favoured the JDC and Saly Mayer for a number of reasons. The JDC provided crucial funds to the ICRC and in many respects shared a similar philosophy about concrete humanitarian aid work and discretion with the Geneva-based institution. Schwarzenberg described Mayer as an 'experienced and discreet friend of our house'[18] and went on to say: 'Saly Mayer is really the only one who does something and is really useful to us.'[19] As a result, cooperation between the Jewish organizations sitting in New York and Geneva and the ICRC soon increased. The former would provide financial support and the supplies, and the Red Cross would take over transport and delivery of the food supplies. Relation between the parties could be difficult at times, but also achieved some significant successes, especially later into the war.

Turning Point: 1944

In January 1944, the US Department of the Treasury was charged with the administration of the newly founded War Refugee Board (WRB). The WRB was created to help civilian victims of the Nazi regime, particularly Jews.[20] The creation of the WRB was a turning point for the ICRC's rescue efforts for civilian Nazi victims. Like the Allied joint declaration on German mass murder of Jews and other civilians of 17 December 1942, the founding of the refugee board seemed to send a clear if belated signal: the United States had now taken a more concerted interest in the fate of Europe's Jews.[21] From early 1944 onwards, government agencies such as the WRB took action and coordinated rescue efforts for Jews.[22] It received support from private aid organisations, prominent among them the American Jewish Joint Distribution Committee, which provided much of the funding for rescue operations of the government board.[23] Furthermore, the WRB began putting considerable pressure on the ICRC to act and intervene, arguing that the ICRC should not limit itself to the letter of international humanitarian law, but should provide concrete aid in the spirit of Red Cross philosophy. With the foundation of the refugee board the status of many Jewish aid organizations in Europe began to change in the spring of 1944.[24]

Jewish relief organizations like the JDC turned out to be valuable partners of the first US agency to be founded with the explicit purpose of saving civilian victims of war and the Nazi genocide. The funds from Mayer along with pressure from the WRB spurred the ICRC to undertake more relief efforts in Eastern Europe. As part of the goal of becoming more active in German-occupied and satellite countries, the ICRC attempted to gain access to concentration camps and ghettos like Theresienstadt. In March 1943 Max Huber assured Saly Mayer that the ICRC would do what it could for Jewish victims and was exploring the possibility of sending ICRC delegations to Budapest, Bucharest, and Bratislava.[25] At the same time the ICRC considered an intervention with the British government to allow more emigration to Palestine for 'Israelites' in Central and Eastern Europe. London should increase the visa quota to British controlled Palestine, for those with close relatives in Palestine and with an exit visa granted.[26] In a Meeting of the Committee in November 1943 Burckhardt proposed that Schwarzenberg prepare missions for Romania, Hungary, and Slovakia. 'The development of the Jewish problem makes it necessary and urgent to send a mission to Central and Eastern Europe', Burckhardt stated.[27]

In January 1944, the US Ambassador to Switzerland, Leland Harrison, forwarded a message from the newly established WRB to ICRC president Max Huber at the ICRC in Geneva:

> We are familiar with the report [...] to your Washington delegation concerning possible feeding programs in Romania, Theresienstadt, Slovakia and Croatia, and the need of funds therefore, and desire information as to the areas in which you could operate immediately, assuming that necessary funds are made available to you to provide food and medicines to Jews and other persecuted group in German occupied areas who are denied the facilities available to the rest of the population. Please advise where food, medicines and other supplies can be purchased and how much money is needed. We are prepared to see that funds are made available at once for necessary operations.[28]

On 11 February 1944, the US legation in Switzerland followed up with Max Huber that the War Refugee Board was requesting more information about the ICRC's relief operations on behalf of Jews and other persecuted groups. At the top of the list were relief efforts in Croatia, Slovakia, Romania, Hungary, and the Theresienstadt camp north of Prague.[29] And indeed the ICRC followed up with rescue missions in these locations.

The Red Cross sent a delegate to Romania and Romanian-occupied territories, distributed foodstuffs, and in 1944 intervened with the Romanian government in favour of the remaining Jewish population. 1944 was also the year, when the ICRC became very active for the relief and protection of Hungarian Jews, as we will see later in this chapter.

Money was key, because all these plans and new efforts had to be financed. The JDC through Saly Mayer made the needed funds available, granting $100,000 (300,000 Swiss francs) for the project. The ICRC was to buy food and clothing and otherwise carry out the relief work. The WRB was to be fully informed about the action taken by Geneva.[30] The US legation in

Switzerland promised full support when it stated: 'In accordance with instructions received from the Department of State, the Legation will be pleased to offer you all possible cooperation in this matter.'[31] The news made Schwarzenberg euphoric: 'This is amazing; 100,000 dollars for free is fantastic. This changes everything; now one has to pursue this work seriously... I have to tell Huber that this has to get done now.'[32] Schwarzenberg began to hope for more active interventions, perhaps even a proper office for Jewish affairs. Meanwhile, the ICRC started to give in to more demands by Jewish organizations and Allied governments. In February 1944 Mayer wrote to Max Huber that he was thankful for all the support given by the ICRC so far and shared his relief that the United States had at last officially acted. He also expressed his hope that the blockade restrictions against Nazi-controlled Europe might be liberalized in order to allow for more aid supplies and money for rescue operations.[33] US support for Jewish organisations continued. In March 1944 the JDC received a license from the US government to dispatch $300,000 a month to Mayer in Switzerland. Mayer was basically given free rein to use the money wherever he deemed necessary, but he was instructed to inform the War Refugee Board about everything.[34] The money provided by the JDC through the WRB buoyed up the activities of Jewish organizations. It also complicated the ICRC's role in such activities. According to Schwarzenberg, Saly Mayer was willing to use legal and illegal means (maybe a reference to bribery or legally questionable protection papers) to save as many people as possible; the ICRC remained more cautious.[35] It still put its energies into the food parcel scheme and hoped for its extension, with WRB support. The ICRC appealed again to the American Red Cross for lifting the blockade for food deliveries to concentration camps. This renewed attempt would have been quite understandable, if the WRB of the Treasury Department had not already allowed the transfer of $200,000 to the ICRC 'for the purchase of supplies for these concentration camps'.[36] In early 1944 the American Red Cross made clear that there was still no change of policy in Washington regarding the blockade: 'The American Red Cross (AMRC) has followed the practice of not endeavouring to influence the decision of the Blockading Authorities [...]' 'I believe you have already approached the Blockading Authorities without successful results, so that it appears there is little further that we can do at this moment concerning this problem.'[37] An internal AMRC memo stated at that time that the State Department was strictly against sending food supplies to concentration camps where ICRC delegates were not allowed access.[38] The US authorities wanted to make sure that food packages filled with precious coffee, cigarettes and meat would not fall into enemy hands. These were understandable concerns. Who could stop SS guards from taking advantage of the situation and simply taking the shipments for themselves? Distribution of Red Cross food parcels under the supervision of the ICRC was seen as the best way to prevent such an abuse of rescue aid. Access to the concentration camps and ghettos therefore seemed crucial.

Thus it was seen as a big step in the right direction when the Nazi authorities finally agreed to an ICRC inspection of the ghetto-camp in Terezín (Theresienstadt) near Prague. The camp had been the focus of relief operations for quite some time, not just on the part of the ICRC, but also for the Danish and Swedish Red Cross. The Swedish Red Cross had been sending large numbers of gift packages to Norwegian internees and Danish Jews in Theresienstadt for some time.[39] The 23 June 1944 visit of a delegation of the ICRC and the Danish Red Cross was carefully orchestrated by the SS, who presented a very sanitized view of 'normal' camp life. Occupied Denmark should be kept quiet and the vital imports from neutral Sweden continued. Therefore the well-being of Danish prisoners in Theresienstadt and elsewhere was of particular concern to the Nazi leadership in the final stages of the war. In preparation for the visit the SS was kept busy. Weak and sick people were deported to Auschwitz to reduce numbers in the completely overcrowded camp, houses painted, streets and parks cleaned, and flowers were planted. The delegates were shown a school, a soccer game, and a children's theatre performed for them. The deception seemed to have worked, and the Nazis were very pleased with the ICRC's favourable report of the good treatment of Jews in German camps. But this came at a time when the public in neutral and Allied countries was already well informed about the ongoing genocide. Encouraged by the successful propaganda trap they had laid for their visitors, the Nazis decided to produce a 'documentary' about Theresienstadt that became known as *The Führer Gives a City to the Jews*. Most inmates appearing in the film were deported and murdered in Auschwitz shortly after the final scenes were shot. In Nazi propaganda Theresienstadt was portrayed as a 'spa town' where elderly German and Austrian Jews could life out their lives in peace. The example of Theresienstadt was meant to refute news about deportations and systematic killings in death factories.[40] The ICRC's 1944 report about Theresienstadt certainly discredited the organization as being either naive or complicit in a cruel fiction,[41] even more so as the responsible ICRC delegate Maurice Rossel continued to defend his views many decades later. When in 1979 the French documentary film-maker Claude Lanzmann interviewed Rossel for his epic film *Shoah*, Rossel stated that he confirmed the excellent conditions in the camp and probably would do so today as well. And there was more. After his visit to Theresienstadt, Rossel gained access to Auschwitz but didn't realize its function as a killing centre.[42] In April 1945 the ICRC came back to the ghetto-camp Theresienstadt for another visit. The Nazi authorities, including Adolf Eichmann, who were hosting the Swiss, denied the genocide and showed them the propaganda film about Theresienstadt.[43] While the ICRC endured the farce staged for them about Theresienstadt, British and American troops were liberating concentration camps such as Bergen-Belsen and Buchenwald. The Allied film footage about the reality of these camps shocked the world. On 2 May 1945 ICRC delegate Paul Dunant managed to move into the Theresienstadt ghetto and negotiated its protection under the ICRC flag. On 8 May 1945 he handed the surviving inmates over to the Czechoslovakian authorities.

The Neutrals Change Course

While humanitarian agencies like the ICRC were feeling the Allies' pressure to become more active in their work, so too were neutral countries feeling the pressure to conform to the Allies' demands. The Allies saw various neutral countries' policies as detrimental to the war effort and called for change. The US government wanted neutral nations to side with them and help them to defeat Nazi Germany.[44] Sweden and Switzerland had faced harsh criticism for not being really neutral and instead lending support to the Axis powers. According to the Allies, Swiss non-participation in the war against the Nazis was at best seen as an act of selfishness. Western governments saw Switzerland as a weasel, skilfully avoiding taking a stance. Even worse, with raw materials and supplies from the neutrals, Germany made weapons that killed Allied soldiers. Therefore, although technically in line with legal standards of behaviour for neutral countries, the Allies considered Swiss economic co-operation with Germany to be a shabby business. Swiss fears and appeasement strategies towards Nazi Germany were accepted initially, but after the German surrender at Stalingrad in February 1943, the Allies lost patience. US Secretary of State Cordell Hull stated in 1944 that the Swiss had to cease 'purchas[ing] protection against aggression by furnishing

aid to our enemy'. Like Switzerland, until 1943, neutral Sweden, tried to
appease Germany. It allowed German troops to march through Sweden
and allowed the German navy the use of Swedish territorial waters.
It also delivered important raw materials (such as iron ore) for use in
Germany's war industry, and adopted Switzerland's indirect suggestion of
stamping German Jews' passports with the infamous 'J'. A few hundred
Swedes even volunteered for Hitler's Waffen SS and fought against the
Soviets.[45] Historian Paul Levine stresses the Allied pressure on Sweden
when he writes: 'From early 1943 forward, the Americans demanded in
increasingly strident tones an immediate end to what one U. S. representative called "the very substantial aid you are giving the Germans every
day." '[46] Winston Churchill showed little sympathy either: 'Neutrals who
have played a selfish part throughout ought to be made to suffer in the
postwar world.'[47]

Because both countries were slow to comply with Allied requests, the
Americans became increasingly frustrated. In the words of US Secretary of
State Dean Acheson: 'Both Swedes and Swiss are among the most inde-
pendent-minded, not to say stubborn, people in the world. . . . If the Swedes
were stubborn, the Swiss were the cube of stubbornness.'[48] The neutral
countries would in due course be forced to react to the demands of the
emerging victors.

The Allies sought the help of all neutrals in turning the tide against
Germany. Their aim was to damage the enemy from all possible angles.
Economic warfare played an enormous role in the total war effort. To crip-
ple the enemy, foreign trade was disrupted and imports of raw materials cut
off. To achieve these goals, the Allies had to force the neutrals in Latin
American and European countries into line with the blockade policy. Those
nations after all were major suppliers of the Axis powers. But many loop-
holes allowed the neutrals to continue their trade relationships. Ultimately,
by 1944 the Allies demanded that all exports of the neutrals to Hitler's Germany
had to end and threatened severe sanctions. As Germany's neighbours, the
role of neutral Switzerland and Sweden was thus of particular importance
in this strategy.[49]

By the end of the summer of 1943, Sweden had given in to many Allied
requests.[50] Switzerland long resisted, but eventually had to give in, too.[51] By
pleasing the victors, Switzerland (and other neutrals like Sweden) hoped for
better settlements in postwar economic questions. One of these issues was
the fate of German government assets held in Switzerland.[52] Another issue

was German gold, worth millions (including looted gold), sitting in the vaults of the Swiss national bank. The Swiss had little interest in surrendering these assets. Yet a change of policies was imminent, because the Allies' leverage was increasing. Starting in 1944, for instance, food deliveries from harbours in France and Italy to landlocked Switzerland came to depend almost completely on Allied goodwill.[53] US intervention in the European war and advocacy for victims of Nazi atrocities also meant that the neutral countries were under pressure to defend their wartime activities. The Swiss and the Swedes now had to adapt to a new geopolitical constellation.

For Sweden, a long-term realignment of its foreign policy and economy would be necessary if it was to prosper after the war. Until 1942 the Swedish government showed very little interest in the fate of European Jewry and accepted only a small number of refugees.[54] The rescue of the Danish Jews by Sweden in 1943 certainly marked a major turning point in its stance. But the Danish Jewish community was small, comprised of a few thousand people, mostly with a strong Scandinavian identity. The way to safety for them was relatively easy, merely a short trip in a fishing boat over to the coast of Sweden. The situation of millions of Polish and Eastern European Jews was quite different.[55] But Sweden's humanitarian successes could not erase its failures, nor conceal its partially selfish motivations. 'Sweden's admirable record of support for humanitarian activities notwithstanding, few would argue that a sovereign nation-state engages in such actions without their own interests firmly in view.'[56]

The case was much the same for Switzerland, which also had to demonstrate the contributions a neutral country might make to postwar Europe as it rehabilitated its image with the Allies. Switzerland had to change its foreign policy priorities—not to look to Berlin anymore but to the new emerging superpowers, the United States and the Soviet Union. Improving relations with these countries meant not only a new foreign policy but also new diplomatic personnel (including a new foreign minister).[57] A majority of the Swiss parliament saw humanitarian aid as one of Switzerland's most effective foreign policy tools.[58] High-ranking Swiss government officials repeatedly discussed how Switzerland might use humanitarian aid for refugees—including the services of the international Red Cross—as a bargaining chip for extracting foreign policy concessions and economic favours and relief from the Allies.[59] Hungary became an obvious place to start, since in 1944 it remained home to the last large surviving Jewish community under Axis control.

Hungary: A Humanitarian Proving Ground for Civilian Aid

Most of Europe's Jews in Nazi hands had already perished by 1944. Hungary now became the last chance to save a large community on the continent. A brief outline of the rescue activities of Sweden, the ICRC, and Switzerland reveals the complex motivations, both self-serving and selfless, of the neutral countries, as they sought to aid Hungarian Jews and curry favour with the Allies at the same time. Hungary lost most of her territory as a result of the First World War. The now small and landlocked country was led by an authoritarian regime under Admiral Miklós Horthy, who eventually sided with Mussolini and Hitler. The Hungarian government introduced antisemitic laws and drafted young Jews for slave labour brigades, but did not give in to German demands for the deportation of its Jewish population. After the catastrophic defeat of German, Italian, Romanian, and Hungarian troops at Stalingrad in early 1943 and the Allied advances on all fronts, Horthy was looking for a way out of the apparently already lost war. His government was now trying to secretly broker a separate armistice with the Western powers. Hitler suspected as much and took precautions to keep his ally in line. In March 1944 German troops occupied Hungary, and soon thereafter Adolf Eichmann coordinated the deportation of the majority of the country's 800,000 Jews in Hungary and its newly acquired territories to Auschwitz.[60] This number also included an estimated 100,000 Christians of Jewish ancestry and converts to Christianity, who had been defined as Jews under the Reich's 'racial laws'.[61]

At that point in the war the reality of the 'Final Solution' of the 'Jewish question' as mass murder was no longer a well-kept secret, if it ever had been. In Hungary, the genocide unfolded while the world was watching and reporting on every step of the deportation process. Even before Eichmann and his SS murderers began the deportations, the WJC informed the WRB about the planned genocide of the Hungarian Jews. The *New York Times* reported on 10 May 1944, that the Hungarian government 'is now preparing for the annihilation of Hungarian Jews'. On 18 May, a few days after the start of the deportations, the *Times* in London reported about the first transport of Jews to the 'murder camps in Poland'.[62] In the second half of June 1944, little more than a month after the deportations from Hungary had begun, the international public learned details about the systematic killings in Auschwitz-Birkenau. Based on reports by two escapees from Auschwitz,

a detailed report about the 'frightful happenings in these camps' was prepared for Allied governments and Christian aid societies in June 1944. The
WRB confirmed the authenticity of these reports: 'It is a fact beyond denial
that the Germans have deliberately and systematically murdered millions of
innocent civilians—Jews and Christians alike—all over Europe. This campaign of terror and brutality, which is unprecedented in all history . . . even
now continues unabated. . . .' The WRB was in favour of making the
Auschwitz reports public because, it 'should be read and understood by all
Americans'.[63] The reports were eventually widely distributed and covered
by the press.

Detailed descriptions of these horrific events were accumulating on the
desks of neutral and Allied governments, international aid organizations,
and the Vatican. The genocide was now as obvious and recognizable as the
approaching and certain defeat of Nazi Germany. In June 1944 the Allies
landed on the beaches of Normandy and marched on central and northern
Italy, while the Soviets were advancing towards the eastern German provinces. Eichmann's trains continued to roll, but the informed world was
beginning to take some action to help civilian victims of the Nazis.

The WRB and the State Department now turned to the neutral countries, the ICRC, and the Vatican in order to press the Hungarian government to halt the deportations.[64] The Swedes already had a remarkable
humanitarian record, established when they admitted and therefore saved
most of the Danish Jewish community in 1943.[65] Swedish humanitarian
Raoul Wallenberg was now sent to Hungary in order to save thousands
more lives.

Sweden reacted earlier and with more determination than the ICRC,
something which was noted by the WRB. A letter from the WRB director
to Secretary of the Treasury Henry Morgenthau reads: 'We requested neutral powers and the International Red Cross to increase the size of their
missions in Hungary. Sweden complied with our request and appointed a
special attaché at Budapest who is in direct communication with our representative in Stockholm and has, in many ways, been extremely helpful to
the Board.'[66] Wallenberg was widely travelled, spoke a number of languages,
and had studied in the United States.[67] Together with his fellow Swedish
diplomats, he began issuing 'protective passports' that identified the bearers
as Swedish subjects. The documents had very little legal standing, but were
nevertheless often respected by the Nazis and the Hungarian authorities.
With money from the WRB, Wallenberg and his associates rented thirty-two

Figure 3.1. Arrival of Jews from Hungary in Auschwitz-Birkenau in May 1944; women and children are photographed on the selection platform.

buildings in Budapest and put them under the protection of the Swedish government. Large signs at the entrance doors and oversized Swedish national flags helped with the deception and provided safe havens for many Jews in Budapest. But it was often simply Wallenberg's personal courage and personality that saved thousands of Jews from deportation and certain death.[68] Meanwhile the ICRC was carefully following every step of the 'Swedish representative in Budapest'.[69] From the perspective of the ICRC's leadership, Wallenberg, handpicked and supported by the WRB and the Swedish government, had now turned out to be a serious 'competitor'.[70] The Americans were certainly counting ·on Wallenberg as the unofficial representative of the WRB.

In May 1944 the ICRC sent their own small delegation to Budapest. The WRB insisted that the more neutrals were in place the better. Washington expected that a net of aid workers and diplomats from neutral nations would hinder the deportations. At the outset of the crisis in Hungary, WRB director John W. Pehle stressed the importance of the ICRC acting in Hungary,

Figure 3.2. Protective document from the Swedish Red Cross issued to the Hungarian teenager Erika V, 1944. (United States Holocaust Memorial Museum, courtesy of Erica & Joseph Grossman)

and the US government communicated its expectation that the ICRC would send a special delegation to Budapest immediately. 'Failing this, we are asking that Intercross [the international Red Cross] be advised of our conviction that an immediate enlargement of the Intercross delegation in Budapest and throughout Hungary, especially in the localities in which Jews are being concentrated, is an elementary humanitarian obligation of that organization.'[71] Although the appeals were not ignored, disagreement within the ICRC leadership delayed the agency's response to the crisis. It was mainly up to courageous individuals to hold the Swiss and Red Cross flag high in the Hungarian capital. Among the humanitarian heroes of Budapest were ICRC delegate Friedrich Born and Carl Lutz from the Swiss Legation. The ICRC's record in Hungary benefited greatly from the personal commitment of Born, who often acted on his own initiatives and went beyond the more timid instructions from Geneva. The ICRC in Budapest soon followed the Swedish example and handed out letters of protection to Jews and put Jewish hospitals, clinics, hostels, and soup kitchens under the protection of the organisation.[72] According to the ICRC, 30,000 letters of protection were issued and 3,000 Jewish children found food and shelter in homes in Budapest.[73] English author Alex Kershaw wrote: 'But of all the neutral diplomats, Wallenberg was the one who had placed himself in the most danger, directly in the firing line, in the crosshairs of the SS and the Arrow Cross' [the Hungarian fascist, proto-Nazi party].[74] The American historian Randolph L. Braham comes to a similar conclusion: 'Raoul Wallenberg provided a heartening and rare example of great personal courage and self-sacrificing humanitarianism.'[75] The Swiss, it seemed, could not match the success of the Swede.

As the crisis continued, more neutrals intervened on behalf of the Hungarian Jews. Pope Pius XII asked Hungarian leader Horthy for a personal intervention in favour of the deported civilians, although he never explicitly mentioned Jews in his plea. President Roosevelt joined in and clearly threatened Hungary with serious consequences, while the King of Sweden appealed to Horthy in the 'name of humanity'. The ICRC risked reneging on its humanitarian mission if it failed to act. Max Huber finally bowed to the wishes of the majority of the committee and intervened directly in favour of the Hungarian Jews. In June 1944 he wrote a letter to Horthy and asked him to stop the deportations, declaring that they would damage the humanitarian tradition and reputation of the Christian Hungarian nation if continued.[76] With this letter, the ICRC officially broke its silence and made a plea for the remaining Jews in Budapest. Historian Arieh Ben-Tov speaks about the motivations behind this important step: 'In my opinion, Max Huber decided to address the Hungarian Regent directly in order to save the honour of his country in the eyes of its citizens, of the world and of history. It was essential to try to save the Hungarian Jews in order to protect these values.'[77] But this change of policy came too late for the 400,000 Hungarian Jews who had already been killed by this point.[78] After all these pleas and Allied pressure, the deportations were halted in July 1944, at least for a time. While the Soviets moved towards Hungary, the ICRC, Jewish organizations and diplomats from neutral countries continued their efforts to save Hungarian Jews.

The Swiss government now finally decided to take action. Foreign Minister Pilet-Golaz, like police chief Heinrich Rothmund, was concerned about the impact that inaction in Hungary would have on the Swiss public and especially on the public in the United States.[79] Pilet-Golaz wrote to the Swiss ambassador in Hungary and ordered that action be taken, saying that the Swiss public was very shocked about news of the antisemitic measures introduced in Hungary, and asking the ambassador to inform the Hungarian government how deeply affected the Swiss people and the Swiss government had been by these developments. The Swiss government was now considering how to help at least some Hungarian Jews,[80] urging Burckhardt to use his contacts with German diplomats to get to them.[81]

Huber, however, was not willing to give up his cautious position of non-intervention. The increasing expectations of the Swiss government caused him concern, as evidenced by his remarks during a public talk in 1944: The 'integrity of humanitarian activities is not to be tainted by considerations of the future prestige of our country in the postwar world'.[82] Huber stressed that the ICRC was only at the service of individuals in need, not states or countries. 'Its activity has to be purely *humanitarian*. It can't allow itself to be instrumentalized in any way for political gains', Huber said.[83] With this statement, he was subtly criticizing Burckhardt, too, who saw the ICRC as a forum for his own career ambitions in international politics. Burckhardt was aware that Huber appraised him critically, remarking: Huber 'thinks that I am a "lone wolf", a man with dictatorial tendencies. That is untrue.'[84] Huber again pointed to the absence of a legally binding mandate and argued for non-intervention in the 'internal affairs of a state', but Swiss government officials made clear to the ICRC that rescue efforts in Hungary were of great importance for their foreign policy.[85]

The ICRC was also eager to redeem some of its reputation before the end of the war, and Burckhardt was concerned about the Swedish competition: 'we must avoid another organization beating the committee'.[86] He was certainly not alone among the ICRC leadership. From London, Ruegger also stressed the importance of his Red Cross colleagues' intervention in Hungary and the status of the ICRC in British government circles. In September 1944 he reported back to Burckhardt: 'The question of the Jews in Hungary is watched with great interest here [in London]. Bit by bit they realise here what the work of the ICRC really means in this and other areas. You can tell our honourable president [Huber] that it was . . . not possible to present a true picture of everything achieved by Geneva. [Foreign Secretary] Mr. Eden of course knows the work done by the International Committee and you.'[87]

Burckhardt also seemed to have given in to increasing demands by Jewish aid organizations. Paul Guggenheim from the WJC made an 'energetic and serious representation' reminding Burckhardt of the ICRC's responsibility.

Jewish circles were disappointed by the ICRC's 'great inactivity'. The WJC had little understanding for such hesitation, 'despite changed political situation and necessity of their rendering account when war is over'.[88] A few weeks later, US ambassador Leland Harrison informed Washington that the ICRC was now sending more delegates to Hungary. The ICRC had assurances that the deportation of Jews was being halted and that they could provide relief, and Burckhardt and Harrison had talks about the ICRC's plans to send more representatives to Budapest, as is evidenced in the following cryptic sentence: 'Burckhardt intimated that there might be possibility arranging dispatch to Hungary one or two capable Swiss persons as confidential WRB representatives, probably attached to ICRC mission.'[89] Already in July 1944 Burckhardt was asked by Jewish representatives to investigate in Berlin about the whereabouts of ransomed Jews from Hungary.[90] By August 1944 Jewish leaders in Switzerland communicated to Mayer that their hopes for these kinds of negotiations now lay with Burckhardt and the ICRC. Although they found themselves in a moral dilemma about negotiating with the 'murderers of millions of people', there seemed 'only one hope of rescue'. The ICRC now entered immediately into direct and open negotiations with the SS. Burckhardt was depicted as a man of action and was lauded for his initiative in briefing the representatives of various Jewish organizations about the initiatives of the ICRC for Jews in Hungary.[91] Rescue efforts in Hungary were now high on Burckhardt's priority list, considered as 'highly important for the future of the ICRC',[92] although he suggested to Ruegger that results could only be achieved in secret negotiations with Germany.[93]

On 8 August 1944 Burckhardt invited the various Jewish aid organizations (among the addressees were Mayer, Riegner, and Roswell McClelland of the WRB) to meet in Geneva at the ICRC headquarters. He wanted to brief them personally about all the rescue missions and activities of the ICRC in Hungary. Burckhardt could now show how active he was.[94] Meanwhile Burckhardt and his aide Bachmann used their networks to keep the Swiss press informed, particularly about the ICRC efforts in Budapest.[95] According to Jewish aid organizations in Geneva, Burckhardt stated that ICRC had to avoid all illegal activities and focus on realistic aims. After the halting of the deportations, the ICRC wanted to increase its delegation in Budapest and bring food and clothing into the ghettos and camps. At the same time Burckhardt warned against too much optimism, especially regarding emigration of Jews from Hungary. However, some concrete rescue missions were on the table. The Swiss government had signalled that it would accept a transport of 1,000 children from Hungary. At the end of the meeting Max Huber declared that the ICRC would do its best to help reduce the suffering of humanity.[96] But public appeals were still out of the question for Huber at this time. In 1944 he still defended the ICRC's policy of discretion when he wrote in a law journal:

> For this reason the committee does not regard its purpose as actively involving itself in public appeals and protests to governments or, even less so, the world public. If it appeals to the collectivity of states or the wider public it does so in a warning, preventive way, and not in a way that could be understood as judging recent acts. A protest is by nature an anticipation of a verdict, in which, at least in most cases, the preconditions for an independent investigation are not present.[97]

Huber wanted to help, but relied on negotiations and a policy of small steps.

The Swiss association of Rabbis thanked Huber and Burckhardt for organizing the meeting and all their efforts for Jews in Hungary. They realized that Hungary was a last chance operation: 'Millions of our brothers in the faith have become victims of a campaign of extinction. Our community in Europe has been decimated to a hitherto unprecedented extent.' The ICRC, the Swiss Rabbis went on to say, now protested against the killing in Hungary and the Red Cross constituted a high moral authority ('*eine hohe moralische Instanz*'). The Rabbis stressed that they trusted in the ICRC's work in the name of humanity. They also warned of the need for vigilance. The ICRC had to make sure that the promises made to them by the Hungarian authorities were kept.[98] At the same time the Jewish communities increasingly made sure that the ICRC was keeping the promises it had made to them as well. Jewish aid organizations and the Americans knew about president Burckhardt's diplomatic ambitions and now relied on him. The very next day after the meeting between Burckhardt, Huber, and the Jewish aid groups, WRB Director John W. Pehle acknowledged the efforts of the ICRC and Switzerland. He identified part of the motivation behind the rescue operation: 'The ICRC [is] in general very proud of their success in [the] matter [of the] Hungarian Jews which they very much needed for their political position.'[99]

As historians Michael Barnett and Thomas G. Weiss have concluded, 'The ICRC silence during the Holocaust led to accusations, and self-recriminations, that its position of neutrality meant that it had acted as an accomplice of the Nazis.'[100] Burckhardt knew full well that he and the ICRC were not always

viewed kindly by what he considered 'Jewish circles'.[101] The ongoing pressure from various advocacy groups annoyed ICRC leaders and revealed
mounting tensions between the parties. In August 1944 Burckhardt expressed
irritation about the public protests demanded by some Jewish organizations:
'We are not the judges of the world; we help individuals. We don't use
the press for moral protests.'[102] The frustration Burckhardt expressed also
revealed the ICRC's enduring inability to see clearly for what it was the
particularly terrible fate meted out to Hitler's Jewish victims. In a meeting
with the ICRC in August 1944 Riegner made clear what the priorities
were, urging that the most important thing for the time being was to stop
the deportations of Jews from Hungary.[103] For Riegner and the Joint
Distribution Committee, the partnership with the ICRC had proven to
be a mixed experience, and overall they felt that Geneva could and should
have done more.

In autumn 1944 the humanitarian situation in Hungary suddenly spi-
ralled out of control. In October 1944 Horthy was ousted by the Germans,
who set up a Hungarian puppet government, formed by Hungarian Fascists
known as the Arrow Cross Party. The Arrow Cross gangs immediately initiated a reign of terror against the remaining Jewish population in Budapest.[104]
In the Budapest ghetto, hunger was common, and its residents were almost
completely at the mercy of the SS and the Hungarian fascists. An exhausted
Wallenberg tried to be everywhere at the same time and intervened where
he could.[105] Together with delegates of other neutral states such as Spain,
Portugal, Switzerland, and the Vatican, Swedish diplomats now became very
active in issuing pledges for visas and setting up soup kitchens, homes for
children, and hospitals.

In December 1944 the Soviets closed in on Budapest, but the battle raged
for two more months until the last parts of the city were conquered by the
Soviet army and its Romanian allies.[106] In the last weeks of the German
occupation, some 40,000 Hungarian Jews were forced to take part in death
marches in western Hungary. Thousands of Jews were killed by the SS
guards, local mobs, or starved to death. When the Red Army finally liberated
all of Budapest in February 1945, 120,000 Jews in the city were still alive.[107]
Their rescue was certainly due in part to committed men like Wallenberg,
as well as men such as Friedrich Born and Carl Lutz, amongst others.[108]
When the Red Army assumed control, Wallenberg made his way to the
nearby Soviet headquarters. He then vanished without a trace. It is widely
assumed that he was arrested by the Soviets in January 1945 and died a few

years later in their captivity.[109] The Soviets might have been suspicious of Wallenberg because of his close ties to the Americans.[110] In any case, the tragic circumstances of Wallenberg's disappearance made him even more *the* hero of Budapest.

The reasons for the Soviets' actions are not obvious and varied from country to country. The Soviet attitude towards the ICRC's presence had become obvious earlier in Romania, where Soviet forces advanced in the summer of 1944. By March 1945 McClelland from the WRB reported from Switzerland that 1 million people in Romania needed relief. He had concluded that while Soviet authorities were tolerating the work of voluntary humanitarian organizations in Romania, they were not giving them any kind of support.[111] The situation in Hungary was worse. Soon after the Soviet capture of Budapest, Friedrich Born had to leave Hungary.[112] At the beginning of May 1945, the Soviets told Hans Weyermann, the last ICRC delegate in Budapest, to leave the country within twenty-four hours. The Soviets had little sympathy for the Swiss and accused them of collaboration with the Nazis. A report by US diplomats in Budapest from May 1945 reads: '[Weyermann] believes action is largely based on the fact that International Committee is composed of Swiss citizens. . . . As Weyermann is the sole representative of the International Red Cross here, that organization's work would stop with his departure.'[113] Weyermann held out in Hungary until April 1946.[114] The Red Army's pressure on humanitarian aid officials in Budapest was not unique. Around the same time, Soviet authorities arrested the delegates of the ICRC in Berlin. After three months in a Russian gulag, they were finally released and returned to Switzerland. This was the first time that delegates of the organization had been taken into custody, as Max Huber bitterly remarked.[115]

Competing Humanitarians

As the case of Hungary illustrates, the Swiss, like the Swedish, were eager to secure their 'humanitarian credentials', and the rivalry between the two nations hardened. Sweden, like Switzerland, wanted to demonstrate to the victors how valuable its services as a neutral intermediary had been; its intervention in Hungary offered one avenue to showcase the quality of those services. Although some Swiss diplomats and ICRC delegates in Budapest had worked tirelessly to protect Jews, the Swedes ultimately appeared to

overshadow the Swiss in their rescue efforts. In a report of May 1944 about
the Hungarian situation, WRB Director Pehle drew a very favourable picture of Sweden, while giving Switzerland fewer high marks. He acknowledged that Switzerland had taken in thousands of refugee and emigrant
children during the war, but Sweden's activities seemed far more impressive
to Pehle, who cited the fact that Finnish, Norwegian, and Danish Jews had
all found a safe haven in the latter country.[116] The Israeli historian Yehuda
Bauer is more direct, pointing out 'This aid was undoubtedly due in large
measure to real humanitarianism, and it also reflected a desire to gain favour
with the Americans, whom the Swedes considered to be very concerned
about the Jews.'[117]

This competition between Sweden and Switzerland, between the
Swedish Red Cross and the Swiss-based ICRC, also turned into a competition between two ambitious men: Carl Jacob Burckhardt and the vice president of the Swedish Red Cross, Count Folke Bernadotte. Bernadotte, a
nephew of the Swedish king, was a widely travelled and sophisticated person, a real establishment figure in his Swedish homeland. He also enjoyed
excellent connections to the United States: his wife was American, and in
1939 he had even been made an honorary chief of a Native American tribe
in Montana.[118] Count Bernadotte and Wallenberg knew each other, and
both were favourites of the Americans' WRB.[119] Ambitious and eager to
prove himself in the service of the Swedish Red Cross, it is telling that in
1943 he created a very fanciful and special officer's uniform with red crosses
on the lapel for his new post.[120] Like Burckhardt, Bernadotte saw his activities on behalf of the Red Cross primarily as a means to play a role on the
international stage and make a name for himself.[121]

Burckhardt understood the emerging power dynamics as the war drew
to a close. He had seen the Hungarian crisis as a highly welcome opportunity
to improve the ICRC's and his personal standing in the world.[122] One
opportunity to do so arose out of the events that had taken place in Hungary.
Saly Mayer and the JDC became involved with ransom negotiations initiated by SS leader Heinrich Himmler and put into motion by his underling,
SS officer Kurt Becher. The Reichsführer SS wanted to secretly open up a
contact with the western Allies in order to negotiate a separate surrender on
the Western front. The SS Chief believed that Hungarian Jews had a direct
contact to their brethren in the United States. And in the Nazis' conspiracy-
theory worldview the American Jews were running the US government. In
other words, by talking to Saly Mayer the SS could eventually engage in

Figure 3.3. Count Folke Bernadotte, the humanitarian from Sweden.

secret negotiations with Washington and London. Himmler cherished the illusion that this would be the first step towards an alliance with the British and the Americans against the Soviets. Mayer played for time and his negotiations saved some lives. A total of 1,684 Hungarian Jews made their way from Budapest to Bergen-Belsen to Switzerland in two separate transports as a result.[123] In autumn 1944, the press had reported details about Mayer's talks with SS leaders that had led to the liberation of some Hungarian Jews. As a result, others saw an eleventh-hour chance for improving their image through similar rescue deals. Prominent among them was former Swiss president Jean-Mary Musy. The aging Musy was an ultra-conservative politician and an early admirer of Hitler who now also saw a chance to improve his reputation. After his talks with Himmler, 1,200 inmates from Theresienstadt were released to Switzerland in February 1945.[124] Burckhardt certainly realized the public relations value of such a success. It appears that Mayer had kept him informed as the talks were taking place. Records in

Mayer's archives indicate that the ICRC was supposed to play a mere supporting role in Mayer's negotiations.[125] Burckhardt, however, was not one to share the credit with men such as Musy or Mayer.

The moment for the ICRC to play an active role seemed have to come when Himmler contacted Burckhardt and hinted at possible peace negotiations. On 2 February 1945, Burckhardt received a letter from Himmler's office inviting him to come to Germany for a meeting. Two weeks later, Burckhardt replied to the 'highly esteemed gentleman' that he was ready to meet Himmler for talks.[126]

When Burckhardt informed Mayer about Himmler's invitation, Mayer encouraged him to meet the SS chief: 'Now S.[aly] M.[ayer] proposed that Minister Burckhardt should certainly and by all means go ahead and meet with H. Himmler. These contacts of course have to take place with the knowledge not only of the [Swiss] Federal Council, but also the Allies, who would have to concur, if the step were to be useful.'[127] Washington supported this plan and encouraged the ICRC. In January 1945 the War Refugee Board and the State Department advised their representative in Switzerland to 'urge' the new Swiss Foreign Minister Petitpierre and ICRC president Burckhardt to do everything they can to keep the remaining Jewish victims alive. Washington encouraged McClelland to check with Petitpierre and Burckhardt what they could do in order to take concrete steps in that direction.[128] Burckhardt certainly considered himself the right man for the job. In a letter to a Swiss diplomat in Paris, Burckhardt stated that he was the 'only man who can still talk to the Germans vigorously and in plain language—in other words the personality that was in charge of all the negotiations concerning the issues of prisoners in the last five years'.[129] Meanwhile, Burckhardt kept in close contact with the new Swiss Foreign Minister Petitpierre and stressed that his negotiations with the Nazis were a matter of Swiss national interest.[130] In February 1945, as they debated what action to take in Hungary, the humanitarians in Geneva were clearly seriously concerned about the future standing of the ICRC. In March 1945 Burckhardt wrote to Ruegger about last-minute rescue operations on behalf of Jews and his ongoing doubts about the ICRC's standing after the war: 'I am deeply concerned about the future of the ICRC.'[131] Spokesmen from the WJC made it clear to Burckhardt that it was in the ICRC's own interest to increase its rescue efforts for Hungarian Jews.[132] Around the same time Riegner, speaking on behalf of the World Jewish Congress, also thanked Burckhardt's assistant Hans Bachmann for everything that the ICRC had

Figure 3.4. After the Musy-intervention: Swiss Red Cross workers and Swiss army reservists organize the documentation for Jews released from Theresienstadt and brought to safety in Switzerland.

achieved for the Jews in Budapest.[133] But this and similar statements were made before the end of the war, at a time when decisive rescue operations from Burckhardt and the ICRC were still expected.

Expectations were very high, and Burckhardt did everything to encourage this perception of a huge success at hand. Direct negotiations with the Nazi leadership should finally allow the ICRC to have access to concentration camps in Germany and in all of Nazi occupied Europe (or what was left of it in 1945). It was wishful thinking on Burckhardt's part to imagine that his efforts could stop further deportations, initiate widespread relief in the concentration camps, permit the dispatch of delegates to camps, or enable the transfer of a large number of camp prisoners to Switzerland and other countries. Nevertheless, the ICRC decided to announce German concessions in favor of deportees in the press and on the radio.[134] The Swiss and international media covered these events widely, and further hinted at possible political talks, to the extent that Burckhardt felt it necessary to issue an official denial.[135] In a personal letter to Ruegger in March 1945, he complained that leaks from the press had almost sabotaged his efforts. But he was able to repair the damage and continue the negotiations with Himmler. Burckhardt then bragged to Ruegger about the results as a fait accompli: 'Permanent delegates of the ICRC in all camps, even the camps for the Jews ("*Judenlagern*"), exchange of various categories of a larger number of hostages. All of this is just the beginning.'[136] Burckhardt was seeking a grand success, not the rescue of a single transport of people. In fact, his only success was convincing others that his efforts would soon bear fruit. The Jewish Telegraphic Agency in London reported in March 1945 on a meeting of Dr Leon Kubowitzky from the WJC in New York with Swiss President Eduard von Steiger and Burckhardt. Kubowitzky received assurances that 'the Swiss Government and the Red Cross will use all their influence to assist in the rescue work. Switzerland will offer hospitality to evacuees from Germany within the limits of its capacity'.[137]

Burckhardt, driven by his desire for a place in history and for the power to shape world events, hoped for talks with Himmler and possibly even Hitler himself. The ordinarily solid *New York Times* had already reported 'Burckhardt Sees Hitler. Red Cross Head Reported Pleading for Allied "Hostages"'.[138] This proved premature, since Himmler eventually chose to deal with Bernadotte, the Swedish humanitarian, over Burckhardt.[139] Himmler sent his underling Ernst Kaltenbrunner to Burckhardt, while he himself met with Bernadotte. In the meeting with Burckhardt on 13 March 1945 General Kaltenbrunner showed himself not well informed about the various agreements and correspondence between German authorities and the ICRC in recent months. Kaltenbrunner could not pledge to anything. Instead, he just promised to forward the demands and practical questions of the ICRC to Himmler and the German Foreign Office.[140]

Nevertheless, Burckhardt still kept promising that a successful deal was imminent. On 6 April 1945, Roswell McClelland, head of the WRB in

Switzerland, wrote to US General William O'Dwyer about the various negotiations with Himmler and concluded:

> After Burckhardt's discussions with Kaltenbrunner of the SS, by which negotiations for the release of large categories of "*Schutzhäftlinge*" were more or less officially opened between the German Government and the International Committee of the Red Cross, it is not surprising that Musy's dealings should become secondary if not of less importance. It is my feeling—and hope—that ICRC's present negotiations on this broader basis will now supersede and replace the previous subordinate negotiations carried on through the Saly Mayer–Becher and Sternbuch–Musy "hook-ups".[141]

By the end of the talks, Burckhardt had achieved very little. Kaltenbrunner agreed that food parcels might be distributed to concentration camp prisoners under the supervision of the Red Cross. However, it was not until the last days of the war that ICRC delegates were actually allowed to enter some of the camps.[142] For further concessions, Kaltenbrunner referred to Count Bernadotte, who, as Kaltenbrunner made clear, had direct access to Himmler.[143] This last remark from Kaltenbrunner must have caused some unease in Geneva, because it made clear that the ICRC and Burckhardt did no longer had such privileged access to the SS leader and that they might in future have to go through Bernadotte instead.

Meanwhile, Himmler's concessions allowed Bernadotte to undertake some last-minute humanitarian aid initiatives.[144] The rescue mission of the Swedish (and Danish) Red Cross between March and July 1945, the now famous 'white buses' under the Swedish flag and large red crosses, saved thousands of Scandinavians (Danes and Norwegians) and Jews of various nationalities. Based on Bernadotte's agreement with Himmler, they could be picked up from selected concentration camps like Neuengamme and brought to safety in Sweden.[145]

The count lost no time in publicizing his successes. His book, *The Curtain Falls*, already published in autumn 1945 in the United States, became a bestseller translated into eighteen languages. In it, he describes the rescue of Scandinavian prisoners at a concentration camp on the outskirts of Hamburg: 'We drove up to the entrance of Neuengamme, where the gates were opened for us and closed as soon as we were inside: I was the first representative of a neutral humanitarian organization to visit a concentration camp.'[146] We can only imagine how Burckhardt felt when he read these lines. It was he, after all, who had already visited Nazi concentration camps

Figure 3.5. Lübeck, Germany, April 1945: Swedish Red Cross staff meeting with Folke Bernadotte.

back in 1935.[147] Burckhardt tried to sell the meetings with Kaltenbrunner as a great success, but they paled in the shadow of Bernadotte's more spectacular achievements.[148] Being overshadowed by Bernadotte and the Swedes chafed.

Burckhardt expressed his resentment in private, suggesting that the WRB, the US State Department and Jewish organizations inside and outside of Europe had made impossible demands and that the Jews were ungrateful. In a personal letter of February 1945 'about everything we did for the Jews', Burckhardt wrote to the ICRC delegate in London, Charles de Watteville: 'Dear friend...regarding the aid efforts for Jews as a whole, we achieved sheer miracles in the Hungarian sector, 80% of the lives saved, in the midst of an ordered program of extinction! For this these people should be grateful. I am asking myself if their [the Jews'] resentment, of which you write, is not at least in part due to certain efforts of the League... This is truly a private letter, the kind one writes on a Sunday morning. Burn it.'[149] De Watteville did not burn the letter, and it survived in Ruegger's personal archive in Switzerland. The letter is unusual in that Burckhardt rather openly reveals some of his fears and thoughts concerning the League and Jewish critics of the ICRC.[150]

Figure 3.6. Jewish women who have recently been liberated from Ravensbrück concentration camp, cross the German–Danish border on their way to Sweden. Photograph #10859.

Figure 3.7. Liberation of the Mauthausen concentration camp in May 1945. ICRC delegate Louis Haefliger drove to the nearby US forces and led them to the camp. He is the man in civilian clothing standing in front of the entrance to the underground armament plant "Bergkristall" in St. Georgen/Gusen.

Burckhardt's complaints were not limited to the actions of Jewish organizations, however. In a letter to Ruegger in May 1945, Burckhardt responded to critiques of the ICRC by emphasizing that in 1934 the ICRC had informed the future Western Allies that an estimated 200,000 German citizens were imprisoned in German concentration camps; back then, he noted, the Western powers had not reacted. Yet those same states were now criticizing the ICRC for a lack of action.[151] Ruegger, of course, did not disagree with his confidant. In a written response to his 'dear friend', he declared, 'Your information is of particular value to me. Foremost your hint on what the ICRC already had pointed out in 1934—5 years before the war. It is very useful and important to note that unjustified attacks against the ICRC in the English press—in contrast to the North American press—were downplayed by the Foreign Office itself.'[152] But Ruegger, the Swiss ambassador in London at the time, did not seem particularly interested in rehashing the Allies' supposed failures or burnishing the role of the ICRC and Switzerland during the war. He was more interested in damage control and 'damping down' international criticism.

For Burckhardt, helping the Jews ultimately became a way to please the Allies, especially Washington, as they moved toward victory. It had become clear to him that only a striking humanitarian 'success', even one only carried out in the waning days of the war, would quiet some of the criticism that had been increasingly directed against the ICRC and Switzerland. But his attempts to quickly repair, at least partially, his organization's poor record in providing aid for Nazi victims and engaging in back-door diplomacy late in the war, met with only marginal success. In the days and weeks after the fighting ceased, ICRC delegations provided relief in a number of camps. In Austria, ICRC delegate Louis Haefliger helped to liberate Mauthausen—the largest and most notorious concentration camp in the region.[153] Given the widespread last-minute mass shootings and death marches this was not a small achievement, but far from the great success that Burckhardt had hoped for.[154]

Inter Arma Caritas

The important and valuable work of the ICRC for on behalf of POWs is outside the main focus of this book, so only a short and general overview must suffice here.[155] When the Second World War broke out in Europe in

1939, the ICRC staff grew rapidly and by 1944 included about 1,500 staff members in Geneva and 800 in the rest of Switzerland, in addition to about 180 envoys (delegates) and their deputies deployed in various countries.[156] Despite a relatively small staff, the ICRC focused its energies on helping the millions of wounded soldiers and POWs covered by its international mandate. More than 11,170 visits to camps is a clear testimony to the ICRC's efforts on behalf of prisoners of war.

In this arena, the ICRC proved quite effective and had an impact on the conduct of war, especially in Western Europe. The major belligerents in the Western hemisphere had signed and ratified the Geneva Conventions of 1929, with the Soviet Union being the major exception. It was not least thanks to the Geneva Convention and the work of the ICRC that the survival rate of US and British POWs held in German and Italian captivity was very high.[157] US soldiers in German POW camps were treated humanely, indeed 'infinitely better' than other war prisoners and civilians, as the *New York Times* concluded on 1 May 1945. The Geneva Convention was respected in most cases.[158] Nazi ideology played a role in this as well. 'White' US-Americans and British soldiers were considered fellow Germanic, and therefore 'Aryan', people in the racist hierarchy. The killing of American POWs in Belgium during the battle of the Bulge by SS forces was more an exception than a rule.[159] However, in the last months and weeks of the war in Europe, the situation in POW camps in Germany grew dramatically worse, leading to serious concern on the other side of the Atlantic. As the Nazi government began collapsing and the German train and road system suffered major damage through repeated Allied bombing, it became ever more difficult for Red Cross food shipments to reach POWs. The dangers of starvation for GIs, British and Canadian POWs grew ever larger in the final months of the war.[160] By March 1945 the regular flow of food parcels from the ICRC to POW camps was almost entirely suspended.[161] The US government denounced the 'Reich's Cruelty to US Captives' and warned that 'the perpetrators of these heinous crimes against American citizens and against civilization itself will be brought to justice'.[162] Despite some failures, the Geneva Convention nevertheless remained in high regard and US media outlets lavished much attention on the Geneva humanitarians in the last months of the war. The Geneva Conventions—and the humane treatment of German POWs in American camps—were credited with having secured better treatment for GIs held in Germany.[163] In June 1945 the *New York Times* reported that '99% of US Captives in Reich Survived, Red Cross

Reports'. The ICRC stressed that this was in great part thanks to the Geneva Convention and the Americans' faithful adherence to its principles. ICRC president Burckhardt told the US press that Hitler had given orders to kill all American and British airmen in captive in Germany. One reason why this was not done, according to Burckhardt, was because the British and American authorities had followed the Geneva Convention and because the German military leadership also saw itself as bound to Convention principles.[164] Soon after the war, the American Red Cross also stressed this aspect: 'No better illustration of the value of the program of relief to American prisoners of war in Europe can be found than this fact: Aside from normal mortality, over 99 percent of those captured were returned safely to their homes.'[165] The Geneva Convention even protected those British and US POWs in Nazi hands with a Jewish background. A very recent example for this was made public recently. In December 2015 Yad Vashem Holocaust Memorial in Jerusalem honoured the first US soldier as a Righteous among Nations. Master Sergeant Robbie Edmonds was the senior officer of a larger group of American POWs taken prisoner during the battle of the Bulge in 1945. When Nazi officials demanded that all Jewish GIs identify themselves, Edmonds refused. Instead he asked *all* American POW's to step forward. The Nazi officer in charge threatened Edmonds with a pistol, who responded that 'according to the Geneva Convention, we only have to give our name, rank and serial number. If you shoot me, you will have to shoot all of us, and after the war you will be tried for war crimes.' Finally the German Kommandant gave in and let the men be.[166] The ICRC was very eager to protect these provisions of the Geneva Conventions not to discriminate against POWs based on their religion, but was not always successful. Jews were at times singled out in German captivity, imprisoned in separate POW camp areas or worse.

The popular film *Unbroken*, based on factual wartime events, recently made the fate of US POWs in Japanese captivity known to a wide audience. Unlike Germany and Italy, the Japanese government had signed but never ratified the Geneva Convention of 1929 and therefore was not legally bound to it. Although the Japanese government indicated that they would nevertheless respect the Geneva Convention on POWs, it made little effort to implement it. The militaristic culture of 1930s Japan did not leave much space for humane treatment of POWs and wounded enemies. As in the case of the Nazis, humanitarianism was considered 'weak sentimentality'.[167] Not surprisingly, therefore, the American Red Cross stressed that the situation for US POWs in Asia was often worse than in Europe: 'If the amount of relief which reached them seems small in comparison to what was achieved in Europe, it must be remembered that, in spite of all Allied government and Red Cross representations, Japan showed very little understanding either for the welfare of prisoners or for the maintenance of the Geneva Convention. Consequently, it was much more difficult to get supplies to the Far East.'[168]

Another major blackspot in the protection of POWs during the Second World War was on the Eastern Front. The Soviet Union never ratified the Geneva Convention of 1929, giving the ICRC little legal leverage. A further result of the Soviets' non-ratification was that the Nazi government felt even less constrained in its treatment of captured Soviet soldiers. An estimated 3 million Soviet POWs were either shot or starved to death in German captivity.[169] Nazi racial policy planned the death of millions of Soviet citizens from the very beginning of the German invasion. An estimated 27 million people, mostly civilians, were killed during the war. This was by far the highest death toll of an Allied nation. The ICRC considered its failure to aid Soviet POWs to be one of its greatest failures during the war. Nevertheless, the ICRC tried everything to highlight its successes in the protection of POWs, especially to Washington and London, to show them that the ICRC was still an active and useful organization.

In the end, it was not the ICRC and Switzerland but the Swedish Red Cross and Sweden that received most of the credit for rescuing Jews. It was not Burckhardt or Huber, but Bernadotte and Wallenberg who became the postwar stars of international humanitarianism. The ICRC found itself in a major existential crisis and faced being completely restructured or even dissolved. Its reputation had been damaged and its financial situation had become critical. Moreover, after Burckhardt's retreat (he became the Swiss ambassador to Paris in February 1945), Geneva was left without a strong leader. The national Swedish Red Cross, on the other hand, was an active, fresh force that promised change inside the Red Cross family. It now rivalled the ICRC for status within the humanitarian firmament. But what if the 'world's humanitarian headquarters'[170] during the Second World War had been in Stockholm? Would the humanitarian organization have intervened to save lives much earlier and with more determination?

4

The Red Cross in Crisis

In 1945 there was a big question—would the humanitarianism of the nineteenth century still have a place in the postwar world? Would the 'moral conscience' of the world have a future after Auschwitz? If the humanitarian idea was to survive, who should now carry the torch passed on by Henry Dunant, Florence Nightingale, and Clara Barton? Neutral Sweden's aid record looked so much better and its national Red Cross leader, Bernadotte, was a leading light in humanitarianism. Would it not be a logical choice to have Sweden take the lead? In other words, would the Red Cross turn (symbolically speaking) into a blue cross on a yellow background after the Swedish flag? And would the Geneva Conventions one day be called the Stockholm Conventions? Indeed, the humanitarian competition established during the Second World War between Sweden and Switzerland was to continue after 1945 and almost changed the world of international humanitarian law for good.

The International Committee of the Red Cross (ICRC) faced numerous obstacles after the war in maintaining its status as the world's leading humanitarian organization. Some of these constituted elemental threats to the organization's entire legacy and history of accomplishments. Others presented opportunities for the ICRC to leave its contested past behind and resume its leadership position, by now, above all, also championing the rights of civilians in wartime. The immediate postwar years became a period of intense challenges for the ICRC, propelled by criticisms of how its officials had handled crises during the war, its cozy relationship with the Swiss government and even the Nazi regime, and its limited aid for Soviet prisoners of war (POWs). The failure of the ICRC in not speaking out against the Holocaust and providing only limited aid to civilians was discussed at the time. A crisis in leadership and diminishing funds hampered the organization's ability to respond to external attacks, even as it issued a number of

publications defending its recent record. Another major issue for the humanitarians was the position of the new superpowers. The Soviet Union was
among the most outspoken critics of the ICRC and Switzerland. The US
government held no strong opinions about the matter, but the American
national Red Cross was at the same time very ambitious to stake its own
claims.

In considering the two to three years running up to the critical Stockholm
Red Cross conference of 1948, we have to look at both the ICRC's internal
conflicts and fissures and the formidable opponents they faced in Europe
and further afield.

The Second World War and Its Challenge to Humanitarian Ideals

The atrocities committed during the Second World War by the Nazi regime
shook the philosophical foundations of the international Red Cross organizations. The world was shocked when the war in Europe ended and the
concentration camps were liberated. Knowledge about the mass murder of
Jews was not wholly new, but the images and reports that now became
available made the full scale of these crimes visible. On 14 April 1945, an
American Red Cross (AMRC) representative reported back to Washington
what he had seen in Buchenwald: 'The stench and the groans from those
sick and dying skeletons need not to be described here. Suffice it to say that
the scene was more horrible and damning than death itself. In the other
parts of the hospital area were men hobbling around on legs with absolutely
no flesh on them—ghastly! Great running sores covered the faces and bodies of others. Many showed signs of extreme physical punishment.'[1] In the
face of this complete breakdown of humanitarian laws and standards—and
the Red Cross's failure to intervene—many national Red Cross societies
were now deeply concerned about their future, particularly as the revelations about Nazi atrocities cast one of their sister organizations, the German
Red Cross, in an especially problematic light.

Around the same time that Buchenwald was liberated, the acting president of the German Red Cross, SS-Obergruppenführer Ernst Robert
Grawitz, committed suicide in Berlin by blowing himself and his family up
with hand grenades. Meanwhile, in southern Germany, Walther Georg
Hartmann, head of the Foreign Section of the German Red Cross (DRK)

and himself a Nazi Party member, tried to carry on the work of the German Red Cross as a national and centrally organized Red Cross Society, even appealing to the Americans for help. In a letter to the AMRC in June 1945, he proposed the steps needed for 'preserving the union of a Red Cross in Germany'. The ICRC's chief delegate in Berlin, Roland Marti, supported Hartmann's efforts for 'negotiations' with the AMRC. In a memorandum on the reorganization of the Red Cross in Germany, the self-appointed 'acting president' Hartmann made almost no mention of past mistakes or of the impending denazification of its staff and screening of its personnel. In Hartmann's eyes, only a few changes seemed necessary: the restoration of the German Red Cross's non-political attitude predating 1933 and some reorganization of the leading staff would, he felt, suffice. The swastika in the German Red Cross emblem had only been faintly crossed out with a blue pen on the letterhead of Hartmann's correspondence. But the organization's Nazi past was not so easily left behind.[2] In May 1945 Jewish-American voices openly demanded that the leaders of the German Red Cross were to be punished as war criminals.[3] The ICRC too was well aware of the involvement of the German Red Cross in Nazi crimes. One ICRC delegate in Germany in June 1945 wrote to Max Huber that the German Red Cross (DRK) had been a paramilitary organization deeply influenced by the Nazi Party since 1937.[4] At that point the DRK was torn apart and in chaos, its future uncertain. Some local and regional offices were allowed to function, while Allied authorities refused to let others continue their work. The ICRC now at least had to clarify the situation.[5] One underlying aspect of Geneva's interest in Germany lay in its concern about the future of the national German organization. In August 1945 Huber sent a memorandum to Secretary of State Byrnes on precisely this topic. In it Huber described the ICRC's ongoing contacts with the German Red Cross, especially the foreign affairs service headed by Walther Georg Hartmann. Cooperation between Geneva and elements in the German Red Cross had remained mostly positive, even under the Nazi regime, at least according to Huber. In Huber's opinion, the remnants of the German Red Cross should be permitted to maintain operations and its chief officers should be allowed to continue to carry out their duties, especially the ones who had already been in office before the Nazis took power.[6]

Despite both Hartmann's and Huber's efforts, it quickly became clear that the Allied occupation powers had no intention of allowing a centralized German Red Cross to be active across Germany. The irony and reality of a humanitarian organization operating under a genocidal regime was not lost on the Allies, who soon classified the German Red Cross as a deeply Nazified organization. As a result, the Allies dismantled the national organization, although it continued to exist on a local level. Shutting down a national Red Cross was unheard of in its long history. Furthermore, the German Red Cross Society's complicity with the Nazi regime now threatened to invalidate the work and future of the entire Red Cross network.

What was at stake went far beyond the violation of standards of conduct and even criminal acts by one national Red Cross society. Did the Geneva Conventions and the nineteenth-century ideals of Henry Dunant still have a place in the era of large-scale genocide and nuclear weapons? Who or what would enforce them? The annual report published by the AMRC in June 1945, only weeks after the liberation of the last concentration camps, caught the mood of the moment well: 'The toll of anguish and misery exacted from the armed forces by any war is frightful. World War II is no exception. But in terms of the suffering of civilian populations, this war has established a grim record never approached before.'[7]

Figure 4.1. April 1945 Nordhausen, Germany, concentration camp prisoners and soldiers of the US Army and medical personnel in a ruined building.

Figure 4.2. American Red Cross personnel with Holocaust survivor from the slave labour camp Mittelbau Dora - Norhausen, April 1945.

The ICRC was very well aware of the new realities of total war, as Swiss law professor and ICRC official Maurice Bourquin indicated soon after the war ended: 'Neither rockets nor atomic bombs make any distinction between "combatants" and "non-combatants". They spread death over vast areas, and their effects cannot be limited to a definite target. Nothing is safe from them.'[8] Burckhardt sounded very pessimistic as well when reflecting on the possibility of effective humanitarian action in the Second World War, writing: 'In a hopeless war against the world people at the front, behind the front, in the cities, in the countryside, were destroyed in large numbers by all available types of explosive force or simply rounded up and gassed.'[9] In order to address these monumental changes in the world, the ICRC leadership in Geneva sought refuge in traditional concepts. In his 1943 book *The Good Samaritan*, Max Huber had appealed to the leaders of the fighting powers to embrace the joint pillars of humanity and Christianity, a very unrealistic, almost naïve, approach in the midst of a total war and genocide.

With dictators like Hitler and Stalin in charge, such appeals had little chance to be heard. Huber was 'quite simply, overwhelmed by the scale of the war and the depths of its inhumanity'.[10] He had become very pessimistic because Christian values were no longer the basis of an international ethos.[11] Huber expressed his frustrations to Burckhardt. 'The spirit of the times', Huber wrote, 'makes me helpless. Often I see everything in imminent decline. Law is trodden underfoot all over the world'.[12] It was not clear to Huber if 'Dunant's dream' was still up to meeting the challenges of the time.[13]

The Guardians of Humanity Had Failed

In the aftermath of Auschwitz the world reflected not just on the general defeat of humanitarianism, but specifically on the shortcomings of the ICRC. The ICRC was after all meant to be the guardian and promoter of humanitarian principles and laws. At the war's end it was only to be expected that Jewish organizations, and Jewish communities in general, would be disappointed by the ICRC. Whatever the ultimate reasons, the ICRC decided not to speak out against the genocide committed by Nazi Germany and its allies against the Jewish people. True, in the last months of the war the Red Cross in Geneva acted with more determination and individual ICRC delegates and aid workers did all they could do to help. The survivors of the camps and their families were grateful for these efforts. However, these achievements paled when confronted with the millions murdered in a systematic extermination campaign. The genocide was too enormous to be kept a secret, but the humanitarians had kept silent. It is understandable that Jewish communities and their leaders concluded that the 'moral conscience' of the world, the Swiss-based guardians of humanity had failed them. The critique soon focused on the ICRC's silence on the Holocaust.[14] In some cases the Jewish critique was stated openly and in the press. One of the earliest postwar-articles of this kind was published in May 1945, just weeks after the liberation of the last Nazi concentration camps. The introduction of this book opened with the powerful first sentences of the article, titled 'The International Red Cross Was Silent' published in the New York-based *Jewish Frontier*. The author, Siegfried Kantor, was a prominent Jewish lawyer from Vienna, who fled the Nazis and found refuge in the United States, and who seems to have had a particular interest in the work of the ICRC.[15] It is worth taking a closer look at the arguments laid out in the article. It is also interesting to get some glimpse into the ICRC's reaction to it. The first paragraph of the article reads:

> When future historians are able to analyze the circumstances which made possible the annihilation of one-third of the Jewish people—the bulk of European Jewry—as well as the barbarous slaughter of untold masses of other civilizations during the Second World War, there is one set of problems which will give them the greatest difficulty: Where was the enlightened, civilized world, particularly the humane, neutral influences, while all this was going on? Where above all, was the International Red Cross Committee? For the IRCC [ICRC] has a specific obligation, owing its essential character as laid down in its statutes, to safeguard the hard-won principles of civilized conduct in war-time.[16]

The disappointment with the Red Cross was not extended to the entire movement, but to the ICRC specifically. The author immediately follows the opening blow against the ICRC with a glowing praise of the AMRC.

> The International Red Cross Committee must not be confused with the American National Red Cross, for example, whose spectacular work within its own sphere will be for ever praised and admired.[17]

This distinction made by the American-based Jewish author is quite remarkable. While the ICRC came out of the war with its reputation among Jewish communities tarnished, the AMRC was blameless, or so it reads. The long article showed the author to be well informed about the work, the legal basis, and the philosophy of the ICRC, pointing out that while the ICRC helped POWs, it did not do much for civilians. This was even more surprising as this contradicted decisions taken in the interwar years at the all Red Cross conferences since 1921. With this the author pointed particularly to the 14th Resolution of the 10th International Red Cross Conference (1921), according to which civilians and political prisoners would fall within the ambit of the Red Cross. Kantor also pointed to the presence of government representatives at these Red Cross conferences. He took these circumstances as proof for the 'existence of an international customary law' for 'domestic civilian internees, deportees, and hostages' securing 'humane treatment of all political prisoners'. But 'prudence and discretion' reigned in Geneva, while millions were victimized: 'One cannot but be struck by the peculiar attitude adopted by the Committee in the face of the wholesale extermination of civil populations.'[18] According to Kantor, national Red Cross societies would do a much better job. With the exception of shipments of food to Theresienstadt, the ICRC had achieved little. The article clearly shows that it was written by a lawyer with a background in international law. 'This international customary law cannot be abrogated by the unlawful capture and execution of hostages, nor can a new customary law of mass or individual deportation, mass or individual starvation, be created by the mass crimes of Germany and her allies. Passivity and resignation have proved to be the worst defense against such flagrant violations of the "natural rights of man" to which the International Committee appealed in a statement of July 24, 1943.'[19]

This article did not escape the attention of the ICRC. Under the heading 'Press attacks on policies of the ICRC', it stated that a Jewish newspaper in the United States would criticize the ICRC and its policies The ICRC office in Washington recommended to headquarters: 'We feel that this false information should be stopped and sincerely hope that it will be possible for the Committee to issue statements which will make the truth known to all the world.'[20] But Jewish organizations and prominent individuals continued to criticize the ICRC for its shortcomings during the war. The ICRC started to feel the heat. 'The Jews will cause us troubles. Their influence is big in the Anglo-Saxon countries', stated a memorandum prepared for a conference in London in the summer of 1946 at which Jewish aid organizations were expected to bring the ICRC to book.[21] Jewish activist Gerhart Riegner repeatedly criticized the ICRC for not considering enough the recent tragedy of European Jews. In a letter to Max Huber of July 1946 Riegner addressed the ICRC in the name of the World Jewish Congress in New York. He reminded Huber of the horrible fate of the 6 million Jewish men, women, and children. These civilians were enslaved, deported, and murdered in a 'systematic extermination' campaign, made possible in part because of missing legal protection for non-combatants in the existing Geneva Conventions.[22] Riegner's letter was sent just before the opening of a Red Cross Conference in Geneva in the summer of 1946, where the drafting of a new convention dealing with civilians of enemy nationality was on the agenda.[23] Riegner wanted to make sure that the fate of the civilians was not overlooked when drafting new humanitarian law. At a meeting convoked by the ICRC immediately after the conference of the League Board of Governors in Oxford in July 1946, Gerhart Riegner was not willing to uncritically support a resolution proposed by one delegate that the charitable relief organizations present thank the ICRC for all they had done for POWs and civilian internees. Riegner, representative of the World Jewish Congress in Switzerland, had worked closely with the ICRC during the war. He knew about the achievements, but also the limitations, of Geneva. As we have seen in earlier chapters, he was often frustrated with the ICRC. He was probably the wrong man to be called to its defence. Riegner was quite surprised and found himself in a 'delicate position', but requested that the reference to civilian internees be taken out of the text. 'The meeting erupted in turmoil', reported Riegner.[24] The ICRC was well aware that it would have to face critical questions in the months to come—and not just from Jewish circles, but also from inside the Red Cross family.

Infighting in the Red Cross

The ICRC faced an even greater possible consequence—its potential dissolution at the hands of its own Red Cross family. In 1946 during the conference of the League Board of Governors in Oxford, some of the participants proposed that the ICRC be closed down and simply replaced by the League of Red Cross societies. This added to Geneva's precarious position.[25]

Count Folke Bernadotte, the shining star of international humanitarianism at the end of the war, led the voices criticizing the ICRC. By so doing, the Swedish Count was clearly seeking to strengthen the position of Sweden and the Swedish Red Cross. In the words of political scientist David P. Forsythe: 'Mixed in his criticism of the ICRC were his own personal ambitions, which were not small, and the ambitions of his co-nationals who wanted the Swedish Red Cross to become a power center—if not *the* power center—in the Red Cross Movement. [...] As is frequently the case, policy debates were affected by egos, individual and collective.'[26] Even if the Red Cross did not move its centre to Stockholm, Sweden's role in the humanitarian arena would become increasingly decisive. Switzerland, by contrast, was poised to lose its humanitarian flagship. Sensing a shift in power, the AMRC, which like Sweden was ready to take on a greater role in the humanitarian organization and which already played a leading role in the League of Red Cross Societies, joined Bernadotte in his plans for reorganization.

The ambitious League members with Bernadotte as their leader, now used this momentum and confronted the ICRC with its failures and with numerous demands.[27] Sweden and the League, led by the Americans, were largely on the same page. Bernadotte argued that Switzerland had not really been neutral during the war and had given in to German demands. In any case, the geographic location of Switzerland made it very vulnerable to German demands, the critics were eager to point out. The various motivations underlying the internal critiques within the wider Red Cross family at this time were complex. National Red Cross organizations disliked the ICRC's privileged discretion to recognize new national societies and of course its unique status as promoter and guardian of the Geneva Conventions. The ICRC's peacetime work was seen as competition for the League. At the same time, national societies were expected to provide some of the funding for the central organization in Geneva. The critics also had a different understanding of the purpose of the Red Cross. The ICRC saw its goal as rendering war less inhumane, while the League under American leadership initially had aspirations for the Red Cross to be an important and active instrument of peace. Bernadotte thought along similar lines. He was supported by Basil O'Connor, president of the AMRC as well as chairman of the League of Red Cross Societies.

President Franklin Delano Roosevelt appointed Basil O'Connor head of the AMRC in July 1944.[28] A lawyer turned humanitarian, O'Connor was an old and trusted friend of the president.[29] Basil O'Connor had an Ivy League education and stemmed from an Irish-Catholic family in Massachusetts.[30] He had founded his own law firm in New York in 1919 and met Franklin D. Roosevelt in the early 1920s, becoming his legal adviser. In 1925 the two men opened a joint law firm. Philanthropic work also brought the men together. O'Connor became deeply involved in the fight against polio not only because of Roosevelt's struggle with the disease, but because of that of his own daughter.[31] When Roosevelt discovered the positive effects of therapeutic waters at Warm Springs, Georgia, he bought the resort in 1926 and his friend O'Connor became head of the Warm Springs Foundation.[32] O'Connor subsequently became very actively involved in work for charitable foundations, which eventually led to his career as a philanthropist.[33] From 1946 to 1950 he served as the elected chairman of the Board of Governors of the League of Red Cross Societies. In addition, he was outspoken in the fight against discrimination, serving as an active member of the executive committee of the National Conference of Christians and Jews and the African-American Tuskegee Institute in Alabama, where he was a Board of Trustees member.[34] With Roosevelt serving as the (honorary) president of the AMRC, O'Connor may well have kept him closely apprised of Red Cross affairs and goals.[35] Under O'Connor's leadership, the AMRC soon became very centralized, leaving local offices with little say, but at the

Figure 4.3. Portrait of Basil O'Connor in his later years.

same time still expected to support the headquarters in Washington with their fund-raising efforts. O'Connor's leadership style was thus remembered as being at times hierarchical and less democratic.[36] The AMRC also expended in numbers and activities during the war.

The AMRC followed US troops from Europe to the Pacific. It took on ever more ventures and was running a huge operation when the Second World War ended.[37] The AMRC had first begun to work outside the borders of the United States during the First World War,[38] and during the Second World War it began to play a part in international relief operations for civilians. After 1945 it continued this work, but on a smaller scale. While engaged in international relief for civilians, the AMRC leadership remained 'the agency of the American people in expressing their voluntary interest and concern in the well-being of civilians in need in foreign countries'.[39] But many new intergovernmental humanitarian organizations were now also competing for the same territory.

The AMRC thus had to fight to remain a force in the humanitarian arena on the world stage. In part this was possible because humanitarian foreign aid became part of President Truman's Cold War containment doctrine. Seeking to win the sympathies of world public opinion against communist governments, the US government created new institutions that would show 'American efforts to relieve, rebuild and reorder the world' in the best possible light.[40] The organization also worked to find a niche alongside the new initiatives sponsored by the United Nations such as the United Nations Relief and Rehabilitation Administration (UNRRA) and its successor, the International Refugee Organization (IRO), and in November 1946 the UN General Assembly even adopted a resolution to encourage the cooperation of national Red Cross societies. O'Connor played a key role in nurturing good working relations between the UN and the League.[41]

American ambitions caused tension between the two international Red Cross networks—the ICRC and the League.[42] It was not clear how work in the international humanitarian field would be divided between them after 1945 and who would be in charge of the necessary reform work. The competition between the League and the ICRC can be seen playing out on many levels and in many arenas. Both organizations were competing for consultative status within the Economic and Social Council of the United Nations. The League leadership discussed whether an application for joint status as one Red Cross representation would be beneficial and should be discussed at the coming Stockholm meeting. The secretary general of the League warned Basil O'Connor, its chairman and president of the AMRC, that recent criticism of the ICRC might hinder a joint application.[43] A 'struggle of prestige between the two institutions' loomed on the horizon.

Sweden and the League Charge Ahead

To the ICRC the League no doubt looked like an ambitious upstart American project.[44] It comes as no surprise that Burckhardt quickly pointed an accusatory finger at the League. He was aware of the ambitions of certain national Red Cross officials and societies, and showed he felt disappointed, even betrayed by the League. Burckhardt thought that postwar relief work together with the League could have been of value.[45] But at the same time he blamed the League for claiming all the recognition for joint projects. In a 1946 letter to the former police chief and current Swiss representative in refugee organizations Heinrich Rothmund, Burckhardt wrote that the cooperation between the League and the ICRC during the war had 'brought us nothing'. On the contrary, he lamented that the League had exploited the international committee's aid for their own purposes, while ignoring the ICRC's contribution. He went on to say that the joint aid efforts for civilians had increasingly come under the influence of the League and were thus mostly controlled by the AMRC under Basil O'Connor. As a result, the ICRC suffered 'unforeseen disadvantages'.[46] During the Oxford meeting of the League in 1946, the Joint Relief Commission (a joint venture between the League and ICRC) was dissolved.[47] Burckhardt made clear that the dissolution of the Joint Relief Commission was an 'American manoeuver' and criticized Huber as being too soft in this matter.[48]

The letter was quite typical of the ICRC president's private correspondence at the time. Burckhardt did not have many good things to say about Bernadotte either. This is hardly surprising. When Bernadotte made his proposals to reform the Red Cross movement and internationalize control of the ICRC earlier that year, he deeply offended Geneva and drew Burckhardt's ire. The Swiss diplomat called Bernadotte 'a peacock count' and accused him of not being informed about the history and the traditions of the Red Cross. Burckhardt then went on to say that Bernadotte's suggestions were 'not even worth discussing'.[49] Others, however, were eager 'to discuss such things'.

At the meeting of the League's Board of Governors in Oxford in July 1946 and at a preliminary Red Cross conference in Geneva a few weeks later, delegations began raising strong grievances against the ICRC. O'Connor was very much concerned that the Red Cross maintain 'freedom of action, unhampered by governmental interference or political pressure'. As chairman of the League, he expressed concern not only about Red Cross societies in the Soviet zone of influence, but also about the ICRC's independence from the Swiss government.[50] The criticism at times grew so sharp that it appeared tantamount to a 'request by certain delegations to set up what amounted to a tribunal to try the International Committee', the official minutes noted.[51] While Max Huber insisted that the ICRC would not cooperate with such proceedings, he stressed that the committee was willing to look back at its errors and learn from them for the future. In collusion with League officials, however, Count Bernadotte took the lead and proposed a 'Special Committee to Study the Ways and Means of Reinforcing the Action of the International Committee of the Red Cross'.[52] This committee was the framework through which Bernadotte sought to enlarge the all-Swiss committee to include members from neutral countries, thereby strengthening the role of neutral Sweden inside the Red Cross movement.[53] And it had some leverage, partly because some of the ICRC's financial support came from national societies.[54] In addition, national societies often viewed ideas and proposals by Sweden positively, not least because of the high reputation that Bernadotte and the Swedish Red Cross had earned in the final stages of the war.[55] Swedish nationals would probably have been among the first candidates for a leadership position in a reformed ICRC, most likely even Bernadotte himself. Although his proposals found widespread support, much remained to be done.[56] When the new Special Committee first met in Paris in November 1946, the directness of the discussions and 'undiplomatic language' exchanged during the meeting seemed unprecedented. These meetings were dominated by representatives of the League and by Bernadotte, who was also responsible for putting together the agenda. In preparing for the 17th International Conference of the Red Cross in Stockholm, the critics wanted to ensure that they and not the ICRC would be in control of the final deliberations.[57]

The proposed changes caused the Swedish and Swiss camps to square off in advance of the Stockholm conference, scheduled for August 1948. Bernadotte felt that the working group he initiated should study 'different alternatives of organisation of the International Committee of the Red Cross' and seek ways to reorganize the movement to make it more effective. The proposals were to serve as a basis for discussion at the Stockholm conference. At the first meeting of the Special Committee, Roger Gallopin of the ICRC began by saying that because the 'ICRC itself is the subject of this meeting', the two ICRC delegates had no authority to bind the ICRC in any way whatsoever. Gallopin promised, however, that the ICRC delegates would work with the committee in a spirit of cooperation. An alternative plan for restructuring the movement came from Pierre Depage, president of the Belgian Red Cross and a leading League representative. He envisioned implementing firm oversight of the ICRC by a Red Cross assembly and moving the organization's base from Geneva, should Switzerland's neutrality be compromised. Not surprisingly, Depage and Bernadotte coordinated their efforts and ideas.[58] James Nicholson from the AMRC joined in the critical voices. For him, the commission was originally set up to complete an 'investigation of activities of the International Red Cross Committee during the war'. Although the AMRC had been quite happy with its relationship with the ICRC during that time, the allegations made against the ICRC were serious and needed to be discussed. The Americans were especially concerned about charges made that the ICRC had turned into a foreign policy instrument of the Swiss government.[59]

Back at their headquarters in Geneva in the fall of 1946, ICRC officials concluded that their governing body was about to become internationalized and have its authority curtailed, and that it would henceforth operate under outside supervision by the League and remain in Geneva only temporarily. These proposals constituted a great humiliation for the ICRC. In response, Roger Gallopin from the ICRC's General Secretariat made clear that he and the ICRC's legal expert Jean Pictet would refrain from any voting on these proposals. The danger to the ICRC was obvious—indeed, it was so great that it now became uncertain whether the ICRC would remain the promoter and guardian of the Geneva Conventions.[60]

The ICRC's prospects appeared to darken further when it became clear that the US government itself was beginning to question the committee's competence and trustworthiness. One of the leading experts of international humanitarian law in the US government, State Department official Albert E. Clattenburg, reported in 1947 that many governments were 'unwilling to accept the ICRC as a trusted neutral agency...[So] it was clear enough that a new agency had to be formed which would not embody the same objections or pretexts'.[61] Draft documents at that time for the new Geneva Conventions would not name the ICRC as its guardian but refer simply to the 'competent international organisation'.[62] This was clearly a slap in the face to the ICRC and the Swiss.

The Soviets and the Left Join the Fray

The Soviet Union basically boycotted the Swiss-run organization by not attending conferences and meetings organized or co-organized by the ICRC and by avoiding direct communications with the committee.[63] Cooperation between the League and the Soviet alliance of the Red Cross and Red Crescent Societies was difficult too, but they continued communicating with each other and holding meetings. To make matters worse, Swiss–Soviet government relations had turned icy long before the Second World War broke out. After the Bolshevik Revolution in 1918, Swiss assets inside Russia were confiscated and the Swiss embassy in Petrograd plundered. Later, the Swiss broke all diplomatic ties with Soviet Russia. In 1934 Switzerland voted against the admission of the Soviet Union to the League of Nations, and after the Soviet invasion of Finland in October 1939, the Swiss welcomed their exclusion from the League. The relationship between Moscow and Bern continued to be chilly even after the Siege of Stalingrad. In late 1944 Swiss attempts to reach out to Moscow ended with a diplomatic slap in the face for Switzerland. Moscow insisted that the Swiss were conducting a pro-fascist policy and had to change course. A few days later Swiss Foreign Minister Pilet-Golaz, an outspoken anti-communist, stepped down.[64] Meanwhile in 1945/46 the Swiss Foreign Office had to deal with the killings and kidnappings of Swiss citizens, as well as the destruction of Swiss property by the Red Army in Czechoslovakia and Eastern Germany. There was little that the Swiss could do about it and it certainly did not help bilateral relations.[65]

The ICRC reacted somewhat differently than the Swiss government to the Rusisan Revolution, keeping a delegate in Moscow until 1938 and seeking contacts with the Soviets on several occasions. In 1921 it recognized the Red Cross Society of Soviet Russia and never completely broke off relations, even as Moscow often reacted in ways that made it less than approachable.[66] As the Second World War drew to a close, the Swiss government now wanted to use the ICRC's best offices in helping it overcome its international isolation and re-establishing relations with the Soviets.[67] An initial suggestion in 1944 of improving the relationship between the Red Cross and the Soviets through cooperation in relief operations in Yugoslavia proved 'totally out of the question'.[68] But after a number of rocky attempts, diplomatic relations between the Alpine republic and the Soviet Union were eventually re-established in 1946. In this context, it is hardly surprising that the long-standing chill between the two countries affected the work of the ICRC and its ambitious reform plans.

At the 1947 conference of European Red Cross Societies in Belgrade, the Soviet delegation made serious accusations against several Western national societies, but against the ICRC in particular.[69] Yugoslavia was the most aggressive of the Soviet Union's allies in expounding exactly the same litany of accusations and complaints against the ICRC as the Soviets (but added to them the ICRC's handling of Yugoslav Nazi collaborators in Displaced Person camps and other camps in Italy and Austria).[70]

The ICRC's refugee policy, especially its help for Nazi collaborators, was repeatedly attacked in the press. Léon Nicole, head of the Swiss Communist Workers Party, had already accused the ICRC of issuing 'false passports for Nazis' in August 1946, but without going into much detail.[71] Problems concerning the abuse of ICRC travel papers for refugees in Italy also caused something of a stir in left-wing newspapers. The ICRC had been aware for some time of the scandals that now further threatened its credibility and, therefore, the reform of the Geneva Conventions. Evidence of travel document fraud filtered out via the ICRC's internal channels, confidential diplomatic meetings, and even the press.[72] By late January 1947, the widely read communist Italian daily, *L'Unità*, reported on a group of forty Nazi criminals who were under the protection of the Vatican Commission for Refugees. The 'suspicious persons' all carried manipulated ICRC 'passports'. Under the headline 'Passports for SS Men and Collaborators', *L'Unità* informed readers that police had arrested a number of former SS soldiers in the Italian port city of Genoa. Up to that point the whole group had been furnished with travel documents by the ICRC, supported by the Vatican Commission for Refugees, and been hosted in Catholic institutions.[73]

The story spread rapidly, and various European news outlets reported on the scams, including the Swiss left-wing press.[74] The ICRC in Geneva took careful note of all these media reports.[75] One Swiss newspaper concluded with tough questions about culpability: 'Now we wait anxiously for an explanation from the ICRC' which engaged not just in providing aid to POWs but also aid to 'bandits of the Waffen SS [...]' 'Who is guilty: the Vatican Commission or certain high ranking officials of the ICRC?'[76] This kind of news report about the ICRC's involvement with war criminals and collaborators only seemed to confirm Soviet suspicions.

The Soviets also made sure that their views were made public and they now launched a press campaign against the ICRC. In December 1946 an article appeared in the widely distributed Soviet daily *Trud* (*Labour*) about the ICRC. The author of the piece showed disdain for the Geneva humanitarians: 'Democratic world public opinion has more than once expressed its indignation that several leaders of the International Committee of the Red Cross (Geneva) were advocates of fascism.'[77] The ICRC, according to *Trud*, had not defended the Geneva Conventions, but on the contrary 'remained silent on bestial fascist conduct and, in essence, covered up crimes of the Hitlerite invaders'. After proffering these allegations, the Soviet newspaper concluded that the ICRC was not just reactionary, but also unfit to address the challenges of the postwar world. The Soviets thus demanded a strengthening and transformation of the League of Red Cross Societies to turn it into an effective tool for peace. In other words, Moscow refused to offer any support for the ICRC, arguing that the committee should be replaced by the League.[78] Even the left-wing Swiss newspaper began repeatedly echoing the critique from Moscow.[79] The Zurich-based magazine *Die Tat* succinctly concluded that the ICRC had failed to discharge its full duties, was essentially bankrupt, and had to resort to the Americans and others for financial help. After listing the ICRC's failures and shortcomings, the magazine concluded sharply: 'Its disgusting actions are not really criminal but rather attributable to unsoundness of mind due to senility.'[80]

The Soviet Union remained the country most hostile to the ICRC.[81] It criticized the organization for having done nothing to help Soviet POWs in German camps. This accusation was quite hypocritical, for the Soviets had not actually ratified the Geneva Convention of 1929. The ICRC in coalition with the 'bourgeois' states was accused of preventing Soviet POWs from returning to the Soviet Union, where they would allegedly be welcomed warmly. Beyond this, left-wing critics claimed the ICRC was helping Nazi collaborators to escape justice. A harsh critique of the organization's failure to protect civilian victims of the Nazis also appeared in the Soviet magazine *Literary Gazette*. Among other issues, there were mutterings of reports about concentration camps (most likely a reference to Rossels' visit to Theresienstadt): 'During the war, the "investigators" of the Geneva Committee foully deceived world opinion with their printed reports which sought in every way to conceal the truth about the fascist death camps.' The State Department evaluated these reports and harboured few illusions about the Soviets' intentions regarding the Geneva Conventions:

Figure 4.4. Finland 1942: a delegate of the ICRC was able to distribute 5,000 Red Cross food packages to Soviet POWs.

'The Soviet attitude toward the International Red Cross [Committee], so clearly set forth in this article is indicative of the degree of cooperation to be expected from the Soviet Union in any international undertaking, even in one of so purely humanitarian and non-political a character as the Red Cross.'[82]

The *Neue Zürcher Zeitung* served as one of the platforms used by the ICRC to fend off attacks.[83] The paper stressed that the Russian suspicions were unfounded and that the Red Cross 'in absolute neutrality and impartiality' had helped Soviet POWs as much as it could.[84] The ICRC in order to explain its position issued a number of publications, many of them merely scholarly but some also intended for a wider audience.[85] In preparation for the Stockholm conference—but also addressing both attacks from the left and other political quarters—the Geneva-based organization also published a detailed report about the ICRC's activities during the Second World War in anticipation of some of the criticism it expected to encounter during the meeting.[86] In 1947 the ICRC published perhaps its most effective report about its wartime activities, *Inter Arma Caritas: The Work of the International Committee of the Red Cross during the Second World War* by Frédéric Siordet, one of its staff members.[87] The text laid out in detail what the organization had done to support POWs and deportees. In its effort to shape public opinion and garner support for the ICRC, Siordet's book was a careful balancing act that both highlighted successes and acknowledged failures. In the opening passages of his book Siordet pointed proudly to the committee's 8,000 visits to POW camps, 36 million food parcels sent, and 120 million messages from POWs delivered to their families. But the author mentioned defeats as well. The fate of Soviet POWs and Axis soldiers captured by the Red Army were described as a 'total failure'. Siordet admitted to not doing enough for concentration camp inmates or deported civilians. But he was quick to add that little could have been done for those victims, arguing, first, that the ICRC did not know much about the fate of those civilians and, second, that it had lacked a legal basis on which to intervene.[88] Ultimately, Siordet was surely right when he stated that in the face of the extermination centres in the East 'the civilized world itself had failed'.[89] Yet many a critical reader could not have avoided the conclusion that the ICRC had failed along with it.

Because *Inter Arma Caritas* was aimed at a wider audience, it appeared simultaneously in German, French, and English. English editions of ICRC publications were not common at the time, a clear hint that Geneva had an international audience in mind. In fact, the target audience was largely named in the foreword: 'The International Committee of the Red Cross will present to the Seventeenth International Red Cross Conference, which will be held at Stockholm in August 1948, a detailed General report on the whole of its activities in the course of the Second World War and during the immediate post-war period.'[90] Max Huber and the ICRC leadership wanted to make sure that *Inter Arma Caritas* was as widely distributed as possible.

Ship without a Captain

In addition to its damaged reputation and attacks from the left and its close affiliates, the ICRC was suffering from a serious leadership deficit. When long-time president Max Huber was about to retire and Carl Burckhardt was elected to succeed him in January 1945, Burckhardt suddenly accepted the Swiss ambassadorship in Paris. Burckhardt's decision created an uncertain situation, which became more complicated when he failed to give up his title as ICRC president. As a result, his presidency lay dormant while he served as a Swiss diplomat. This less-than-ideal situation left Huber no choice but to continue to represent the ICRC temporarily. In the midst of a serious crisis, the ship lacked a strong captain: in 1945 the new president was largely absent, while the old president was definitely past his retirement date.

The correspondence between long-time police chief Heinrich Rothmund, Burckhardt, Huber, and Ruegger from this period reveals that they considered the crisis within the ICRC to be deeply intertwined with the broader crisis of Switzerland. In his correspondence with Burckhardt, Rothmund sounded pessimistic, although he still saw opportunities for a positive outcome, telling his colleague: 'The Swiss government should realize that this is a chance for Switzerland to save its position rather than allowing itself to be attacked from all sides for having made this or that wrong decision or for generally being suspected of helping the Nazis.'[91] Rothmund, however, was very surprised and seemingly disappointed about Burckhardt's decision to become the ambassador in Paris. Rothmund stated that he was disappointed because he had been very much looking forward to working with Burckhardt in his new function as Swiss delegate in the Intergovernmental Committees for Refugees in Geneva. He then asked Burckhardt for advice about which people in the ICRC he should work with.[92]

The Red Cross family watched closely as the ICRC tried to find a more suitable president. In February 1947 the American ambassador in Bern reported to the AMRC that Huber was finally stepping down as the ICRC's de facto president. Washington government circles followed the situation with great interest, and the US diplomat Leland Harrison reported from Switzerland about the Soviet reaction to Huber stepping down. Would Burckhardt now finally take over his duties as ICRC president, or would another solution to this crisis of leadership arise? The question remained unresolved, and the ICRC essentially remained without a president for some time. The Swiss press also commented on these developments in the ICRC's chain of command. Martin Bodmer and Ernest Gloor were appointed as vice presidents to direct the ICRC in the interim, while the Swiss communist and socialist press bluntly began to speculate about its chances of survival.[93]

Observers on the other side of the Atlantic tried to ascertain what direction the rudderless vessel might take. The US State Department detailed Bodmer's and Gloor's backgrounds. While Bodmer was from a wealthy family and politically conservative, Gloor had been active in the social democratic movement in Switzerland. Their appointments signalled that the ICRC was going through a fundamental transition.[94] For the traditionally conservative, Christian, traditional leadership of the ICRC, the election of a social democrat was unusual. It seemed to indicate that the Committee had made some compromises with their old antagonists on the left in Switzerland. Internal correspondence of the AMRC in Washington also registered the crisis. A report to the executive vice chairman of the AMRC read: 'The left-wingers, I am told, have continued to badger the International Red Cross Committee to the point that considerable doubt exists as to whether the Committee will long be able to persuade the Swiss National Council to appropriate, as it has in the past, substantial sums for the use of the Committee.'[95]

With the internal and external crises continuing and the Red Cross conference in Sweden in summer 1948 looming ahead, election of a successor became pressing. Burckhardt made it clear that he thought he could serve Switzerland's immediate interests better by serving as Swiss ambassador in Paris than serving as the ICRC's president.[96] But at the same time, he wanted to keep all options open and indicated that he might return to Geneva. Hans Wolf de Salis from the ICRC delegation in Rome in January 1948 wrote to his friend Burckhardt that he still hoped for Burckhardt's return to

Geneva, noting that Burckhardt was, of course, the best candidate, but that Ruegger would be a good second choice for a strong presidency.[97] Meanwhile in London Ruegger had begun a closer correspondence with Burckhardt, as the two worked both for the defence of the ICRC and on behalf of Switzerland. Burckhardt clearly saw no conflict of interest in combining ICRC business and Swiss foreign policy in his communications with Ruegger.[98] The ICRC leadership recognized that the next president must be strategically chosen.

In the autumn of 1947, the Swiss government's delegate for international aid work and ICRC member, de Haller, observed that it was 'supremely important for the ICRC and indirectly for Switzerland, given the significance of the committee's fate for Swiss foreign policy' for the committee to appoint a 'president who could not only equal Bernadotte in caliber, but who would effectively assume his role' before the Stockholm conference.[99] In a memorandum for the Swiss foreign minister, de Haller too was very troubled about the future standing of the ICRC. He identified the ambitions of the US–AMRC and Sweden as the main causes underlying the Geneva humanitarians' crisis, particularly the Americans' desire for power: 'There is a will to take command of the International Red Cross. In effect, the U.S. has always had its hands on the League of Red Cross Societies. There is but one stumbling block on the road: the International Committee.'[100] Sweden had its own barely disguised ambitions, he opined.

> Sweden has been envious of the role played by Switzerland during the entire war, be it in matters related to the Red Cross or as protecting power. Apparently it has the ambition to ensure a position for itself similar to our own for the future, if not to replace us altogether. We have tradition on our side, but Sweden has the advantage of being a member of the United Nations, of possessing a dynamic national Red Cross presided over by a member of the royal family and having the support of the nation. It is likely that Count Bernadotte is in cahoots with Mr. O'Connor, the president of the American Red Cross.[101]

Faced with these forces, de Haller conceded that some changes inside the ICRC would be necessary to counteract American and Swedish schemes. Retaining Burckhardt as head of the ICRC proved unacceptable for Moscow, for the Soviets saw him as pro-fascist. Under his presidency, it would have been difficult to improve relations with the Soviets, but also with some Western governments, such as the United Kingdom. Because Burckhardt had been the target of such strong criticism and the enduring view that he was at heart a pro-Nazi, Ruegger seemed to be the better candidate. The latter was willing and able to defend the status of Switzerland and its human-itarian flagship. 'In this critical hour', Ruegger wrote to the head of the Federal Political Department (Foreign Office) Petitpierre, 'we must make every attempt to maintain the institution to which our country is so closely tied and on which much of Switzerland's prestige depends'.[102]

Even as he prepared to leave the presidency, Burckhardt exerted consid-erable influence on the choice of the man to succeed him.[103] In November 1947, he decided to give up the presidency for good, insisting that he wanted to remain ambassador in Paris, and made melodramatic references to the effect that the coming months could be critical for Switzerland's existence as a nation.[104] In the case of a new war, however, Burckhardt declared he would be willing once again to offer his services to the ICRC. Retrospectively, his offer seems more self-serving than selfless, for another war would have given him the chance to play a leading role in world events and attempts to play power broker again. Burckhardt made clear that he wanted to be where the big decisions were made, and this was Paris for the time being: 'The current problems, committee—national societies—League, appear to me from a distance as fleeting, compared to the real duties [we face] here and now.'[105] In the end, Burckhardt spoke in favour of appointing Ruegger as his successor.[106]

In February 1948 Ruegger was elected ICRC president with the support of his lifelong mentor Huber but also with Burckhardt's blessing.[107] The news was met with great interest at the headquarters of the AMRC in Washington.[108] The *Journal de Genève* of 10 February 1948, celebrated Ruegger as an outstanding choice, as a leading Swiss diplomat, and likely a bulwark against attempts to internationalize the committee's leadership.[109] This is certainly a correct assessment. In reports from London to his supe-rior, the foreign minister Petitpierre, he showed himself to be both a Swiss patriot and Cold War hawk.[110] At the same time he was a careful diplomat and would serve well as ICRC president. Swiss foreign minister Petitpierre certainly had no doubts about this either and congratulated Ruegger on his new position as ICRC president 'in the interest of our country'.[111] Soon after his election, Ruegger sent a letter to British Foreign Secretary Anthony Eden in which he reflected: 'My decision to accept the presidency of the International Red Cross Committee in Geneva was, as you can imagine, not an easy one to take, but it had to be done. The present moment is serious, and the committee had felt that Carl Burckhardt, who had accepted in 1945 but not exercised the presidency of the committee (as he left then almost immediately for abroad) had somewhat grown apart from the problems of the committee in this moment, and it was therefore unavoidable to accept the final appeal which I had tried to direct to other channels. One chief problem of the next months and weeks will be to try to bring about a settlement of the Red Cross problems as regards Eastern Europe.'[112] With Ruegger's appointment, a new start in the relationship between the ICRC and the Soviets became more likely. In 1948 he expressed to Stalin his strong interest in regular cooperation between the Red Cross in Geneva and the Soviet Union.[113] Clearly Ruegger was focused on resolving the ongoing critiques coming from the left and the Soviet Union, though he no doubt had the ICRC's internal problems and financial crisis on his mind as well.

Financial Insolvency

As soon as the leadership crisis had been addressed, the urgency of addressing the ICRC's financial position took precedence. Geneva was short of funds. The organization's finances were in dire straits owing to developments at the end of the war. During the war, the belligerents themselves had financed many of the ICRC's activities, including food parcels and other relief. With the end of the war, this funding all but ceased.[114] Payments from Germany and Japan stopped with their capitulation and funding from Jewish aid organizations ended a few months later. In 1946 several governments likewise informed the ICRC that they would stop payments to the committee because their POWs were now safely back home. The cessation of these payments severely limited the ICRC's capital and provoked great anxiety within the organization. In private, Burckhardt complained bitterly that the belligerent countries had behaved very opportunistically in their support of the ICRC and its aid to POWs. The national governments would support the committee as long as they needed to show their voters that they were taking good care of their fellow countrymen in captivity, he said. Once this need was gone, no further funds could be expected from these foreign governments. (Burckhardt was mainly referring to the United States and Great Britain.)[115] But such complaints would do nothing to restore the funds needed to continue the ICRC's work in peacetime.

With its funding drying up or in dispute, the ICRC was forced to ask the Swiss government for help. General Eisenhower had allowed for the care of German POWs still held in Germany and France and therefore needed twenty-five more ICRC representatives for this purpose. This additional activity made its position even more difficult. In his letter to the Swiss Finance Department, de Haller repeatedly underlined the urgency of the crisis.[116] Because the work of the ICRC was in the Swiss interest, the government did give some emergency funds to the organization, which made the ICRC even more dependent on it. Yet the funding was not overly generous, at least not in Burckhardt's opinion, writing in early 1946: 'The Swiss federal government advanced the ICRC five million. These five million are not designated to put large aid projects together, but rather to enable the committee to liquidate its work in a decent manner and to wrap up the last obligations still remaining.'[117] Rothmund agreed with his friend and expressed his own lack of optimism about the future of the ICRC: 'If the Red Cross does not realize that, if the worst comes to the worst, it won't be allowed to put itself out of its own misery but will have to submit to being killed, then it would be better not to give it a little bit of money to stay afloat for [even] a short while.'[118]

The Swiss government was, however, embroiled in its own difficult negotiations with the Western Allies about Nazi gold and frozen German property and was not always happy about the additional burden of the ICRC's requests for funding. In the spring of 1946 a Swiss delegation was invited by the British, Americans, and French to Washington to discuss a number of issues flowing from the Paris Reparations Conference. Foremost was the buying and storing of German and German-looted gold during the war, among other German property sitting in Switzerland. The US government boycotted Swiss firms which had traded military goods with the Axis powers. In addition, the assets of German–Swiss companies in the United States were frozen. Now, after the war, the Swiss needed to free these assets and to lift the 'blacklist' of Swiss companies allegedly collaborating with the Germans. While the Americans proved tough negotiators on these issues, the British and French were more lenient and very eager to return to business as normal. For the Swiss officials involved, the ideal outcome of the Washington talks would have been a solution that respected Swiss sovereignty 'and also helps to end the suspicions shared among the Allies against Switzerland', as an internal Swiss government memo described it.[119] It was hoped that swift Swiss action in the war's immediate aftermath would enable the country to salvage its reputation with the Allies.

In February 1946 the Swiss Foreign Office prepared a number of suggestions for its minister, Max Petitpierre, to prepare for these important negotiations. It suggested contacting US policy-maker and spymaster Allen

Dulles before the meeting, who was known for his friendly feelings towards Switzerland, his home for much of the war. The president of the Swiss-based Nestlé company also had good connections with certain figures in the US government, especially the Treasury.[120]

In the summer of 1946 Winston Churchill visited Switzerland with his wife Clementine and met with many influential Swiss leaders. The Swiss Foreign Office was very much interested in this visit, although it was undertaken as a private trip and the Conservative leader had been voted out in office in the summer of 1945. Swiss banks and business circles organized and paid for parts of the Churchills' tour, but their intentions were not merely benevolent. The visit was also intended to boost the image of Swiss banks and business circles, and help remove them from Allied blacklists. The Swiss foreign office reported on his every move in detail and the Swiss newsreels also seized on the opportunity to publicize the couple's movements. Churchill also found time for a short visit to the ICRC headquarters. Burckhardt was among the prominent Swiss politicians Churchill met in private. As a Swiss government report later noted, their discussion was harmonious.[121] Publicly, Churchill expressed understanding for Swiss neutrality. The former British prime minister was highly respected and his presence indeed appeared to improve the country's standing in the Western world.[122] Churchill's visit took place after the first Washington talks between Switzerland and the United States, but many issues were still far from resolved, including those relating to the ICRC, and so there was strong interest in getting Churchill to help argue the Swiss position.

The main sticky issue was Allied claims to German assets held in Switzerland. Given the total surrender of and disintegration of the Nazi government, the Allied Control Commission in Germany (consisting of the United States, the Soviet Union, France, and Great Britain) declared themselves the de facto German government. They laid claim to all German property, even that held in Switzerland. Switzerland was the most important safe-haven for German assets during the war, in gold, jewellery, bank accounts, and property. Switzerland also served as the main hub for Nazi Germany's financial operations. The Nazi government's (often looted) gold reserves would be exchanged for Swiss francs or stored in Swiss bank vaults. The amount of gold bought by the Swiss banks from the Nazis was considerable. At the end of the war the US government estimated its value at $400 million. Swiss officials rejected the Allied claims to German assets in Switzerland and took the stance that Bern should continue to oversee German properties such as embassies, consulates, and border train stations until a new German government had formed. They sought to convince US politicians in particular that the demands for German assets in Switzerland were unjustified.[123]

Looted Nazi gold was a particularly touchy subject, one on which US and Swiss positions sharply diverged. The Swiss calculated a much lower value of German gold stored in Swiss vaults and were disingenuous in claiming that they did not know that some of the 'Nazi gold' had been expropriated from occupied countries such as Belgium and the Netherlands. The president of the Swiss National Bank insisted they had acted in good faith and that German officials had informed them that all of it had been German pre-war gold. This of course was not the case, and Swiss officials either knew or at least suspected its problematic origins long before the Washington meeting.[124] The negotiations were tough, but eventually a compromise was found. In exchange for a lump-sum payment, the Allies gave up any claim related to other transactions involving Nazi gold to Switzerland.[125] The Swiss government, however, never recognized the internationally binding legal basis of the agreement and never fully implemented even the Washington provisions. The Swiss eventually offered to hand over $58 million's worth of gold, a compromise which the Allies accepted. The liquidation of German assets, however, turned out to be more complicated and politically tricky. In 1952 the Swiss government finally agreed to pay a lump sum for these assets. This sum was already lower than agreed in Washington, but was even further reduced to $4.7 million. For Bern it was merely a politically motivated bilateral agreement in order to show good will. It interpreted the payments it made as the Swiss contribution for the reconstruction of Europe.[126] In other words, the Swiss government of the late 1940s never admitted any wartime wrongdoing. The whole gold issue was highly politicized at the time and was detrimental to Switzerland's image, but quickly faded.[127]

A major unresolved issue that had a direct impact on the ICRC was the large sum transferred at the end of the war from the German and Japanese governments to the ICRC, which the Allies were freezing for the time being. The ICRC reached out to the Swiss government and asked for support in this matter. The negotiations in Washington in 1946 would also reveal the financial problems facing the ICRC. Max Huber demanded that a member of the ICRC should be present at the Swiss delegation in Washington to talk about German and Japanese blocked contributions to the ICRC.[128] The German Reich had set in motion a transfer of 15 million Swiss francs to the ICRC shortly before the German surrender, but the Allies had the transfer stopped.

In August 1945, shortly before its capitulation, Japan had also transferred $2.5 million to a Swiss bank, money that was allegedly meant as a gift to the ICRC from the Japanese empress. The Allies also blocked this transaction. De Haller pushed the issue with the Swiss government by pointing out that the financial situation of the ICRC had become extremely difficult and the funds should be treated as a high priority. Various other governments only promised money but delayed payment, which made the situation worse.[129]

The Swiss government also supported the ICRC's claim for freeing up the Japanese and German funds. Walter Stucki, Swiss diplomat and a leading negotiator in the Washington talks, stressed that the Swiss government supported the release of 10 million Swiss francs that were transferred by the Japanese government to the ICRC in the last moment prior to the surrender. The Swiss request received a very negative response from Washington.[130] In late 1945 the ICRC in Geneva reported in detail to the AMRC, as well as the US State and War Departments, about its fragile financial situation and a delegation lobbied on its behalf in Washington for release of the funds.[131] In June 1946 the dispute about the Japanese funds was referred to the Allied Far Eastern Commission, which oversaw the terms of surrender for Japan. It decided that the ICRC had no rightful claim to the money.[132] However, this was not the end of the story. The problem of the alleged gift from the Japanese government to the ICRC kept the State Department busy for many years to come.

In conclusion, we can say that the ICRC faced myriad internal and external threats in the immediate aftermath of the Second World War. Some of these issues were products of the war and some products of a new postwar order. The attacks from Jewish and communist circles had a huge impact on the ICRC, because theirs was a critique that was to a large degree shared by Western Red Cross societies as well, particularly the Swedish Red Cross. In contrast to Sweden, the ICRC had no strong leadership—certainly nobody who could rival Bernadotte, who was still undermining Geneva as the Stockholm meeting drew closer. The ICRC was also close to being bankrupt and depended on the goodwill of its main sponsors. Initially, the ICRC had very few allies; Switzerland could be counted on, but was itself under pressure and had limited resources. Among the ICRC's strongest allies were the Vatican and the other Christian churches. But, ultimately, the ICRC *had* to ensure that it got the backing of powerful governments as well, especially the new superpowers of the day, the United States and the Soviet Union.

5

Between Nuremberg
and Geneva

It was not long after the end of the war that the Swiss had convinced themselves that it was the strength of their army and their humanitarian politics which had spared them from war and German invasion. As the Swiss *Neue Zürcher Zeitung* expressed it in September 1945: 'We had been spared [from the war], thanks to God's will and thanks also to our willingness to defend ourselves militarily, and certainly also because the International Committee of the Red Cross as a Swiss institution could offer its services—which both sides of the conflict depended on in the same way—only from its basis in neutral Switzerland.'[1] 'The humanitarian spirit had triumphed',[2] and the idea of Switzerland as a 'country of mostly courageous and right-eous people' became the dominant national narrative in the postwar years.[3] Former sociology professor, Swiss politician, and UN official Jean Ziegler criticizes Switzerland's post-1945 elites harshly but probably fairly when he declares that 'their failures during World War II were now fabricated into big lies'.[4] An independent commission of historians concluded not much differently: 'Outwardly and domestically, the image of the Confederation was to a large extent founded on its tradition of granting asylum, its good offices, humanitarian aid, and the services provided by the Geneva-based International Committee of the Red Cross (ICRC).'[5] In the immediate aftermath of the war, this narrative of humanitarian neutrality would not be easy to defend. A series of Allied allegations, dramatic revelations, trials, and media reports in these postwar years challenged Switzerland's much-vaunted record of neutrality time and time again. The French term '*malaise suisse*', suggesting emotional unease, crisis, or internal conflict among the Swiss, began circulating.[6] The term *malaise suisse* also implied a series of insinua-tions and accusations against a number of prominent individuals. These affairs would distract from the larger issues at stake, but were at the same time part of the overarching question as to how the nation would save face and fare in the emerging Cold War.

Swiss politicians in the immediate postwar years took pains to stress how imminent the danger of a wartime German invasion had seemed. They did so in part to find justification for their own accommodation of Nazi Germany during the war. Scandals related to the wartime activities of the Swiss and the ICRC began to erupt as the world assessed the legal and moral culpability of individuals, organizations, and countries during the war crimes trials in Nuremberg in the years 1945–1949. The very participation of Swiss and ICRC officials in such proceedings as witnesses for the defence raised questions about the political sympathies of leaders in the Alpine republic and its most celebrated organization. Revelations about Swiss and ICRC efforts to broker peace during the war through secretive 'diplomacy' had the effect of placing the nature and viability of Swiss neutrality—and a neutral ICRC—in question.

Burckhardt's 'Diplomacy'

The public learned at this time that Burckhardt had been identified as a potential wartime negotiator between the Swiss and German and Allied circles. In July 1947 the Swiss socialist newspaper *Vorwärts* reported in a lead article on Burckhardt's attempts to arrange a peace deal between Nazi Germany and Great Britain. In response, Burckhardt's friends in the ICRC commented that 'historical falsehoods have become the object of bad journalism and bad policy'.[7] But the news was indeed true, at least at its core.

During the war, Burckhardt's attempts at diplomacy on behalf of the ICRC and Switzerland were guided by his conviction that National Socialism could have been tamed and deradicalized with 'European ethics'. He asserted that the Western Allies had started the war without 'sufficient legitimation',[8] and he took the line that war had not been necessary to 'overcome' the Nazi regime, claiming that it would ultimately have destroyed itself anyway.[9] From Burckhardt's point of view, the Hitler regime appeared to be only a temporary threat when compared to Communism, which he saw as the real danger for Europe and the world.[10] Burckhardt's engagement as a peace negotiator dated back to his time as high commissioner in the Free City of Danzig from 1937 to 1939. In that period he had gotten his first taste of high-stakes politics, meeting with Hitler and high-ranking German and British diplomats. Burckhardt sought to shape Europe's destiny and defend Germany and the continent from Soviet domination, believing that he could single-handedly prevent another world war.[11] He had contacts in high-level British diplomatic circles until the war, but the installation of the Churchill government in 1940 changed this.[12] A friend of and politically aligned with the former British foreign secretary Lord Halifax, Burckhardt disliked and disapproved of his successor, Anthony Eden. Burckhardt accused Churchill of being shortsighted in focusing on the defeat of Nazi Germany. In Burckhardt's view, Churchill was completely underestimating the communist threat to Central Europe. Thus he embarked on his own diplomatic mission.

Burckhardt's criticism of the Allies was not limited to Great Britain, for he was not pleased with US objectives in Europe either. President Roosevelt's European policy, he argued, was largely influenced by his extreme anti-German Jewish advisers. The formula of unconditional surrender for Germany to which the United States and the United Kingdom had agreed in 1943 seemed to Burckhardt to be a confirmation of his pessimism.[13] Burckhardt's diplomatic efforts show that he was not merely acting as the president of the ICRC, but as something approaching an unofficial 'foreign minister' for his nation, attempting to affect the strategy and outcome of the war.

In his role as negotiator, Burckhardt attempted to connect the German anti-Hitler opposition with British politicians and was at times a self-appointed 'messenger of hope for the German resistance'.[14] Ulrich von Hassell, one of the most prominent proponents of the conservative anti-Hitler opposition, considered Burckhardt an intermediary for possible separate peace negotiations with Great Britain. Hassell was a high-ranking German official and German ambassador to Italy until 1938 who had hoped that once Hitler was eliminated by the internal German opposition, the Western powers would be willing to make a negotiated peace with Germany. Hassell hoped to elicit such guarantees from the British in order to strengthen the anti-Hitler opposition, and envisioned becoming foreign minister of the new Germany and reinstating the monarchy.[15] What Burckhardt and Hassell could not have known was that Churchill had no intention of seriously considering these 'peace feelers'.[16] Ultimately, Burckhardt probably never had viable contacts or leverage with Churchill's government because he was acting on his own initiative and not as an official spokesman of the Swiss government.

His objectives and actions mirrored those of some members of the Swiss government. In 1941–1942 Swiss foreign minister Marcel Pilet-Golaz concurred with Burckhardt's aim of keeping communism out of Europe. When Burckhardt travelled to London in late 1941, he used Red Cross business as a cover in part for his attempted peace negotiations. He shared Pilet-Golaz's belief that the British and the Germans should fight side by side against the Soviets because the main deadly enemy was communism, and that if Hitler could be removed, such an alliance would be possible. Burckhardt was thinking along the same lines as Hassell and hoped to convince the British to follow suit. He made no secret that his mission was not just about humanitarian questions.

Despite Burckhardt and Hassell's hopes, neither Prime Minister Churchill nor Foreign Minister Eden was even prepared to meet with Burckhardt. Eden already openly disliked Burckhardt for his pro-German attitude. It is not surprising therefore that a few years later any notion of considering Burckhardt as the new Swiss ambassador to the United Kingdom was out of the question, for Eden had 'strong objections'.[17] Stalin had never stopped suspecting that the British might attempt to broker a deal with Germany against the Soviets, and talks between prominent British leaders and Burckhardt would only have confirmed such suspicions. While Churchill made clear that Burckhardt's visit would be confined to 'Red Cross business only', Burckhardt's activities were obviously leaked to the press. The *Manchester Guardian* ambiguously reported in November 1941: 'Some people jumped to the immediate conclusion that the vice-president of the Red Cross might be concerned with a peace move by Germany.... Although he is keenly interested in politics and has many influential contacts in Germany, there seems to be no reason to think that Professor Burckhardt's mission is other than it purports to be.'[18]

The month spent in London at the end of 1941 turned out to be disappointing for Burckhardt's political ambitions and detrimental to Swiss–British relations. In the months following his visit, Burckhardt complained bitterly that the 'administrative wasteland' of Red Cross business would prevent him from advancing his own political and academic endeavours.[19] On returning to Switzerland from England, he met Ulrich von Hassell in Geneva in January 1942. He did not inform Hassell that his diplomatic mission to England had been a fiasco, but instead claimed that some British circles were still interested in coming to an understanding with 'respectable Germans', which fed the diplomat's wishful thinking.[20]

Burckhardt's secret diplomacy while serving as vice president of the ICRC also had a huge impact on British views of Burckhardt and the ICRC at the time. Churchill and Foreign Secretary Eden's deep mistrust of Burckhardt increased as a result of his clumsy visit, which British intelligence watched closely. Some British officials not only suspected Burckhardt of harbouring pro-German sentiments, but questioned whether the ICRC was an instrument of the German intelligence services and whether the Swiss were pro-Nazi.[21] In this way, Burckhardt's attempted peace-brokering during the war placed both his own and the ICRC's reputation at risk.

Burckhardt's role in the case of Rudolf Hess serves as a further example. In May 1941 Hitler's deputy Hess famously parachuted into Scotland, saying that he wanted to negotiate peace between Germany and Great Britain. The reasons for Hess's flight to Great Britain remain mysterious, but it is very likely that Hess hoped to organize a common front against the Soviet Union. He probably acted on his own initiative, and his deteriorating state of mind may have been one factor in this spectacular move, taken just before Hitler's invasion of Stalin's empire.[22] Hitler was outraged when he heard the news; he had obviously not been informed of Hess's plan. In any case, the British immediately arrested Hess and his initiative failed completely. In the words of Holocaust historian Gerhard Weinberg: 'In spite of various speculations and the suspicions of the Russians, nothing was planned and nothing ever came of this startling adventure.'[23] The British government also made it quite clear that they wanted to put him on trail as a war criminal after the end of the war. Convicted at the main Nuremberg trial in 1946, Hess would spend the rest of his long life in jail, dying in Spandau Prison in 1987.

Intriguingly, Hess had contacted the ICRC's 'foreign minister' through an intermediary in 1941 less than two weeks before he left on his flight to Scotland. Hess picked Albrecht Haushofer, a German geographer and diplomat who had contacts with wavering Nazis and right-wingers who wanted to end the war with the Western powers, as the intermediary for his mission to Geneva.[24] Haushofer and Hess probably knew Burckhardt from his earlier attempts to facilitate an understanding between Germany and Great Britain. Hess's emissary wanted to learn more about possible contacts in England.[25] Burckhardt pointed to possible British 'friends of peace'. Beyond that, he apparently did not provide much concrete help, but did promise his support for the initiative.[26] Hess, who was convinced he could persuade British opponents of Churchill to come to an arrangement with Hitler, parachuted to a location near the estate of the Duke of Hamilton, a friend of Albrecht Haushofer's. Hess never seemed to have talked about his connection to

Burckhardt while in captivity, but Burckhardt's involvement came up during the Nuremberg trials in 1946, as we will see later in this chapter.[27]

The ICRC's president from 1948 to 1955, Paul Ruegger, had been involved in the Hess case as well. As the newly appointed Swiss ambassador to the United Kingdom, Ruegger visited Hess in Wales on 20 December 1944. Hess considered himself a POW and therefore asked neutral Switzerland to ensure his personal safety.[28] He wanted to be taken to Switzerland and interned there. Ruegger tried to explain to him that this would not be possible, well aware of the fact that much more than humanitarian interests were involved.[29] The British Foreign Office would never have agreed to release Hess to Switzerland, and the always suspicious Soviets wanted to put Hess on trial. One of the concessions that the British finally made to their prisoner and the Swiss was to permit limited correspondence, especially to his wife who was then in Switzerland. Hess's family correspondence was forwarded through the ICRC in Geneva and thus landed on Burckhardt's desk before being sent on. Burckhardt also handled the letters directed to Hess. Although Burckhardt had a keen interest in Hess's case, his motivation was political and personal, not simply humanitarian or based on an interest in legal questions.[30] Furthermore, his support of Hess's requests to the British was not the end of his own attempts to negotiate with German officials and to reach out to the Allies. Burckhardt continued his behind-the-scenes political activities in a range of ways. For example, in November 1943 he delivered a report about conditions in Germany to Allen Dulles in Bern. The well-connected Dulles was outpost chief in neutral Switzerland of the US wartime intelligence 'Office of Strategic Services' (OSS) and later director of the CIA.[31] Even in the last weeks of the war, Burckhardt played the part of secret diplomat. In his talks with SS-Obergruppenführer Ernst Kaltenbrunner in April 1945, Burckhardt gave the impression that he had influence with Anglo-American policy-makers, thereby exploiting Nazi preconceptions that he was influential.[32]

The Humanitarians and Allied Justice

As the war ended, the Allies agreed to destroy Nazism for good and to make sure that Germany would never be a threat again. One way to do this was to hold Germany—its leaders and its people—accountable for the war and the Holocaust. With the desire for revenge in the air, the Western Allies (especially some US leaders) nonetheless honoured the rule of law and opted for putting the top Nazi leaders on trial in the city of Nuremberg.[33]

As American historian Richard Breitman notes: 'From the beginning, future war-crimes trials were an American project. Some Washington officials considered the very announcement of trials in which offenders would be treated as common criminals, not political officers, an important element in a campaign of psychological warfare.'[34] In a way, these trials can also be understood as a compromise between vengeance and forgiveness.[35] Nuremberg had many shortcomings and was far from perfect, but it was much better than the available alternatives. In hindsight it proved the right decision and was eminently preferable to demands for the summary execu- tion of Nazi leaders without trial or for the collective punishment of the German people as a whole. Insisting on the rule of law, in other words legal proceedings with due process, the right to a lawyer and defence witnesses, helped to set new standards. The sentences varied from death penalties to prison sentences and acquittals.

Nuremberg would help to draw a clear dividing line between dictatorship and a democratic new beginning. But the Americans did not limit themselves to punishing criminals in the strict legal sense. People who had not commit- ted specific crimes but who had been Nazi Party members and held offices in Hitler's Germany were made to face denazification courts. Offenders were placed in different categories and faced sanctions such as being barred from the professions or from public office for a number of years. Denazification procedures became the Allies' chief programme for scanning and punishing the large numbers of Germans and Austrians who were high- and low-level Nazis. In short, Allied policies in Germany after the war—from holding war crimes trials to denazification courts—sought to develop a democratic and pro-Western Germany, even if that meant turning a blind eye to the culpa- bility of some former Nazis now considered useful to the Allies.

While the ICRC had no formal role in these Allied actions, its leaders found themselves drawn into the war crimes trials, whether reluctantly or proactively. Despite this involvement, the ICRC leadership was always highly critical of them. The organization's distaste had already become obvi- ous before the end of the war, when the Soviets held a few of their own trials of German officials and Nazi collaborators. The Soviets were the first to organize war crime trials of captured German prisoners of war (POWs), beginning with the public trials at Krasnodar in July 1943. In December 1943, 6,000 people watched another war crimes trial at the Kharkov theatre.[36] During this trial, three German *Einsatzkommando* officers and one Soviet collaborator were found guilty and hanged. The men accused were most likely guilty, but such trials violated Western standards of justice, as the judgement appeared foreordained and the defence was severely constrained. Stalin's propaganda, by contrast, would depict the trial as a triumph of justice. Moscow therefore made sure that a lot of publicity accompanied the proceedings; the trial was filmed and Western journalists were present.[37] In defending their actions, the Soviets explicitly referred to the Moscow Declaration of 1943, in which the Allies agreed to judge Nazi war criminals in the countries where they had committed atrocities.[38] Furthermore, the Allies concurred that 'major war criminals whose crimes... have no particular geographical localisation' such as the high command of the German state, the Nazi Party, and the SS, for example, 'should face joint international trials'.[39] Kharkov therefore held special significance because Moscow presented it as its model for future war crimes trials.

The Soviet trials evoked a response from the West, but that response was far from uniform. US Treasury Secretary Henry Morgenthau congratulated the Soviets on the trials, but the State Department was more cautious, fearful that the Germans would retaliate against American POWs.[40] The ICRC, however, criticized the Soviets for not adhering to the rules of the Geneva Conventions and launched an appeal in December 1943, arguing that captured German soldiers should be treated as POWs until their guilt was proven in a trial. Moscow's response came promptly. The Soviets accused the ICRC of defending German fascists who committed atrocities against the civilian population.[41] Soviet newspapers attacked the Red Cross on the 'question of war criminals', saying that the ICRC was choosing to ignore the massive breaches of human rights and international law by Hitler's forces in the Soviet Union and to downplay the atrocities they had committed, which had claimed millions of civilian victims. Moreover, the Soviets charged, the ICRC's silence and its so-called 'impartiality' would only help the perpetrators of these crimes;[42] the Soviet people would not accept any outcome in which German soldiers would not be held responsible for crimes they had committed. These soldiers would not be treated as POWs, the argument ran, but as criminals undeserving of the protection of international law. Thus, Soviet officials argued, appeals by the ICRC on behalf of these Nazi criminals should be thrown 'on the rubbish heap of history'.[43]

The ICRC and Nuremberg

The ICRC leadership was no less critical of the Nuremberg trials against some of the leaders of the Nazi regime. ICRC President Burckhardt opposed the trials not only because he thought they had a negative effect on a democratic Europe and created a distraction from the communist threat in Eastern Europe; he also considered them to be part of a Jewish vendetta against Germany 'disguised' as justice. Several statements he made in 1946 point to this conclusion. According to Burckhardt, Nuremberg was part of an overall strategy to wipe out 20 million Germans through ethnic cleansing and deportations from their homelands. He referred to a 'Colonel Rosenthau' in Nuremberg who had allegedly made such a statement in the presence of British political scientist and Marxist Harold Laski.[44] There was, of course, no official named 'Rosenthau' in Nuremberg. Burckhardt, always the secretive diplomat, was very careful in his statements, and it was up to the recipient to understand the message. According to historian Paul Stauffer, 'Rosenthau' was really the Jewish American lawyer Samuel Irving Rosenman, a special counsel to Presidents Franklin D. Roosevelt and Harry S. Truman from 1945 to 1946.[45] Rosenman was of Russian-Jewish descent and—according to Burckhardt—he thirsted for revenge against the German people. Burckhardt's transformation of 'Rosenman' in to 'Rosenthau' may also have been an oblique reference to Roosevelt's Secretary of the Treasury Morgenthau, who in some German eyes became synonymous with a vengeful 'victor's justice'. Morgenthau, for instance, had in 1944 proposed dismantling Germany's heavy industry after the war.[46] Furthermore, Morgenthau had urged Roosevelt to adopt a policy calling for the summary execution of German leaders and the pastoralization of Germany.[47] Roosevelt only partially gave in to such demands and in the end most of Morgenthau's plan was never implemented.

Burckhardt obviously considered such notions outrageous and fixed on some of Roosevelt's Jewish advisers who thought in terms of collective German guilt. He also saw himself as a target of Jewish attacks and expressed anger over the role he thought American Jews played in denazification and the prosecution of Nazi crimes. According to Burckhardt, US prosecutor Dr. Robert M. W. Kempner, a Jewish lawyer originally from Berlin who had fled Germany and eventually emigrated to the United States,[48] was the leader of this perceived 'anti-German' group that also included Rosenman and Morgenthau. Burckhardt never held back in expressing his dislike for the trials and the men he saw as responsible for them, opposing the whole process as an expression of 'victor's justice'.

Burckhardt was not the only official Swiss with a distaste for the Allied war crimes trials; another Swiss critic of Nuremberg with ties to the ICRC was Paul Ruegger. At the time of the trials, the former assistant to ICRC president Max Huber was in London serving as Swiss ambassador. Part of his duties involved reporting on events in Great Britain as well as on the general mood and reactions to current events. The first Nuremberg trial was no exception. Ruegger expressed his official position on the International Military Tribunal trial in Nuremberg in his 3 October 1946 report entitled 'The Judgment at Nuremberg' ('Das Urteil in Nürnberg') to Swiss foreign minister Max Petitpierre.[49] At the beginning of his report, he acknowledged the massive crimes committed by the Third Reich and the necessity of punishing the perpetrators. Yet at the same time he criticized the legality of Nuremberg, explaining that he felt 'a certain uneasiness about the legal premises on which the "law" has been applied'.[50] Although Ruegger summarized positions and opinions he had genuinely heard expressed in various circles in London, his selection and emphasis nevertheless obviously reflected his particular bias. In his report to the Swiss Foreign Office, he pointed out: 'I have to repeat again that nobody seriously challenges the necessity of the suppression of the massive crimes substantiated again during the Nuremberg trial.'[51] Ruegger, however, never referred directly to Jewish suffering. He did, however, refer to the Soviet Union and its crimes against humanity, referring to Stalin's terror and the Gulag system. Ruegger also reminded the foreign minister about the joint German–Soviet attack on Poland in 1939. Put bluntly, he thought that Soviet leaders should also be put on trial.[52]

The United States and Great Britain put significant pressure on Switzerland to ensure that it would not grant asylum to war criminals and fascist leaders. In November 1944 the Swiss parliament issued a statement in response, which satisfied the Western Allies.[53] As Swiss ambassador in London, Ruegger was confronted with the practical implications of this decision. After talking to the legal adviser of the United Nations War Crimes Commission, which was founded in late 1943 to collect evidence on Axis war crimes, Ruegger reported his findings back to Bern: 'Given that Switzerland is not a member state of the United Nations it does not participate in the works of the War Crimes Commission and it is not legally bound by the commission's decisions. The listing of individuals on the war crimes list does not automatically mean that such a person has to be extradited.'[54] This point of view was likely not shared by London or Washington. Ruegger then went on to say that fair trials in political cases were unlikely. For Huber, Ruegger, and particularly Burckhardt, Nuremberg would call into question both their personal allegiances and their credentials as neutrals.

The ICRC: Discretion and Direct Testimony at Nuremberg

The ICRC as an organization did not ignore the question of war crimes, but officially investigating and prosecuting war crimes had never formed part of its mission. The victims of war and atrocities might 'want justice, but the ICRC and other humanitarian organizations who look after them are not in the business of justice' as one scholar put it.[55] Though committed to creating new standards of wartime conduct, the organization paradoxically avoided speaking publicly about war crimes and war criminals. Protecting the conventions—not punishing those who violated them—always remained the ICRC's main concern. In the wake of Nuremberg, however, while the ICRC was preparing for the new Geneva Convention, it defined grave violations of the Geneva Conventions as de facto 'war crimes' that would qualify for universal jurisdiction. A small but highly specialized working group of ICRC war crimes experts chaired by Max Huber also addressed this issue. The Geneva Conventions were seen as a minimum standard of behaviour for any member country of the international community. Therefore, most nations wanted to see these standards protected. In the end, punishment of those who violated the conventions was spelled out in the Geneva treaty of 1949.[56]

Still, punishing or even publicly denouncing perpetrators of such crimes never featured centrally in the ICRC's agenda. On the contrary, over time the ICRC adhered ever closer to a policy of discretion. In cases of conflict, humanitarian organizations have often found that discretion was the price they had to pay for access to the victims. This was a genuine dilemma for the Red Cross, which would become even more acute in the context of the Holocaust. In the words of Dutch philosopher Eva Wortel: 'History shows that the moral dilemma of humanity versus justice is not new. On the one hand, it is difficult to remain silent in the face of acts of injustice; while on the other hand, the condemnation of these acts could have a negative impact on the trust of authorities and consequently lead to humanitarian access being blocked. This has been identified as one of the most fundamental dilemmas faced by the Red Cross Movement, and has evolved as an important discussion within the humanitarian community.'[57] Critical media in 1945 showed little understanding of the ICRC's 'plea of discretion' when it came to Nazi war crimes; on the contrary, there were clear expectations that the ICRC would provide information about atrocities and share its knowledge with the prosecution in Nuremberg and elsewhere.[58]

For the ICRC, as Burckhardt and Huber always stressed, practical aid came first and publicity had to be avoided. They feared provoking the perpetrators of war crimes and genocide or causing them to fear that ICRC personnel would eventually testify against them. Over time, international criminal courts came to respect this ICRC policy and they have not forced ICRC officials to testify in criminal cases.[59] The standards of 1945, however, were different. And if Huber preferred the organization's officials to adhere to a quiet role, Burckhardt enjoyed being in the spotlight. Despite these contrasting positions, not only Burckhardt and Ruegger, but also Huber were to play a role in the very public trials held at Nuremberg.

Even after Germany's defeat, Burckhardt continued to warn against both Soviet plans and the fallout from harshly punishing the Germans. The Germans, he argued, would soon be needed as allies of the Western powers in the fight against communism. Therefore, they need to be treated 'fairly', and he strongly rejected all notions of collective guilt in his correspondence with Swiss Foreign Minister Petitpierre.[60] Given these views, Burckhardt was, therefore, fundamentally opposed to the Nuremberg trials.

Burckhardt's desire to prevent what he saw as a miscarriage of justice and a diplomatic mistake caused him to embrace the possibility of testifying for the defence at Nuremberg. In February 1946 he wrote to the ICRC's acting president, Huber, that Joachim von Ribbentrop's lawyer in Nuremberg had mentioned Burckhardt as a potential witness for the defence. So far nothing had come of this, and it seemed unlikely that he would be asked to testify, Burckhardt stated. But if asked, he would answer the call: 'Yesterday the Apostolic Nuncio [the Pope's ambassador to Switzerland] approached me on this agenda and said it would probably be a matter of conscience for me. He allowed himself to say that if someone can serve the truth in this questionable process, then one must do so.'[61] Former German Foreign Minister Ribbentrop ultimately did request a number of prominent witnesses—Burckhardt among them. Ribbentrop even asked for the king of England, Churchill, and Molotov. These were, of course, unrealistic demands that only served to irritate the court. But Burckhardt was a good bet for a number of Nuremberg defendants, given that he was inclined to assist them.

Burckhardt's popularity among the defendants at Nuremberg greatly concerned Max Huber. When Huber learned through the newspapers that SS leader Ernst Kaltenbrunner had asked for three Swiss witnesses, among them Burckhardt,[62] he reacted strongly. Burckhardt's eagerness to testify alarmed him. Burckhardt was very likely aware of this and citing the apostolic nuncio's approval may have been a clever strategy, for Huber was a devoted Christian open to the notion of forgiveness. Huber wished to keep ICRC officials off the stand because of the ICRC's traditions of neutrality and discretion. But he was fighting a losing battle because the attention-grabbing Burckhardt was so eager to testify. He probably felt from early on that it wouldn't be easy to make Burckhardt stay away from Nuremberg. In a letter dated 15 March 1946 Huber asked Burckhardt about his intentions regarding Nuremberg and concluded somewhat pessimistically: 'A right to official secrecy for the ICRC [officials] of course does not exist in any international law, nor in any national law.'[63]

In his testimony during the Nuremberg trials, Burckhardt stepped onto an international stage. He felt that he could only benefit from testifying and, at the same time, improve the humanitarian record of the ICRC. On 18 March 1946, Burckhardt informed his 'dear friend' Huber that he might be called to testify in Nuremberg by Ernst Kaltenbrunner as well as Ribbentrop. Burckhardt declared himself willing to take the stand in the case of Kaltenbrunner, Himmler's subordinate and mass murderer. He wrote to Huber: 'As of today I was not approached by the authorities with an official request. Personally I am of the opinion that one should provide testimony whenever possible, especially if human lives are at stake.'[64] In the case of Ribbentrop, Burckhardt stated that a statesman in great danger deserved help. However, he initially seemed less enthusiastic about extending a hand to Kaltenbrunner, at least it appeared so in the letter to Huber: 'In Kaltenbrunner's case, there is not much to say about the personal and active role played by this representative of Himmler's. Ultimately he only served as courier between his superiors and us and made concessions only to the extent that they were already included in his instructions.'[65] But Burckhardt was soon willing to speak in Kaltenbrunner's defence as well. This may have been an attempt to set the record straight, for Kaltenbrunner had made some inaccurate statements about the ICRC president. Kaltenbrunner claimed at Nuremberg that Burckhardt had had meetings not only with Ribbentrop, but also with Hitler during the war, which

Burckhardt insistently denied: 'I never even saw the Chancellor of the Reich during the war years.'[66]

In contrast to statements he had made to Huber, Burckhardt in his witness statement repeatedly underlined that he assumed Kaltenbrunner had had the best of intentions and that he had communicated all the humanitarian requests made by the ICRC to his superiors, as requested. Burckhardt even recalled that the SS Obergruppenführer said he was against the persecution of the Jews in a handwritten note: 'Kaltenbrunner said, "That's the biggest nonsense ... we should release all Jews. That is my personal view." '[67] While Burckhardt chose to support the defence of some defendants at Nuremberg, the testimony of one of the accused put him on the defensive himself.

Rudolph Hess's revelation that Burckhardt had secretly attempted to broker a peace between the Germans and British was a bombshell that Burckhardt sought to defuse. Burckhardt, of course, denied any connection with Hess's mission. He even said that he had never even met or known Albrecht Haushofer, the go-between for Hess. Conveniently for Burckhardt, Haushofer never had an opportunity to contradict these statements, for he had been killed by the SS a few days before the war ended.[68] Burckhardt's involvement in secret diplomatic talks between the Third Reich and Great Britain had been a complete breach of ICRC principles. If the secret negotiations that Hess revealed had been deemed credible by the public, the ICRC and Burckhardt's reputations could have suffered severe setbacks. The fact that Burckhardt managed to deny Hess's testimony diffused the bomb in the short-term, but the accusation nevertheless affected the ICRC's relationship with the Soviets.

Despite his personal political beliefs and his testimony at Nuremberg, Burckhardt knew, of course, that the ICRC needed to stress its apolitical humanitarian mandate. In 1947 Huber again made clear that it was 'essential that the Committee should keep its activities *untouched by politics in any shape or form*'.[69] But Vice President Burckhardt was not a man to tailor his actions to support a philosophy he found impractical. 'Today we know that Burckhardt mainly paid only lip service to the doctrine of an apolitical Red Cross', the historian Paul Stauffer has concluded.[70] Burckhardt could even be considered the 'organisation's chief wartime violator of the standard of non-political involvement'.[71] He certainly had long aspired to a grander role. But Burckhardt did not occupy the right position to make that happen.

He was not the secretary of state of a nation, but a mere representative of a humanitarian organization that was committed to impartial, neutral, and essentially apolitical aid to war victims. What remained open to Burckhardt was humanitarian diplomacy, which sometimes—given his personality— amounted to some highly politicized diplomacy.[72] Plausible deniability and the absence of any corroborating witnesses ultimately allowed him to pro- tect his reputation and that of the ICRC temporarily. However, this would do little to silence the critics, particularly those inside the Soviet Union, who saw the Swiss government and the ICRC as virtually one and the same.

Intervening against Nuremberg: *The United States v. Ernst von Weizsäcker et al.*

After the conclusion of the international Nuremberg trial, the United States continued to prosecute former Nazi officials in twelve subsequent Nuremberg trials without the participation of the other Allied powers. Burckhardt continued to play a role in the defence of the accused at these trials, notably in the case of Ernst von Weizsäcker. His decision to testify seemingly resulted from his distinction between 'good' and 'bad' Nazis. German officials who shared his views and helped him in his humanitarian or political dealings, especially in forming an alliance with Britain against the Soviet Union, became his 'good Germans'. Some of them were even his friends, and Burckhardt would come to their rescue against what he saw as 'Jewish revenge' that was 'disguised' as Allied jus- tice. The case of Ernst von Weizsäcker, one of the highest-ranking offi- cials in the Nazi German Foreign Office and later German ambassador to the Vatican, exemplifies this. Weizsäcker was the main defendant in the 'Ministries case', officially case no. 11 of the later Nuremberg trials. Weizsäcker's high rank in the Nazi regime made him a top candidate for Allied prosecution. It is not a coincidence, therefore, that this trial against a number of former German diplomats and other high-ranking officials (including SS officer Schellenberg) was officially designated *The United States v. Ernst von Weizsäcker et al.*[73]

Burckhardt's interest in the case was neither purely political nor purely humanitarian. The Weizsäckers and Burckhardts had known each other since the early 1930s and had on occasion even spent Christmas together.[74] In September 1939 Weizsäcker praised Burckhardt for his attempts to keep the peace in Danzig and regretted that the conflict between Germany and Poland would be decided militarily.[75] On several occasions Burckhardt and Weizsäcker had also discussed possible ways to bring about peace with Britain and forge an alliance against Stalin's Soviet Union. Weizsäcker wrote after the war: 'I was in favour of peace, and it did not really matter on what basis. I doubt that any person with a heart and common sense could have thought otherwise'.[76] But it was Weizsäcker's wartime service, not his tardily expressed views on peace, which made him the focus of the Allies' legal proceedings. Weizsäcker, the cautious foreign policy strategist, was eventually pushed aside by the group of Nazi newcomers around Ribbentrop, who replaced Konstantin von Neurath as foreign minister in 1938. Weizsäcker's influence diminished from that point on and in 1943 he was made German ambassador to the Vatican.

After the war ended, the Allies ordered all German diplomats back to Germany. Weizsäcker did not comply and remained at the Vatican until 1946. Only after long negotiations did he eventually return with his wife in a Vatican limousine to Germany, where he was arrested.[77] He had advocated peace, but had never engaged in active resistance against the regime. His opposition was rather, in the words of Klemens von Klemperer, 'that of a tired servant of the old school rather than of an outraged man of principle; it was resistance devoid of firm resolve and conviction'.[78] At his trial, Weizsäcker presented himself not merely as a more cautious and moderate politician, but as an enemy of Hitler and even as an active anti-Nazi. In 1950 he published his memoirs, in which he stressed his role in the anti-Hitler opposition.[79] Historians remain divided over the sincerity and motivation of Weizsäcker's anti-Hitler efforts, some believing that he may have exaggerated his connections to the German resistance during his trial.[80]

In any case, Ernst von Weizsäcker had been one of the highest-ranking diplomats of the Third Reich. Although not the most fanatical, the ambitious Weizsäcker was nevertheless a member of the Nazi Party and held a (honorary) high officer's rank in the SS.[81] In his résumé of 1938 he stated: 'In the summer of 1933 after the takeover of the government [Machtergreifung], I was sent as diplomat to Switzerland. From the summer of 1936 until the spring of 1937, I was acting director of the Department of Political Affairs of the Foreign Office. From May 1937 to March 1938, I was director of the Political Department; at the beginning of April [1938], I was appointed state secretary [Staatssekretär] in the Foreign Office.'[82] This hardly sounded like the career of an anti-Nazi, and when he joined the SS in 1938 he must have taken the oath: 'I promise to promote and support the [Nazi] movement with all my powers.'[83] However, it was not so much Weizsäcker's membership of the Nazi Party but his involvement in the deportation of Jews that played a major role in his prosecution and eventual conviction.

In the run-up to the trial, Switzerland and the ICRC had to decide on an appropriate public position. Hans Frölicher, Swiss ambassador in Berlin during the Nazi years, showed great interest in the trial. In a report to his successor he expressed strong hostility toward the court in general and the American prosecutor Robert Kempner in particular. He wrote to colleagues to say that because Swiss diplomats could not appear in the court, he would write a statement on behalf of Weizsäcker.[84] Frölicher considered Weizsäcker a friend of Switzerland and he was not alone in this view. In October 1947, just two months before the trial began, several Swiss politicians also argued that Swiss honour would be damaged if Switzerland did not make at least a limited effort on the defendant's behalf. Officially not much could be done, of course, but individual politicians could act 'privately' on behalf of the accused Nazi official. The note addressed to Swiss Foreign Minister Petitpierre lists Burckhardt, among others, as a potential witness for Weizsäcker's defence at the trial.[85]

When the chance arose for Burckhardt to come to Nuremberg in 1948 and testify in defence of his confidant, he at first refused. One reason was US prosecutor Robert M. W. Kempner, who was—according to Burckhardt—head of a Jewish pressure group that would see the ICRC 'foreign minister' as a 'red flag'.[86] However, other avenues to come to the defence of his friend appeared to be available. In August 1941, Weizsäcker had had a long conversation about politics with Burckhardt in Berlin. In a purportedly verbatim statement from memory of this meeting, Burckhardt gave the impression that he had written it up immediately afterwards, while it was still fresh in his mind. Paul Stauffer suggests that Burckhardt in fact produced this document in 1947–1948 for Weizsäcker's defence.[87] The defence exhibit index of the Weizsäcker trial lists 'Extracts from secret diaries of Carl J. Burckhardt (For Reference only)' as well as an affidavit by Burckhardt.[88] The affidavit was written on the letterhead of the Swiss ambassador to France and Burckhardt stated that he was submitting 'true copies of diary notes'.[89] The court however objected to this 'evidence' and it likely was of little value to the defence. During their stroll in the Tiergarten park in Berlin in August 1941, Weizsäcker allegedly said to Burckhardt among other things that: 'The Americans absolutely must learn how matters stand within Germany, what great powers of interior resistance exist in Germany against the mob of gangsters which wields power and is driving us and the world into a calamity whose extent is unimaginable.'[90]

These statements were meant to whitewash Weizsäcker, portraying him as a man of the anti-Hitler group in the Foreign Office who was also a friend of the United States and had hoped for its support against the Nazi leadership. Burckhardt's statement had some truth to it, but Weizsäcker had never been enamoured of the United States; on the contrary, one could not expect much sympathy from what he had once deemed the 'disgusting Americans'.[91] According to Burckhardt, in 1938 Weizsäcker had already felt that Hitler should be removed. The German diplomat wanted to preserve peace with Britain and was in touch with the leaders of the German opposition: 'It was certainly a conspiracy with the potential enemy with the aim of keeping the peace, a double game of extreme danger', as Burckhardt stressed.[92] In his memoir about his time as high commissioner in Danzig, Burckhardt mentioned Weizsäcker more than thirty times, which leaves no doubt about their close relationship in these years. Burckhardt watched the trial against Weizsäcker with disbelief and displeasure. The proceedings also put Burckhardt's own policies and negotiations for a Europe united against the Soviets on trial. Weizsäcker's wife wrote to Burckhardt that all the efforts of the two 'close allies', Weizsäcker and Burckhardt, were 'misunderstood or else abused'. How could the US prosecutors proceed, when even Churchill had called the proceedings against Weizsäcker a 'deadly error'?[93] In March 1948 Huber also sent an affidavit for the defence of Weizsäcker, but as a private individual and not in his capacity as former ICRC president, as he made very clear at the end of his letter. But the letter itself was all about his work as ICRC president and his cooperation with the German Foreign Office at that time. At the end of the four-page letter Huber then stated that he couldn't comment on Weizsäcker's role in the Foreign Office, but was convinced that it was beneficial for the Red Cross. Given Huber's cautious position and his worries about Burckhardt's eagerness, this letter is somewhat surprising. At the time of writing, Huber was still honorary president of the ICRC and still very active indeed.[94]

Moreover, Max Huber and Burckhardt were not the only Red Cross representatives coming to the aid of Weizsäcker. Walther G. Hartmann, the former high-ranking German Red Cross official, also provided an affidavit in Weizsäcker's defence. In it he stressed his connections with the League of Red Cross Societies, which 'was heavily under American influence' and traditionally always headed by the president of the American Red Cross, as

Hartmann pointed out at the beginning of his statement. Hartmann then stated that the SS wanted to cut off all ties with an American-run organization. It was only thanks to Foreign office officials like Weizsäcker, according to Hartmann, that the German Red Cross maintained its contacts with the League.[95] Johannes Schwarzenberg, who had worked for the ICRC during the war and was then made Austrian ambassador to Italy, also seems to have shared Huber's sympathies for Weizsäcker. He wrote of Weizsäcker that 'he can be accused of cognizance but not of complicity'.[96] Among those providing the affidavits for Weizsäcker, Christian conservative politicians and Christian dignitaries figured prominently, including Pope Pius XII, but also Karl Wolff (himself a prisoner in Nuremberg), who at the time of his statement for Weizsäcker in 1947 was still stating his profession as 'General of the Waffen SS'.[97]

The trial *The United States v. Weizsäcker et al.*, with twenty-one defendants, ran from the end of 1947 until the April of 1949, and took place in a period when the Cold War was rapidly heating up. In 1948 the Soviets blocked all access by land to Berlin. That same year the communists staged a coup in Prague, and the Soviets walked out of the Allied Control Council for Germany, which had brought the four occupying powers together at one table. As a result, the United States sought to exploit all available resources in its showdown with the Soviets. Some former enemies now turned into allies, and now, three years after the war had ended, the confrontation between the United States and the Soviet Union appeared to have reached a 'point of no return'.[98] The Americans' fear of communism now far outstripped their fear of a resurgence of Nazism and German militarism. Germany and the Germans were henceforth needed to defend 'the West'. Nuremberg and its lessons had fallen out of fashion, and the remaining proceedings were wrapped up in a hurry. As the chief Nuremberg prosecutor Telford Taylor explained: 'By 1948, there had arisen a widespread feeling that the Nuremberg trials should be brought to an end at the earliest possible time, as indeed they were the following year.'[99] Given the new priorities, it came as a surprise to many when Weizsäcker was convicted in 1949 and sentenced to seven years in jail.

In response to Weizsäcker's conviction, in August 1949 Burckhardt and Huber sent a letter to US president Harry S. Truman, asking him to nullify or suspend Weizsäcker's Nuremberg conviction because he had aided the ICRC on several occasions during the war. Burckhardt sent the letter via the US embassy in Paris and sent a similar communication to US High Commissioner John J. McCloy; both letters spoke in favour of leniency for

'M. d. Weizacker [sic], who was recently condemned at Nuremberg', as U.S. Ambassador David Bruce reported. Their letter to President Truman began: 'As leading members and former presidents of the International Red Cross Committee in Geneva, we have had intensive and daily necessity to deal, throughout the second World War (1939/45), with the fate of war victims and especially of prisoners of war'. The opening sentence reveals that Huber and Burckhardt were not appealing merely as private individuals, but as former presidents of the ICRC. This was surprising, first because it is an instance of the ICRC leadership's direct intervention in war crimes trials. No less surprising was the fact that Burckhardt managed to get Huber to sign the letter. At the time this letter was written, Burckhardt was the Swiss ambassador to France. Thus it seems very likely that the Swiss government had given its blessing to this letter-writing campaign, partly because Burckhardt was using diplomatic channels to forward the letter. The letter went on to urge Truman 'to consider the possibility of revising the sentence either by its annulment—thereby wiping out the implied stain on his char-acter—or at least suspension of the penalty'.

It is remarkable that the two former ICRC presidents would intercede for a high-ranking diplomat who had served the Nazi regime. Weizsäcker may have been a more moderate Nazi official, but the frankness of Burckhardt and Huber's request to the US president is nevertheless striking: 'We believe that such a revision is justified by what M. de Weizsäcker has done, under personal danger, to make possible the activity of the International Committee in favour of the Allied Prisoners of War and of the population of occupied countries, activity which was undertaken to a considerable extent on the wish of the American government and of the [American] Red Cross'.[100] In closing, Burckhardt and Huber even made it appear that the United States was indebted to the ICRC. The intervention did not have the desired effect, but Weizsäcker's time behind bars would not last long. He was released from Landsberg prison after serving only eighteen months of his sentence. Burckhardt's interventions here as an ex-president of the ICRC appeared less than neutral.

The Fallout from Nuremberg

The Swiss press followed the Nuremberg trials closely, especially when prominent Swiss conservative and right-wing politicians were involved, as in the case against of Weizsäcker and Schellenberg. SS Brigadier General Walter Schellenberg, head of Nazi foreign intelligence, proved to be one of the biggest scandals. Schellenberg, was the man who suggested that the SS leadership open up peace feelers to the Western powers and use concentration camp prisoners as bargaining chips for that purpose. It was ultimately Schellenberg who put out channels for Himmler to Count Bernadotte, former Swiss president Musy, and Burckhardt for the rescue of thousands of Nazi prisoners. Schellenberg finally made his way to Sweden, where he stayed for a few weeks at one of Bernadotte's estates.[101] Not unlike Weizsäcker, SS officer Schellenberg too styled himself as someone internally in opposition to the Nazi leadership and its goals, who only stayed in office in order to prevent worse things from happening. And of course he stressed his part in last-minute rescue operations: 'There was also the humanitarian side which had always moved me deeply, and about which I felt something absolutely had to be done.'[102] In June 1949 Schellenberg was sentenced to six years in prison, but was released in 1950 on medical grounds. A number of politically dubious Swiss politicians defended Schellenberg, including former Swiss President Musy. This defence of 'innocent' figures such as Weizsäcker and his colleague Schellenberg would severely harm the reputation of Switzerland, the Swiss left-wing press argued.[103] Swiss President Etter's defence of Hitler's State Secretary Weizsäcker caused a great stir. Such actions were not helpful in improving Switzerland's image in the eyes of the Allies. The Swiss government eventually forbade Swiss officials from testifying at Nuremberg. Etter then later added to his affidavit, which carried the letterhead of the Swiss president, that he did not write it in his role as the president, but as a private citizen.[104]

The Social Democrats challenged Etter's statement that Weizsäcker had been a true and honest friend of an independent Switzerland. They published documents which were intended to show that Weizsäcker was not a friend of Switzerland at all, but had on the contrary used blackmail and threats to support Nazi German demands for Swiss compliance.[105] The communist newspapers found even clearer words: 'It is a disgrace for our country, that a member of our government and a number of our staff officers speak in defence of a man complicit in Hitler's barbaric regime, who was complicit in the horrible suffering and misery which the war brought to the whole of humanity!'[106]

The guilty sentence against Weizsäcker was widely covered by the Swiss media, both the right and the left.[107] Weizsäcker was sentenced for his role in the preparation of an aggressive war and crimes against the civilian population. The *Neue Zürcher Zeitung* reported in detail the motivation of the sentence under the headline 'Shared Guilt of Weizsäcker in the Murder of the Jews'. In the opinion of the court, Weizsäcker knew much about the 'Final Solution'. The German Foreign Office played an important role in the deportation of Jews to the extermination camps in Nazi-occupied Poland. Weizsäcker signed a letter in 1942 in which the Foreign Office told the SS that it had no objections against the deportation of 6,000 Jews from France to the East. All this was proof enough to convict Weizsäcker.[108]

The role of the Swiss authorities and specific ICRC members in the trials at Nuremberg confirmed for critics inside Switzerland the charges levelled against the republic and its flagship humanitarian organization; the neutrality of both seemed a fiction and they had turned a blind eye to the excesses of the German dictatorship when it suited them. The fact that men charged with serious crimes sought the testimonials of ICRC officials and received them seemed only to confirm the critics' suspicions. It also revealed how the personal loyalties and ambitions of ICRC officials undermined the reputation of their organization, opening it up to still further criticism, especially from the Soviet Union, and placed its future effectiveness in jeopardy.

Ruegger's critique of the Nuremberg trials was legal in nature. Traditionally, one could be convicted of a crime only for acts that were illegal at the time they were committed. The Nuremberg trials violated this traditional legal principle by applying *ex post facto* new international law. Crimes against humanity and waging a war of aggression were newly defined offences that unlike war crimes were technically not punishable under international law. This critique was shared by a number of renowned law scholars, even scholars from Allied countries.[109] Ruegger also hinted at the fact that only Axis crimes were on trial, but not Allied ones. He argued that Stalin and his associates could also have been tried for aggressive war (Poland 1939), crimes against humanity (gulags, famine), and war crimes (for example, the treatment of German POWs). While Ruegger's opposition to the Nuremberg system was based on legal arguments, Burckhardt's critique originated from a very different place. His assistance towards Weizsäcker was at least in part motivated by friendship. But it also reflected Burckhardt's *Weltanschauung* in which the Nazis were anti-Bolshevik fighters, who were helping to defend Western (European) civilization. Burckhardt's help for Kaltenbrunner was then likely motivated at least in part by his distaste for Allied 'victor's justice' and his anti-communism.

Burckhardt's statements for the defence in the Weizsäcker trial did not go unnoticed in the mainstream media.[110] Harsh attacks from the Soviet camp kept coming. The widely read Soviet newspaper *Trud* (*Labor*) wrote in 1946: 'Fascist lawyers counted on depositions from the Geneva Committee, which during the war was in league with the Hitlerites and remained a tool of reactionary forces after war.' The Soviet press reserved particular opprobrium for one individual: 'It is not difficult to disclose the sources of this reactionary policy conducted by the Geneva Committee; it is sufficient to reveal names of certain of its leaders. First among them, for example, is the well-known Carl Burckhardt, closely associated with German reactionary forces.'[111] The Stalinist communist rhetoric and wording aside, *Trud* provided a quite accurate description of Burckhardt's background and activities. We see here an overall Soviet strategy to discredit the ICRC and lower its standing in the world of Red Cross families.[112] As a result of the ICRC's lack of responsiveness to Soviet demands and its criticism of the Soviet war crimes trials, Switzerland's relationship with the Soviet Union remained tense; official diplomatic relations were non-existent. Moscow accused the Swiss of embracing a 'pro-fascist policy' by collaborating with Nazi Germany. After Stalingrad, Swiss foreign policy-makers attempted to re-engage the Soviets. But in November 1944 the Soviets harshly rejected such attempts in broadcasts on Radio Moscow. Ruegger's talks with the Soviet embassy in London also led nowhere.[113] Normal relations were only slowly re-established, with formal diplomatic relations between Moscow and Bern finally resuming in March 1946.

As his wartime activities became public, Burckhardt found that the other Allies, not only the Soviets, were distancing themselves from him. The cool response Burckhardt received when he sought support for his denials that he had acted as a secret diplomat made it clear that he was now ploughing a lonely furrow. The postwar priorities of the European powers had shifted. Burckhardt's role in the attempted German–British peace talks did not remain a secret for long, and he was desperate short to salvage his reputation after being denigrated as a 'Hitler-appeaser'. In March 1946, Burckhardt asked the British ambassador in Paris, Alfred Duff Cooper, who was a former secretary of state for war in 1935–1937, to help him with a public denial. The British ambassador's response did not prove very encouraging. He urged Burckhardt to lay low when confronted with rumours about his role:

It has taken the Foreign Office a long time to reply to the dispatch which I addressed to them at the beginning of last month, and in which I suggested that they might have a question asked in the House of Commons which would produce a denial of the allegation that you ever took any part in Anglo-German peace conversations during the war.... The [British] Secretary of State for Foreign Affairs writes that he feels such a question, if it were put now in the House of Commons, would be more likely to draw attention to this malicious report than to put an end to it. He therefore feels, while he is fully aware that the rumour is quite without foundation, that it would be wiser to let it die a natural death rather than to revive it by fresh publicity. I hope very much that you will be able to share his view.[114]

The British Foreign Office was wise not to issue a denial because the allegations were indeed true.

Burckhardt's personal influence diminished as a result of his reputation for having been very pro-German. As a result, his nomination as new Swiss ambassador to France in February 1945 caused heated debate, where his alleged affinity for National Socialism was stressed, as was his involvement in many political scandals.[115] The communist newspaper *La Voix Ouvrière* organized a full-fledged press campaign against him in February 1945, which it renewed after the revelations made by Karl Haushofer (Albrecht's father) during the Hess trial at Nuremberg became widely known. In 1953 the official 'Documents on German Foreign Policy' were published for the period 1918–45, and they finally corroborated the claims about Burckhardt's dealings with German officials. After these new revelations, Burckhardt's critics felt further vindicated in their hostility to him.[116] The files of the German diplomats showed Burckhardt to be a friend of Germany and the Nazis, and an admirer of Hitler with antisemitic views.[117] Burckhardt was embarrassed and outraged. He immediately protested in London to the British chancellor of the exchequer, Rab Butler, who answered as follows: 'You wrote to me about the distress which you feel over the publication of the "Documents on German Foreign Policy" [which] "naturally, present all these events and personages as seen through German eyes"... It is open to you to publish your own account of these events, and I believe that the British, American, and French editors-in-chief of the documents would welcome such a publication.'[118] Many years later, Burckhardt would finally clarify some of his positions and defend himself in his memoirs, *Meine Danziger Mission*. Burckhardt cited former German diplomats like Ernst von Weizsäcker to make his case that he had used his position as a mediator for peace and as an opponent of the Nazis.[119] Burckhardt the historian knew how history is written. In a small 1950 monograph series about 'European personalities', Burckhardt was described as 'a good European' in the 'service of humanity'. This is probably how Burckhardt saw his own activities: work undertaken in the interest of preserving European civilization.[120] It appears that the former ICRC president remained forever focused on his personal legacy and reputation, failing to see or care enough how his actions might affect the Red Cross or Switzerland.

6

The ICRC and Aid Politics in Ruins

The postwar emergency presented the International Committee of the Red Cross (ICRC) with a host of familiar challenges, from protecting millions of German prisoners of war (POWs) now in Allied hands to helping freed prisoners of war return to their homelands, and creating a way for the relatives of former prisoners and forced labourers to trace missing family members.[1] Unsurprisingly, the ICRC helped liberated Allied POWs and provided aid to former combatants still detained by the Allied powers. Once the war had ended, the committee was particularly active in providing care for German POWs in France. When 750,000 former German soldiers were rounded up and sent to France, the ICRC was allowed to use food supplies from the American military to help them.[2] The longer-term fate of Axis POWs also troubled the committee's leaders. According to the Geneva Conventions, they should have been freed as soon as possible after an armistice. But because no armistice had been signed, no peace treaty was in sight and Germany had ceased to exist as a state, the ICRC grew concerned that the Allies could hold German POWs indefinitely.

The ICRC also took the rather unusual step of becoming active in civilian relief after the war. Helping civilians in the immediate postwar years was primarily the domain of the Allied forces and a limited number of international agencies. In 1938 the Intergovernmental Committee on Refugees (IGCR) had been founded on the initiative of President Roosevelt to support Jewish refugees, and in 1943 it began to extend its services to all victims of the Axis powers. The year 1943 also saw the creation of the United Nations Relief and Rehabilitation Administration (UNRRA), mobilized to provide war-torn nations with medicine and food supplies. In 1946 its successor, the International Refugee Organization (IRO), was founded, taking over the duties not only of UNRRA but the IGCR as well. These major aid providers collaborated with and relied heavily on the resources of a host of philanthropic endeavours, often organized as faith-based initiatives: the National Catholic Welfare Conference, the American Jewish Joint Distribution Committee, and the Quakers, among others. In addition, the Red Cross League and national Red Cross agencies supported these efforts with infusions of aid to regions devastated by the war.

The ICRC, by contrast, was traditionally seen as an organization for war-time and not peacetime humanitarian aid. However, its leaders were eager to get in on the game, part of a strategy to prove the committee's viability and postwar relevance. And it had done so already in the wake of World War I, caring for refugees and displaced POWs. Committed to the principle of neutral humanitarian intervention, its leaders in 1945 felt it could provide a valuable service by filling gaps in relief and by lobbying for improved living conditions for the civilians of the defeated nations—areas and categories of people not covered by the Allies. This included in particular citizens of former Axis countries and a newly arrived wave of ethnic Germans from the east.

Occupied Western Germany seemed like fertile ground for the Swiss committee's entrance into civilian relief projects, not least because UNRRA's and the IRO's restricted mandate prevented them for aiding the general German population. Here the ICRC devoted special efforts to aiding ethnic Germans, expelled from East European countries that had long suffered under the Nazi war machine. These were striking, even risky choices on the part of the ICRC. Communist countries harshly criticized the ICRC's sup-port and protection for Germans and other ex-enemy nationals as taking sides with 'fascist people'.[3] The committee's relations with the Soviets reached a new low point, and thus the very initiatives that were intended to cement Geneva's place in the postwar world also ironically threatened to undermine many of its future plans.

Helping German Civilians

The ICRC's main vehicle for providing material relief for civilians together with the Red Cross League had been the Joint Relief Commission of the Red Cross, created in 1941. At the end of the war this cooperation contin-ued to operate for a time—particularly in Western Europe—and ICRC delegates supervised the distribution of joint aid with significant results. The Joint Relief Commission 'was able to dispatch to the populations of the various countries further millions of kilograms of supplies—more even than through-out the whole duration of the war'.[4] These efforts continued until November 1946, when the venture was dissolved, a decision taken at the Oxford meeting of the League. The ICRC did not want to give up the initiative, but it had no real resources of its own, finally conceding, 'The feeding of the civilian popu-lations is a matter for governments'. With what limited resources remained, the ICRC decided that 'since the end of the hostilities, events have obliged the Committee to act chiefly on behalf of the nationals of the defeated countries', particularly those stranded in western zones of Germany.[5]

The ICRC ultimately worked alongside and often at cross-purposes with the Intergovernmental Committee on Refugees, UNRRA, and their suc-cessor organization, the IRO. While these Allied relief agencies excluded Germans and ethnic German refugees from aid, the ICRC was, by contrast, free to implement its own aid policies and refused to adhere to these dis-tinctions. With the German state essentially out of operation after the war, the ICRC began to cast itself as the de facto 'protector of the Germans'.[6] Small wonder, then, that West German chancellor Konrad Adenauer would later thank the ICRC 'for everything that [it] did in those difficult years', not only for German POWs but also for German civilians and refugees.[7]

Attempting to capitalize on its relationship with US officials, the ICRC began to work toward securing a larger role in postwar relief efforts in Germany, which required permission from Allied authorities. In August 1945 Max Huber had sent a memorandum to the American Red Cross and the US government seeking permission to provide aid to ex-enemy dis-placed persons (DPs) who were on German territory and in desperate need of relief—the nationalities involved included Balts, Bulgarians, Romanians, Hungarians, and Italians, but not Germans.

He used the committee's past work for Allied POWs as a springboard, and reported that the ICRC's warehouses in Switzerland contained food parcels that had been donated by various countries for their POWs. Now that the war was over and the POWs had been liberated, these remaining packages could be used for new relief purposes.[8] Huber stressed in a mem-orandum to US Secretary of State James Byrnes the work that the ICRC was now performing for former POWs and Holocaust survivors in Germany.[9] Initially Huber's attempts proved fruitless and the State Department was well aware of the ICRC's frustration: 'At the time of Germany's defeat,

Intercross had hopes of being invited by the occupation authorities to take over the function of providing relief to displaced persons in Germany....To their great disappointment Intercross was not permitted to take over this work. The military authorities decided to do the job themselves with the assistance of UNRRA in whom ultimately it was hoped full responsibility in this regard could be vested.'[10] While the State Department was aware of Red Cross ambitions, it realized that it could not decide this issue, because military authorities controlled this domain.[11] Undeterred, the ICRC's efforts to gain a foothold in relief work in Germany continued.

In September 1945, a letter signed by US military governor for Germany, General Lucius D. Clay, granted the ICRC the authority to work with DPs under UNRRA's care. In February 1946, the US military government in Germany, Office of Military Government, United States (OMGUS), gave the Swiss committee permission to provide relief assistance to the general German population as well. By 1946 the ICRC had been given co-responsibility for an estimated 320,000 uprooted people in Germany, Austria, and Czechoslovakia.[12] According to an OMGUS memo, US military authorities would later express their satisfaction with the new relief work for civilians of the ICRC, though they were aware the American Red Cross and the League of Red Cross Societies had questioned the organization's new role.[13] But the main task of managing the large numbers of DPs was still carried out by others.

The United Nations General Assembly approved the establishment of the IRO in December 1946,[14] giving it the critical mission of aiding victims of the Nazi, fascist, or quisling regimes who could not tap their own governments for assistance.[15] UNRRA was replaced because it was equipped to provide short-term relief, not resettle large numbers of refugees. When the IRO, with its headquarters in Geneva, finally went into operation on 1 July 1947, it took over the care and protection of more than 700,000 people, the majority in Europe.[16] In order to qualify for aid, those in need had to meet certain criteria. And here the Allies continued to distinguish between two categories—'displaced persons' and 'enemy or ex-enemy DPs'. According to the IRO and Allied occupation authorities alike, enemy nationals, ex-enemy nationals, and Nazi collaborators remained ineligible for this form of international aid.[17] In December 1947, ICRC official Roger Gallopin asked the American Red Cross for its support when the ICRC petitioned the US authorities to change its policy about access to detainees. Gallopin's intervention with General Clay in fact was aimed at the general's 'removing the current restrictions in visiting the civilian internee enclosures' in Germany, but with limited access.[18] The ICRC's special efforts for these people found little approval in some quarters. An official of the US War Department noted: 'In his reply General Clay stated the principal reason for refusing to permit the International Red Cross to inspect the civilian internment camps and to provide relief assistance is that they are of a national and not of an international character. They are German detention camps. For the international Red Cross to provide relief to these camps of former active Nazis, when there is so great a need for relief outside of the camps, would be inconsistent with the purpose of the camps, and certainly not understandable to the suffering Germans outside of such camps.' The ICRC, he continued, should not be 'providing relief to Germany's criminals [Nazis]'.[19]

The ICRC and the Expulsion of Ethnic Germans

Shortly after the war ended, the major Swiss daily *Neue Zürcher Zeitung* declared that the 'diplomacy of humanitarianism had achieved great successes', but suggested the work of the ICRC was hardly complete. The article continued that new duties awaited the Red Cross in the field of relief aid for civilians, especially those expelled from their home countries for good.[20] And, indeed, the ICRC soon began expressing concern about the German expellees living in camps in Germany under poor conditions. By 1944 Soviet troops had gained the upper hand against the Germans. Advancing rapidly, they reached the eastern borders of Nazi Germany in August. Now the brutal warfare waged by Hitler's troops in the east would find its way back into Germany. German civilians became the targets of the Red Army's revenge for the decimation of the Soviet Union.[21] An estimated 27 million Soviets perished during the war, the overwhelming majority of whom were civilians.[22] On their way westward Soviet soldiers also plundered, raped, and killed on a massive scale.[23] This outburst of violence left up to 500,000 German civilians dead and an estimated 1.5 million German women victims of sexual violence.[24] Millions of Germans desperately tried to escape this fate and moved westward, away from the approaching front. With cars, horse carriages, and often on foot they moved through the devastated countryside in the midst of a harsh winter. Those who stayed behind and survived the first wave of violence were soon forced out of their houses and towns for good.

When the Allied leaders met again at the Potsdam Conference near Berlin in the summer of 1945, the expulsion of Germans from the east was already well underway.Vowing that German minorities would never again become a potential threat, countries such as Czechoslovakia and Poland sought to rid their lands entirely of ethnic Germans. Germany's pre-1938 eastern border was also redrawn. Although the British and Americans disliked the brutality of the expulsions and called for the 'orderly and humane' transfer of ethnic Germans, they avoided a direct confrontation with Stalin over this issue.[25] Thus, the German-speaking populations of eastern and south-eastern Europe, from Yugoslavia to the Baltics—at least 12 million German nationals and ethnic German civilians—were forced from their homes for good.[26]

Those who made it to what remained of a defeated, largely destroyed, and occupied Germany had their history written on their faces and forms: newsreels from 1945 show a beaten people. Given the shortage of food, heating materials, and housing, these now homeless Germans were not welcomed with open arms by local populations.The German town or district authorities were ordered by the occupation powers of their zones to provide housing for the new arrivals. Expellees were often housed in improvised camps and old military compounds, or found space in war-damaged buildings.With the German recovery from the war years slow, life in such camps continued for years for these people.The expulsion of ethnic Germans at the end of the Second World War remains controversial to this day.[27]

In 1949, roughly 8 million German expellees were still living in western Germany, most of them in camps or barracks.[28] These ethnic Germans were classified as 'ex-Enemy Displaced Persons', and thus did not fall under the IRO's mandate, which excluded persons of German ethnic origin, be they German nationals or members of German-speaking minorities from other countries.[29] As political scientist Michael Barnett writes: 'The allies created the UNRRA [and the IRO] to help the victims of *German* aggression so there was little interest in giving equal weight to the needs of the Germans.'[30] And, indeed, in the period 1946–1952, neither UNRRA nor its successor, the IRO, would ever completely change this policy.[31]

The Allies' refusal to provide protection for these Germans presented a huge obstacle and left them in a legal vacuum. 'Paradoxically', writes the historian R. M. Douglas, 'the women and children who made up most of the expellee population occupied a legal status far lower than that of members of the SS, who as former servicemen of the German armed forces, were protected by the Geneva Convention'.[32] The ICRC was clear on the status of expelled civilians and stated that they should in principle be treated and protected like POWs. The ICRC was allowed to visit camps in Czechoslovakia and in Denmark, but given the overall dimension of the problem, the lack of resources, and 'the animosity felt towards the racial minorities',[33] the ICRC could achieve very little in this field.[34]

Nevertheless, the Swiss committee's delegates in Czechoslovakia, Romania, Denmark, and elsewhere intervened on behalf of this population.[35] In July 1945, for example, the ICRC informed the interior minister of Czechoslovakia that more than fifty ethnic German children had been interned in an improvised prison with so little food that some had starved to death. At first, the relevant authorities simply ignored most such requests, yet the ICRC continued to press for intervention.[36] In the spring of 1946, the head of the ICRC delegation in Prague, Walter Menzel, sent a letter to Czechoslovak Foreign Minister Jan Masaryk. 'It would go against my conscience', Menzel wrote, 'to continue keeping silent about the conditions prevailing in the camps in Czechoslovakia'.[37]

In a departure from the standard Red Cross practice of 'quiet diplomacy', Menzel had leaked information to the British government about the terrible conditions for German civilians interned in some camps in Czechoslovakia. And with the Cold War heating up, the ICRC could count more and more on increased sympathy and support from the western powers for refugees and expellees from Communist countries. The pressure had some effect, at least in Czechoslovakia. Finally, in 1947 the government in Prague publicly asked the ICRC to inspect its camps. By then, however, most of the ethnic Germans had already been expelled and only a few camps remained open. But those facilities in fact improved significantly as a result of the ICRC inspections.[38] The ICRC leadership certainly had differing opinions about how much to engage in aid for civilians. Given its own problems and the scarce financial resources available, these activities were disputed. ICRC president Burckhardt was, after all, pursuing a calculated gamble in defending Swiss interests, whilst at the same time resisting Soviet and American demands.

Burckhardt and Germans as Victims

ICRC President Burckhardt was fervently committed to using his organization to help German refugees and expellees. In October 1945 Burckhardt wrote to ICRC member Jacques Cheneviere (later the organization's vice president) that it was vital for their organization to make at 'least an allusion to the drama of German refugees from the East'.[39] Doing more would be not only financially risky for the organization, given their sheer number, but politically risky as well. In a 1946 letter to Heinrich Rothmund, the Swiss delegate of the Intergovernmental Committee on Refugees and long-time national police chief, Burckhardt acknowledged: 'The real task of the International Committee of the Red Cross is to help prisoners of war in armed conflicts; in other words, we go where no other institution can go ... Should we risk the true nature of our institution and with it, its future existence, by taking over a boundless endeavour; just to lose eventually all the sympathy we [have] earned over the years?'[40] Still, Burckhardt had no intention of pulling back at this juncture, writing to his Red Cross colleague Huber: 'Nowhere is it written that the purpose of the committee has to be reduced to the care of POWs; such a reduction would contradict the absolute humanitarian principle which gives the Red Cross its fundamental right to exist.'[41] But Burckhardt also remarked that the ICRC's help for civilians could only be limited, given the scarce resources at its disposal and the giant task. He stressed that aid for civilians had to come from the Allies, for they had the necessary infrastructure and resources to tackle the 'largest state of emergency the world has ever seen'.[42] In the midst of an organizational crisis and confronted with criticism from all sides—especially from the Soviets—the ICRC's prudence in this matter may have been appropriate. But Huber was the cautious man, not Burckhardt.

While the Allies took a tough stance on the question of German expellees, the Red Cross family also remained divided over this issue. The ICRC was keenly aware of the international mood and therefore cautious early on when seeking aid for the *Volksdeutsche* (ethnic Germans).[43] Initially only three small neutral states—Switzerland, Ireland, and Sweden—allowed the funds that they provided to the ICRC to be used in assisting forced German migrants from the East.[44] The American Red Cross, in line with US government policy, denied aid to these *Volksdeutsche*. Burckhardt complained that the American Red Cross was not only unwilling to help, but that it was ready to prevent other agencies from doing so:

> The American Red Cross had protested energetically and in a threatening manner against our modest attempts to intervene with humanitarian aid against these horrible events, which will also not end this winter'. Continuing in the same vein, he added that 'James [the American Red Cross representative

in Geneva], who is a nice man in private—an impression I also have of many Nazis I've met, by the way—told me very directly during a short stopover in Paris that aid efforts to benefit Germans are not wanted. If such a proposal should be made, the American Red Cross will oppose it with all its power.[45]

Burckhardt made clear that there was no hope of getting support in the United States to expand aid operations. 'I hear that the appeal of the Committee was badly received in America', he wrote.[46] No support would be forthcoming from Britain either, or from the Scandinavian countries or their national Red Cross societies. Burckhardt also wrote to Huber confirming that no help could be expected from the League or the American Red Cross. The ICRC should have declared on VE Day that it would claim the right to help the civilian population as it saw fit. He then attacked the American Red Cross: 'My experience with Americans, they only respect you if you return their blackmailing coldness with coldness.'[47] What Burckhardt did not say was that even in Switzerland, the willingness to aid Germans remained rather faint in those years. Germany had acquired such a bad reputation that even in Switzerland few people were willing to ask for relief measures for German civilians.[48]

But Burckhardt had no intention of capitulating to the Americans and the Soviets on the matter of providing humanitarian aid to the German civilian population and German expellees. He had identified many possible sources of assistance from South America, where a number of countries were willing to provide aid. South Africa, Canada, and Australia were also potential hosts for German emigrants. In his correspondence with Rothmund, Burckhardt noted the particular support of Argentina for ICRC interventions on behalf of Germans. It was, he wrote to Rothmund, basically a matter of convincing the countries of South America that helping the Germans was a way of pushing back against 'American imperialism'.[49]

The correspondence between Burckhardt and his successor Paul Ruegger offers further insight into the ICRC president's thinking. Two of Burckhardt's assumptions become clear—that Germans were victims of the war and that a Jewish vendetta existed against the Germans. The claim by Germans and Austrians that they also were victims became ever more commonplace in the Cold War years. In Austria, this stance focused on the fact that the Germans had 'overrun' their country when they annexed it in the 'Anschluss' of March 1938. In West Germany, claims to victim status focused on the wartime suffering of the German population, which was allegedly taken hostage by Hitler and his gang. Many in West Germany and Austrian clung to the assertion that only a small number of their top leaders had been responsible for wartime atrocities, while the rest of the population was innocent and had been forced into obeying orders. Burckhardt assumed this commonplace position as well, assuming that only a handful of (criminal and insane) leaders such as Hitler and Himmler were responsible for the war and wartime crimes. In January 1946, Heinrich Rothmund, the national police chief and Swiss delegate to the Intergovernmental Committee on Refugees, wrote to Burckhardt, lamenting that millions of German and ethnic German lives would ultimately be lost that winter in Germany and countries in the east because of forced expulsion, hunger, and violence. Rothmund objected strongly to exacting revenge on the Germans for the mass crimes committed during the war: 'It is certainly understandable that the nations that suffered the most under the organized terror still today have a hard time understanding that whatever happens to the German people now will eventually be re-visited upon them.'[50] Burckhardt most likely broadly agreed with Rothmund here and went even further in his reply: 'Organized nastiness is not just a specialty of the Nazis, but of our generation in general.'[51]

In 1946, Burckhardt even suggested that the Jews had gotten a kind of 'revenge' against Germany with the brutal expulsion of millions of Germans from their traditional homelands in Central and Eastern Europe. In his correspondence he argued that the Jewish influence on governments, especially in the United States, had enabled Jews to bring about this revenge.[52] And in his January 1946 'confidential and personal' letter to Rothmund quoted above, Burckhardt wrote that: 'The death of millions in the East and in Germany is due to a very influential group that is in power in the world today. All of this [has been] consciously planned and desired, and not something that could be described as "destiny".'[53] Burckhardt's writings depict both the tragic fate of ethnic German expellees and the Nuremberg trials as signs of a Jewish vendetta, asserting that for the ICRC 'to do something in this area'—and he believed that it should—it would need to muster 'the courage to confront the forces I have just hinted at and to put them in their place'.[54]

The ICRC president suggested that Jews and communists would now murder German expellees in Eastern Europe without interference from the United States, and he believed that the ICRC should not support the Allied powers' policies on the treatment of German expellees. Rothmund seems to have held similar views. A seasoned diplomat, Burckhardt avoided using the word 'Jews' in his correspondence, instead hinting at 'certain forces'. But Rothmund surely knew to whom Burckhardt was alluding; it had been Rothmund himself who first raised the issue of the fate of the German people in a letter sent to Burckhardt just a week earlier. That letter was forwarded to the Swiss ambassador in London Paul Ruegger as well.[55] In striking contrast to the men's eagerness to help German expellees, Rothmund and Burckhardt appeared rather reluctant to extend assistance to Jewish survivors. In February 1945 Rothmund was appointed as a delegate of the Intergovernmental Committee on Refugees and worked in that capacity for more than two and a half years, stepping down in 1947. When Rothmund was offered this new role as Swiss delegate for the refugee organization, he asked his close friend Ruegger for advice and received encouragement.[56] 'In St. Gallen I have arranged a meeting with [Jewish Joint-representative] Mr. Saly Mayer', he wrote. 'I want to know what the Jewish circles think about this as well. They might be thinking, "Now they have sent a fox to guard the geese".'[57] The metaphor was apt. In his new role, Rothmund intended to defend Swiss interests by ridding the country of the often stateless Jewish refugees who had found a temporary safe haven there from the Nazis.[58]

The Allies and Forced Repatriation

Another policy involving uprooted people in Europe sorely tested the wartime alliances and support for the ICRC in these years. Many but by no means all displaced civilians in Europe wanted to go home. Some were forced to return to their countries of origin because of provisions in postwar Allied agreements. Before the war ended, the Allies had concluded a number of agreements specifying how different groups of people would be handled after the war. The Declaration of German Atrocities (known as the 'Moscow Declaration'), signed at the Moscow Conference on 1 November 1943, required war criminals to be returned to the countries where they had allegedly committed their crimes. The Moscow Declaration distinguished between small-scale perpetrators, who were to be dealt with by national courts, and 'major war criminals'. The most prominent among the latter group, those whose atrocities generally were not limited to one particular country, were to be tried jointly by the Allies after the war.[59]

In February 1945, at the Yalta Conference on the Black Sea, Churchill, Roosevelt, and Stalin had agreed on the terms of postwar prisoner exchanges and the repatriation of their respective nationals. Using the British and US POWs whom the Soviets had liberated from German camps as a bargaining chip, Stalin got the British and Americans to agree to the repatriation of all 'Soviet nationals', meaning not just POWs, but also civilians who had been deported by the Germans as labour, as well as Soviet citizens who had collaborated and fought with the German forces.[60] The agreement required all former Soviet citizens to be handed over to Moscow—regardless of what the people concerned wanted. Whoever had his or her residence in the Soviet Union on 3 September 1939 had to be repatriated to Moscow's empire. The Soviets insisted that this would include former residents of Soviet-occupied eastern Poland and the Baltic countries (Latvia, Estonia, and Lithuania), a notion that the western Allies rejected.

At first the western Allies stuck to their agreements with Moscow. In the months following the German surrender in May 1945, large numbers of former POWs and Nazi collaborators, such as Lithuanian and Ukrainian soldiers who had served in the Waffen SS (the military wing of the SS), were returned to their homelands by force. Although the fate of these repatriated East Europeans varied greatly from country to country and changed over time, repatriation very often resulted in either harsh prison sentences or execution. The Iron Curtain would soon divide Europe, but for now the wartime alliance was still in place.

In June 1945 the Western Allies handed over approximately 40,000 Soviet and Ukrainian Nazi collaborators and their families to Soviet authorities in southern Austria. Many of them were anti-communist Cossacks who had fought in the Wehrmacht against the Red Army. The group also included many Cossack women, children, and elderly people who had surrendered to British authorities, begging for protection.[61] The British and Americans were already well aware of what repatriation to the Soviet Union would mean for these individuals. A month earlier, future British Prime Minister Harold Macmillan, who had travelled to Austria to discuss the situation, wrote in his diary: 'To hand [the Cossacks] over is condemning them to slavery, torture, and probably death. To refuse is deeply to offend the Russians, and incidentally break the Yalta agreement. We have decided to hand them over.'[62] Indeed, the Cossacks in question either committed suicide to avoid falling into Soviet hands, were sent to Siberian gulags (forced labour camps), or were executed.[63]

By the end of 1945, more than 2 million POWs and civilian DPs had been transferred to the Soviet Union. At that point US policy towards forcible repatriation of DPs from Eastern Europe slowly began to change, as did that of the Allied refugee organizations and other western governments. By the time the war with Japan ended formally on 2 September 1945, British and American POWs in the Soviet occupation zones of Germany and Austria had been sent home, weakening Stalin's hand. Rapidly deteriorating relations between the East and West, reports of the brutal treatment of returnees, legal questions, and protests by churches and dignitaries against forced repatriation all contributed to a policy shift.[64] In December 1945 the US authorities banned the forced repatriation of civilians who had not been Nazi collaborators. The decision came too late for most. Millions of civilian DPs and POWs had already been sent back to Stalin's empire or emigrated elsewhere.[65]

By the time the IRO was established, tensions between East and West over how to handle the East European DPs and Soviet refugees had grown visibly.[66] Because the United States was the major financial backer of the IRO, Washington took the lead in regulating postwar migration.[67] Seeing the organization as 'an instrument of the West', the Soviet Union withdrew from the IRO on its first day of operation, ending the 'short-lived era of Grand Alliance humanitarianism' (in the words of the historian Gerard Cohen) that had begun with the establishment of UNRRA in 1943.[68] In Moscow's view, the Soviet refugees and East European DPs who remained in the camps of western Europe were nothing less than traitors and war criminals. And thus, as far as Moscow was concerned, there was no 'refugee problem'. At the founding of the IRO, the Soviets had stressed that 'in their view all men of goodwill, since the defeat of the Axis Powers, could return to their home countries; quislings, war criminals, traitors, fascists, and undemocratic elements who opposed [the] governments of their countries should not receive any assistance from an international organization'.[69]

The parties on both sides of the table nevertheless understood and agreed that the IRO was not to interfere 'in any way with the surrender and punishment of war criminals, quislings, and traitors, in conformity with international arrangements and agreements'.[70] Western representatives attempted to reassure Soviet diplomats by promising to support the repatriation of the East European refugees within the parameters of the IRO agreement.[71] At the same time, Moscow claimed that the West was supporting the formation of anti-communist movements and groups in the camps, and that the British, Americans, and French were exploiting DP labour. Moscow's suspicions and allegations were not always unfounded. A number of DPs from countries now falling into the Soviet orbit had in fact been recruited for anti-Soviet propaganda and intelligence work. And it was not long before numerous former SS men and Nazi collaborators from Eastern Europe had been taken under the wing of the US and British intelligence agencies.[72]

Although suspected war criminals remained excluded from IRO aid and potentially subject to extradition, the western Allies softened on this policy. Starting in 1946, in every single case, they first asked for 'submission of evidence supporting the substantiality of the presumption of guilt based upon reasonable particularity as to time, place, and nature of offenses and perpetrator thereof' before extraditing an alleged perpetrator to a communist country. The US government continued to comply with the Moscow Declaration if a 'prima facie case' could be made that a person had committed war crimes or voluntarily collaborated with the enemy. But in cases where doubt existed, the western Allies would not forcibly repatriate the person in question.[73] By adopting this process, the western Allies technically tried to honour the Moscow Declaration and avoided openly challenging the Soviet Union on this issue. Moreover, while the IRO for the most part abandoned forced repatriation of East European DPs, its field administrators continued to apply psychological pressure to individuals in an effort to persuade them to return to their home countries.[74]

The ICRC's Stance on Forced Repatriation

Against this backdrop the ICRC adopted a different stance, a stance that held ramifications for the larger ICRC agenda. Based on its principle of neutral humanitarianism, the organization had opposed forcible repatriation from the very beginning, putting it at odds with Allied policies stemming from the Moscow and Yalta agreements.[75] The brutal reality of forced repatriation reached the ICRC in Geneva early through its field delegates. In June 1945 an ICRC delegate in Germany reported on the fate of Russians, Ukrainians, Lithuanians, Estonians, Poles, Hungarians, Yugoslavs, and Armenians fearful of repatriation to the Soviet Union, where immediate arrests or worse awaited them. The ICRC delegates on the ground then asked if these unfortunates could not be helped to get papers to emigrate overseas.[76] It was not just news reports and the reports of delegates from the field that troubled Red Cross officials, but also reports from people who had themselves been targeted for repatriation against their will.

Burckhardt and the ICRC received letters from East Europeans stranded in Germany and Austria asking the ICRC for protection.[77] A letter from a Latvian Aid Committee in Germany read: '99% of Latvians do not want to return to their homeland given the present circumstances. They consider themselves as political emigrants and citizens of the independent, democratic Republic of Latvia.'[78] In January 1945 Burckhardt made clear in a meeting with ICRC delegates that Armenians, Azerbaijanis, and Georgians stranded in Germany should not be forcibly returned to the Soviet Union. The ICRC agreed to help with repatriations, but only if they could be guaranteed that their return would be voluntary.[79]

In order to press its agenda, the ICRC attempted to influence other relief agencies to resist seemingly punitive repatriation policies. In August 1945 Max Huber, the interim president of the ICRC, contacted Sir Herbert Emerson, director of the Intergovernmental Committee on Refugees, on the issue. He submitted a memorandum explaining the situation of East European refugees who were under threat of being sent to their countries of origin unwillingly. The list of groups was long but incomplete and included pretty much all the East European nations. Huber expressed the hope that all refugees would be included without discrimination in resettlement aid, and appealed to Emerson about the problem of large numbers of refugees from Eastern Europe seeking to emigrate and start a new life in the western zones of occupation.[80]

In August 1945 Huber also held a meeting with Heinrich Rothmund, ICRC official Paul Kuhne, and Gustave G. Kullmann from the League of Nations Refugee Office to determine the situation of refugees. They learned that holders of the interwar Nansen passports remained under the protection of the Intergovernmental Committee on Refugees and that UNRRA would provide housing and food, but was not in charge of finding new home countries for these refugees generally. Asked about the issue of forced emigration, Kullmann stated that based on humanitarian principles he opposed it, but that the Soviets would insist on the enforcement of the Yalta agreements. Kullmann made clear that, according to its mandate, the Intergovernmental Committee on Refugees was 'only in charge of refugees who had been persecuted by the Nazi regime'. This sentence is the only sentence underlined by hand in these minutes preserved in the ICRC archives. The ICRC then referred to a number of special groups that should be included and not counted as Soviet citizens, such as the Baltic DPs. Kullmann declared he would propose an international agreement to the IGCR for the introduction of an identity document, much like the former Nansen passport, for people who definitely would not be able to be repatriated.[81]

The ICRC continued to follow the developments in Allied refugee policies carefully and pushed to make its position heard. Max Huber was repeatedly invited as an observer at the sessions of the plenary committee of the Intergovernmental Committee on Refugees in London.[82] Beyond making official appeals against the policy of forced repatriation, the ICRC inspected camps and documented the food and health situation. They also intervened with authorities on behalf of some former Yugoslav POWs and Baltic DPs who had been threatened with the loss of their ration books.[83] The committee viewed all DPs, refugees, and expellees as deserving of humanitarian assistance. To bolster its argument, the ICRC cited the Geneva Convention, which deems the wearing of a uniform to be the main indicator of belonging to an army, and by that logic, Russians and other East Europeans wearing Wehrmacht or Waffen SS uniforms merited treatment as German POWs.

To the ICRC's disappointment, the meetings of the Intergovernmental Committee on Refugees showed no change in attitude and refugee status was still granted only to victims of fascism and Nazism.[84] In a note for its delegation in Berlin, the ICRC showed great concern about non-repatriable refugees and intervened for them with the Intergovernmental Committee, but also with the Allied authorities on the ground in western Europe. Thus, for instance, the ICRC delegation in Salzburg contacted the American authorities in the course of 1945 to halt the forced repatriation of Hungarian refugees. Although forced repatriation was now on the wane, there was still reason to be alarmed. The ICRC in Geneva received a copy of an order from the American headquarters in Frankfurt am Main from November 1945 that all nationals of former enemy countries were to be repatriated. In this context, Geneva was naturally eager to learn if the United Nations intended to intervene with a solution for all refugees and support the end of forced repatriation.[85]

Max Huber reached out to prominent members of the United Nations delegations—Eleanor Roosevelt included—in curtailing forced repatriation.[86] It was a great success for the ICRC when the General Assembly of the UN in their Resolution of 12 February 1946, voted to stop the practice of forced repatriations except for 'war criminals and traitors'.[87] And, in December 1946, the ICRC in Geneva had further good news to share. The Intergovernmental Committee of Refugees fell in line with the UN decision and finally agreed that forced repatriation would no longer be an option, with the exception of cases concerning war criminals or traitors.[88] As the western Allies slowly changed their policies in 1946 on forced repatriation, the ICRC no longer stood alone. Geneva hoped that the resources of the newly created IRO would soon extend to all refugees, even former enemy nationals. Motivated by decisions taken at the United Nations, the ICRC took the next step. On 6 May 1946 the committee officially appealed directly to the governments of the western Allies to stop forced repatriation.[89]

While the ICRC's stand on forced repatriation initially drew fire and little sympathy, its position on aid to Axis collaborators proved even more controversial. The ICRC did not exclude any refugees and expellees from defeated nations from its aid programmes. In the context of its tradition of neutrality and impartiality, this was hardly surprising. For all practical purposes, it did not even distinguish between perpetrators and victims of the Nazi regime.[90] As noted above, the Allied-sponsored IRO and the western Allies were only willing to help the identifiable victims of fascism and Nazism but not their long-time oppressors.[91] Despite their many differences, all the Allied powers agreed that 'war criminals and traitors' should be repatriated. On this point the ICRC disagreed. The ICRC stressed that it 'could extend its help without discrimination to all refugees, without any consideration of political opinion, nationality, race or religious belief'.[92] As one historian put it, the organization was 'dedicated to an extremely broad principle of humanitarian aid'.[93] The ICRC's policies here essentially undermined denazification efforts and the Allied agreements on the repatriation of Nazi criminals and collaborators.

ICRC Policies in the Shadow of the Cold War

While the ICRC never abandoned its principle of neutral humanitarianism, the Allied refugee organizations did gradually change their goals and standards. By 1947 they still denied international aid to Nazi collaborators, but at the same time now opposed blanket forced repatriation. In a June 1947 report about its practical application of the regulations, administrators of the Intergovernmental Committee of Refugees finally declared that persons who fought voluntarily for the Germans but were not involved in war crimes were 'ineligible for international aid, but not liable to forcible repatriation'.[94]

Uncertainty nevertheless persisted. Internal memos show that the regulations often remained unclear and confusing, even more so for refugee organization officials in the field. Yet they also show that decision-makers grew more lenient as time passed. With the Cold War heating up in the wake of the Communist takeover of Czechoslovakia in 1948 and the Soviet blockade of road and rail traffic to Berlin, former fascists and Nazi collaborators at risk of being prosecuted always chose to make their homes in the West. Anti-communist criteria soon became an important factor in the IRO's decisions in individual cases, and the organization's rules for forcible repatriation therefore changed significantly.[95]

By 1947 the western Allied governments had for the most part had stopped extraditing DPs who originally hailed from Communist-controlled countries. And their opposition to the forced repatriation of East Europeans had become unambiguous by 1948.[96] The clearly formulated US position stated that the agencies they oversaw were making concrete efforts 'to rehabilitate and resettle these unfortunates so that they may live as free men'.[97] The IRO may not have issued a blanket pardon for war criminals, but the Cold War's anti-communist focus clearly had an impact inside the IRO. The organization's screening teams now considered the 'moral intention' of applicants, and thus fear of persecution and anti-communist conviction helped swing decisions. If Nazi collaborators claimed that they had been forced to fight for the Germans, they became eligible for aid and protection. Indeed, many remaining East European soldiers of SS divisions were now eligible on these grounds.[98]

The US government nonetheless enacted strict immigration laws that prevented Nazis and Nazi collaborators from entering the United States. On 1 July 1949 the US Displaced Persons Commission, which administered resettlement of a certain number of European DPs, declared that 'membership at any time in the Communist, Nazi or Fascist parties automatically disqualifies a person seeking eligibility for admission into the United States under the Act'.[99] Under the US Displaced Persons Act of 1948, former SS soldiers and Nazi Party members should technically never have been allowed to enter the United States, nor should any Nazi collaborators. Despite these provisions, the US immigration authorities' interpretation and application of the law had in fact become increasingly more relaxed when it came to immigration and visas for European fascists. This new policy applied to former soldiers of the Baltic Waffen SS units and the Ukrainian Waffen SS 'Galizien' Division who were seeking DP status. In September

1950 the US High Commission for Germany decided that 30,000 Estonian and 60,000 Latvian Waffen SS soldiers would be considered freedom fighters against the Soviets and not simply Nazi collaborators. This logic suggested that they had never been *real* members of the Waffen SS. The Displaced Persons Commission decided that 'the Baltic Waffen SS units (Baltic Legions) are to be considered as separate and distinct in purpose, ideology, activities, and qualifications for membership from the German SS, and therefore the Commission holds them not to be a movement hostile to the Government of the United States'.[100] Unsurprisingly, numerous Nazis and SS men ultimately found their way into the United States after the war. Historians can only estimate very roughly how many war criminals were among them. The situation for certain categories of ethnic Germans— *Volksdeutsche*—also now began to change slowly. Under the Displaced Persons Act, ethnic Germans from Czechoslovakia fleeing the communists were allowed to receive US visas.[101]

The message was clear. The new focus had become to mobilize all useful forces in the fight against communism and the Soviets. By the 1950s, the United States had decided to 'let sleeping Nazis lie'.[102] Even former Holocaust perpetrators now had little to fear. The case of Iwan (John) Demjanjuk provides a case in point. A 22-year-old Ukrainian who served in the Red Army, Demjanjuk was captured in 1942 by the German Wehrmacht. Perhaps because life as a POW in German hands was often extremely harsh, he decided to switch sides. He was sent to an all-Ukrainian unit of the Waffen SS that later merged with General Vlassov's 'Russian Liberation Army'. Demjanjuk became one of many Ukrainians serving as concentration camp guards. Despite allegedly having been a guard at the Sobibór extermination camp when the war was over, he easily blended into the masses of DPs stranded in Germany at the end of the war. In order to avoid repatriation, he lied to the IRO and identified himself as a former forced labourer from Poland.[103] By the late 1940s he was living in a DP camp in Germany with the aid of the IRO and found a job as a truck driver for the US Army.[104] In 1952 Demjanjuk immigrated to the United States, where he lived undisturbed for decades.

Another prominent collaborator who managed to avoid forced repatriation was Michael (Mischa) Seifert, an ethnic German from Landau (Shyrokolanivka) in the Ukraine. Seifert had been an SS guard at the Bolzano concentration camp in northern Italy. After the war, Seifert went to Germany and joined the many East European refugees living there temporarily. He finally migrated in August 1951 to Canada via the German port of Bremerhaven. The minimal information about him on an index card of the International Tracing Service of the Red Cross suggests that the IRO helped him to immigrate: 'IRO International Movement Office Bremen-Grohn. Lfd. Nr. 489, Az. Emigration Bremerhaven.'[105] Seifert lived in Canada with his wife, Christine, bought a house in Vancouver, and acquired Canadian citizenship by claiming that he was originally Estonian. Only many years later did his wartime past as the notorious 'Beast of Bolzano' catch up with him.[106]

Increasingly lenient IRO policies helped several war criminals and Holocaust perpetrators to escape justice, as the official historian of the organization, Louise Holborn, has pointed out: 'A certain number of persons who have effectively and voluntarily helped enemy forces have succeeded, by concealing their actions, to be recognized within our mandate.'[107] By 1950 Allied refugee organizations had begun actively assisting refugees who had been labelled as Nazi collaborators and 'doubtful cases'.[108] In keeping with this shift, the United Nations High Commission for Refugees' 1951 Convention Relating to the Status of Refugees, was custom-built for (European) anti-communist refugees, regardless of their past lives. It recognized anyone as a refugee with a 'well-founded fear of persecution' in his or her home country.[109] Furthermore, by the 1950s, newly founded refugee organizations began focusing exclusively on refugees from Communism. The postwar practice of categorizing refugees as either victims or perpetrators of the Nazi regime had ended.

Once the Cold War set in, the West's predominant concern was no longer old Nazis but the communists.[110] It took longer, however, for the western powers to finally view German and ethnic German expellees (some of whom had been Nazi perpetrators) as war victims. Although it remains difficult to pinpoint exactly when the rigid divisions of the Cold War were finally set, the confrontation between the United States and the Soviet Union had reached a 'point of no return' by 1948.

Carl Burckhardt, at the helm from 1945 to 1948, was an early 'Cold Warrior', and he welcomed the shift in focus 'from "victors' justice" to anti-communism'.[111] Burckhardt was clearly opposed to forced repatriation to the Soviet Union. He opposed any compromises with the Soviets on the handling of DPs and he believed that the committee should take a clear stand on the matter.[112] Burckhardt had always considered the Soviet Union to be Europe's main enemy. After US president Truman adopted a foreign policy doctrine of 'containment' in 1947 to prevent Communist countries from spreading their influence, and with the outbreak of war in Korea in 1950, the IRO and ICRC were once again mostly on the same page when it came to the refugee question. The fate of ethnic Germans from outside Germany remained one exception to this concord. The IRO never completely reversed its policies on these refugees. According to the 1947/8 United Nations *Yearbook*, although individual *Volksdeutsche* were granted IRO assistance, an overall decision regarding the eligibility of this group was still pending. 'In September 1948, the General Council of IRO decided that, in view of its other more urgent problems, the Organization was still in no position to resolve this problem.'[113] Despite many setbacks, the ICRC continued to lobby the IRO on behalf of these ethnic Germans' eligibility for international assistance.

Despite a shift in political sentiments, many such Germans remained in limbo into the 1950s. Andreas (Andrej) B., a young *Volksdeutscher* from Yugoslavia, is an example of the IRO's continued stance on this group. His story also illustrates the limits of IRO categories, which often failed to accommodate complicated questions of identity. On 12 September 1950, Andreas B. applied to the refugee organization for aid. In his interview, he stated that he was born in 1928 in Yugoslavia, was drafted into the German army when he was 17 years old, and had to fight on the Austrian front in the last weeks of the war. Captured by Tito's partisans, he remained a prisoner until October 1948, when he was finally released and landed in a refugee camp in Trieste. According to an IRO officer, Andreas had no intention of going back to Yugoslavia, the country of his citizenship before the war, after having experienced the 'communist paradise' for three years in its camps. On the one hand, the officer stated that the young man had lost his citizenship and could not be forced to return Yugoslavia. On the other hand, as a *Volksdeutscher* and former German soldier, Andreas B. was technically 'ineligible' for IRO aid. With no Allied help to emigrate overseas, he wanted to settle in Germany, although his German was weak. According to a note on his application form, he 'speaks German but his Serbian is much better'.[114] This case illustrates well the complicated nature of determining each person's ethnic identity, their status as war criminal, collaborator, refugee, or DP, for the categories often overlapped and reality was more complicated than these categories allowed. The question of who was a victim and who was a perpetrator, especially when it came to ethnic Germans, did not always have a clear answer, despite attempts to categorize individuals and groups as one or the other.

The decisions made by both the IRO and the ICRC had very real implications for the people concerned. On the one hand, the ICRC applied 'humanity without limits', ignoring any distinction between victims and perpetrators.[115] Thus, even the distinction between Nazi camp guard and camp inmate became blurred in questions of postwar aid. This was the inevitable consequence of the ICRC's neutral humanitarianism. The Allied-sponsored IRO, on the other hand, applied a form of collective guilt that excluded even German expellee children from its help. Both decisions may seem morally questionable. The ICRC allowed many who were guilty of crimes during the war to get away, while the IRO punished many who were innocent. But there is a major difference between the two policies. In contrast to the ICRC, the IRO tried to maintain the key distinction between victims and perpetrators. The IRO attempted to withhold aid from Nazi war criminals and Nazi collaborators by categorically excluding all Germans, and it installed a sophisticated screening process for East European DP applicants for aid. The organization's eligibility definitions were challenged in the political arena and changed over time, but its starting assumptions were never completely abandoned. First and foremost, it was the victims of the Nazi regime who deserved assistance, not the perpetrators. The ICRC, on the other hand, upheld its principle of 'humanitarian neutrality', even when confronted with men and women who had implemented genocide.

In the immediate postwar months the ICRC proved very active in civilian relief. Its leaders took the radical step of expanding its mandate so that it could assist DPs in Europe, an obvious and urgent humanitarian challenge to emerge as the war drew to its close.[116] The organization at this time began sending representatives to DP camps, and providing food parcels and tracing and emigration services for dislocated people all over central and western Europe. The ICRC also provided aid to countries in the Soviet sphere of influence, although on a far more limited basis.[117] National Red Cross societies (especially the American Red Cross) and the Red Cross League provided most of the material relief. The ICRC served as an intermediary and helped distribute the food parcels, clothing, and medicine through its delegates. With the dissolution of their Joint Relief Commission in late 1946 this phase came to an abrupt halt. The ICRC was all but bankrupt and lacked the means to continue this programme on its own. Burckhardt remarked bitterly that the dependence on the (American-dominated) Joint Relief Commission was a big mistake and complained

Figure 6.1. Harry Weinsaft of the American Jewish Joint Distribution Committee, hands out Red Cross packages to Jewish displaced persons in Vienna, Austria.

about the Red Cross League's leadership. The ICRC now concentrated its limited resources on aid and protection for German civilians and expellees. It also lobbied against forced repatriation, flying in the face of Allied government policy, natural expediency, and prior agreements. Both ICRC decisions were controversial at the time. While Huber had more humanitarian and tactical grounds for doing so, Burckhardt seemed to be propelled above all by his strong anti-communism. He had no intention of giving in to Soviet demands, even if the ICRC had very few means at its disposal to resist them. With the establishment of the IRO in 1946, the limited refugee material aid programme of the Red Cross was downsized even more. With the establishment of the United Nations High Commission for Refugees (UNHCR) in 1950, the ICRC—now under Paul Ruegger— finally took note that providing aid to displaced civilians was not within the Swiss based organization's portfolio. Still, that did not mean it could not continue intervening on behalf of the interests of refugees in extraordinary situations and emergencies.

The ICRC attempted to insert itself in civilian aid initiatives to expand its portfolio after the war and remain 'relevant', to extend its *raison d'être* in times of peace. The Geneva Convention reform offered one promising path; this was another. The choices made in fact exposed the ICRC to even more criticism, especially from Soviet quarters and the communist countries. The ICRC's foray into civilian relief work was, then, a terrible gamble in the end, especially as Soviet support remained critical for successfully completing the reform of the Geneva Conventions.

Some of the organization's forays into civilian aid projects and advocacy were outright failures, such as the attempt to change the IRO's eligibility principles for Germans or early attempts to reach out to suspected Nazi war criminals being held in internment camps. Other ICRC excursions began badly and drew much fire from the new powers in Europe, yet were later embraced by those same powers as being fully in harmony with the new Cold War climate, with new Cold War priorities and alignments. Blocking involuntary repatriation of East European and Soviet citizens after the war was a prime example of how the ICRC's unpopular choices could evolve into something viewed as positive. Still, as we shall see, the Geneva organization could ill afford to offend or alienate the Soviet government in pursuing its larger agenda.

7

The Humanitarians
and the Nazis

After the Second World War many war refugees were unable to return to their old homes for reasons ranging from the difficulty of crossing borders to the communist takeover of their home governments to the actual disappearance of their former countries due to redrawn borders and new occupying powers. Thus many people no longer had valid travel documents and remained in limbo. Although some people were happy enough to have emerged from the war alive, others wanted to emigrate in order to begin life anew. But in order to do so they needed internationally recognized travel documents in which the visas of the immigration countries could be stamped. Initially, the United Nations (UN) sought to address this need through the International Refugee Organization (IRO). As stated earlier the IRO served only what it considered to be 'genuine' refugees; this meant it refused help to those who might have committed war crimes or collaborated with the Axis powers. Using strict screening methods, the IRO was able to root out collaborators and criminals who tried to falsify their identities and wartime histories. But its vetting process was by no means foolproof, and the agency sometimes ended up assisting the very individuals it sought to exclude from aid. Given the narrow scope of refugees that the IRO would assist, the International Committee of the Red Cross (ICRC) saw both a pressing need for travel papers for those excluded from IRO aid and a way to improve its record of assistance to war victims by providing such papers. As a result, the ICRC developed its *titres de voyage* and made them available to virtually any applicant. Implementing few requirements and conducting virtually no screening procedures, the ICRC made it possible for large numbers of Nazis, war criminals, and collaborators to emigrate, and de facto ensured that many would never have to answer for their actions during the war. In this way, the ICRC's principle of neutral humanitarianism put it at odds with Allied policies. Intended to improve its standing with the Allies, its work on behalf of uprooted war victims actually threatened to damage its reputation and therefore backfire. The ICRC soon tried to withdraw from issuing travel papers, but a number of factors meant that this was easier said than done.

IRO Travel Documents for Victims

Given the growing numbers of refugees of various backgrounds, the Intergovernmental Commission for Refugees took on more and more responsibilities towards the end of the war. One of the new duties discussed in 1943 was 'securing travel documents for stateless refugees or persons who do not enjoy the protection of any government'.[1] However, from 1946 (when it was founded), it was ultimately up to the IRO to deal with the immense problems faced by war refugees. Recognizing refugees' need for travel documents, in October 1946 twenty-one countries signed the 'London Agreement', which created the IRO's so-called 'London travel document'. The United Nations Yearbook reported:

> As a result of considerable work undertaken by the Intergovernmental Committee on Refugees, an international convention was adopted in London on October 15, 1946, concerning the issuance of a travel document to refugees and displaced persons coming within the mandate of IRO. This convention covers those refugees who were unable to obtain a travel document because they did not come under prewar international arrangements which were concluded for the benefit of the so-called 'Nansen' refugees.[2]

By 21 September 1948, some twenty-eight governments had begun issuing or recognizing the IRO travel documents.

According to the agreement, a person had to fulfil certain conditions to receive identity papers from the IRO. The applicant had to be a genuine, deserving refugee according to agency's standards, which meant the person was either de facto or legally stateless and had a legal residence permit in an IRO member country.[3] The IRO would handle the resettlement and the issuance of the required travel documents for such refugees.[4] The IRO supported and protected 'the nationals of Allied countries, the Jews and the victims of the Nazi regime regardless of their nationality. as the ICRC headquarters noted.[5] These conditions in principle excluded Germans, war criminals, and Nazi collaborators and the Allies put a screening system in place that was intended to enforce this policy.[6]

In preparing to launch the IRO, the United Nations discussed ways to '(1) define measures so as to avoid giving assistance to war criminals etc. (2) [...] to recommend to the Council [of the UN] to do everything possible to make the competent bodies speed up in the screening, segregation and surrendering of these undesirables'.[7] Historian Gerard Daniel Cohen stresses that the policies used by the IRO were strict, concluding: 'Precise guidelines and uniform jurisprudence were supposed to shield its staff from improvisation and arbitrariness.'[8] The presence of people with an undesirable past among the millions of displaced persons (DPs) was obviously not a secret. It was also widely assumed that Nazi collaborators had found their way among the refugees.[9] Eastern bloc countries therefore demanded that 'more effective provisions should be made ensuring that war criminals would not receive any aid from the IRO'.[10]

Yugoslav delegates in the Preparatory Commission for the IRO voiced some of these concerns. In 1946, for instance, a high Yugoslav official complained that DP camps in Italy, Germany, and Austria were 'in the hands of war criminals and quislings, including "*Volksdeutsche*"'.[11] A delegate from Yugoslavia at the United Nations pronounced: 'You can well imagine that if any part of the 25 million dollars intended for refugees is spent on war criminals, collaborators, quislings and others who do not belong to a genuine refugee group such as Jews, Spaniards [refugees from the Spanish civil war], etc. there will be that much less for the latter—hence there is an injustice to them.'[12] In reply the US delegate reminded the subcommittee meeting that they were not talking about enforcing criminal justice, but only about ensuring that assistance would not be given to the wrong people: 'Clearly, we have no power or mandate to set up any kind of court.'[13]

The IRO undertook a screening process to weed out the undeserving or those who were not genuine refugees.[14] According to Cohen, many parallels can be found between denazification on the one side and the filtering of 'false' refugees on the other; both processes were a form of punishment: 'If the granting of DP status was an international recognition of victimization, its denial was tantamount to a guilty verdict.'[15] If one didn't get DP recognition, secure housing and food rations were denied by some Allied refugee organizations.

The IRO set up regional offices to issue these new travel documents. Their personnel translated foreign-language documents and set in motion research to confirm the identities of the applicants, and assessed any gaps that existed in an individual's story about their recent past. National and local authorities were also tapped to confirm personal details. The screening was ultimately a massive undertaking, especially in the American Zone of Germany, with vetting teams working six days a week and conducting up to forty interrogations a day. Despite the wartime damage and the fact that many local and regional institutions were not yet fully functioning again, the process appears to have been largely effective. It did indeed help to identify many undesirable applicants and thereby provided a measure of security to host countries.[16]

Along with interviews and documents checks, the IRO's purge of unlawful DPs relied in part on lists compiled by the Allies in preparing the Nuremberg trials and for denazification bodies such as the Berlin Document Center. The discovery and arrest of war criminals, however, was left up to the intelligence units of the Allied military forces such as the Americans' Counter Intelligence Corps. The UNRRA and IRO screening teams limited themselves to seeking out interlopers in the DP camps who had lied about their backgrounds and wartime past. Evidence of collaboration could sometimes be found on the very bodies of the applicants—SS blood group tattoos for example. But despite these efforts, the precise background of East Europeans who had fought alongside the Germans in the war was difficult to uncover.[17] In many cases, it was close to impossible to prove that they had enlisted voluntarily and were not forcibly conscripted, as they claimed. Jewish refugees were normally immediately recognized as DPs and not subjected to long screening processes.[18]

Although the IRO was not given the task of investigating war criminals, its representatives in Italy often worked with the Allied occupying forces and the postwar government officials who did so. Historian Louise Holborn has shown that co-operation between the government and the IRO went much further in Italy than elsewhere, for 'the organization prepared the documents for refugees and transmitted them to the appropriate department of the Italian Government for validation before issue'.[19] The Italian government in turn wished to become involved with the 'human flotsam and jetsam of war' as little as possible and had no desire to pay for their upkeep.[20] Therefore, the new government in Rome had a great interest in the smooth passage of refugees through Italy and concluded that travel documents should be easily available. Nevertheless, in Italy too the screening of refugees initially remained very thorough. In 1946, the Allied authorities

Figure 7.1. Travel Document for Refugees of the International Refugee Organization (IRO). (ITS Bad Arolsen)

there examined 20,000 Ukrainians and Yugoslavs to identify and arrest any possible war criminals. At the same time, the Allies and the IRO exerted pressure on the refugees 'so that as many dissidents as possible returned to their homelands'.[21] As late as January 1947, a special British screening team was assigned to evaluate the Ukrainians and Yugoslavs. This commission, headed by Fitzroy Maclean, the former leader of a British military mission to Tito's partisans in Yugoslavia, carried out the investigations. As head of the screening mission, Maclean proved very thorough in rooting out Croatian Nazis and collaborators.[22] Seeking refuge through the IRO thus became a less and less desirable option for Nazi collaborators and war criminals who hoped to establish a sanitized wartime history.

Although Germans were not eligible, some nevertheless sought assistance from the new agency. They had many reasons for doing so, mostly of a practical nature, to meet their most basic and urgent daily needs. For example, DP camps had much better infrastructure and resources than the camps run by local German authorities for expelled *Volksdeutsche*. Thus DP status was soon very much in demand. Although the DP camps were generally geographically close to major German population centres, the living conditions there as well as overseas emigration opportunities were beyond the reach of most Germans. Even an expellee German with a documented anti-Nazi past did not often qualify as a recognized DP in Germany, Austria, or Italy.[23] A way out of this difficulty was to change one's primary affiliation. Ethnic Germans seeking assistance sometimes registered as members of the dominant ethnic groups of their former home countries—as Poles, Czechs, and Romanians. IRO review boards checked the ancestry of applicants, and German-sounding family names alone became cause for suspicion. Nevertheles, mastery of a non-German language often helped to convince IRO officers of claims, transforming an individual into a person with the desired ethnicity.[24] The screening may retrospectively seem somewhat absurd and unjust: two refugees from the same Romanian town could be treated completely differently—one was an ethnic Romanian and the other as an ethnic German, ineligible for displaced status.

Despite the attempts of some refugees to exploit weaknesses in the system, the IRO screening process was initially very effective, as the many detected former collaborators in the Waffen SS—such as Latvians, Bosnians, or Ukrainians—would suggest. The detailed information that the IRO (and UNRRA) was often able to assemble is impressive.[25] The effectiveness of the screening process is even more astounding given the chaotic circumstances and large numbers of uprooted people circulating at this time, with few if any personal records.

Rejected petitioners could appeal, and a special IRO review board was dedicated to revisiting their cases. Often the board in fact revealed the petitioner's background as a Nazi collaborator rather than a victim, as notes in IRO files suggest. Typical was the conclusion: 'appellant having voluntarily assisted the enemy forces is excluded' from aid.[26] In other cases, suspicion that an applicant came from an ethnic German background was grounds to decline or suspend a decision indefinitely, as files marked 'Petitioner is declared not within the mandate of the organization' indicate.[27]

The many cases preserved in the International Tracing Service archives prove that people tried time and again to obtain IRO eligibility by stressing their non-German ethnic backgrounds. The case of a woman from Latvia who was a naturalized German, only having moved to Germany in 1939, is quite typical. The entire family was resettled in German-annexed Poland, and his son-in-law even served in the Wehrmacht. The family members were expelled from Poland after the war and found themselves in occupied Germany. The IRO did not accept them as DPs, stating: 'As a German citizen in Germany she cannot be considered a bona fide refugee by IRO definitions.'[28]

However, despite all the IRO's efforts to prevent abuse, significant numbers of Nazi collaborators did slip through the cracks and received help from the UN agency. In May 2013 German authorities belatedly arrested a 93-year-old suspected Nazi war criminal.[29] The alleged camp guard in Auschwitz, Hans Lipschis, was originally from Lithuania, a fact that would play a critical role in his case. While under investigation, he pleaded innocent, claiming that he had simply worked as a cook in Auschwitz and was, therefore, not an accessory to murder. One year after the Soviet occupation of the Baltic states in 1940, the Lipschis family had left for Germany—Germany's eastern border was only a few miles away from his family farm. It is not surprising, then, that Hans spoke both Lithuanian and German, although his German was rather weak. In 1941 Lipschis joined the Waffen SS and in 1943 became a German citizen. He advanced to the rank of SS *Rottenführer*, as a service list of 1945 proves.[30] At war's end, he was taken into British custody in a prisoner of war (POW) camp and released in the summer of 1945. A year later, he presented himself as a DP to the Allied authorities. In order to be eligible for status as a DP and IRO aid, the former SS man claimed to be an ethnic Lithuanian civilian labourer and used the Lithuanian form of his name, Antanas Lipsys, on his application. He did not mention his time in Auschwitz and left his wartime activities rather vague. He stated that he had moved to Germany in 1941 out of fear of the Russians and worked as a 'farm labourer' and 'trench digger' until 1945. Lipschis must have felt comfortable enough to make such false statements to the IRO, but his move was not without risks.

By 1949 the screening officers of the IRO had found out about his German citizenship and his service in the Waffen SS, as handwritten notes on his IRO file indicate: 'First information false', 'naturalized 1943', and 'served in the Waffen SS'. The captured German records that the Allies collected and microfilmed for screening purposes contain enough material about Lipschis to document his involvement with the Nazi regime. Confronted with these facts, Lipschis stated that he had been given German citizenship without his knowledge and that he had been forced into the German military. The screening officers probably had little problem finding Lipschis' request for German citizenship in 1941 in which he stated: 'Ich bekenne mich zum deutschen Volkstum' ('I swear allegiance to the German People'). In his citizenship application, he stated that he was an ethnic German in order to facilitate his request. Even more evidence existed, for Lipschis had signed these documents, proving that he had full knowledge about his German citizenship.[31] Once the IRO discovered the truth, he was deemed 'ineligible' because he was 'not within the mandate of the organization' as the IRO document states. A few years earlier, the quite effective screening process could have been damning for Lipschis. As a self-declared *Volksdeutscher* and German citizen, he would have been excluded from IRO aid and as a Nazi collaborator threatened with extradition to Lithuania, which was now part of the Soviet Union. In any case, he was neither the first nor the last SS man from Eastern Europe who received IRO support for at least a short time by lying about his background.[32] Lipschis expressed 'fear of persecution by Russians' and apparently managed to keep his 'refugee status', at least according to new guidelines established by the US government in the 1950s. Under the terms of the US Refugee Relief Act of 1953, he was finally able to leave Europe behind. As in the cases of alleged Ukrainian extermination camp guard John Demjanjuk, he emigrated to the United States in the 1950s, where he settled in Chicago and became a permanent resident. But in April 1983, Lipschis was the first alleged Holocaust perpetrator to be deported by the United States to Germany for concealing his role in the SS. This notwithstanding, he lived undisturbed in Germany for the next thirty years despite his deportation.[33] The German authorities could not pick him up at that time because it could not be proven that he had personally murdered anyone. In early 2014 a German court finally deemed Lipschis unfit for trial because of signs of dementia.

The ICRC's Travel Document for All

Initially the ICRC had no international mandate for issuing travel documents of its own.[34] This did not prevent the organization from taking action. Its priority had always been to meet the basic human needs of those affected by war or other disasters. The ICRC never allowed its activities to be limited by the tenets of international humanitarian law; instead, it relied on its own basic principles, and the priorities of its leaders. In the tradition of the Red Cross, the ICRC took actions first and sought to codify these actions in international law later.[35] ICRC president Max Huber raised the issue of travel documents for non-official refugees soon after the war. In a letter of August 1945 to High Commissioner for Refugees Herbert Emerson, Huber stressed that a solution for East European refugees of various nationalities, including Jews, had to be found. Huber felt that the Allied refugee organization should introduce identity papers for such refugees and model them on the Nansen passports.[36] Huber knew what he was talking about. He had been after all president of the Nansen Office for Refugees until 1938. But the policy Huber sought was never realized, for the Allies had different priorities and the IRO different principles than those of the Swiss humanitarians.

The ICRC now decided to intervene in what it saw as a humanitarian emergency believing that 'non-recognized' refugees, especially expellee Germans, had no real alternatives. In the first postwar years, given that there was no central German government in place, German passports were difficult to obtain. Local German authorities could issue identity cards, but they were not accepted for international travel. There were also very few aid organizations that would help Germans to emigrate overseas, most of them non-governmental. So, the ICRC decided to introduce its own travel documents. Madame Elisabeth de Ribaupierre, director of its Division for Prisoners of War and Civilian Internees in Geneva, summed up the difficult situation of 'non-recognized refugees' in a memo:

Because these people enjoy no support or protection from the government of their country of origin, or indeed from the institution set up especially to this end, the ICRC has actively concerned itself with their fate. [...] The International Red Cross Committee seeks to ease their departure for a host country, helpfully dealing with their situation by issuing a travel document to them, to which the necessary visas can be applied.[37]

Although providing travel papers was not traditionally one of the tasks and responsibilities of the ICRC, it began to issue them due to what the leadership viewed as an unprecedented and desperate situation at the beginning of 1945.[38] In a 1948 'Report of the International Committee of the Red Cross on its activities during the Second World War', the ICRC made its own motivation for the introduction of these temporary-documents clear: 'In view of the distressing situation of these applicants, the ICRC took steps in February 1945 to establish a "Travel Document" (bearing the number CICR 10.100), for issue by its delegations abroad to former detainees who applied to them'.[39] According to Roger Gallopin, one of the top officials of the ICRC at the time, the travel papers were issued 'in response to the request made by several of its delegates stationed in liberated countries'.[40] Gallopin further explained that 'the ICRC created its travel document, which it placed at the disposal of its delegations abroad, in order that the latter could issue it to former internees who applied to them and thereby to enable these persons to receive on an ad hoc document the necessary visas for the return to their country'.[41] In other words the papers were initially intended to help POWs and other prisoners with new identity documentation after their release.

These travel documents may have seemed to be an unlikely undertaking for the ICRC, but they were not. The ICRC had in the interwar period gained some experience with migration issues and travel papers for refugees.[42] After the Russian Revolution in 1917 and the breakdown of multinational empires such as Austria-Hungary, the ICRC played a particularly important role in initiating the so-called Nansen passports for stateless refugees and political émigrés.[43] In 1921 the League of Nations initiated a High Commission for Refugees led by the Norwegian explorer Fridtjof Nansen. Refugees stripped of their former citizenship became a mass phenomenon in the interwar years.[44] In the era of nation-states, no one was responsible for stateless people and the creation of the Nansen passport thus represented a breakthrough.[45] Not only did the ICRC initiate the Nansen passports, but Red Cross officials also managed the League's refugee office for some time.

Therefore the ICRC under Max Huber could rely on some previous experience. As early as July 1944 the Prisoners of War and Civilian Internees Commission of the ICRC began examining the possibility of issuing 'travel documents'.[46] In September 1944, Renée-Marguerite Frick-Cramer from the ICRC wholeheartedly agreed with Johannes (Jean) von Schwarzenberg, the Austrian in charge of the concentration camp food parcels programme, that a certificate for travel needed to be introduced. She pointed to the fact that the ICRC had been involved in providing papers for stateless refugees in 1920–1922. In addition, Hans Wolf de Salis who headed the ICRC delegation in Rome, would issue papers for Croats.[47] Eventually, in February 1945, a 'very unusual travel document' was designed at the Red Cross headquarters in Geneva.[48] A few months before the end of the Second World War, the ICRC thus began to issue simple, improvised travel papers called *titres de voyage*. These Red Cross travel documents originally served as 'one-time travel papers'.[49] The ICRC's *titres de voyage* were a kind of substitute passport because the Red Cross had never been a government agency and could not issue proper passports. By the end of 1951, the Red Cross had issued an estimated 120,000 such papers.[50]

Given the ICRC's previous relief work for refugees, its post-1945 work in this field hardly comes as a surprise.[51] But its postwar activity in this field differed in at least one important respect: although the organization had previous experience with travel papers for stateless refugees, it had not always issued these documents itself. It was the League of Nations, international refugee organizations, or national governments who had the authority to do so. But Nansen passports did not fit the even more complicated situation following Second World War which found many refugees wanting to emigrate permanently and build a life somewhere new.[52] Thus the Red Cross remained a long-term presence in the area of refugee aid and was willing to 'undertake emergency assistance programmes until other machinery could take over'.[53]

The introduction of the new ad hoc travel document service was probably intended to improve the ICRC's own record of aid for civilians, in this case refugees. It was introduced at the same time as the ICRC's announcement of its commitment to revising of the Geneva Conventions. Schwarzenberg appears to have been in charge of this new task. He was a member of an important Austrian aristocratic family and held not only Austrian but also Swiss citizenship.[54] ICRC President Burckhardt did not think very highly of his colleague Schwarzenberg. In a private letter to ICRC delegate Charles de Watteville dated February 1945 and forwarded to Ruegger as well, Burckhardt made his opinion about the man very clear: 'Schwarzenberg is perhaps not the best man for this. He is not the director of the division for deportees. The boss is Roger Gallopin. Schwarzenberg has good old-Austrian qualities of a public servant, but no "esprit de corps". He pushes all work off on his superiors and staff; he talks a great deal about nothing, exaggerates, and complains a lot about Switzerland.'[55] In the same letter, the president also made it clear that he did not trust Schwarzenberg with big decisions, so everything of importance had to be approved by Burckhardt personally. The date of his letter coincided with the introduction of Red Cross travel papers.

The timing of the ICRC's passport initiative is of interest. In the same letter, Burckhardt referred to the attacks on the ICRC's record in helping Jews. He stressed the necessity of pointing out all the efforts the ICRC had made on behalf of Jews and told Ruegger that Schwarzenberg would prepare a report to this end. There can be no doubt that the ICRC wanted to highlight and improve its aid to civilian victims of the war. The exact reasons and decision-making process for the travel papers are still not well documented. However, Burckhardt's views on German expellees and German suffering provide some insight. As his letter to Rothmund showed, he was not solely motivated by humanitarianism.

Another clue about the reasoning behind the inception of the travel papers can be found in ICRC administrative documents. The ICRC in Geneva clarified its position on Red Cross travel papers in a memo to all delegations: 'Within the context of the "Intergovernmental Committee", certain governments, which signed an agreement in London in October 1946, issue travel papers under certain circumstances. But unlike these passports, the ICRC travel papers are available for all refugees regardless of race, nationality, faith, or political conviction.'[56] In an official publication of the ICRC, Elisabeth de Ribaupierre, who had taken over Schwarzenberg's duties, talked about the humanitarian emergency involving refugees, a group of 'war victims' that deserved attention. In this situation, the ICRC had created the *titre de voyage* for all those who had lost their identity papers or could not renew their passports. The intention was that obtaining such a titre de voyage should be a rapid process without delays.[57] De Ribaupierre stressed the neutral humanitarian principles that formed the basis of this aid, underlining that: 'The main feature of the *titre de voyage* is that it is for free for anybody asking for it, given that the person fulfills the three requirements I mentioned above, it is available to all without regard to race, religion, mother language, or political conviction.'[58] The message from Geneva was quite clear: each person who applied for a travel document would get one for free if the person fulfilled the rather vague conditions of lost papers and a promised visa from the country of intended immigration.

In practice, however, even these minimal policies were often ignored. The ICRC made it clear that 'political conviction' was not a reason to exclude anybody; therefore, Nazis would get the papers as easily as communists. Based on the principles of humanitarian neutralism, the ICRC believed that a greater injustice was inflicted when the innocent were punished together with the guilty. A former ICRC official in Rome expressed this attitude clearly, stating: 'We were, after all, an "aid" organization, not detectives. In the end, the most important thing was to help the many for whom our help was legitimate.'[59] Thus neutral humanitarianism would not even exclude war criminals, as ICRC Vice President Jean Pictet stated unequivocally:

> Guilty persons themselves are not excluded from this assistance if they have need of it, a fact which has sometimes not been well understood. The Red Cross does not, however, interfere in any way with the administration of justice; its action does not run counter to the essential right of a state to suppress violations of its laws. What the Red Cross does demand is that each person shall be humanely treated.[60]

The ICRC introduced only a few basic guidelines, although these seem to have varied over time and from delegation to delegation. 'One condition for the issuing of the documents is that the applicants come personally to the delegation. The ICRC then examines the documents presented (identity cards, residence permits, papers issued by the Italian authorities). The data of the applicant are to be registered in a form; we keep a copy and put them in alphabetical order, a copy is made available to them [ICRC headquarters]', the ICRC delegation in Rome summarized in 1945.[61] But in many cases the applicant did not in fact appear personally and his or her forms were sent by mail instead. The applicants also often had no identification documents to present. Contrary to de Salis' assurances, the ICRC stated repeatedly that screening applicants was not its job. The organization went even further, stating that it would give no guarantees of the identity of the applicant. The ICRC *titre de voyage* itself even states: 'The present document has been established at the request of the bearer because he has stated that he possesses no regular or provisional passport and that he is unable to procure one. This document is no proof of the bearer's nationality and has no effect on the latter.'[62]

The guidelines proposed in 1945 reflect good intentions more than they do reality. In 1950 de Ribaupierre made this quite clear: 'This document, known as Travel Document 10,100b, was issued on request to all who could give proof of: (1) lack of valid passport, (2) authorization had been granted for the applicant to leave the country in which he was then living and (3) agreement had been obtained from the diplomatic or consular authorities of the country to which the applicant wished to proceed, to grant a visa.'[63] De Ribaupierre did not explain however, how an applicant would prove the lack of a valid passport. The ICRC also did not check if an applicant was in fact allowed to leave his or her place of residence; for example, former members of the Nazi Party or the SS were not allowed to leave Germany in the first postwar years under Allied regulation. An ICRC report published in May 1948 also stated: 'The main condition required of the applicant is to produce the written promise of a visa granted by the consulate of the country where he wishes to go, and an authorization to leave his country of residence.'[64] This main condition was also often overlooked, for the Red Cross papers were issued without proof of a secured visa. A letter of reference from the Vatican with the desired destination of the applicant might serve this purpose. The Vatican Aid Commission for Refugees in Rome soon collaborated closely with the ICRC for this purpose. A US State Department official remarked: 'The investigation of the I.R.C. further revealed that a close supervision of the application is not given and that too much reliability is placed upon the letters of identification issued by Vatican delegates.'[65] It was no secret that some of the clergymen operating under the umbrella of the Vatican Commission of Refugees were Nazi sympathizers, including men such as the Austrian Bishop Alois Hudal. But the word of clergymen was accepted, for as Madame Dupuis of the ICRC in Rome pointed out: 'How could we refuse to accept the word of priests'?[66] The many letters of recommendation issued by the Vatican Commission of Refugees and now preserved in the ICRC archives show how common the practice of issuing these identification letters had become.

Another indisputable precondition for the Red Cross was the stateless status of the applicants—at least theoretically. But data such as nationality or country of origin were often missing from applications. In many cases, the information given was contradictory at best. A proper screening process was neither implemented nor planned. The vague guidelines and the non-existent screening process for obtaining ICRC travel papers allowed for all kinds of abuse. The whole issuing process was ramshackle in the extreme and led, in many cases, to inaccurate or blatantly false identification papers. A US State Department report criticized the absence of screening by the ICRC officials sharply, declaring:

> It is to be noted that although these International Red Cross passports are recognized as perfectly valid identity documents, they in fact identify nothing. The name appearing on the passport is invariably fictitious and often is one of several aliases used by the person whose picture it bears, who in turn might have in his possession numerous other passports and identity documents bearing identically the same picture which he uses at different times, under varying circumstances, for his personal benefit. It is also noted that the picture is affixed to the passport with ordinary paste. No seal is impressed through the picture or anywhere else on the passport, making the practice, which is in common usage in Italy, of transferring or changing pictures, a very simple one. This is likewise true with the thumb print which is affixed. The thumb print is never clearly made nor legible. It is made from ordinary ink pad and never 'rolled' but rather only pressed, thus making a classification count impossible.[67]

There was also no way of examining and checking the ICRC travel documents because the applications were sent immediately to Red Cross headquarters in Geneva. Once archived there, they remained under lock and key. US State Department official Vincent La Vista noted with some resignation: 'Unfortunately, the International Red Cross makes it a practice to send all its records to their headquarters in Geneva, as soon as practical after each case is closed there, thus making it impossible for the investigation to continue along these lines here. It is the opinion of this writer, however, that an examination of the records in Geneva of all passports issued by the International Red Cross would reveal startling and unbelievable facts.'[68] The ICRC archives in Geneva were not opened until fifty years after La Vista's report was completed. Their contents prove La Vista to be right: the documents reveal the ICRC's involvement in the escape of SS men and Nazi war criminals.

Once the programme went into effect, ICRC travel papers were in demand by non-recognized refugees, namely Germans seeking to get out of Europe, *Volksdeutsche* and East Europeans. The communist world soon realized that the ICRC was undermining Allied agreements, particularly those related to the extradition of war criminals and collaborators, through the issuing of its travel papers. The Soviets were certainly eager to attack the Red Cross for its help to Eastern European refugees, but the Red Cross continued to insist that its aid was completely impartial and available to everybody in need.[69]

While large numbers of *Volksdeutsche* and East Europeans not eligible for IRO aid began approaching the ICRC delegations for travel papers, Jewish survivors of the Holocaust normally sought help and travel documents through the IRO, not so much the ICRC. Yehuda Bauer's standard work on the American Jewish Joint Distribution Committee (JDC) and Jewish DPs in the postwar years makes no mention of Red Cross travel papers playing a major role in refugee aid for Jews.[70] One reason why ICRC travel papers were seemingly not as much in demand by Jews in Europe was that the United States, unlike Argentina, Syria, Egypt, and other countries, did not recognize ICRC travel papers as valid for overseas travel.[71] However, archival research shows that the ICRC did help Jewish DPs with travel papers.[72] For example, on 27 June 1949, Jacob S. from Romania applied at the ICRC delegation in Genoa for a *titre de voyage*. He stated he was Jewish and had been imprisoned from 1941 until 1944 in Ferramonti, a camp initially established in fascist Italy in 1940 in order to round up the foreign Jews in the country. Jacob S. had been born in Bukovina, which at the time of his birth was an Austrian province, although after 1918 it changed hands several times. At the end of the war in 1945, Jacob and his family found themselves stranded in Italy, considered stateless by Italian authorities. They had no intention of going back to Romania. Jacob declared that he and his family wanted to emigrate to Israel, and the information on his application form was signed and confirmed by the American Jewish Joint Distribution Committee in Genoa.[73] The Jewish family would have been eligible for IRO aid, but an ICRC document might have been seen as a faster solution.

The Positive Consequences of Success: Recognition of the ICRC's Travel Papers and Aid to Refugees

Some governments shared views similar to those of the ICRC. As a result, many states soon recognized the Red Cross travel papers as a kind of substitute 'passport' and often referred to them as such. But the ICRC's activities as a de facto passport authority were only tolerated and not yet enshrined in international humanitarian law like the Geneva Conventions.

Although ICRC delegations in cities such as Prague, Vienna, Innsbruck, and Salzburg had begun issuing travel papers, Rome and Genoa created by far the most such documents. Italy remained a crucial transit country for people seeking to leave Europe.[74] According to historian Catherine Rey-Schyrr, the ICRC delegations in Rome and in Genoa alone had by August 1949 issued 67,500 travel papers, especially to Ukrainians, Yugoslavs, and Germans, out of a total of an ICRC total of 90,000.[75] The following year ICRC official de Ribaupierre also reported that more than 100.000 travel documents had been issued, mostly by offices in Prague, Vienna, Salzburg, Innsbruck, Paris, Cairo, Shanghai, Madrid, Genoa, and Naples. But the numbers were highest in Rome.[76] Indeed, the Italian delegations had long faced a storm of refugees.[77]

The ICRC delegation in Rome under Hans Wolf de Salis established that the help of all ICRC delegations in Italy was necessary and desirable for the distribution of travel documents, but control of the central card system would be retained by de Salis's office in Rome. Rome alone wanted to issue the documents, although applications could be made to the individual offices, to which Rome sent the final *titres de voyage*. In this way, de Salis was eager to assume control of the travel documents process and central filing system. It was chiefly up to him and his ICRC staff in Rome to determine what form the practice and control of the issuing of travel documents would take.[78] In addition to the Rome office, the ICRC in the important port town of Genoa soon became particularly active and autonomous in the issuing of travel documents. Attempts to improve the procedures when issuing the documents also occurred, too; in August 1945, the ICRC had introduced some control procedures. Lists were drawn up of the documents issued, and the completed and signed application forms were eventually sent back to Geneva, where they remain today. The travel documents themselves were handed out to the applicants at the ICRC delegations, mostly in Rome and Genoa.[79]

The recognition of the ICRC papers and their practical use ultimately depended on their recognition by immigration countries. Mme de Ribaupierre pointed out that the *titres de voyage* were neither passports nor official papers, and thus the diplomatic services of countries of immigration had complete discretion about whether to accept the ICRC travel papers or not and stamp their visas on them.[80] In August 1948, the Genoa ICRC delegate Dr Leo Biaggi de Blasys investigated which countries were according recognition to Red Cross travel documents. He wrote to a large number of consulates and embassies in Italy and got back an extremely positive response. Almost all the Latin and South American countries recognized the ICRC's travel papers. Particularly encouraging was the answer from the consul general of the Republic of Argentina in Genoa: 'This consulate always accepts your travel documents; our visas are always affixed to your travel documents, and these ICRC identity cards are accepted by us as travel papers and by the Directorship General for Immigrants as entry documents.'[81] The Genoese ICRC official could thus report to his headquarters in Geneva:'Our identity cards are recognized in principle as travel documents by Argentina, Bolivia, Chile, Cuba, Paraguay, Peru, Spain, Egypt, France, Mexico, Switzerland, Uruguay, and El Salvador'.[82] South American countries were interested in skilled laborers and highly educated personnel from war-devastated Europe. They were willing to allow a certain number of Europeans to immigrate, as long as they were anti-communist. A fascist or Nazi past was not considered an obstacle, sometimes even the opposite.[83]

In a 1948 'Report of the International Committee of the Red Cross on Its Activities during the Second World War', the ICRC also stated that the issuing of these documents was in de facto agreement with the immigrant countries and shifted the responsibility to them:

> The work of the ICRC in this field depended on the attitude of the Consulates of the immigrant countries, and could be pursued only in countries where consular services had been speedily re-opened. In Germany, the country, which has the largest numbers of DPs, Travel Documents have been issued only in a few cases, owing to the almost total absence of foreign consulates.[84]

The ICRC also referred to the 'approval of the Allied and local authorities' and probably meant the de facto recognition of the papers by national governments and the IRO.[85] However, the 'recognition' of the ICRC travel papers still varied somewhat from country to country.

The French and Swiss authorities remained cautious.[86] In June 1945, only a few weeks after the end of the war in Europe the ICRC informed Rothmund (at the time serving as delegate of the IGCR) about the new travel document. The Red Cross stated that the *titres de voyage* was not an identity document, but was intended only to facilitate the repatriation of all prisoners of war, civilian internees and deportees.[87] Swiss police authorities were aware of the danger of abuse, but still tolerated the documents. According to historian Christiane Uhlig, the issuing of ICRC travel papers for Switzerland was accomplished in coordination with the Swiss immigration authorities (*Fremdenpolizei*) who felt the ICRC should only issue travel documents 'in cases where the police authorities are not willing to issue substitute passports'. Oskar Schürch, deputy director of the Swiss police department, had little interest, however, in hindering the ICRC's work as a quasi-passport authority because, as he wrote to his superior officer Rothmund 'under certain circumstances and in individual cases, we might have an interest that the ICRC issues an identity card and not the police authorities'. In which cases this could have been in the interest of the *Fremdenpolizei* under the leadership of Rothmund remains unclear.[88] But the attitude of the Swiss authorities varied. The branch of the Swiss police that dealt with forgeries remained very cautious in its treatment of ICRC identification papers, well aware of the practice of giving false information, noting that '[t]he ICRC formally gives out these cards without any guarantees and generally relies only on the petitioner's information'.[89]

Although the ICRC's travel documents originally served as single-use passes allowing refugees to return to their homes or travel overseas to settle in a new country, the ICRC in some cases extended the life of these documents for years. De Blasys explained that some countries also regularly extended the duration of the validity of the ICRC documents. South American states pressed for the most extended validity of the ICRC papers. The positive attitude from South American countries that De Blasys reported was not a coincidence and most likely had to do with the attitude of some of those countries toward the US–dominated IRO. In spite of the IRO's responsibility for the refugees and their documents, its authority in this matter was often undercut. Some South American states recognized the ICRC documents, but not the IRO identification papers. Even the Swiss authorities sometimes questioned the validity of IRO papers, despite the fact that the IRO's own headquarters were located in Geneva.[90] The IRO was, thus, ironically repeatedly forced to ask the Red Cross for *titres de voyages* for immigrants to South America. This state of affairs was somewhat incongruous, given that the IRO had refused to take responsibility for 'ethnic German refugees' or Nazi and fascist collaborators.[91] Because the IRO was understaffed and the bureaucracies soon had other priorities, the agency eventually put up few objections to the ICRC travel papers, or so it seems.[92]

Despite these successes, as early as 1946 the ICRC was looking to get rid of this function soon as soon as possible, and was looking for an alternative organization to take over, stating that the postwar chaos had lifted somewhat and that therefore delegates should confine themselves to strictly essential duties. The ICRC hoped that the Intergovernmental Committee on Refugees (IGCR) would now introduce a travel paper for all refugees and it wanted to know what the IGCR's point of view on this issue was.[93] IGCR Director Herbert Emerson explained that this was to be a major project for the soon to be operative new refugee organization, the IRO. The eligibility criteria were also on the agenda for discussion. Given that the introduction of IRO travel papers was only in the planning stage, the ICRC should continue to distribute its document for a few months longer.[94] The ICGR could help with the distribution of ICRC documents in Germany, Italy and Austria. But the ICRC in response pointed to their principle of aiding those in need, without reference to political, racial, or religious criteria, and argued accordingly that 'it would be difficult to grant our travel documents only to persons falling within such category determined by another entity other than us'.[95]

The Allies obviously had some concerns that the ICRC travel document was being abused. One ICRC official explained: 'You must be aware that our travel document is issued with the authorization of the local governments, and on the basis of the promise of a visa. In our opinion, these conditions, together with the investigation conducted on the spot by our delegates constitutes a sufficient guarantee, that the document is not being issued in any manner that might lead to criticism.'[96] As we will see later, that optimistic assumption proved wrong. The Allied refugee organization and the ICRC were clearly not in sync with each other. The ICRC officials kept repeating that the fundamental principle of Red Cross action was complete neutrality, whether political, racial or religious. By repeating this mantra, the ICRC officials just kept confirming the differences in principle between the two organizations. The ICGR was willing to provide funding for the ICRC refugee services, but only for recognized refugees. 'Such being the case, we ask ourselves whether it would not be wiser to abandon the idea of calling upon the funds managed by the Intergovernmental Committee, unless this body should decide to make an exception in favor of the International Committee, by taking the fundamental principles of the Red Cross into account.'[97] This did not happen for a while, and the ICRC was therefore on its own with the financing of its travel papers for the time being.

What had begun as an ICRC project to relieve suffering eventually became an official prerogative of the humanitarian agency. In May 1950 Ruegger and Honorary President Huber again appealed to the IRO and other humanitarian organizations such as the 'Joint' organization in New

York to authorize care for non-recognized refugees and issue travel papers for them. The magnitude of the problem remained so enormous that something had to be done, and the ICRC felt it had to speak out publicly on behalf of the many displaced and stateless persons who remained in Europe: 'The International Committee considers itself obliged by its special position to devote particular attention to those cases in distress which, because of exceptional circumstances, are outside the scope of any other authority or organization.' The ICRC sought to make permanent its services in Europe and the Near East that 'provided refugees and stateless persons with travel documents which allow them, as they choose, to return to their countries, to emigrate', and to ask sovereign governments if they would grant the ICRC all facilities to care for refugees in cases where no other authority was recognized to do so.[98] The ICRC eventually succeeded, and the ad hoc travel papers introduced during Burckhardt's presidency were codified by international law in 1951. Under the terms of the International Refugee Convention of 1951, the ICRC in special cases was permitted to issue 'an emergency one-way travel document for humanitarian purposes, although foreign-country immigration officials are not obligated to recognize such documents'.[99] As a result, the papers survived for decades and are still being issued today by the ICRC and used in various crisis zones worldwide.[100]

The Drawbacks of Success: ICRC Travel Documents as Aid to Criminals and Collaborators

The aid agencies knew of the presence of many men who fought on the Axis powers side among the people stranded far from home. Nevertheless, the process of issuing travel papers was not able to, or in the case of the ICRC intended to, root out war criminals and collaborators. While the IRO responded to this challenge with intensive background checks verified with scattered authorities and lists of suspected war criminals maintained by the Allies and the UN, the humanitarians in Geneva adopted a much more generous approach: the Red Cross accepted any pretext and no background check was required. Although guidelines existed, the process was largely arbitrary and not overly exacting.[101] It should therefore come as little surprise that ICRC papers were soon in high demand amongst people with a problematic past.[102]

How were many Nazis able to escape postwar justice? One part of the answer lies in the choice by Red Cross officials to ignore information on ICRC applications that should have raised red flags. This lack of scrutiny is illustrated well by the case of Herbert Bauer, a prominent and highly decorated officer in the Nazi Luftwaffe during the Second World War. As a teenager Bauer had already become a fanatical Nazi, and his activities in the Hitler Youth repeatedly got him into trouble with the Austrian author-ities.[103] After the Nazi annexation of Austria in 1938, Bauer was ready to serve his Führer heart and soul, joining the Nazi Party as a 19-year-old.[104] In the autumn of 1944 Hitler decorated Bauer with the Iron Cross with Oak Leaves, one of the highest recognitions for a Nazi warrior.[105] Bauer would not disappoint the trust Hitler put in him and fought for his Führer until the end of the Third Reich. After the war, however, he was taken POW, eventually seeking to leave Europe behind and make a fresh start. With the help of local former SS officers, he crossed illegally into Italy in 1948 and applied for an ICRC travel document in Rome under his real name.[106] Bauer had been born in the Austrian town of Innsbruck as he correctly stated, but in order to prove his alleged statelessness, he gave Czechoslovakian as his original nationality on the application form. He may have been trying to pass himself off as a *Volksdeutscher* from the Sudetenland. Innsbruck is situated on the Italian–Austrian border and was nowhere near Czechoslovakia, a fact that the ICRC officials in Rome would certainly have known. The Vatican Commission for Refugees nevertheless confirmed Bauer's informa-tion. Bauer therefore had no problem emigrating to Argentina, where he joined a large circle of former Luftwaffe and Nazi comrades, all of whom had obtained ICRC documents.[107]

One of many other examples of the ICRC's failure to investigate further applicants whose information should have raised questions is that of Austrian SS *Hauptsturmführer* Hubert Karl Freisleben. In August 1947 Freisleben, born 1913 in Amstetten, Austria, completed an application for an ICRC travel document at the organization's delegation in Rome. He presented himself as a Sudeten German *Volksdeutscher* who was now stateless. Freisleben used his real name and birth date, even including the fact that he had been born in Austria. The 'chemist' wanted to emigrate to the Dominican Republic or South America with his wife Gertrude and their two children. He con-firmed his identity with a 'Viennese driving license with photograph' dated 5 August 1944. The Vatican Commission for Refugees in Rome supported his request with a letter of recommendation, but referred to him as a holder of German citizenship,[108] a contradiction that in and of itself should have raised eyebrows. In reality, Dr Freisleben had been a hardcore Nazi. After the annexation of Austria, the doctor had become leader of the national socialist student organization for Southern Germany ('Reichsführer Südost der Reichsstudentenführung') based in Vienna, and in February 1938 he had joined the SS. The SS *Hauptsturmführer* was not merely an opportunist, for he had joined the Nazi Party as early as 1932.[109] His reasons for emigration are unclear, perhaps he had to face denazification or the loss of his Austrian citizenship. In any case, he stated all his biographical data correctly, with one important exception: his Sudeten German background appears to have been completely invented. It would have been easy for IRO screening teams to check his background because they used the same files as this author to establish the background of applicants. But even without a thorough screening, the case should have raised suspicion. Why would somebody born in Lower Austria suddenly turn into a *Volksdeutscher* from Czechoslovakia? The ICRC should have rejected cases such as this one in which it was blatantly apparent that the applicant was an Austrian or German citizen and not stateless, but it did not. As an Austrian citizen and former SS and Nazi Party member, Freisleben was very likely not allowed to travel abroad at all. By not checking the background of applicants, the ICRC made illegal emigration easy.

The ICRC's failure to investigate questionable information on applications for travel documents helps to explain in part how wanted men were able to escape justice. Another part of the explanation lay in the ICRC's decision to use witnesses to establish an applicant's identity, a convenient but corruptible system. The first, less detailed ICRC travel papers were called 10.100 forms. To receive a 10.100 document, all one needed were two witnesses to confirm one's data. This made for a rapid turnover, but led to falsification on a large scale. Friendship and contacts were formed in POW camps, and people readily helped one another by confirming each other's real or false identities. Consequently, no limits to potential abuse existed. All in all, then, questionable evidence and a procedure that was vulnerable to manipulation characterized the issuing of the early *titres de voyage*.

The whole casual procedure of confirming identity with witnesses and issuing travel papers is illustrated clearly by the example of Austrian SS officer Hermann Duxneuner. Duxneuner was an engineer and had joined the SS in June 1937. He belonged to the hardcore Nazi leadership of western Austria and was in charge of 'de-judaization' there. On his 1939 CV he stated: 'After the [Nazi] takeover I joined the economic office, and I am in charge of the Aryanization of the Tyrol Gau.'[110] In other words, he was in charge of the systematic plundering and stealing of Jewish property in the region. SS *Unterscharführer* Duxneuner also provided lists of Jews to be assaulted and murdered during the 1938 November pogrom in the Austrian city of Innsbruck.[111] At the end of the war, he went into hiding in northern Italy. As early as December 1946, Duxneuner applied for a 10.100 travel document in order to emigrate to 'Holland or Brazil'. Duxneuner used his real name, described himself as a 'former Austrian' who was now stateless, and gave his profession as engineer. His stateless status was probably real, for he may indeed have lost his Austrian citizenship because of his Nazi past. Authorities of the postwar Austrian Republic often denied the re-admission to the country's citizenship to hardcore Nazis. This was particularly true for leaders of the illegal Nazi movement in Austria before the Anschluss in 1938. Many of them had fled Austria for Germany after an attempted Nazi putsch in 1934. These actions were seen as high treason by the Austrian government, and the citizenship of such Nazis was revoked and not automatically reinstated after 1945. Suspicions about the accuracy of his application would have been well founded, but in any case ICRC delegate Hans de Salis signed Duxneuner's papers personally. Duxneuner even presented a letter of recommendation from the Vatican to support his application for a 'passport of the International Red Cross'.[112] With his identity now firmly established and travel papers in his hands, Duxneuner could now vouch for others. While in the Fossoli di Carpi camp, a former Nazi concentration camp turned refugee and internment camp for stateless foreigners, Duxneuner appeared as one of three witnesses for a 10.100 travel document confirming the identity of a certain Kurt Baum, a former member of the elite SS *Leibstandarte* 'Adolf Hitler'. SS *Unterscharführer* Baum was from Danzig, a city that became part of postwar Poland. Like so many Nazis and SS officers, Baum and Duxneuner stated their names, birth places, and birth dates correctly, so it would have been easy to double check the background of these men. But the former SS officers had no screening or checks to fear. Thanks to Red Cross documents, Baum and Duxneuner could emigrate to Argentina.[113]

There are also many more prominent cases of Holocaust perpetrators such as Josef Mengele or Adolf Eichmann who managed to escape justice with Red Cross travel papers. On his Red Cross travel paper, Dr Josef Mengele, the former Nazi camp doctor of Auschwitz–Birkenau turned into a certain 'Helmut Gregor', a *Volksdeutscher* from Italy.[114] As the war ended Mengele was already wanted for atrocious crimes, especially his cruel experiments on twins. Like the other medical staff in Auschwitz, Mengele also performed 'selections' of prisoners on the ramp, determining who could be exploited for labour and who would be murdered immediately in the gas chambers.[115] At first he managed to hide among the millions of German prisoners of war and later he worked as a farmhand in Bavaria. Mengele's escape led him to Genoa, the Italian port town on the Mediterranean, where on 16 May 1949 he applied for a Red Cross travel document. Mengele declared he was 'stateless' and based his story on his alleged background as an ethnic German from northern Italy.[116] Mengele consequently managed to receive all the necessary papers to escape to South America. Josef Mengele, 'the angel of death of Auschwitz' and one of world's most wanted Nazi criminals, escaped earthly justice when he died in 1979 in the course of a bathing accident.

Like Mengele, Adolf Eichmann followed the so-called 'ratline' through the Alps to Genoa and South America and received assistance from local Nazis, Catholic clergy and the ICRC on the way. However, he did not ultimately succeed in eluding justice as Mengele did. Eichmann was an important organizer of the Holocaust. From his desk, the Nazi bureaucrat coordinated deportations, gathered statistics, and directed the implementation of systematic and centrally organized murder in millions of cases. At the war's end in May 1945, like Mengele, Eichmann, too, blended into the masses of German POWs in Allied custody and eventually lived under an assumed name in Germany. In 1950 he made it to Italy and applied for an ICRC travel document under the name of 'Ricardo Klement', born in 1913 in Bolzano. Eichmann reinvented himself as an ethnic German from Italy and was, therefore, considered 'stateless'. He finally embarked to Buenos Aires from Genoa. There he started a new life, but not without difficulties. He often switched jobs and lived in modest circumstances. In the meantime, he was wanted worldwide. Finally, in 1960 he was discovered living in Buenos Aires and was kidnapped and taken to Israel. The subsequent trial against him in Jerusalem drew worldwide attention and revived international interest in the Holocaust. It is surprising, however, that the question of how Eichmann managed to escape justice in the first place was hardly addressed at all during the trial.[117]

Ludolf von Alvensleben, Heinrich Himmler's adjutant and, as SS *Gruppenführer, Generalleutnant der Waffen SS and Police* the highest-ranking Nazi in Argentine exile, followed in Eichmann's footsteps as well. He had other reasons than just his high rank in the Nazi regime to escape overseas. He had been involved in major war crimes in Poland and the Crimea.[118] In

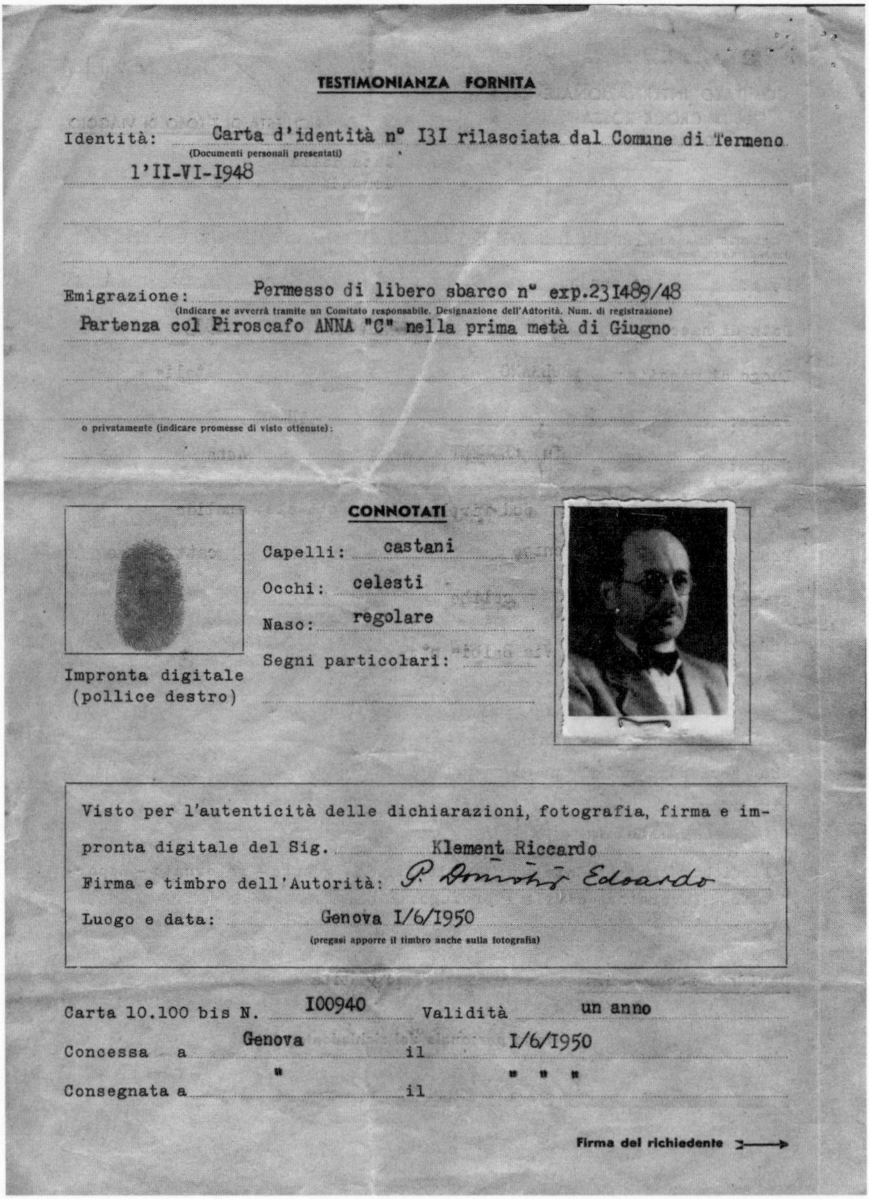

TESTIMONIANZA FORNITA

Identità: Carta d'identità n° I3I rilasciata dal Comune di Termeno
(Documenti personali presentati)
l'II-VI-I948

Emigrazione: Permesso di libero sbarco n° exp.23I489/48
(Indicare se avverrà tramite un Comitato responsabile. Designazione dell'Autorità. Num. di registrazione)
Partenza col Piroscafo ANNA "C" nella prima metà di Giugno

o privatamente (indicare promesse di visto ottenute):

CONNOTATI

Capelli: castani

Occhi: celesti

Naso: regolare

Segni particolari:

Impronta digitale (pollice destro)

Visto per l'autenticità delle dichiarazioni, fotografia, firma e impronta digitale del Sig. Klement Riccardo

Firma e timbro dell'Autorità: P. Domoter Edoardo

Luogo e data: Genova I/6/I950
(pregasi apporre il timbro anche sulla fotografia)

Carta 10.100 bis N. I00940 Validità un anno

Concessa a Genova il I/6/I950

Consegnata a " il " " "

Firma del richiedente →

Figure 7.2. Application of Holocaust perpetrator Adolf Eichmann alias Riccardo Klement for an ICRC travel document, 1950.

Poland alone his '*Volksdeutscher Selbstschutz*' unit killed an estimated 20,000 to 30,000 people, including Polish intellectuals, Catholic priests, Jews, and other civilians.[119] After the war, the Polish authorities sentenced him to death in absentia and he was wanted in West Germany.[120] He obviously had good reasons to evade justice. For his Red Cross papers, he, too, purported to be an ethnic German from Italy. In October 1949 he applied for an ICRC travel document in Genoa under the alias of 'Teodoro Kremhart'. As an ethnic German who had lost his citizenship, he could be technically considered stateless. Alvensleben spent some time in Italy playing hide and seek with the authorities before 'Teodoro Kremhart' managed to travel with his ICRC papers to Argentina, where he joined up with Eichmann. Alvensleben died in 1970 in South America without having been brought to trial.[121]

Tens of thousands of former SS members, Nazis, fascists, and their collaborators from all over Europe started a new life overseas after the war. Many of them used travel papers from the ICRC in order to emigrate.[122] According to the ICRC, more than 100,000 travel documents were issued between 1946 and 1950, most of these in Italy.[123] Exactly how many war criminals, Nazis, and their collaborators fled overseas with ICRC papers? It still remains difficult to pin down precise numbers, for much depends on the definitions of who committed crimes under national socialism and fascism. One must distinguish between (1) high-ranking Nazis and SS officers, (2) those who implemented and carried out war crimes and anti-Jewish measures, including mass murder, and (3) fascists and Nazi collaborators from all across Europe.[124]

The groundbreaking research of the Argentine journalist Uki Goñi, German historian Bettina Stangneth, and others has brought many details about the escape of Holocaust perpetrators, Nazis and fascists to Argentina to light.[125] Thus Argentina is currently the best documented destination for Nazi emigration. Through his research, Goñi counted approximately 300 Nazi perpetrators from all over Europe who came to Argentina.[126] Goñi argues that the actual numbers were likely much higher. Historian Volker Koop estimated in 2009 that 600 Nazis and military experts from Germany and Austria immigrated to Argentina alone.[127] According to the Commission of Historians in Argentina in 1999, some 180 prominent or seriously implicated Nazi officials and SS officers entered the country from Europe through Buenos Aires harbour on the Río de la Plata River alone. According to German scholar Holger Meding, the largest number of German-speaking immigrants came to

Argentina via Italy, approximately 30,000 by his estimate.[128] Meding estimates that between 300 and 800 high-level Nazis, including some 50 known war criminals and mass murderers, were among them.[129] They were joined in that country by thousands of collaborators and fascists from Italy, Hungary, Slovenia, Belgium, and especially Croatia. Their numbers include such prom- inent figures as Ante Pavelić, the former Croatian head of state. Some sources speak of at least 30,000 people, mostly Croatians, who were smuggled out through Italy and provided with ICRC papers. Many of them had a fascist past and belonged to the Ustaša, the Croatian fascist movement.[130]

In the emerging Cold War, the desire to flee now-communist homelands proved a powerful justification for church officials to assist many in securing ICRC travel documents. In her 2007 book *De Yalta à Dien Bien Phu*, the historian Catherine Rey-Schyrr concluded that about 90,000 ICRC travel papers were issued for DPs from all over Europe, among them many Holocaust survivors. Rey-Schyrr also points to the important role of Italy as a transit route and the ICRC delegations in Genoa and Rome.[131] Christiane Uhlig has discussed the travel papers of the ICRC in the context of the Swiss Independent Commission of Historians's volume on the Second World War (the final report was published in 2002). Uhlig refers to the issu- ing of 'travel papers to a number of Germans with a tainted past' and lists nine of the most prominent cases (including, of course, Mengele, Eichmann, and Gestapo-official Klaus Barbie).[132] Uhlig also points out that it is hardly a secret that a considerable number of Nazis emigrated to Argentina after the war. ICRC spokesmen repeatedly stated that Nazis used ICRC travel documents in only a few isolated cases.[133] This was certainly not the case. As German author Bernd Biege has suggested, the escape of Nazi criminals like Eichmann and Mengele with ICRC travel papers are just 'the tip of a (mostly unresearched) iceberg'.[134]

Argentina was hardly the only desirable destination for fugitives; Spain, countries in the Near East, or those in North and South America—includ- ing the United States and Canada—all appear to have been sought-after places to relocate. That is why some 9.000 Ukrainians from the former Waffen SS Division Galizien found their way through Italy to Great Britain and from there to Canadian shores, where they passed themselves off as agricultural settlers ready to work on Canada's vast farmlands. Thanks to the intervention of British and Vatican officials and the help of the ICRC, they managed to leave the past behind.[135] Approximately 90,000 Baltic Waffen SS soldiers and Nazi collaborators were in 1950 classified as 'freedom fighters against the Soviets' and allowed to emigrate to North America.[136] A clearer statistical picture concerning those who fled abroad with ICRC travel papers will only emerge when records have been thoroughly examined for all major countries that accepted new immigrants, not just Argentina. However, there can be no doubt that the numbers of SS members, fascists, Nazis, and Holocaust perpetrators from all over Europe who fled with ICRC travel documents is higher than is often assumed.[137]

The *titres de voyage* programme showed the ICRC's committment to the principle of neutral humanitarianism. It was also an easy and cheap way to provide some concrete aid for undocumented war victims, particularly the ones not cared for by Allied organizations. Problems with the papers could be foreseen, but this was a calculated risk and looking for war criminals was not the ICRC's agenda anyway. But eventually the criticism from various angles that this attracted became a burden—and financial support from London and Washington was crucial. Given its financial problems, the ICRC wanted to get out of the business of issuing travel papers rather sooner than later. But the Allies' reluctance to care for all nationalities and ethnic groups compelled it to go on doing so. At the same time, the ICRC urgently needed support. The ICRC's advocacy of reform to the Geneva Convention and the upgrading of the international protection of war victims for potential future conflicts turned out to be a successful strategy in this regard. This project found shared interest in Washington, London, and eventually even in Moscow. But the ICRC had to wait for a window of opportunity to open in order to put this agenda into practice.

8

A Window of Opportunity

The emergence of the United States and the Soviet Union as the world's superpowers had a profound effect on events in Europe as the war ended. At the same time, the still fluid conditions of these years presented unique opportunities for collaboration before these powers retreated into hostile, entrenched positions. US State Department officials, anticipating a major future conflict with the Soviets, chose to give reform of the Geneva Conventions strong backing. Their interests meshed well with the long-held aspirations of the International Committee of the Red Cross (ICRC) to improve the conventions' protection of prisoners of war (POWs) and to place civilians under their protection. A good working relationship between the State Department and the ICRC helped move the reform process forward, despite considerable obstacles. But given the weakened standing of the ICRC, it remained unclear which Red Cross organization was actually in charge of making the necessary preparations. The League of Red Cross Societies and the national Red Cross societies challenged the ICRC's leadership, and confusion and uncertainty ensued for a while. Various Red Cross conferences discussed reforming the Geneva Conventions before government experts met for the first time at a conference in Geneva in 1947.

The credibility of the ICRC as the institution leading the reform became critical, for without it a number of nations might not have taken part in the reform process or ratified its draft proposals. In fact, refusal by the Soviets to participate constituted a real danger, and many other countries involved in the process—including France and Sweden—questioned the ICRC's ability to persuade the Soviet Union to join in the initiative.

But would the State Department back the ICRC at any cost? US officials clearly feared that a full-blown scandal over ICRC-issued travel papers might erupt and derail the entire reform proposals. As luck would have it, just such a scandal erupted between the Geneva meeting of spring 1947 and the critical meeting in Stockholm later that year, a gathering where the shape of the future conventions would be finalized. Though the travel papers scandal was but one of many which affected the Red Cross family and its leadership, this particular scandal presented an especially serious threat to the very status and future viability of the ICRC and to securing support for the conventions. Soviet non-participation remained a central problem that had to be resolved. The conventions essentially had the status of international treaties, even if they were the initiative of a private philanthropic, non-state organization. They ultimately required the signatures of governments, not just philanthropic organisations, be they national or international. Formally Red Cross conferences were kept apart from the diplomatic meetings concerning the Conventions, but in both cases government experts were present. Trust and cooperation between Red Cross and government officials were thus critical, and the support of the United States for the humanitarian project would prove decisive.

Washington and Geneva

The US State Department had long taken a robust interest in the ICRC and at times even intervened in its activities. Career diplomat Albert E. Clattenburg, head of the Special Projects Division and chairman of the Prisoners of War Committee in the State Department, was an expert in the problems arising out of practical application of the Geneva Conventions. A Philadelphia native, Clattenburg (1906–1987) joined the foreign service after graduating from the University of Pennsylvania in 1928. During the war years he became assistant chief of the Special War Problems Division of the State Department, which entailed extensive policy work on refugee questions.[1] Many officials in the State Department at the time looked unfavourably upon bringing increased numbers of Europe's Jewish refugees into the United States. Clattenburg likewise showed little sympathy for the growing numbers of Jews seeking refuge abroad and failed to grasp the dangers confronting them in Nazi-occupied Europe. And he favoured post-war repatriation even of those who did make their way across the Atlantic. In a meeting with Jewish aid groups in September 1945 Clattenburg argued that German Jewish refugees already in the United States wanted to return to their former homeland, which—he asserted—was now free of antisemitism. This stance suggests that Clattenburg probably shared some of the prejudices and policies of the man who had been his boss, Assistant Secretary of State Samuel Miller Breckinridge Long. Breckinridge Long had long worked to keep prospective Jewish immigrants out of the United States and at times even undermined rescue efforts, until he retired in 1944.[2]

Clattenburg's career at the State Department continued after the war and in 1945 he was appointed assistant chief of the Special Projects Division. In that capacity, he became involved in the discussions about revising the Geneva Conventions from an early stage and continued to participate in policy discussions about them while serving as first secretary and consul in the US embassy in Lisbon from 1947. Clattenburg's superior by that stage, George C. Marshall, Secretary of State from 1947 to 1949, was deeply involved in Red Cross politics. A hero of the Second World War, General Marshall made his lasting mark on postwar history as father of the Marshall Plan for the recovery of Europe. After his tenure as Secretary of State in September 1949 he was appointed president of the American National Red Cross, succeeding Basil O'Connor.

Clattenburg and the State Department had been working closely with both the ICRC and the American Red Cross on expansion of the conventions. The

Figure 8.1. Washington, DC, May 1950: ICRC president Paul Ruegger and General George C. Marshall, American Red Cross president, discuss business.

government was willing to work with any international Red Cross body as long as results were achieved. American diplomats were now most troubled by the possible non-participation of the Soviets in the reform initiative and expended much energy to bring Moscow to the negotiating table. With the Cold War heating up, time seemed to be running out. Central to their efforts to make the Soviets a signatory to new Geneva treaties was the treatment of US soldiers in a future war, particularly one in which the United States and USSR had become adversaries. To achieve that goal, the State Department stood ready to intervene in what had essentially begun as a private, philanthropic initiative.

Outreach between State Department officials, including Clattenburg, and the Red Cross had in fact begun long before the end of the Second World War and was not limited to protecting POWs. By 1944 the State Department together with the Treasury Department's newly founded War Refugee Board had organized some limited humanitarian operations for Jews in Hungary and other Nazi-occupied territories in cooperation with Jewish agencies, the American Red Cross and the ICRC.[3] The ICRC even had a special delegation set up in Washington to maintain this bridge. Urgently interested in getting humanitarian aid to American POWs still in Japanese captivity, Clattenburg's men followed every move of the Swiss and Swedish humanitarians in the critical last months of the war. This included keeping close watch on the three-month-long travel odyssey undertaken to Tokyo by ICRC delegates Marcel Junod and Marcel Straehler; they finally arrived there in August 1945, just before the fighting in the Pacific ceased.

Harbouring far-reaching interests and multiple agendas, State Department officials found themselves engaged in postwar diplomacy on behalf of diverse partners in philanthropic circles. After the Soviet capture of Berlin in May 1945, for example, Geneva was cut off from the remaining group of Red Cross workers in the devastated German capital. Concerned about the welfare of its Berlin delegation, the ICRC asked the State Department to use its diplomatic channels to obtain news of the team. The Swiss-based organization preferred not to contact Moscow directly, for its relations with the Soviets had turned sour. As Clattenburg soon realized, the rapport between the ICRC and Switzerland on the one hand and the Soviet government on the other had reached an all-time low point when the war ended.[4] The close relationship between the State Department and the ICRC can be seen at other junctures as well. In September 1945 State Department officials wanted to express its thanks to Geneva for all it had done for

American POWs during the war in an official capacity, and considered organizing a US congressional resolution along these lines. Realizing that some members of Congress were extremely critical of the committee as well as of Switzerland, the Department ultimately opted for a more modest letter of thanks.[5] In the end US Secretary of State James Byrnes wrote Max Huber, extending 'warm personal thanks' for all the ICRC had done for American POWs, especially those in Europe.[6] This expression of gratitude concerned wartime feats, but the ICRC clearly aspired to play a major role in postwar relief as well. Max Huber knew the support of the US government was vital for the future status of the ICRC. In a letter to Byrnes, Huber declared that the Americans' support was the ICRC's 'most valuable asset and guarantee that the labours of the International Committee will be successful'.[7]

The State Department and Clattenburg's division ultimately played a crucial part in the revision of the prisoners of war convention and simultaneous adoption of the convention planned for protecting civilians in wartime. Reform of the Geneva Conventions had been on the ICRC's agenda for quite some time. Given the unsettled shape of post-1945 Europe the issue became even more pressing. This was a goal that Huber repeatedly stressed, as in 1944, when he stated that it was 'of particular importance' that the ICRC 'have the right and the real possibility' to initiate 'new international [humanitarian] law.'[8] The project was in part self-serving, for Huber and the ICRC leadership wanted the Committee to remain the most respected humanitarian organization in the postwar world. Remaining a key player through new initiatives would help secure that goal.

The State Department was first drawn into the reform process before the war ended, when it received a letter from Carl Burckhardt written on 15 February 1945. In the attached memorandum, the ICRC president informed governments that were signatories of the Geneva Conventions about the planned reforms. Max Huber followed up in September 1945 with a letter to these governments calling for a preliminary conference of government experts. The United States had a huge ongoing interest in the welfare of its POWs and its experiences in the Second World War confirmed its commitment to making the Geneva Conventions work. Clattenburg wrote about the timing of the reform efforts: 'The attached letter from Judge Huber suggests the desirability of assembling, while their experience is still fresh, representatives of the principal belligerent states who have dealt during the war with problems connected with prisoners of war and civilian internees for a discussion of possible revisions in the applicable Conventions.'[9] And the United States was clearly prepared to embrace this opportunity to strengthen international law. The State Department soon turned to the Navy, the Army, and the Departments of Justice and the Interior, as well as the American Red Cross, requesting that each party submit suggestions and recommendations regarding the conventions.

The problem of where to meet for the necessary conferences caused some headache. Clattenburg was at the time working closely with Basil O'Connor, chairman and president of the American Red Cross (AMRC). The State Department needed the AMRC for its expertise on POWs, but also needed the organization to act as its liaison to the League and the ICRC. From the start, O'Connor was not shy in voicing his opinions to American foreign policy officials on the matter. In a July 1945 message to the State Department, his ambitions for the League and the American Red Cross already seem obvious. He proposed that the next meeting of the League of Red Cross Societies should be held in the United States, not least because the League drew its chief financial support from the AMRC. He noted, however, that the Swiss were pushing for Geneva as the conference venue. O'Connor also made clear that the Soviets harboured little sympathy for the Swiss and the ICRC. 'I am informed', he told the State Department, that 'the Russians would prefer that meeting be held in the United States and will not attend if held in Geneva. If this is true and if that position were conveyed to [the] temporary Chairman of League the meeting might be assured in the United States. Communications should be entirely informal on this subject. Your assistance would be appreciated.'[10]

Geneva 1947: The Diplomats Meet

O'Connor lost this round. Although the board of governors of the League met in Oxford in 1946, Geneva remained the preferred meeting location for Red Cross business. The ICRC and Swiss government scheduled a preliminary conference of government experts for April 14 to 26, 1947, in Geneva. At this semi-official meeting, experts were to prepare revisions to the convention. There, government experts from interested countries should discuss the drafts, prepared mainly by the ICRC. State Department officials accepted the ICRC's invitation, but were troubled that the Soviets had declined to participate. Clattenburg announced that the preliminary meeting of government experts could take place without the Soviets, but he declared, 'Participation by the USSR in a formal revisionary conference would, of course, be essential. Likewise it would be essential that the USSR ratify any instruments resulting from such a conference.'[11]

Clattenburg was appointed head of the US delegation of seven, which consisted of officials from the War Department, Department of State and US Army, with one observer from the American Red Cross. Networking in informal meetings and dinners played an important part in such international gatherings, and in this the Geneva gathering would be no different. On the way to Switzerland, Clattenburg cabled to the State Department 'to facilitate entertainment problem can you arrange ship in our use one case each scotch, gin, bourbon, all out of bond'.[12] Sailing on the 'SS Marine Perch' the party left the United States at midnight on 28 March 1947. After eleven days at sea the delegation arrived safely and even earlier than planned in the port of Antwerp, but the trip from there to Geneva required much last-minute improvisation. Once in Geneva the American team learned that conference space was limited. The delegation was forced to set up its office headquarters in the hotel bedroom of Chairman Clattenburg, 'which was sufficiently large for the purpose, and such typing as could be done by the stenographer made available to the delegation on a part-time basis by the American Red Cross was done in that room'.[13] By day the assembly point in the 'Maison des Congrès', attached to the beautiful Palais Wilson, now a United Nations building, was much more impressive. Apart from the Americans, government experts from Great Britain and its Dominions, France, the Netherlands, South Africa, Poland, Czechoslovakia, Belgium, Norway, Australia, India, New Zealand, Canada, and Brazil all answered the ICRC's invitation. Meeting in one large conference room and two committee rooms at the Maison des Congrès over the next two weeks, they exchanged views and made recommendations concerning the treatment of POWs, enemy civilians, the sick and wounded and medical personnel.

The meeting in Geneva proved very productive, with the resulting materials and documents submitted weighing in at a total of 45 kilos (99 pounds). Once back home, Clattenburg prepared a detailed report for Secretary of State George C. Marshall, underlining the importance of the continuing negotiations.[14] Attached to his official letter, he sent Marshall a secret communication as well, for 'there were various aspects of the meeting in question which cannot suitably be discussed in an unclassified paper'.[15]

The secret attachment made clear how sharply fear of the Soviet Union was shaping the demands and discussions of the participants. The meeting proceeded with a focus on technical details, but a number of topics caused heated debate. One was the definition of conditions which would permit partisans to be protected as POWs. Countries formerly occupied by the Germans and their allies felt very strongly about including this provision. Clattenburg pointed out, 'Behind what they said openly one could sense the apprehension that a new occupation of their countries might occur at any time. This scarcely-concealed fear was as strong in the presumably Soviet-oriented delegations of Poland and Czechoslovakia as in the Netherlands, Norwegian and Belgian delegations and in the at least partly Communist-influenced French delegation.'

The anxiety plaguing the European delegations is reflected in their 'Insistence upon legislation to outlaw actions by any future occupying power which might even superficially resemble the actions of the Germans in attempting the crime of genocide.'[16] These fears certainly had some foundation, since countries such as Czechoslovakia were still fending off Soviet influence in April 1947. A year later the communists would seize total power in Prague. Clattenburg pointed to the very charged atmosphere created by the use of hostile political labels, such as when Polish diplomats accused the ICRC of having joined forces with fascism. A resolution by the Polish delegation condemning war was defeated by Western bloc countries, because it clearly contained less than neutral terms and was seen as a propaganda move by the communist bloc. This tension notwithstanding, the Polish and Czechoslovak delegates expressed their belief that the Soviets would participate in the Stockholm Red Cross conference scheduled for the following year.[17]

The Soviets and Yugoslavs continued to mistrust the ICRC—and with good reason—suspicious that the Swiss organization was aiding quislings from Yugoslavia residing in Italy. The puzzle of how to bring the Soviets to the table preoccupied Clattenburg, who concluded, 'No delegation or delegate was willing to envisage the possibility that the Soviet Union would finally refuse to come into a conventional system for the protection of war victims. All knew that no such system would have any value without Soviet participation. How to obtain that participation was a question most often discussed in private conversations among delegates.'[18] Clattenburg regarded the ICRC as conservative and traditional and cast some doubt on whether it would be able to resolve the dilemma.[19]

Bringing the Soviets to the Table

The importance of securing Soviet participation and the Soviets' absence at the 1947 preliminary meeting made the question of which agency should lead the reform movement critical and fueled Swedish aspirations to claim a larger international role. In his more confidential communication to George C. Marshall, Clattenburg reported that some delegates were 'unwilling to accept the ICRC as a trusted neutral agency in its traditional field' and, as a consequence, the delegates had fallen back on the rather vague expression 'the competent international organization'. Clattenburg thus concluded, '[And so] it was clear enough that a new agency had to be formed which would not embody the same objections or pretexts.'[20] This was a delicate turning point, for the ICRC and the Swiss were hosting the conference. For all its efforts, the ICRC's future looked no brighter during and immediately after the diplomatic conference it organized in April 1947. Nevertheless, the participants never reached a real agreement about the identity and character of a new agency that might oversee the launching of the new conventions. The tensions in Geneva intimated by Clattenburg came out into the open when plans for the next meeting emerged.

The next meeting of the International Red Cross was scheduled for August 1948 in Stockholm. Apart from the location and date of the conference, much remained in dispute, including the question of when and where the official signing of the treaties by government representatives should take place—the final step in this whole process prior to ratification. While the Swiss and the ICRC pushed for Geneva, other nations wanted to avoid that option. Spurred on by the Soviet boycott of the Swiss, behind the scene negotiations went on and coalitions were formed. After Geneva, some participants plotted to have an additional preliminary meeting in Paris so that a Soviet presence would be more likely. These included the French Foreign Ministry, Basil O'Connor, Count Bernadotte of the Swedish Red Cross, and the Belgian Red Cross president Pierre Depage.[21] Bernadotte agreed to this plan because the official signing ceremony could then still take place in Stockholm. The Americans were amenable to the proposals, although they were also well aware of the fact that with such a move the historical role of Switzerland in the arena of humanitarian law would be undermined.[22] Bernadotte must have rejoiced, for the Geneva Conventions might soon be called Stockholm Conventions. But for the Swiss and the ICRC these

developments must have been alarming. The Swiss were also busy counteract-
ing Swedish efforts and reached out to the State Department with an alternative idea. During a diplomatic conference in Geneva they proposed that the
Dutch should lead in law of war and neutrality, while the Swiss delegation
would deal with Red Cross matters. The Swiss embassy enquired if under this
format the US government would 'approve the calling in Geneva of a diplomatic conference to confirm and adopt the texts of the new conventions'.[23]

For the Americans, however, Soviet attendance had priority. If this could be
arranged in Sweden, then Washington would go ahead with that location.
O'Connor advised the State Department not to follow the recommendation
adopted by government experts to call together a formal diplomatic conference before April 30, 1948. While government experts argued that the drafts
had already been considered in detail and nothing would be gained for wait-
ing until after Stockholm, O'Connor disagreed. Basil O'Connor told Secretary
of State George C. Marshall that the formal meeting of the diplomats should
be held after Stockholm to give the experts more time to finalize the drafts.[24]
O'Connor and his American Red Cross were also very much in favour of
keeping the Red Cross family gathering in Stockholm separate from the diplomatic conference.[25] The State Department eventually followed O'Connor's
advice. Clattenburg too fell in line with O'Connor and argued that there
would not be enough time to prepare the drafts and bring the Soviets on
board before April 1948. The US government nonetheless hoped that *some
government* would send out an invitation for a conference to sign the
Conventions sooner rather than later. By 'some government', the Americans
probably had France and Sweden in mind rather than Switzerland.[26]

The British Foreign Office and the State Department debated how best
to proceed at Stockholm. The United States wanted full British participation in the Stockholm conference. State Department officials argued that a
strong western presence would be necessary to fight off Soviet scheming. To
the Americans' disappointment, the British eventually decided not to send
an official delegation to Stockholm, but rather be present with observers
only. From the US point of view this would weaken the western bloc and
therefore only play into communist hands. The State Department also made
clear to the Foreign Office in London that the ICRC would play a prominent role in Stockholm, not least through its crucial work in preparing the
draft conventions now used as working papers for Stockholm.[27] The Foreign
Office was more hesitant to grant the ICRC a prominent role in the process,
preferring to have seen a strong Swiss government lead. As US embassy

officials in London explained, 'It is understood that the principal reason why the Foreign Office desires to have a clear delineation between the governmental discussions and the Red Cross Conference is that they anticipate an attempt by iron curtain Red Cross Societies to turn the Conference into a political sounding board by the introduction of propaganda type resolutions'.[28]

The Foreign Office therefore sought to separate a prospective diplomatic meeting from the main International Red Cross Conference. Whitehall had always seen the ICRC and Red Cross societies as merely private humanitarian organizations, not suited for taking on functions claimed by sovereign governments. The British therefore would not accept invitations sent out from national Red Cross societies such as the Swedish Red Cross to expand intergovernmental treaties.[29]

The Swedish humanitarians also shifted their position during these months of planning. As time passed Bernadotte watered down his critique of the Swiss humanitarians and by 1948 he stated that he had never intended to dissolve the existing international committee. His plan now was to strengthen the ICRC with representatives from other nations, which in case of war could be replaced by some representatives from neutral countries.[30] Even if this was in fact the case, other nations and personalities wanted to keep all their options open. Questions about the future of the ICRC therefore remained on the table.

Distractions from Reform

Even as the international diplomatic community moved closer to supporting reform of the conventions, external events threatened to derail the process. On 24 June 1947, Max Huber, former and honorary president of ICRC, wrote to Clattenburg thanking him 'for the most valuable and efficient help afforded during the Geneva meeting by yourself and by the United States Delegation'.[31] Preparations for the meeting of the Red Cross organizations in Stockholm were taking shape and the related diplomatic conference (at which the final formalities would be dealt with) was planned for soon afterwards, Huber informed him. The efforts of Clattenburg and many others were seemingly paying off, although Soviet participation still remained uncertain. But other issues now began to trouble Clattenburg. A few days earlier, a top secret report from Rome had come to his attention with the potential for undermining the efforts to reform the conventions. The papers referred to a number of top-secret reports from US military intelligence and the State Department. On January 20, 1947, the US consul in Vienna, Laurence C. Frank, had written a dispatch to the Secretary of State. Frank's communication focused on 'the indiscriminate issue and use of identity documents of the International Red Cross, to which the Department will wish to give attention particularly as the practice lends itself to possible subversive activity in connection with immigration to other American Republics'.[32]

Attached to Consul Frank's cover letter was a summary dated 16 December 1946, and produced by the G-2 counterintelligence branch of the US Army. It stated bluntly, 'It is possible for any person desiring an identity document to secure an International Red Cross Identity Document thru the assistance of persons operating under the protection of the Vatican. These documents can be secured without any investigation on part of International Red Cross'. Alarmingly, the missive pronounced, 'These documents may be obtained under an alias or with false nationality. Information stated in effect that reports had been received where known or wanted war criminals had reached Italy illegally and applied and received these documents under assumed names and have to date successfully evaded apprehension.'[33]

This document shows that as early as December 1946 US military intelligence and the State Department were well informed about the ICRC's role in facilitating the escape of suspected war criminals from Europe. This was only months after the first Nazi perpetrators succeeded in fleeing justice with the help of Catholic institutions and Red Cross travel papers via Italy. In April 1947 the US consulate in Vienna forwarded this 'summary of information' to the US embassy in Rome as well.[34] Here US diplomats had already started their own investigation. In charge of mapping these underground networks was Vincent La Vista, a young official at the American embassy in the city. His top-secret report on illegal emigration in and through Italy, dated 15 May 1947, documented in detail the role of the ICRC delegations in Rome and Genoa, which in cooperation with Catholic officials had facilitated the escape of wanted men. La Vista demonstrated how easy it was for unscrupulous people—among them war criminals and Nazi collaborators—to obtain Red Cross travel papers, and his report listed many individual cases, including names and the institutions involved. The American official made very clear that not only many legitimate refugees, but also Nazis and SS men on the run, had entered Italy illegally just to obtain travel papers from the ICRC before quickly leaving Europe from Italian ports. With this very detailed information to hand, it should have been easy to stop this underground network 'of known or wanted war criminals' in its tracks. Reports containing La Vista's findings were in fact sent to the US legations in Buenos Aires, Vienna, and Rome.

The recommendations offered up in the report were unambiguous: 'This agent recommends that the investigation of the various cases mentioned here be continued, and that all control points be informed of these events. The undersigned official further recommends that the Red Cross passport service be entirely suspended, and that a unified procedure against illegal emigration organisations be considered. It is also advised that Allied Supreme Command reach an agreement with the Italian authorities about the treatment of dangerous refugees'.[35] La Vista's report initially caused great concern in Washington. American officials confronted the Red Cross in Geneva and Vatican officials with the allegations detailed by La Vista and others.[36] State Department discussions about how to respond continued into June.

When Clattenburg found the facts of the La Vista report on his desk, he was just coming back from the April 1947 conference of international government experts in Geneva that had discussed reforming the Geneva Conventions. He had invested much time and energy in this project and was not eager to see these efforts sabotaged. In response to this threat, Clattenburg wrote a memorandum on 20 June 1947, to a fellow official. He declared:

> As you know, I have spent a good part of the last year working toward a revision of conventions affecting prisoners of war and the establishment of conventions protecting civilians in wartime. The leading organisation in this field upon which the governments depend is the International Red Cross Committee. The enclosure to your memorandum of June 19 indicates that with or without the knowledge of the International Red Cross, activities are being conducted in Italy with the full knowledge of all protagonists in the international political struggle which can only serve to undermine the position of the International Red Cross unless immediately terminated or denounced.

He proceeded to recommend that the American ambassador in Bern talk to the leaders of the ICRC and address this serious issue. It was of 'paramount importance' to keep the Status of the International Red Cross 'preserved and protected', Clattenburg insisted.[37]

During the preliminary meeting about reform of the conventions in April 1947 and in his August 1947 memorandum about it to George C. Marshall, Clattenburg in fact remained sceptical about whether the ICRC could have a reputable future, although he continued his work without taking clear sides. By the autumn of 1947, however, he appears to have increasingly sided with the Swiss-based organization. He now began to argue that it was the agency most competent to promote and supervise enforcement of the Geneva Conventions. Yet he knew that at this difficult juncture in the negotiations, especially with the verbal attacks issuing from the Soviets, it was wise to avoid additional trouble. The Soviets would have exploited the information in the La Vista report, which might have resulted in a further discrediting of the ICRC, even its removal from the reform process. In 1947 the relationship between the Soviet Union and Switzerland appeared to be improving, but remained far from good. The Soviets may not have backed out of the treaty, but might have insisted that a different competent organization take over. Ultimately Clattenburg's main concern, however, became to protect the ICRC's reputation and status. His hopes now rested with the next conference, scheduled for Stockholm in August 1948.[38] But these hopes could easily be shattered.

The absence of a Yugoslavian delegation in Sweden in fact also threatened to undermine reform of the conventions. A month before receiving La Vista's information, John Cabot, US envoy to the Yugoslav capital Belgrade, informed Clattenburg in a confidential letter that he had spoken with the Assistant Minister of Foreign Affairs of Yugoslavia. This high-ranking insider had told him that the Yugoslav government's refusal to participate in Geneva's discussion of reform to POW and civilian conventions stemmed from the issue of Yugoslavian Nazis taking refuge in Italy. Cabot reported, 'For your private information, it appears that we have not behaved well in this matter and after 19 months we are only now carrying out commitments we promised to execute without delay. I do not know exactly where the connection would arise, but if this is really the reason for Yugoslav attitude it may well be a justified one'. Cabot's handwritten note on the letter reads: 'P.S. I am not reporting anything on this officially, so will not write anything to SPD [Special Projects Division]'.[39] The ambassador and Clattenburg soon learned in detail about the role of the western powers, but also the Vatican and the ICRC in Italy, in helping Nazi collaborators. Equally, the Yugoslav critique of the ICRC might also have had to do with the Swiss-based organization's reports on appalling conditions in Yugoslav prison camps for 'enemies of the state'.[40] Tangled motives and allegations added to the complexity of the issue, further threatening the viability of the reform process. Newspaper reports in the spring of 1947 about SS criminals fleeing with Red Cross papers called for urgency.

Unsurprisingly, the ICRC leadership had already gathered back in March 1947 to discuss potential trouble over the papers. Among others, Interim President Huber and Vice Presidents Ernest Gloor and Martin Bodmer were present. Indeed, while ICRC officials enjoyed the silence of some powers, a storm could have erupted if these allegations were given credence in diplomatic circles. In the end, the ICRC chose to refrain from issuing a public response in the spring of 1947, as State Department officials were beginning to understand the contours of the problem.[41] ICRC headquarters did at this juncture make various attempts to address the shortcomings of its procedures and documents. Some Committee members seemed genuinely very committed to turning the corner on these abuses. The Swiss police authorities saw plenty of reason to be concerned as well.[42]

Protecting the Protectors

The mounting evidence of abuse of the system set up to assist legitimate refugees demanded a response from the US government. Not just Clattenburg, but also the US ambassador to Bern, Leland Harrison, had a special interest in ICRC matters and wanted any official response to reflect this. Harrison asked for guidance in a memo to Washington: 'To what extent, if any, may I make available to them [the ICRC] in strict confidence information contained enclosures to subject instruction?'[43] As the State Department memorandum in response indicates, the ICRC was not to be publicly confronted with these allegations, just as in the case of the Vatican; rather, secret, discreet diplomacy would address and deal with the issue. By the summer of 1947 the State Department no longer seemed much troubled by war criminals escaping justice. On July 11, 1947, the Secretary of State wrote Ambassador Harrison a four-page letter classified top secret, which made the US position clear. In it Harrison was ordered to call Huber, Roger Gallopin, Martin Bodmer, and other relevant ICRC officials to a confidential meeting as soon as possible. The report of the State Department stressed that the United States had detailed information about ICRC offices in Italy engaging in 'the political function of issuing passports or other travel documents to alleged refugees, a field in which there is competent international organization, namely the International Refugee Organization, and its predecessors'.

These activities went against the oft-declared claim of the ICRC that it did not engage in political activity and did not serve as a 'protecting power'. In addition, the issuing of these papers had been done in an extremely lax manner. Documents could easily be altered and there was no guarantee that the person was in fact the person claiming to be a stateless refugee in need. Many criminal elements, spies, and other problematic figures were therefore coming into possession of ICRC travel papers. The United States was grateful for the humanitarian work done by the ICRC, but the US government urgently requested that the ICRC put an end to its practices in Italy and discharge and punish the people who might have abused their position in the ICRC.

The State Department made clear its interest in continuing to work for a new Geneva Convention and the importance of the ICRC in this endeavour. The travel papers scandal had become an open threat to these efforts. If the ICRC was the main force behind a new convention, its moral standing and international reputation needed to remain above reproach, not 'arouse suspicion and distrust'.[44] It had placed the US government in a bind and Washington officials thus called for 'immediate and drastic' damage control. Ambassador Harrison in Bern was also provided with a copy of the La Vista report, which gave him a clear picture of the widespread and massive abuse of ICRC travel documents by criminal elements, including fascists and war criminals.

The letter from George C. Marshall's office, Secretary of State since January 1947, to Leland Harrison reveals that ICRC officials were acting as a 'protecting power' by shielding 'persons of interest' from justice. Acting counter to Allied policies, these officials were suspected of shielding former Nazis and war criminals from extradition, repatriation and prosecution.[45] These activities of the ICRC were undermining Allied denazification efforts, even though meting out justice to Nazis was not a central preoccupation of American diplomats at this juncture. An indication of this relative lack of interest in prosecuting Nazi criminals at this time was the memorandum sent to Washington from the State Department legation in Vienna in August 1947. It reveals that the La Vista report had gained widespread attention in US diplomatic circles, but that war criminals and Nazis on the run no longer held particular interest. It was 'illegal Jewish emigration' that was now causing disquiet among many American (and especially British) diplomats.[46]

For American officials in Europe, Cold War considerations had clearly begun overshadowing all questions of postwar justice. Yet some US diplomats remained hopeful that the Swiss humanitarians truly intended to remedy the abuse of the travel papers. Even before meeting with the ICRC leadership for the first time, Harrison asked his Washington superiors for permission to share the information in the La Vista report with the organization. This would enable the ICRC to initiate proper investigations, he argued.[47] US embassy officials in Rome suggested how Harrison should proceed: 'original Lavista illegal emigration report dated May 15, 1947. Suggest you use this as typical case without disclosing name of individual or organization since precisely same procedure followed by all organizations here in obtaining Red Cross identity documents for persons they sponsor'.[48]

Harrison followed the instructions from Washington 'to meet in strict confidence' with the leadership of the ICRC and did so on August 26.[49] On 12 September 1947 Harrison reported to the Secretary of State in Washington about his meeting at ICRC headquarters in Geneva with Honorary President Max Huber, Vice President Dr Ernst Gloor and Director-Delegate Dr Roger Gallopin. Vice President Martin Bodmer was unable to attend, and ICRC president Burckhardt was missing as well. It is quite likely, however, that the absent Burckhardt was very well-informed about the outcome of the meeting and the issues discussed. Nominally Burckhardt was still the ICRC president, even with his presidency essentially lying dormant while he served as Swiss ambassador in Paris. Harrison made clear that the ICRC officials had shown concern and his impression was right on. Harrison's talk with the ICRC officials certainly had an impact. The day after his meeting with Harrison, on 27 August Gallopin met with the ICRC delegation chief in Rome, Hans W. de Salis. De Salis was certainly the person to talk to, because most of the travel papers were issued in Italy. De Salis was very much concerned with the fate of accused and convicted Nazi war criminals and was interested in legal strategies for their defence. He visited former Wehrmacht or SS members in POW camps and Italian camps for interned civilians. He arranged ICRC food parcels for the benefit of the accused and forwarded letters to their loved ones. After the American intervention, Gallopin now confronted de Salis with the American accusations concerning the issue of 'ICRC travel papers for "war criminals"', as the correspondence reveals. De Salis followed up the meeting with a report sharing his views on these matters with Gallopin.[50] Director-Delegate Gallopin included this information from Rome, when he sent Harrison a written report the following week. The report contended that the ICRC had issued the travel documents at the request of the Intergovernmental Committee for Refugees as well as the Italian government. He indicated the organization's willingness to investigate the lax oversight of the programme and to terminate it entirely.[51] Like Clattenburg of the State Department, Harrison was also involved in securing reform of the Geneva Conventions, and thus needed to bring the Swiss organization into line and cut short any further scandals from that quarter. The ambassador in fact went on to lead the US delegation of twenty to the Geneva meeting of 1949.[52]

Gallopin only touched upon the problem with his organization's travel documents in his response, promising further investigation. Shying away from the Americans' central concern, he limited himself mainly to discussing the abuse of ICRC death certificates issued for deceased POWs.[53] Obviously Gallopin seemed more concerned about the fact that death certificates were issued in Italy in the name of the ICRC, but without its permission. Gallopin also attached a memorandum to his letter that detailed the history of ICRC travel papers. The first *titres de voyages* were issued in February 1945, a product of immediate postwar emergencies. Gallopin stressed that these travel documents were neither identity documents nor passports, and that the information stated in them was based solely on statements made by the bearer of the document. Striking a conciliatory note, Gallopin added: 'The ICRC considered that this activity was justified by the necessity to assist war victims deprived of diplomatic or consular protection, but it is naturally determined to suspend it as soon as an official organisation, duly empowered, will be in a position to take over'.[54] Gallopin nevertheless continued to argue for the necessity and legitimacy of the travel papers.

State Department officials were not completely satisfied with the ICRC's response, for they demanded more concrete action. They may have felt that the ICRC had downplayed the extent of the abuse too much. A few weeks later, in September 1947, probably as an outcome of the meeting in August, State Department officials in Washington asked La Vista, at the US embassy in Rome, to prepare abstracts of his report and get in touch with Harrison; La Vista was given the discretion to determine how much information could be shared without damaging his sources.[55] In October US officials held another meeting with Gallopin at ICRC headquarters in Geneva 'regarding the lax issuance and misuse of ICRC travel documents'. The

American passed on details of typical cases mentioned in the La Vista report and pointed out the features of the ICRC passport that could be easily altered. 'Mr. Gallopin expressed his gratitude for this information', they reported.[56] Gallopin in turn told the US officials of his own visit to Rome, the inquiries he had made personally 'and as a result could now state that a new procedure has been drawn up for processing applications for ICRC passports, which it is believed will minimize the possibility of the misuse which had been described'.

Relaying the substance of the meeting to the Secretary of State, Harrison reported that the IRO in Rome and the Italian Red Cross intended to continue issuing ICRC travel documents. However, 'on January 1, 1948, or as soon thereafter as is practicable, the Italian Government would assume responsibility for the issuance of all travel documents on behalf of the refugees. Until this takes place the Italian Government had requested the ICRC to continue this function as heretofore.'[57] If this seemed to be a weak concession, the State Department concluded: 'Under the new procedure the Office of the International Refugee Organization at Rome and the Italian Red Cross, effective October 15, 1947, will assume the responsibility for accepting and making proper examination of each application and will certify all applications which they approve and transmit them to the ICRC delegate at Rome for action'. Promised, too, were additional steps to eliminate the forging of seals on the documents and to reduce the ease with which photographs could be taken out of them and replaced.[58]

This notwithstanding, more bad news about the ICRC travel papers continued to reach Clattenburg from Italy in 1948. George L. Brandt in the US consulate in Naples was one of Clattenburg's close associates and always kept his friend apprised of the latest news. He had asked Brandt, a career diplomat, for suggestions on revising the conventions, for immigration and visa questions were his specialities. In 1938 Brandt had been advisor to the US delegation at the Évian Conference in France, which addressed emigration possibilities for Austrian and German Jews and resulted, among other things, in the creation of the largely ineffectual Intergovernmental Committee on Refugees (IGCR). He wrote that the Geneva Conventions were 'close to my heart as one of real need for the sake of humanity'.[59] Like Clattenburg, Brandt was worried that something would sabotage their progress. In early 1948 Brandt forwarded a report to Clattenburg's Special Projects Division, addressing once again the problem of identity cards issued by the international Red Cross: Italian nationals with fake papers were attempting to travel from Italy to Venezuela with 'identity cards issued by the Comité International de la Croix-Rouge, Via Gregoriana 28, Rome, Italy'.[60] Brandt also attached some Italian newspaper accounts, from *Il Risorgimento* and *Il Giornale*, about alleged refugees who had been arrested at the port in Naples. Many of these purported foreign stateless refugees spoke Italian with a Roman accent and therefore were likely not foreign refugees at all. Reporters had found it strange that the Italian police authorities supervising embarkations to Peru and Venezuela would not notice. Local police officials informed police headquarters in Rome that the departing refugees carried 'passports' issued by the International Red Cross Committee. In some of these cases the ICRC representative appears to have been lax about verifying that applicants were indeed refugees using their real names and with nowhere to go. In other cases, somebody from the ICRC, it was suggested, had outright colluded in producing travel papers for people on the run from justice and using false names.[61] While many cases passed unnoticed, the media was clearly catching on to the problem with increasing frequency.

If the new procedures promised by the IRO in Rome and the Italian Red Cross had been borne of good intentions, the situation in the field remained lax and the implementation of these measures dragged on while the abuses continued. Accounts of the well-structured escape routes for Nazis continued to trickle in. The American consulate in Bremen sent in one such report in early 1949, titled 'Recrudescence of Secret Activities of German Rightist Groups; Underground Route Established by Them via Tirol and Italy to Argentine; Encouragement Given Them by Peron Government'. His informant was the German insider Paul Schmidt, who had worked as chief of the press department of the German Foreign Office under Ribbentrop and Hitler. Even at this late date, the consul concluded that 'a well-established and well-marked route exists, which is enabling many persons illegally to leave not only Germany, but countries of Southeastern Europe as well, for Argentina where they are stated to be welcomed by the Peron government'.[62] Many of Hitler's former followers and SS men as well as former Croatian fascists, French Nazi collaborators, and anti-communists from Eastern Europe—were still making use of these escape structures. And Argentine officials in Switzerland and in the Italian port town of Genoa were helping former Nazis and SS officers. 'The Argentine Embassy in Rome is widely known in SS circles in Germany and Austria as their friend and protector', the consul informed the Secretary of State.[63]

Bowing to pressure from the US State Department, Italy, the ICRC in Geneva, and other concerned powers, tried to find a solution to these ongoing abuses and retreat from the whole travel papers business.[64] In reality, a clear-cut solution would remain elusive.[65] Although the abuse in its Rome and Genoa delegation was well known, the ICRC never ordered a thorough investigation, or so it seems. Despite the problems with the Italian delegations, especially Genoa, there was—at least so far as we know to date— never an internal investigation into the responsible delegates at the ICRC.[66] This is quite surprising, given the massive very concrete and detailed allegations, the pressure of governments and the danger for the organization's reputation. In any case, it seems that Burckhardt and the delegate in Rome, Hans Wolf de Salis were not overly concerned about allegations against the ICRC and felt that the travel papers service should continue.[67] As a result, they continued to be issued in one form or the other until the stream of non-recognized refugees finally abated in the early 1950s.[68] The Independent Swiss Commission of Historians on Switzerland in the Second World War (Bergier Commission) has concluded that the agency actually anticipated the potential abuse. The intention of the ICRC 'was to enable stranded and other people in need to travel overseas. This should be achieved with minimum administrative effort for the ICRC. The ICRC therefore took into account that a considerable space for abuse would unfold.'[69]

In 1947 Vincent La Vista and others had given the institutions and governments involved in rebuilding western Europe plenty of material to stop the escape of Nazis and their collaborators through Italy. The images of the liberation of concentration camps and the reports of the Nuremberg trials against major war criminals were still fresh memories. The La Vista findings could have very easily caused some diplomatic and media storm against the Vatican and ICRC. The consequences of such damage to the ICRC's reputation in the midst of an institutional and financial crisis remain difficult to determine. However, La Vista's findings were scarcely news to the ICRC. It knew already from media reports and internal memos at the beginning of 1947 about the use of travel papers by former SS men and other war criminals. The actual and alleged failings of the ICRC concerning Nazis and their collaborators was a time bomb which the US State Department sought to diffuse, with uncertain results, even as new crises appeared on the horizon.[70] The Cold War and other issues like the reform of the Geneva Conventions increasingly took precedence as time went by.

9

Towards the Geneva Conventions

The US government had a strong interest in the project of a new Geneva Convention, but did not have any interest in participating in the quarrels and jealousies between the various national Red Cross societies and the ICRC. Against this backdrop, Clattenburg and other US officials focused their energies on bringing the Soviets to the negotiating table: Soviet participation had still not been secured and the clock was ticking. Meanwhile, Swiss government officials and the ICRC coordinated their efforts to woo Washington and gain support for their agenda, the defence of the ICRC's traditional role. The fear that the centre of the Red Cross could move to Stockholm for good loomed large in Swiss concerns. As a result, the Swiss organization put out feelers to Washington, trying to curry strategic support in high quarters for its postwar prestige and survival. All the players were well aware that the Red Cross conference scheduled for August 1948 in Stockholm would be very important. No one could have predicted whether the ICRC would be able to defend its position against its challengers and, even more importantly, most of the participants could not have foreseen whether the Soviets would attend and show a willingness to cooperate. Would it be possible to prepare the ground for the subsequent conference of the diplomatic community, at which government representatives could sign the new humanitarian law on warfare? Or would rising Cold War tensions prove all efforts futile? US diplomats and Clattenburg threw their full energies into paving the way for the conference and a more expansive set of Geneva Conventions. This chapter traces the obstacle-strewn path that lay before them and the ICRC in pursuing these goals.

Preparations for Stockholm

The State Department received Bernadotte's invitation for the Stockholm Conference in July 1947. Bernadotte made clear to the invited governments that the discussion of the proposed conventions would be the principal work at Stockholm, not the particularities of the Red Cross movement.[1] Clattenburg addressed the question of why international laws for enforcing humanitarian measures were worth pursuing in an August 1947 letter. 'The nations must set a practicable standard of humanity and morality on these points', he wrote to the Secretary of State, 'or risk allowing acts committed in the past war to receive the sanction of precedent. (The Nuremberg Statute and decisions are far from making a clean sweep in this field)'.[2] Cold War considerations shadowed these conclusions, and the accuracy of his shrewd assessment of the situation soon became evident. A conflict with the Soviets seemed inevitable, yet Clattenburg wanted to ensure that in a new war international law would offer some protection to American soldiers and, therefore, potential POWs.

Clattenburg's division began strategizing for a range of likely scenarios in Stockholm, in part in close cooperation with American Red Cross officials. Unsurprisingly, the hostility to the ICRC demonstrated by Soviet-aligned countries again took centre stage.[3] An additional worry for the State Department was the participation of Spain in the Stockholm proceedings. It was no secret that the Soviets strongly objected to the presence of a Red Cross delegation from General Franco's fascist government, which had been in power in Spain since 1939. Inquiries by US diplomats soon revealed that the Spanish definitely planned to attend, 'despite certain maneuvers by Poland and others to keep the Spanish out'. Bernadotte feared the fall-out and was rumoured to have worked behind the scenes to overcome the communist bloc's opposition to Spain at the conference.[4] Meanwhile, the ICRC also made efforts to bring the Soviets to the table and repeatedly reached out to Moscow. As international legal scholar and diplomat Maurice Bourquin declared in January 1948, 'The increasing opposition between the Soviet and Western systems is making its paralyzing effects felt on all hands. Even the Red Cross, despite its purely humanitarian aims, cannot hope to escape these effects'. And he warned, 'A Convention to which the great majority of the States subscribe, but whose limitations are emphasised by certain absences, thus reflecting the rivalries of the present political scene, would be a most imperfect instrument'.[5] Ruegger was only too aware of this problem. In a March 1948 telegram to 'Generalissimo Stalin', Ruegger proposed a delegation to Moscow to discuss Soviet cooperation with Red Cross work.[6] But these attempts proved futile and the trip did not take place.

In July 1948 the US government approved a carefully selected delegation of fourteen people for Stockholm, mostly representatives of three of the military branches (the air force, navy and army), and State Department officials including Clattenburg. The American Red Cross sent its own delegation of twelve. O'Connor headed the Red Cross delegation and at the same time served as head of the 'United States Delegation', thus wearing two hats. While Albert E. Clattenburg would play a prominent role in the US group, he conceded the first row to O'Connor: the Stockholm meeting remained first and foremost a meeting of the Red Cross family. Still, when appointing its government experts, the US government leaders made clear to them that the revision of the Geneva Prisoner of War Convention and other humanitarian conventions was Washington's main interest.[7] Washington also pointed out that the agenda included proposed changes in the organization of the International Red Cross movement, with potentially drastic consequences for the Swiss: 'It is expected that the USSR or one of its satellites may propose the abolition of the International Red Cross Committee and the assignment of its functions to the United Nations.'[8]

Shortly before his departure for Stockholm, the Secretary of State gave Basil O'Connor detailed policy instructions for the US delegation as well. As chairman of the delegation to Stockholm, O'Connor was directed to make sure that his delegation defended the US position and that the delegation speak with one voice, presenting a 'solid front, expressing the views of the Government of the United States'.[9] One can also discern some pressure to move quickly in the attached position paper. The Red Cross should not be seen as a political instrument for peace, the instructions directed, but should limit itself to purely humanitarian work. Questions relating to atomic weapons should be avoided and deferred to the United Nations (UN). The UN would be addressing questions concerning human rights and war crimes. The UN's committee under Eleanor Roosevelt was at the same time deliberating what to include in what became the Universal Declaration of Human Rights.[10] The American delegates in Stockholm should also avoid any discussion of refugee policies and repatriation, the position paper instructed. If resolutions were offered relating to displaced persons or their repatriation, the delegation should be referred to the competent International Refugee Organization (IRO). Should this turn into a major topic at the meeting, the United States should make clear that it only supported voluntary repatriation.

The refugee policy was one of the areas of disagreement between the ICRC and the American Red Cross. Geneva's relations with the American Red Cross remained tense at this time. The vice president of the AMRC, James T. Nicholson, accused the ICRC of being an instrument of the Swiss government and let it be known that he had sensed a hostile attitude in some members of the Swiss-based organization and its staff towards the American Red Cross during the war and beyond. In his later correspondence with George C. Marshall, Nicholson recommended that Marshall not make any concessions and avoid any reference to the US government's future support for the ICRC. He reminded Marshall, too, of the American Red Cross's position that the ICRC should limit its activities to that of a neutral intermediary in wartime. From these lines it would appear that Nicholson's grievances against Ruegger and the ICRC ran deep.[11] The ICRC leadership was concerned about these complaints, expressed just months before Ruegger's visit to Washington.[12] These tensions were also well-known in Swiss government circles. The Swiss ambassador to the United States, Karl Bruggmann, set out to learn more about the Americans' stance on the International Red Cross in January 1948. As a State Department official summarized his talks with the Swiss diplomat:

> The Swiss [ambassador] asked me today, confidentially, if I could find out and let him know the current attitude of the United States Government and the American Red Cross toward the International Red Cross. He had the feeling that our attitude was rather cool and that the coolness perhaps extended to the Swiss Government on Red Cross matters. He cited the desire of the American Red Cross to have the International Red Cross deal in such matters as recreation for troops, which the latter considered to be a question of military morale and therefore not properly within its competence. He also understood that we favored having the next meeting of the International Red Cross in Stockholm, and feared a possible move to shift its headquarters there.[13]

The report clearly reflected Swiss fears and uncertainties. In the end, the new ICRC president, Paul Ruegger, sought to clear the air by visiting Washington, where he would attempt to woo US support at the highest level. His trip in June 1948 was poorly coordinated with the American Red Cross, which was troubled by the lack of information provided by the ICRC.[14]

Before his meeting with President Harry S. Truman on June 28, 1948, Ruegger also sought to tap the sympathies of the American public with a radio address. It read in part:

> The International Committee may not command material power. Its work is based upon an act of faith. It depends above all on the moral support of the invisible legions. But nevertheless, or perhaps because of this, it was enabled to develop always, and in particular during the last two world wars, its unfailing action in Geneva, and in the field, in favour of victims of the war which no other institution could have fulfilled. Wherefore the most powerful governments enlisted its help and, in particular, the US government gave it its valuable support.[15]

Ruegger's address to the American public foreshadowed his meeting with the president. He expressed his hope that the Americans would support 'the present and proven structure' of the ICRC and the Red Cross movement, and he also spoke out against the planned 'internationalization' of the ICRC, deeming it unworkable. Finally, he asked for the United States to allow the Swiss government to unfreeze Japanese funds earmarked for the ICRC.[16] The US government had misgivings about this claim, and had insisted that the Swiss government block the disbursement of the money.

The British government had their own claims on the money and were curious to know if Ruegger's appeals had any impact on Washington.[17] Ruegger did not in fact meet Secretary of State George C. Marshall on the trip, but sent him a memorandum with a cover letter in which he described the ICRC as 'a moral force'. He also pressed for help in lifting the freeze on funds, urgently needed, given the high operational and administrative expenses of the committee's work in Palestine.[18]

Repeated references to Palestine were not surprising, given that Ruegger was particularly interested in promoting ICRC aid work in the Arab–Israeli conflict of 1948–1949.[19] In 1948 the United Nations had opted for the plan to divide British-ruled Palestine into two states, one for the Arabs, one for the Jewish population. The founding of the State of Israel in 1948 provoked a violent response from the Arab population and their supporters in neighbouring countries. The ICRC soon became very active in providing humanitarian aid to both sides and Ruegger personally managed rescue efforts in war-torn Jerusalem.

The ICRC's involvement in the Palestine conflict started as early as 1947 and was in the final analysis also to a large degree motivated by overcoming its failures during the Holocaust.[20] In response to an appeal made by the

Jewish Agency for Palestine on 21 July 1947, the ICRC approached the British Foreign Office to authorize three ICRC doctors to care for the refugees on the SS *Exodus 47*. The SS *Exodus 47* was packed with Jewish Holocaust survivors destined for Eretz Israel, but stopped by the British navy and sent back to the port of Port-de-Bouc near Marseille, where the ICRC offered its help and negotiated with the British and French authorities. The Jewish refugees on the Exodus eventually were brought back to Hamburg and held in a camp in Germany. The fate of the Exodus drew wide press coverage, caused a huge scandal and worldwide sympathy for the Jewish refugees and their cause.[21] But humanitarian motives were only part of the story behind the ICRC's efforts. The US State Department showed great interest in developments in Palestine as well. Records show that it kept a close watch on ICRC missions and Bernadotte's UN activities there. The political reverberations of this humanitarian intervention did not escape the State Department. The US Legation in Bern cabled 'regarding true activities and plans for Ruegger, ICRC, [Foreign Minister] Petitpierre assured me trip to Near East and Palestine had no political significance and was undertaken for purely humanitarian reasons'. But US foreign policy officials seemed to disagree, as a handwritten note on the cable indicates: 'Reason: Bernadotte leading apparent reorganization ICRC to make representation really international rather than all Swiss. ICR[C] no like.'[22] The ICRC humanitarian mission in the Near East was in fact short-lived and ended in 1951. However, together with the work on the Geneva Conventions, the ICRC hoped that its work in Palestine as a neutral intermediary would win over the US government's support. Over time Ruegger attempted to cultivate a special relationship with Marshall, as his correspondence shows. In a letter to Eleanor Roosevelt, Ruegger later claimed that he and Marshall had always been good friends and that 'there were no difficulties between the top levels of the US government and the ICRC'.[23] Honorary ICRC president Max Huber reinforced these overtures with an article in July 1948 for the prestigious US public policy journal *Foreign Affairs*. There, too, he stressed the utility of an independent, neutral ICRC as the promoter of the Geneva Conventions.[24]

In preparing for Stockholm, Ruegger skillfully took advantage of his high-level contacts in the British government. In a letter to British Foreign Secretary Ernest Bevin he referred to the good time he had enjoyed and the kindness he had received while Swiss ambassador in Great Britain. He then turned the Foreign Secretary's attention to 'our present preoccupations' about the Stockholm conference and the 'really essential question with the future organization of the International Red Cross'. In a real fighting spirit, Ruegger stated that the ICRC delegation in Stockholm under his leadership would vehemently oppose any changes in its traditional structure. Given the important decisions ahead, he asked Bevin to diverge from British traditions and to send a strong official British government delegation to Sweden in order to back the ICRC.[25]

A week later, Swiss diplomacy followed up on Ruegger's intervention. The Political director of the Swiss Foreign Office raised the issue of the ICRC with the Foreign Office. 'He said that the Swiss Government were very much concerned by the Swedish proposal that the Committee should be internationalized. They thought that if this was accepted, it would be the beginning of the end of the International Red Cross.' [...] 'Asked the reasons for the Swiss attitude, he said they were two-fold. First, because the Swedes were anxious to establish their claim to a position of neutrality comparable to that of Switzerland, and secondly, to the personal ambition of Count Bernadotte.' The Swiss diplomat made clear that his government will make a formal representation to the British in support of the ICRC.[26]

Ruegger's intervention, backed by his government, soon triggered some action inside the Foreign Office, as an internal Foreign Office memo of the time shows. This document probably summarizes the general British point of view well, when it states that: 'We have known for some time that Count Bernadotte has had ambitions that Sweden should become a Northern Switzerland, permanently neutral, with himself as head of the Swedish Red Cross, either rivaling or taking the place of the IRCC [ICRC]. The Soviet Government dislikes the Swiss Government and the IRCC, and they may have encouraged Count Bernadotte.'[27] The Foreign Office tended to support the ICRC to stay all Swiss and to focus its work on wartime humanitarianism. They argued however, that Sweden as a second neutral could be a good backup option, if Switzerland is overrun as might have been very much possible during WWII. The conclusion of the memo was however in favor of the Swiss option: 'His Majesty's Government accordingly for their part would not wish to see any fundamental change in its [the ICRC's] character.'[28] Therefore it was decided to give careful support to the ICRC during the Stockholm discussions. Foreign Secretary Bevin accordingly wanted to see 'action to be taken to help the Swiss retain their position.'[29] Contrary to Ruegger's wishes, the British did not send an official government delegation to Sweden, but stuck with their practice of simply sending observers. However, it did decide on some definite action. The Foreign Office telegraphed its Stockholm observer on 23 August about Ruegger's intervention and Bevin advised the British diplomat there to support the ICRC's position by declaring that the British government does 'not wish to see any fundamental change in its [the ICRC's] structure'. The British Red Cross representative in Stockholm Lord Woolton was instructed along these lines in the same telegram.[30] The ICRC seemed prepared to face its critics in Stockholm.

Showdown in Stockholm

The Seventeenth International Red Cross Conference in Stockholm from 20 to 30 August 1948, proved to be a watershed moment. Here the ICRC answered its critics and positioned itself for the future. With the League of Red Cross and Red Crescent Societies and individual national societies seeking to expand their own power in the Red Cross movement, the conference in Stockholm would be a major turning point in determining the future role of the International Committee. The special commission promoted by Bernadotte to study the ways and means of reinforcing the efficacy of the work of the ICRC had postponed its work, leaving matters to be decided at the meeting in Stockholm.[31] In the letter of invitation to the meeting, Chairman Bernadotte formulated the agenda, which included among other things the financial situation of the ICRC, the relationship of and collaboration between the ICRC, the League and the national Red Cross societies, and the future activities of the International Committee of the Red Cross. Other topics on the agenda were the recognition of new Red Cross Societies and, not least, the revision and extension of the Geneva Conventions to cover civilians in war zones.[32] In the run-up to the Stockholm conference, Bernadotte lost no time in making the Swedish Red Cross under his presidency look good. A detailed report by the Swedish Red Cross presented its impressive activity during the war years. The report also included many references to rescue work for Jewish victims, such as those in Hungary: 'Another unique action was carried out in Hungary, where two Red Cross delegates saved thousands of Jews from persecution by swastika and arrow-cross partisans, thanks to special letters of protection issued in the name of [the] SRK [Swedish Red Cross].' The stage was now set for Bernadotte.[33]

The conference gave every sign of being a public relations triumph for Bernadotte and Sweden. Chairman Bernadotte presided over 300 Red Cross delegates from all over the world, many of whom were noblemen, royalty and diplomats. In many ways it became a showcase for Bernadotte's esteem and also for that of Sweden in the postwar world.[34] The American Red Cross delegates were duly impressed and reported, 'The high standard of performance and hospitality set by this conference in Sweden constitutes a real challenge to the American Red Cross to plan a Conference next time that will compare with our magnificent experience in Sweden.'[35] The Americans even praised the chairman's wife, with one US official enthusing 'American born Countess [Estelle] Bernadotte was in charge of social events, of which there were many, all of heart charm and brilliance.'[36] The glamour of royal Sweden had been marshalled, but the opening day was 'the golden hour of Folke Bernadotte'.[37] In his opening statement, Bernadotte told the audience:

> This is the first time an International Red Cross Conference has been held since the Second World War, which in such a devastating manner ravaged both countries and peoples. It is only natural, therefore, that questions of exceedingly great importance will be dealt with here; questions which will have their importance for coming generations, whether, as we hope, countries and people are to live in peaceful relations, or mankind is once again to be compelled to endure the scourge of war.[38]

The tone set by Bernadotte, Sweden's humanitarian record and the Americans' endorsement of him and his country together revealed a shift in the balance of power within the Red Cross. Sweden's fine staging of this important meeting showed once again that it could stand 'very tall in the Red Cross world in those years'.[39] Due to the wartime work of people such as Raoul Wallenberg and Bernadotte, Sweden had already won the delegates' universal recognition and admiration. American Red Cross President Basil O'Connor praised Bernadotte and the Swedish Red Cross in his opening statement and went on to say that the 'prestige of the Swedish Red Cross and its leadership is clearly illustrated by the selection of our distinguished Chairman, Count Bernadotte, President of the Swedish Red Cross, to act as United Nations Mediator in the Holy Land. His untiring efforts to bring peace to that unhappy country, the sincerity and humility with which he approached his difficult task, are known to all of us—and greatly admired.'[40] Bernadotte was to be the first ever UN envoy for peace. In later in-house reports of the American Red Cross, O'Connor had only praise for 'the splendid leadership of Count Bernadotte'.[41] This was hardly surprising, since O'Connor and Bernadotte remained bound by common interests. Reflecting the new power structures inside the Red Cross movement, Bernadotte and O'Connor and their respective national Red Cross organizations clearly dominated the Stockholm conference, not the ICRC. League members from Belgium and the United States agreed with Bernadotte that the ICRC should open its leadership ranks to non-Swiss members. As the host, the Swedish Count could strongly influence and guide the discussion.[42] Belgium played an important role in the League, for the Belgian Count Bonabes de Rouge was now secretary general of the League of Red Cross Societies. Like the Belgians, Bernadotte and Sweden now jockeyed for a leading position among the neutral countries, and were keen to use the conference as a forum to advance those ambitions.

The Soviet absence became the first topic addressed at the conference, typically interwoven with an attack on the ICRC. After opening statements by Presidents O'Connor and Ruegger, Bernadotte called attention to the absence of a Soviet delegation and pointedly read excerpts of the letter that the Soviets had sent to him: 'To begin with, one of the organizers of the Conference is the International Committee of the Red Cross with which the Alliance of the Red Cross and Red Crescent Societies of the USSR does not maintain relations. During the war the International Committee of the Red Cross did not protest against the fascist crimes and against the gravest violations of the International Conventions concerning the sick, wounded and prisoners of war committed by Hitler Germany. It is also a known fact that the International Committee of the Red Cross took up an unfriendly attitude towards the Soviet Union.'[43]

Paul Ruegger reacted with a brief statement, expressing regret over the Soviets' decision and correcting them on various points. The ICRC had helped Soviet POWs when possible, he stressed, and had attempted to establish closer ties with the Soviet Red Cross organization.[44] After airing a harsh critique of the ICRC, some delegations made a surprising motion to hold a vote of confidence in the ICRC. A vote of confidence in the ICRC could easily be interpreted as a hostile act against the Soviets. But after some discussion, the Australian delegation withdrew the motion. The American Red Cross delegation internal report found 'Bernadotte was caught off base—he was quite embarrassed—and finally asked the Australians to withdraw their resolution, which was done and the matter killed off.'[45] Bernadotte had worked very hard to ensure Soviet participation at 'his' conference and planned to bring the Soviet Union into active participation within the Red Cross movement, especially in the drafting of

Figure 9.1. Ruegger, Bernadotte and O'Connor presiding over the Stockholm proceedings, August 1948.

a new prisoners of war convention.[46] Despite this setback, he was partially successful in his efforts to maintain a relationship with the Soviet Red Cross, for—although its delegation did not participate in the Stockholm conference—neither did it abandon its membership. Thus Bernadotte was able at least to avoid an open break with the Soviet Red Cross.[47]

Beyond this, the Stockholm conference was ultimately very successful from the standpoint of expanding the reach of the Geneva Conventions. Although details of the negotiations suggest a complex and contentious process, the key results and the major delegates' reactions to them revealed a high level of satisfaction. The latest drafts for the reform of the existing conventions on POWs and the draft for the new convention for civilians were discussed, amended and prepared for final ratification at the later conference between diplomats. Among the provisions approved were the banning of the torture of POWs, regulations for the treatment of civilian combatants, and the recognition of captured resistance fighters as POWs under certain conditions.

The American Red Cross headquarters in Washington gave the conference a very positive review, particularly its tackling of the conventions: 'This conference was a historic one, and the action taken there particularly significant to Americans interested in the humanitarian ideals of the Red Cross. The conclusions reached in Stockholm affect every American, particularly as they relate to proposals concerning treatment of civilians and prisoners, the sick and wounded in the event of war.'[48] For O'Connor and Clattenburg, the leading American figures in Stockholm, the revision of the conventions was crucial: 'The second world war clearly demonstrated the need of a civilian Convention, and from the experience gained in that war, the International Committee of the Red Cross was able to bring up to date the Draft Civilian Convention for the Protection of Civilians prepared at the XVth International Red Cross Conference held in Tokyo in 1934.'[49] As we saw at the beginning of the book, the Tokyo draft for the protection of civilians of 1934 could not be ratified, and soon afterwards war broke out in China and Ethiopia.

Despite Stockholm's achievements, delegates experienced some disillusionment as well. Members of the US delegation pointed out that the ICRC's critics had failed to push for major changes. Although some reforms were implemented, the ICRC remained an organization run by an all-Swiss group.[50] Pierre Depage's report on ways to increase the efficacy of the International Committee was 'effectively destroyed'. His proposals were heavily rewritten. According to US reports, the Belgian was deeply disappointed and decided to join Bernadotte in his Palestine mission.[51] Bernadotte had been serving as UN mediator in Palestine since early 1948 and his attention was increasingly drawn away from Red Cross business in Stockholm. Soon the Stockholm conference had become a mere forum to promote his new mission in Palestine, as speeches and media coverage from Stockholm show. These ventures were cut short when in September 1948—just a month before the diplomats' meeting to ratify the conventions—radical Zionists murdered Bernadotte in Jerusalem. His proposal for a two-state solution and giving Jerusalem to the Arab part (later he proposed to keep the city under UN administration) had enraged them. Members of the Lehi, also known as the Stern Gang, were soon identified as the men behind the attack.[52] The murder of Bernadotte dominated Swedish newspaper reporting for days after the assassination. As one commentator wrote Bernadotte's death is 'A hard blow for the Swedish people'. He was celebrated as a national hero and 'the first martyr of the UN ideal'.[53] Bernadotte, the first official peace mediator in the history of the United Nations, had carried weight. His enemies, opponents of the count's peace plan, considered him 'a dangerous man' precisely because he carried the weight of an 'international person'.[54] Raoul Wallenberg's biographer Kati Marton has noted, 'For Israel, Sweden, and the United States, the murder of Folke Bernadotte was something to forget about as soon as possible.'[55] With his death, one of the ICRC's most prominent early critics died.

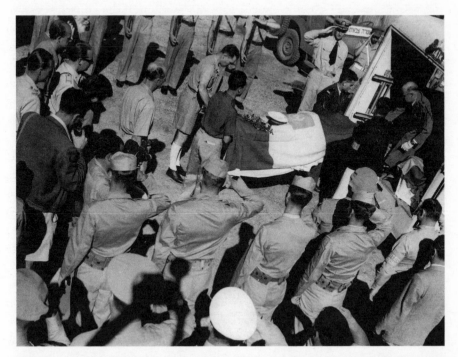

Figure 9.2. Tragic end of a mission: The body of Folke Bernadotte, assassinated in Jerusalem in September 1948, on its way back to Sweden.

At the time of the Stockholm meeting, Ruegger decided to be become active in Palestine as well. Bernadotte had shown that neutral humanitarian intervention to aid Jews and Arabs alike could appeal to American audiences.[56] Red Cross historian Dominique-Debora Junod argues that it was 'political interests more than humanitarian convictions that motivated the ICRC's great projects in the Palestine conflict'.[57] In talks with the American Red Cross, Ruegger 'wished Bernadotte every success in his high political task'.[58] But he may not have always been sincere, in part because Bernadotte had begun using the UN flag as well as that of the Red Cross for his mission, a breach of protocol that deeply upset Ruegger. Given the visibility it would lend the ICRC, Ruegger decided to go to Jerusalem himself in an attempt to steal some of the spotlight. At the same time, the ICRC men hoped to demonstrate that its neutrality and impartiality had impressive benefits in such conflicts.[59]

Before his assassination, Cold War loyalties had increasingly forced Bernadotte to give up his original plan of 'internationalizing' the Geneva committee. He realized that his critique of the ICRC provided ammunition for the Soviets. The world was gradually breaking into two Cold War camps and with it the Red Cross movement. Both the ICRC and Bernadotte strongly opposed allowing the international Red Cross movement to break up. He even remarked in his 1948 book *Instead of Arms*, 'During the Second World War the eastern powers had made rather serious accusations against the International Committee of the Red Cross, accusations which, in my opinion, were highly exaggerated.'[60] Clearly, Bernadotte's critique of the ICRC had softened, although other member societies continued to raise objections. Prospects for the ICRC, however, had begun to brighten. Its harshest critics, the Soviets, had failed to show up in Stockholm (except as observers) and Bernadotte had seemingly given up his challenge to the ICRC's dominant position. The AMRC too, although still very critical of the ICRC, avoided public confrontation from then on. The committee's attempt to insert itself in Palestine showed positive results, and approval of the new Geneva Conventions would further help to improve the position of the Swiss organization. Not least, Ruegger and Eduard de Haller, representing the Swiss government, were now assured that the diplomatic conference for formally signing conventions would take place in Switzerland. There would be no 'Stockholm Conventions', something Bernadotte might once have wished. Now that the Red Cross family had mended some of its rifts, the Swiss government called for a 1949 diplomatic conference in Geneva to ratify the work further discussed in Stockholm.

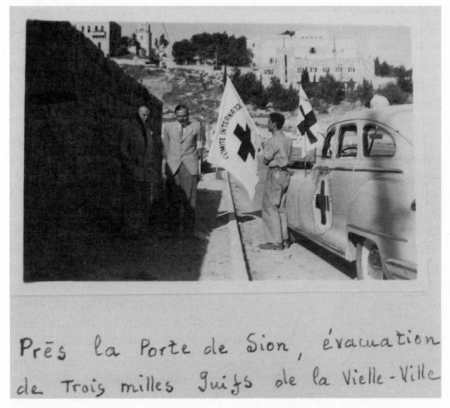

Près la Porte de Sion, évacuation de Trois milles Juifs de la Vielle-Ville

Figure 9.3. Paul Ruegger near the Zion gate in Jerusalem. Evacuation of 3,000 Jews from the beleaguered Old City 1948, Album Delegation of ICRC in Palestine January 1948–July 1949.

Final Complications

Despite the Switzerland's slowly improving relationship with the Soviets, the French continued to be concerned about the possible negative impact of ICRC–Soviet relations on the upcoming meeting of diplomats and its ability to secure the desired expansion of the Geneva Convention. In January 1949 the French embassy therefore suggested sending the invitation to the Geneva meeting through the Swiss government, thereby avoiding ICRC channels and acting 'without taking account of the International Committee of the Red Cross'.[61] Even as 1949 began, the French still questioned the ICRC's leadership, preferring instead to 'see the role of the protecting power entrusted to a new international body composed, for instance, of persons of world-wide repute'. The absence of the Soviets could nullify all the work already invested.[62] The British soon picked up French concerns, and in March 1949 the British embassy in Washington proposed to the State Department that a joint appeal be issued to the Soviet government to participate in the Geneva conference on war victims.[63]

Meanwhile, preparations for the critical 1949 Geneva conference of government delegates continued. President Truman appointed former ambassador to Switzerland Leland Harrison as chairman of the US delegation. Clattenburg joined the US team of nine representatives as an advisor. Clattenburg's Special Projects Division solicited feedback about the draft convention from the World Jewish Congress in New York and discussed possible modifications with the League of Red Cross Societies and the American Red Cross. The State Department was still nervous that Soviet maneuvers might at the last minute sabotage the signing of the conventions. Indeed, there was no shortage of disturbing signs indicating this might happen. The ICRC informed the State Department in April 1949 that it had been approached by Czechoslovakia to arrange the removal of the last remaining 300,000 ethnic Germans in the Sudetenland to western zones, a proposition which the ICRC considered embarrassing; it not unreasonably suspected political motives behind this proposal, yet an ICRC refusal to answer the request for 'humanitarian' assistance could be exploited for negative propaganda. The ICRC was not interested in bad news coverage just before the beginning of the final Geneva conference on protecting civilians.[64] These fears worsened when the Soviets actually made a showing.

Washington was completely taken by surprise when a Soviet delegation of twenty-nine representatives suddenly turned up in Geneva in April 1949. Clattenburg and Harrison could only speculate what the intention of the strong Soviet group would be: 'WE and EE [the West European and Eastern European desks of the department] feel that while the Russian distaste for the International Red Cross is well known and accepted, the Soviets may have some additional motive for participating at the Geneva talks and that they may use them as another international platform in an effort to embarrass us and accuse us of warmongering.'[65] The State Department reacted with urgent messages to Harrison in Geneva: 'DEPT [Department] apprehensive lest Soviets use discussion Convention Protection Civilians occasion propaganda campaign against US and Atomic Energy policy. Please inform DEPT immediately any signs such development. DEPT alerting Specialist Atomic Energy policies for immediate dispatch Geneva is required.'[66] Although the Soviets had only sent observers to the earlier Stockholm meeting, this did not mean they were uninterested in the developments around the conventions; quite the contrary. Moscow saw the humanitarian language of the conventions as useful and actually proved eager to label governments who stalled as 'enemies of humanity'.[67]

Indeed, US officials remained nervous about the Soviets using reform of the conventions for propaganda purposes. Harrison reassured the State Department back in Washington: 'Delegation fully alerted. If any indication Soviet intend introduce this tactic will communicate Department.'[68] During and after the convention, State Department officials followed the media coverage in the Soviet Union closely and found that *Pravda's* readers were being told that Soviet delegates in Geneva sought to improve the conventions while the 'imperialists' were blocking their attempts to do so. British delegates, Soviet readers learned, had supposedly spoken out against the protection of partisans in conflicts, for they obviously had the independence struggles in their own colonies in mind. They also read that the Soviet delegates had proposed protecting civilians against torture and killing, but the United States opposed it.[69]

While the Soviets had many reservations about joining the reform process under ICRC leadership, the British hesitated as well. The British objected to the ICRC's leadership in revising the conventions because Whitehall thought that creating humanitarian law was a task reserved for sovereign states. To the British, the ICRC was just another private humanitarian organization and they held little respect for its traditions, ambitions and unique position enshrined by international law.[70] Under pressure from their American allies, the British eventually gave in. And with Soviet participation assured, the 277 delegates representing 59 states, the ICRC, League of Red Cross Societies and the United Nations (present with observer status), plans for the expansion of the Geneva Conventions could now be finalized.

Despite these advances, much remained unresolved, not just about the limits placed on wartime conduct, but about the watchdogs in Geneva. In his report to the Secretary of State, Clattenburg argued that the Stockholm conference had emphasized rather than solved the problem of finding a neutral agency that would be acceptable to the Soviets as executor and promotor of the new conventions. The important problem of financing the ICRC's work was also still not resolved.[71] Clattenburg remained impressed by the excellent work of the international committee in preparing the drafts of the new conventions, even as it sought reasons to continue its work in peacetime. Still, his overall judgment was rather harsh: 'On the whole the International Red Cross Committee played at Stockholm the part of a conservative and jealous Swiss organization which blandly believes that it can continue unhampered in its humane activities because its activities have always been impartial and humane.'[72] He spoke of the close relationship between the ICRC and the Swiss government.[73] The Soviets would continue to be reliably difficult in the process, seeing the ICRC 'as being partial to fascists' and the Stockholm agenda 'as contemplating war instead of peace'.[74]

Meanwhile, the British and American government experts exchanged their views on the pending reforms. The British considered some of the new provisions as unrealistic in the heat of war, such as the use of POWs for certain kinds of labour. For instance, one of their representatives went so far as to insist that German POWs had performed a great service in clearing mines in recent years, and that bomb disposal and mine lifting were no more dangerous than driving automobiles.[75] The discussions and disagreements between Washington and London continued long after Stockholm, particularly over questions of protecting civilians during armed conflicts. Clattenburg reported that W. H. Gardner of the British War Office, one of the two British government observers in Stockholm, had signaled further sticking points for his government. The British were demanding a reservation be included, 'empowering governments in the interest of national security to deprive protected persons of any or all of the rights prescribed by the Convention'. In other words, he argued the British intelligence services were convinced that under the draft conventions they would be completely unable to operate in a state of war.[76] By autumn 1948, despite such concerns and last-minute hurdles on multiple fronts, the US State department had accepted Geneva as the venue for the forthcoming diplomats' conference, to be called by the Swiss government in the spring of 1949.[77] The ICRC was now firmly in charge of preparations for the spring 1949 conference and the Swiss government would ultimately serve as the repository for all documents relating to the revision of the conventions.[78]

The 1949 Grand Finale

The culmination of all these efforts came in April 1949 with the opening of the diplomatic conference in Geneva. The four conventions were given some final touches and could now be approved by the international diplomatic community: The four conventions covered: (1) 'the Amelioration of the Wounded and Sick in Armed Forces and Field'; (2) 'the Amelioration of the Condition of Wounded, Sick and Shipwrecked Members of Armed Forces at Sea'; (3) 'the Treatment of Prisoners of War'; and (4) 'the Protection of Civilian Persons in Time of War'. The draft agreements prepared for the diplomatic conference in Geneva in 1949 were basically those debated and approved in Stockholm the previous year. The most outstanding achievement of the Stockholm meeting was the creation of a completely new convention to protect civilians in wartime. The protection of civilians had been a long-standing Red Cross goal, but the experiences of the Second World War and its toll on civilians were a major factor in forcing change.[79] Among the main concerns that moved the negotiators was not only the mass torture and murder in concentration and death camps, but also the indiscriminate bombing of cities such as Dresden and London. Intentional killing of civilians was basically done by all nations at war. The Second World War cost the lives of many more civilians than soldiers. While the US lost over 400,000 soldiers and only very few civilians fell victim to the violence, in most other nations the situation was very different. With an estimated 18 million people, the Soviet Union paid the highest toll of civilian victims (out of a total of 27 million Soviet dead in the war). During the Holocaust the Nazis and their allies murdered 6 million Jews and about 5 million other civilians (e.g. Sinti and Roma, Disabled, Gays, Slavic populations). The protection of civilians in wartime was therefore a top priority among victim nations and groups, particularly those nations which had been under Nazi occupation. After the horrors of a world war and a scale of civilian casualties never seen before, the participants felt a sense of urgency to modernize the Geneva Conventions. President Truman's message to Congress during the ratification deliberations stressed 'the urgent necessity for rather extensive revisions of the above-mentioned earlier conventions', particularly 'before the experiences of the Second World War had been forgotten'.[80] Gerhart Riegner from the World Jewish Congress was present in Stockholm as an observer and must have been pleased with the outcome.

Civilians would henceforth be protected from deportations and reprisal killings. The 1949 revisions provided that civilians in enemy hands should be 'humanely treated', protected against acts of violence, rape, torture, 'extermination' and more generally against all 'measures of brutality'. The provisions stipulated, 'Collective penalties and likewise all measures of intimidation or of terrorism are prohibited'.[81] Undefended towns and demilitarized zones were protected from fighting. Civilians in occupied territories should be allowed to receive and send news of a personal nature to their families. Pregnant women and women with young children, as well as children under 15 years old, should get preferential treatment such as higher food rations. An occupying power was not permitted to suppress the religious life of communities and had allow to religious services. These new Geneva Conventions also banned the perfidious use of the emblems of Red Cross societies. At the same time they protected hospitals and ambulances operating under the sign of the Red Cross and the Red Crescent. The other big item on the agenda was the revision of the 1929 POW convention, which was now much enlarged. Article 87 of the new Geneva Convention declared, 'Collective punishment for individual acts, corporal punishment, imprisonment in premises without daylight and in general any form of torture or cruelty are forbidden.'[82] The conventions defined violations and called for grave breaches to be punished, but did not specify a clear procedure for enforcement. National courts, they stipulated, should have jurisdiction or hand violators over to another country for trial.

The public clearly had great interest in this topic and the fate of POWs, and British historian Geoffrey Best even speaks of a 'cult of the POW' at the time, particularly in the United States, which was very much concerned with the fate of imprisoned soldiers.[83] Against the background of the Nuremberg and Tokyo trials, delegates also discussed how violations of these new or expanded international standards should be prosecuted. The trials conducted by the victorious Allied powers after the Second World War had become known as 'war crimes trials'. A majority of the defendants had violated international rules of warfare as defined in The Hague Convention and Regulations and the 1929 Geneva Conventions, and clearly qualified as war criminals.[84] 'Crimes against humanity' however was a new legal concept that came out of the war. The Holocaust was mostly a crime against civilians, and therefore qualified as a crime against humanity. War crimes and crimes against humanity, however, were coming to mean different things on the opposite sides of the Iron Curtain.[85]

One of the most contentious issues in these discussions revolved around whether POWs accused of terrible crimes would enjoy the protection of the conventions. Like the US and British representatives, the Soviets had reservations about exactly who might now be protected under expanded provisions, and how. They argued that possible POW status for defendants during war crimes trials might be acceptable, but after the conviction, the extension of that protected status was unacceptable.[86] The Western powers in particular were concerned that any military conflict between East and West could place Western POWs at risk of being treated as criminals. The main question involved the definition of 'war crimes'. Participation in a 'war of aggression' might be enough to constitute such a crime. The ICRC had up to that point not ignored the question of what war crimes were, but officially these had never been a focal point of the organization's work. Traditionally the committee had tended to avoid the topic and did not speak publicly about the concept or about war criminals.[87] Other controversies claimed centre stage at this final meeting before ratification. One was the forced repatriation of former combatants. In 1949 Moscow was clamoring for the return of large numbers of former Soviet POWs who were still in Europe. Most did not wish to be sent back and some preferred suicide to returning to Stalin's empire. Finally, one of the most heated debates in Geneva about what constituted war crimes erupted during a surprising Soviet resolution to ban the use of nuclear weapons.

What was essentially a formal meeting to finally confirm the new law ended on 12 August 1949. The closing ceremony in Geneva was short, with only three people speaking. Ambassador Leland Harrison signed three conventions for the United States on the same day.[88] The signing of the fourth convention for the protection of civilian persons in time of war was postponed to allow its further review and consideration by the US Government. In December US officials were finally ready to sign this convention as well.

The formal signing ceremony took place at 3:00 p.m. on 8 December 1949, in the Palais du Conseil Général in Geneva. This was a classical building with four massive Corinthian columns at the front, and the Red Cross flag displayed in the middle. Since 1939 the Palais had been used as the headquarters of the central agency of POWs. The final meeting in the large hall of the building was chaired by Swiss Foreign Minister Max Petitpierre. Twenty-eight delegations were present. Delayed by fog in Vienna, the USSR delegation did not actually sign until 12 December. (At the suggestion of chairman Petitpierre its signature was counted as having been added on 8

December.) After the opening speech every delegation was asked to sign and invited to say a few words in turn. Some representatives signed without further comment, while others used the occasion to reiterate their reservations about individual articles or deliver further political commentary. As he signed the convention protecting civilians, US delegate John Vincent again voiced objections raised a few days earlier by the State Department to him. His government reserved the right to impose capital punishment, even if the same offence was not punishable by death in the territory prior to occupation.[89] The representatives of Canada, the Netherlands, and the United Kingdom echoed this concern in their final statements. Soviet bloc countries and the Soviet Union signed and expressed their intent to ratify the conventions, yet unsurprisingly voiced a number of final reservations as well; the Soviet delegate remarked that the civilian convention 'does not cover the civilian population in territory not occupied by the enemy and does not, therefore, completely meet humanitarian requirements'. The Israeli delegate made clear that its medical services would in the future—controversially and against the wishes of the ICRC—use a red Star of David as its symbol. The Hungarian delegate used the opportunity to criticize western countries, stating 'the concrete results achieved by the Diplomatic Conference . . . do not come up to expectations, since the majority of the members of the conference did not adopt proposals of the Soviet delegation concerning the atomic weapon and other means of mass extermination of the population'.

Swiss Minister Petitpierre responded in his closing remarks very directly to the reservations aired in the Hungarian comments: 'Our task was clearly defined. It was not up to us either to draft the Kellogg Pact which had outlawed war, nor to revise The Hague Agreements, which had attempted to establish rules for the limits laid down for us. I think that if we had done so, we would have jeopardized our work. The latter to be effective, had to take account of realities.'[90] He urged the delegates to recommend quick ratification to their respective governments. In what was perhaps a concession to the Soviet bloc and the sharp Hungarian speech, John Vincent reported to his government, 'expressing the hope that the feeling of humanity which gave birth to the idea of the Red Cross would one day be so strong that it would no longer 'limit itself to lessening the evils of war but will undertake the task of fighting the very idea of war and of assuring that peace is finally victorious.'[91] More than fifty-two governments had signed the conventions by the end of 1949.[92] The signature of a nation's delegates was a clear signal that they were willing to support the treaty-making progress. It is also commonly the case that states feel bound by an agreement even before final ratification has taken place. (Ratification normally means the subsequent approval of the sign-ing by a country's parliament or congress, depending on its constitution.) The Geneva Conventions came into force six months after ratification by at least two countries, and the original documents were deposited in the Swiss capi-tal, Bern. The Swiss government also registered the Geneva Conventions with the United Nations. Every time a new country ratified the treaty, the Swiss government informed all other signatories and the Secretariat of the United Nations.[93]

It is not surprising that soon after the signing ceremony was over, the State Department looked carefully into all the reservations the Soviet dele-gates had to the expanded conventions, for the Soviet Union and the United States appeared to be on the brink of a military confrontation. The Soviets had raised, for example, objections to article 85 of the POW convention, arguing the 'USSR does not consider itself bound by the obligation, which follows from article 85, to extend the application of the convention to pris-oners of war who have been convicted under the law of the detaining power, in accordance with the principles of the Nuremberg trial, for war crimes and crimes against humanity, it being understood that persons con-victed of such crimes must be subject to the conditions for those who undergo their punishment'.[94] Article 85 reads, 'Prisoners of war prosecuted under the laws of the Detaining Power for acts committed prior to capture shall retain, even if convicted, the benefits of the present Convention.' The Soviet objection did not come as a surprise, but what troubled Washington was the possibility that the Soviets might accuse and try POWs based on a very broad definition of war criminal.

In the Aftermath of Geneva

The results of the 1949 diplomatic conference in Geneva were overwhelm-ingly positive, despite the many last-minute reservations and objections. Against the odds, a new extended set of humanitarian laws had been formu-lated and ratified by both East and West, and most countries—including communist states—at least officially supported the new laws. The Soviets' presence and collaboration in many areas is remarkable, given the fact that in 1949 the Cold War was rapidly dividing the world.[95] *The New York Times* declared, 'With Russian adherence, all the great powers have approved the new Red Cross conventions that were drafted, Max Petitpierre, Swiss Foreign Minister, said today "on the unhappy assumption that a new war is not impossible".[96] The Geneva Conventions of 1949 were a measure of progress but at the same time would have counted for little in the event of a nuclear war. They in part formed a reaction to past shortcomings and omissions of humanitarian law during the 1930s and 1940s. Laws were desperately needed to provide more effective protection against the horrors of war and to entitle the ICRC to intervene legally on behalf of civilians in war zones. Thus the successful reform effort in Geneva was unquestionably also a big success for the ICRC and its standing in the world. As Caroline Moorehead has emphasized, 'It was both a decided victory over its critics, and something of a surprise, given the Committee's impossible and unhappy position after attacks made on its inaction with regard to the concentration camps.'[97]

Following Geneva, Ruegger and the ICRC leadership were eager to move the ratification process forward in the national parliaments. Most crucial of course was ratification of the reformed Geneva Conventions by the major world powers. Ruegger reached out to George C. Marshall and campaigned for this end, but also again broached the status of the ICRC. He stressed that his work in Geneva demonstrated that the ICRC continued to act as an independent, neutral, universal and impartial body. (Someone at the receiving end, possibly Marshall, underlined the words *neutral* and *impartial*.) Ruegger was hopeful that the position of his organization and its principles would now be more accepted and understood, 'in spite of occasional set-backs'.[98] In fact, both he and Marshall hoped for speedy ratification of the conventions adopted in Geneva. The new Geneva Conventions went into force for consenting states on 21 October 1950.

The Soviet Union ratified the new Geneva Conventions in 1954, while the United States did so in 1955. As of the writing of this book, 194 countries have ratified the Geneva Conventions, in other words, all states on this planet. The president of the American Red Cross, Basil O'Connor, titled his 1949 keynote address 'Can the Red Cross Survive?' He asked the fundamental question whether an organization founded in the remote past of the nineteenth century still had any place in the vastly altered world of the mid-twentieth century. With the completion of the Geneva Conventions, O'Connor's own answer was in the affirmative.[99]

With memories of the horrors of the Second World War still lingering—civilian and POW deaths on an unprecedented scale, the Holocaust—a brief window of opportunity opened between 1945 and 1950 for strengthening international human rights and criminal law. The generation that survived the war was eager to 'create fire walls against barbarism'.[100] These changes and improvements in humanitarian law were part of a larger diplomatic movement. The new Geneva Conventions set a minimum standard of behaviour for any member state of the international community. Political scientist David P. Forsythe underlines the importance of this achievement, concluding 'The 1949 Geneva Conventions were to prove, along with the 1948 Universal Declaration of Human Rights (UDHR) one of the two main pillars for international relations after 1945.'[101] Against the background of the blockade of Berlin and the Communist takeover in Czechoslovakia in 1948, the Cold War turned icy. And with war in Korea breaking out in 1950, the Nuremberg trials concluded, and denazification ended, 'The idea of convicting and punishing criminal enemies lost most of its attraction when enemies became allies.'[102] With the confrontation between the United States and the Soviet bloc escalating, the window of opportunity for addressing human rights and humanitarian law closed again.[103]

The Cold War also ended demands for changes in the hierarchy of the Red Cross world and left the status of the ICRC untouched. At the International Red Cross Conference in Toronto in 1952 the obvious was only confirmed. The ICRC remained an independent humanitarian organization based in Geneva with an all-Swiss leadership. Maintaining this status quo was clearly a victory for the ICRC, and for a time its leaders experienced a sense of triumph that the world had been put right again. For the ICRC, Toronto marked a resolute victory.[104] At the time of the Toronto meeting, Ruegger wrote to a confidant,

Today the position of the ICRC, after the Geneva diplomatic conference and since September 1948 in Stockholm, is quite strengthened in terms of its Swiss composition. Financially, we are not completely without funds; compared to the holdings of 200,000 francs in 1939, the deficit of 3 million francs in 1948, we now have 20 million francs at our disposal. Despite very tough fights on all sides, we move forward. We can do something—at least try—and hold the flag of the ICRC high.[105]

The *Neue Zürcher Zeitung* recognized Ruegger's achievements retrospectively in 1955, pointing out that few people had achieved as much as he had through his extraordinary engagement on behalf of the ICRC.[106] And finally, Hans Haug, president of the Swiss Red Cross and an ICRC committee member, declared in 1966, not without a certain flare of pride, that little

Switzerland had successfully defended its humanitarian flagship in the following terms: 'All attempts to restructure the International Committee and to internationalize it by adding citizens of other countries to it have failed so far or were aborted [...] Today the ICRC as an absolutely independent, neutral and impartial organization enjoys international recognition; no one ignores the necessity and the usefulness of its existence and work.'[107]

Conclusion

There can be little doubt that the momentous decision taken on 14 October 1942 by the Swiss-based International Committee of the Red Cross (ICRC) had long-lasting repercussions. The Committee chose to remain silent about the Holocaust and thereby failed not only the victims but also its founding ideals. The year 1942 might have been a major turning point for Swiss humanitarians had the International Red Cross Committee issued a declaration condemning Nazi atrocities at its October 1942 meeting. It would not have prevented the Holocaust—and we will never know if the move could have saved lives or had any impact on the course of Nazi policy—but it certainly would have protected its moral standing and the major institutional crisis that soon followed would have been less dramatic. Yet despite its failures in the area of civilian aid and protection during the Second World War, the ICRC was quite successful in organizing a critical lifeline for huge numbers of prisoners of war (POWs) in Nazi and Axis hands and in maintaining a tracing service that kept alive some line of communication between dispersed family members.

By 1943 and 1944 the ICRC also became more active in aiding Jews at a time when it became clear that Germany was going to lose the war. But the practical aid the Committee offered was very limited and marked by hesitation. The ICRC could have intervened earlier and with more determination, as the example of neutral Sweden shows. Shortly before the war ended, the ICRC's leaders realized their mistake, but it was far too late. In 1942 Switzerland was surrounded by Axis powers, and its leaders' fear of being overrun was understandable. Yet no public ICRC protests against Nazi atrocities and abuses were made at any point in the final years of the war. There is no doubt that individual delegates of the ICRC did as much as they could to save Jews later on in the war—for instance, in Hungary. However, one cannot help thinking retrospectively that some in the ICRC leadership saw Jewish victims as a distraction from the organization's central mission and, as a result, were not willing to risk more in trying to protect them.

Humanitarian aid formed an important foreign policy tool for neutrals. The humanitarian competition that emerged between Sweden and Switzerland illustrates this in much detail. Once the defeat of Nazi Germany was obvious, Swiss foreign policy adopted a pro-Allied stance and the ICRC leadership had to adapt accordingly. Helping Jews was seen as a way to please Washington, particularly after the Americans created the War Refugee Board in 1944. From 1944 onwards Switzerland began to engage in a 'humanitarian fight-back'.[1] Individual personalities and their ambitions, strengths, and weaknesses played a huge role as well, as the cases of Red Cross leaders Carl Jacob Burckhardt and Count Folke Bernadotte illustrate.

Although the international press had carried wartime stories of German atrocities from time to time, photographs and moving images from the liberation of the concentration camps most forcefully revealed to a broad public the shocking fate of so many Jews under Nazi rule. Through the Nuremberg trials just a few years later, the full extent of the massive crimes committed under the Nazis became visible to the world. As a result, many questions were asked about what the humanitarians and their governments had done to help.

Crisis of Humanitarianism

The ICRC realized early on that the critical voices arising from these revelations were undermining its reputation and, ultimately, its international standing as the premier humanitarian organization. Despite receiving the 1944 Nobel Peace Prize the ICRC had very little reason to celebrate. At war's end the ICRC found itself in a major existential crisis, facing the possibility of being completely restructured or even dissolved. Sweden now openly challenged the Swiss for international leadership in neutral humanitarianism under the Red Cross banner.

After the most devastating war in human history, with the highest number of casualties and an unprecedented genocide, the Swiss humanitarians found themselves in crisis. Not surprisingly, Auschwitz had deeply shaken any vestiges of a nineteenth-century optimism about humanity. Did the Swiss committee still have a future in the world after Auschwitz? The Red Cross network also found itself struggling to stay relevant and viable in peacetime and in the era of a host of new United Nations aid agencies. Historians have recently begun to focus on the founding years of the United Nations and its own sometimes troubled humanitarian projects, but have neglected the interplay of these institutions with the story of the international Red Cross. If Red Cross humanitarianism still had a future in the years after 1945, then who would carry on the torch? Sweden soon challenged the Swiss for leadership.

Bernadotte's immediate postwar proposals to internationalize the ICRC leadership found widespread support among other national Red Cross societies. Along with Sweden, a number of other national chapters—especially the Soviet affiliates—did not trust the Swiss to act as the guardians of the Geneva Conventions any longer. They regarded Switzerland and its fabled permanent neutrality with suspicion, and saw the Swiss as having been overly conciliatory towards their Nazi neighbour during the war. Switzerland no longer seemed like a secure guardian of the Red Cross centre, while Sweden began to emerge as an attractive alternative. In fact, the first drafts of the reform of the Geneva Conventions after the war did not describe the ICRC as the conventions' promotor but instead noncommitally as a 'competent international organization'. With the future seat of the organization left unclear for a time, the ICRC leaders were very well aware of the fact that they would have to fight to retain their decisive central role.[2]

Red Cross leaders in Geneva found a window of opportunity to respond to some of the tragic lessons of the war, while also securing their place in the future of international humanitarian work by making a new and forceful commitment to protecting civilians caught in the crossfire of war. Their new project was also very much tied up with the scramble to survive as an organization and also to save the ICRC's reputation. The troubled path to the expanded Geneva Conventions illustrates that well. As one of the lessons learned from the First World War, the Second World War, and above all the Holocaust, the ICRC pushed for better protection of civilians in wartime and therefore contributed significantly to consciousness about human rights in the postwar world. At nearly the same time the protection of civilians came to the forefront of world attention in the United Nations' Genocide Convention and in the United Nations' Universal Declaration of Human Rights, adopted in 1948.[3] The Genocide Convention defined the destruction of religious or ethnic groups as a crime under international law. While the history of these initiatives is now being widely studied by historians and political theorists, much less attention has been devoted to the part played by the Geneva reforms.

The ICRC also began to take a more active role in intervening on behalf of civilians in its daily operations, supporting refugees not only in

Europe, but also in the war that broke out during the creation of the State of Israel. Because of the postwar refugee emergency the Red Cross had jumped in and started to issue travel papers in Europe as early as February 1945. Committed to neutral humanitarianism, the Red Cross seemed to have been in a dilemma. After the war, criticism from various governments about travel papers for escaping Nazis and SS men put pressure on the organization to stop issuing such documents, which served as de facto passports. But at the same time the committee wanted to help refugees who lacked papers and lacked the means of obtaining them, among them many ethnic Germans. Given the missing screening and controls, the ICRC did recognize that widespread abuse would occur. This was a potentially dangerous problem and added weight to the many criticisms of the ICRC.

As the postwar revisions to the Geneva Conventions were being prepared many accusations emerged that the ICRC had shielded war criminals. The communist countries never tired of airing such revelations, although the problems with Red Cross-issued travel papers were rarely explicitly mentioned in public. And just a few years after the war had ended, the Western powers, and foremost the United States, were increasingly focused on quite different priorities than denazification and war crimes trials. Officials in the US State Department working on the revised Geneva Conventions had no interest in letting this issue get in the way of the successful completion of their project.

The drafting and signing of the new Geneva Convention of 1949 was undoubtedly a great diplomatic success. With this achievement to their credit, ICRC leaders could show the world that it remained a relevant, innovative and active force in shaping international law and humanitarianism. Although all major countries at the time were signatories to the new Geneva Conventions, enforcing the new provisions had mixed results. Applying the conventions remained arguably easier in traditional wars with two clearly identifiable armies squaring off against each other. This would be less the case in guerrilla wars or conflicts with multiple non-state opponents. The new Convention for the Protection of Civilian Persons in Time of War notwithstanding, one thing that has not changed since the Second World War is that civilians continue to suffer the most in armed conflicts.

The regulations of the international Red Cross movement were revised at a 1952 international conference in Toronto. The Swiss could finally relax. The ICRC retained its former status at the helm of the national Red Cross

societies, and the criticisms that had afflicted its leaders in the wake of the
war were largely ignored. Toronto meant a major victory.[4] Geneva became
one of the headquarters of the United Nations, while also remaining the
home base of the international Red Cross. Switzerland retained its place as
an international center for diplomacy and the Swiss could be proud of their
country again.

The critical voice of Count Bernadotte from the Swedish Red Cross
vanished with his murder by Zionist extremists in 1948. But even before his
tragic death he had softened his tough critical stance on the Red Cross in
Switzerland, wary of being used by the ICRC's Soviet critics. Only the
communist countries continued to verbally attack Geneva. With the outbreak of the war in Korea in 1950 the Cold War turned hot. The Soviet
Union and communism became the enemy of the West. The western allies
had to stick together and old conflicts were now pushed aside. Until 1945
Washington at times suspected the ICRC of being Nazi-friendly. Under the
new configuration of alliances, much had changed. Western governments
now supported the ICRC and critical voices around its handling of the
Nazi past were largely silenced. With the decisions made in Toronto the
ICRC had finally overcome its postwar crisis and could focus once again on
daily business in the humanitarian arena.

The humanitarian record of the Second World War had long-lasting con-
sequences for how Switzerland and Sweden were perceived internationally.
Swedish neutrality in the war is still remembered today as 'good neutrality'.
Public places are named after Wallenberg and Bernadotte in many cities and
countries. The square in front of the United States Holocaust Memorial
Museum in Washington, DC, is named after Wallenberg. Wallenberg was
one of the first to be honoured as a Righteous Among the Nations in Yad
Vashem, Israel's Holocaust Memorial in Jerusalem (1963). Bernadotte's
white buses for carrying concentration camp inmates to Sweden are for
good reason prominently displayed at Yad Yashem. Swedish historian Sven
Nordlund has written about Wallenberg and Bernadotte's actions, asking 'Is
it possible that these humanitarian efforts in the final stages of the war laid
the ground for a postwar image of Sweden as a rescuer of Holocaust victims? If this is so, it can be argued that the image of Sweden as a "rescuer
nation" helped to maintain a clear national conscience.'[5] Switzerland, by
contrast, came out of the war with a tarnished international image. Not
surprisingly, the Swiss Righteous Among the Nation honorees Friedrich

Born and Carl Lutz, while honoured at Yad Vashem for rescuing Jews in Budapest, are far less known to a wider general public.

Long Shadows of History

The moving stories of brave rescuers, heroes, and humanitarians have received much attention in recent years. As Jewish Studies scholar Alvin Rosenfeld has pointed out: 'Indeed, these people are now frequently regarded as the "moral heroes" of the Holocaust.'[6] However, in the first postwar years this was different. There was still no widely used term for the systematic mass murder of the Jews and little understanding of their particular fate. In many cases the people we now consider 'heroes' went unrecognized, were unloved, or even worse. ICRC delegate Friedrich Born or Swiss Vice-Consul Carl Lutz were criticized by their superiors at the time for what they had done. Rescuing lives in Budapest had sometimes also meant resorting to bribery, issuing documents with questionable authority and not strictly following orders. On their return from Hungary neither Lutz nor Born received thanks from their Swiss homeland. Instead, Lutz was accused of having exceeded his authority and Born's death in 1963 garnered little notice.[7]

With the end of the Cold War things began to change and a new narrative of the Nazi past and Holocaust began to be written. The long shadows of the war and recent past caught up with Switzerland, as they did in so many countries. Issues such as the fate of Nazi-looted gold reserves, Swiss wartime refugee policies, and the question of bank accounts that had belonged to victims of the Holocaust have been widely and publicly addressed during the last twenty years, above all by scholars working in the Independent Commission of Experts Switzerland—Second World War (Bergier Commission). Former US Deputy Secretary of the Treasury Stuart Eizenstat, who led negotiations about wartime assets still under Swiss control, has written that: 'The Swiss people's mythology about their role as the fearless wartime neutral has been challenged.'[8] It remains to be seen, however, whether these facts will have a lasting impact on Swiss society, or remain in some senses an unresolved chapter, swallowed up in national historical myths.

In these confrontations of the late 1990s, the ICRC too came under scrutiny about its wartime record. The organization—not unlike the Vatican in the Second World War—was criticized harshly for not speaking out against the persecution and killing of the Jews in Nazi-occupied Europe. The British journal *The Economist* called the ICRC's silence in these years the 'most shameful moment' in the ICRC's entire history.[9] German journalist and poet Hans Magnus Enzensberger described it as a 'complete failure of the ICRC... when confronted with the Shoah'.[10] And survivor Elie Wiesel commented on Swiss behaviour, 'When human dignity is at stake, neutrality is a sin, not a virtue.'[11] Robert M. W. Kempner, the eminent deputy prosecutor for the United States at the International Military Tribunal at Nuremberg, called the silence of the ICRC on the Holocaust and the 'protection of mass murderers from punishment by organizing aid to help them escape overseas' as the 'heavy sins of the International Red Cross'.[12]

In the 1990s the ICRC did for all intents and purposes apologize for its silence about the Holocaust and for the limited help that the organization had provided for Jewish victims. When ICRC President Cornelio Sommaruga publicly spoke of 'our share of responsibility', he declared that 'The ICRC of today can only regret the shortcomings and the possible errors of the past.'[13] Moreover, spokesmen for the Committee did not simply wash their hands of ICRC responsibility for allowing prominent Nazis to escape; they suggested that some Red Cross officials might have been involved 'on a local level'.[14] In the late 1990s the ICRC gave 60,000 microfilmed Second World War-era documents to research institutions in Israel, the United States and other countries. Georges Willemin, director of the ICRC archives, said on this occasion: 'Very clearly, the ICRC's activities with regard to the Holocaust are sensed as a moral failure.'[15] But the organization had not always been so open and willing to clarify this chapter of its history. The Committee had long cherished a culture of secrecy and carefully restricted access to files concerning its history.[16] Now, more than seventy years after the war ended, the organization seems far better prepared to face these difficult and controversial chapters in its own past.

A lasting achievement of those challenging years was the reform and expansion of the Geneva Conventions: the reform of the POW convention, new wording concerning sufficient food and housing, provisions covering partisan fighters, and the new convention for civilians in war time. The Conventions were not the only international legal measures that dealt with protection of war victims. As we have seen, at around the same time other provisions designed to safeguard civilians were the subject of far-reaching international agreements, particularly the United Nations' Convention on the Prevention and Punishment of the Crime of Genocide 1948 and the Universal Declaration of Human Rights. Some decades later, these efforts were reinforced with the establishment of a permanent international criminal court in The Hague in 2002. Many recent histories about human rights thinking and policy have ignored the Geneva Convention reforms. In contrast to measures emerging from the new United Nations body, the reforms lacked a high public profile, even at the time they were passed. However, the continuing relevance of such international agreements and the conventions is obvious. Humanitarian emergencies stemming not only from failed economies, environmental disasters, ethnic and religious violence, but also from outright war have continued across the globe since the late 1940s and early 1950s. We now face a refugee problem arising from armed conflict that is greater than any seen since the Second World War.

International agreements and cooperation, particularly between the world's wealthiest nations, between its military superpowers—but also between charities and agencies with an international reach—remain critical in mediating these crises.[17] As this book has shown, major, long-standing humanitarian organizations such as the ICRC have performed their work on a path crowded with political considerations. Leaders of the organization in Geneva made choices and undertook initiatives with geopolitical calculations always close at hand. Their response to the Nazi persecution of Jews and other civilians proved a tragic chapter in the story of those choices, a failure with immense consequences. My account here has focused largely on the immediate aftermath of that tragedy: while the ICRC never fully laid self-serving political considerations or self-exculpatory language to rest, the organization nevertheless put its energies into rectifying its wartime failure for future generations. The outcome was, memorably, a sweeping international convention that extended the principle of protection to civilians during times of war. This book has documented the road to that achievement, even as the long-term impact of the new convention remains an open question, ripe for further exploration.

Acknowledgements

My own work would not have been possible without the studies and efforts of other scholars before me. In particular, the works by Geoffrey Best, Jean-Claude Favez, David Forsythe, Yehuda Bauer, and last but not least Paul Stauffer's books on Carl Jacob Burckhardt. I am deeply indebted to their and many other researchers' contributions to the field. A number of colleagues and friends helped in various ways, by providing critical feedback or suggestions over the years, among them particularly Jan Lambertz (Washington, DC), Guenter Bischof (New Orleans), Michael Dick (Lincoln), David Forsythe (Lincoln), Dan Michman (Yad Vashem), Alfred Steinacher (Nice), and Gerhard L. Weinberg (North Carolina). Suzanne Brown-Fleming, Elizabeth Anthony, and Rebecca Erbelding helped me with my archival research at the United States Holocaust Memorial Museum in Washington, DC and shared some of their own research on the International Tracing Service and also the War Refugee Board with me. Special thanks to Ingrid Lomfors (The Living History Forum, Sweden) and Ruth Müller (Limmattal) for providing materials on the Red Cross. Jennifer Shimek, Tracy Brown, and Elizabeth Stone helped me to improve my prose and helped with the copy-editing.

I am grateful to many archivists and librarians, who helped me finding sources and resources, in particular: Fabrizio Bensi from the International Committee of the Red Cross archives in Geneva, the staff archivists at the Joint Distribution Committee in New York, the International Tracing Service in Bad Arolsen, the University Library in Basel and the Archive for Contemporary History in Zurich, the Swiss Federal Archives in Bern, the Library of Congress, and last but not least the National Archives II in College Park. Natascha Drubek (Regensburg) and Stephan Matyus (Mauthausen Memorial) sent me valuable sources and photos. Special thanks also go to Jeffrey Kozak (George C. Marshall Foundation) and Barbara L. Krieger (Dartmouth Library).

I am grateful for constant faculty support from the Harris Center for Judaic Studies at the University of Nebraska–Lincoln, particularly Jean and David Cahan. I began intensive research in 2009 and spent almost two years as a research fellow at Harvard University studying archival and library sources, and would therefore like to say a particular thank you to my colleagues at the Center for European Studies at Harvard.

I also received financial support from the American Jewish Joint Distribution Committee Archives in New York for this project and was awarded the Fred and

Ellen Lewis JDC Archives Fellowship in 2014. The fellowship is awarded each year to a scholar engaged in promising research about Jewish history and humanitarian affairs. This book manuscript received its finishing touches in the Fall semester of 2015 during my stay as Research Fellow at the International Institute for Holocaust Research at Yad Vashem in Jerusalem. I therefore want to recognize the International Institute for Holocaust Research—Yad Vashem and The Baron Friedrich Carl von Oppenheim Chair for the Study of Racism, Antisemitism, and the Holocaust, founded by the von Oppenheim Family of Cologne for its support. In addition, I was honoured to give the Institute's Danek Gertner Yad Vashem Research Scholarship—Annual Lecture, and greatly enjoyed addressing students of Haifa University's Master's Program in Holocaust Studies as part of a workshop organized by Yad Vashem. The facilities and the working environment of this fantastic research center are priceless. Finally I want to thank Matthew Cotton, editor at Oxford University Press in England, and his colleagues for all the help provided during the final stages of the editing and publication process.

This book is dedicated to Stas Nikolova, my wife and closest companion over many years.

Notes

INTRODUCTION

1. Human rights law and humanitarian law have much in common, such as the ban on torture and slavery as well as the principles of non-discrimination. However, humanitarian law was created especially for times of war to provide basic protection for non-combatants (prisoners of war, the wounded, civilians).

CHAPTER I

1. Michael Barnett, *Empire of Humanity: A History of Humanitarianism* (Ithaca: Cornell University Press, 2011), 1.
2. See Lynn Hunt, *Inventing Human Rights: A History* (New York: Norton, 2008), 15 ff. See Samuel Moyn, *The Last Utopia: Human Rights in History* (Cambridge, MA: Belknap Press of Harvard University Press, 2010), 11 ff. Jenny S. Martinez, *The Slave Trade and the Origins of International Human Rights Law* (New York: Oxford University Press, 2012), 16 ff.
3. Craig Calhoun, 'The Imperative to Reduce Suffering: Charity, Progress, and Emergencies in the Field of Humanitarian Action', in Michael Barnett and Thomas G. Weiss (eds.), *Humanitarianism in Question: Politics, Power, Ethics* (Ithaca: Cornell University Press, 2008), 73–97, here 77. See also Michel Foucault, *Discipline and Punish: The Birth of the Prison* (New York: Pantheon, 1977).
4. David P. Forsythe, *The Humanitarians: The International Committee of the Red Cross* (Cambridge: Cambridge University Press, 2005), 2.
5. Jean-Luc Blondel, 'The Fundamental Principles of the Red Cross and the Red Crescent: Their Origin and Development', *International Review of the Red Cross* 31.283 (July–August 1991): 349–57, here 349.
6. Federic Siordet, *Inter Arma Caritas: The Work of the International Committee of the Red Cross during the Second World War* (Geneva: International Committee of the Red Cross, 1973), 89.
7. Jean S. Pictet, *Red Cross Principles*, Preface by Max Huber (Geneva: International Committee of the Red Cross, 1956). Jean Pictet, *The Fundamental Principles of the Red Cross* (Geneva: Henry Dunant Institute, 1979). See François Bugnion, *The International Committee of the Red Cross and the Protection of War Victims* (Geneva: International Committee of the Red Cross/Oxford: Macmillan Education, 2003), 370 ff. See also Michael Barnett and Thomas G. Weiss, 'Humanitarianism: A Brief

History of the Present', in Michael Barnett and Thomas G. Weiss (eds.), *Humanitarianism in Question: Politics, Power, Ethics* (Ithaca: Cornell University Press, 2008), 1–48, here 3.

8. Forsythe, *Humanitarians,* 22.

9. Geoffrey Best, *War and Law since 1945* (Oxford: Clarendon, 2002),18, 41, 42.

10. Forsythe, *Humanitarians*, 20 f.

11. Julia F. Irwin, *Making the World Safe: The American Red Cross and a Nation's Humanitarian Awakening* (New York: Oxford University Press, 2013), 15 ff. Library of Congress, The Papers of Clara Barton, reel 68, International Committee of the Red Cross, Conferences.

12. Barnett, *Empire of Humanity*, 30.

13. Ibid., 30.

14. Max Huber, 'Principes, tâches et problèmes de la Croix-Rouge dans le droit des gens', *Revue International de la Croix-Rouge* 26.311 (1944): 882–99.

15. Quite recently the Red Cross movement introduced a Red Crystal as an alternative protective sign to the Red Crescent and the Red Cross. Israel uses the Red Star of David as the symbol for its national society inside the country, but the Red Crystal for international operations. In addition to these most commonly used signs, other symbols were used as well. The symbol of the Red Lion and Sun was used in Iran, for example.

16. Forsythe, *Humanitarians*, 30.

17. Forsythe, *Humanitarians*, 32 f.

18. Bruno Cabanes, *The Great War and the origins of Humanitarianism 1918–1924* (Cambridge: Cambridge University Press 2014), 139 ff.

19. Thanks to David Forsythe for his help on this topic.

20. See Julia F. Irwin, *Making the World Safe. The American Red Cross and a Nation's Humanitarian Awakening*, (New York: Oxford University Press, 2013).

21. David P. Forsythe, 'The ICRC: A Unique Humanitarian Protagonist', *International Review of the Red Cross* 89.865 (2007): 63–96, here 85 ff.

22. Forsythe, *Humanitarians,* 35 ff. Barnett, *Empire of Humanity*, 91.

23. James Avery Joyce, *Red Cross International and the Strategy of Peace* (London: Hodder & Stoughton, 1959), 112. Bugnion, *International Committe of the Red Cross*, 366 ff.

24. Best, *War and Law*, 80 ff.

25. Bugnion, *International Committee of the Red Cross*, 214.

26. Michel Veuthey, 'Assessing Humanitarian Law', in Thomas G. Weiss and Larry Minear (eds.), *Humanitarianism across Borders: Sustaining Civilians in Times of War*, (Boulder, CO: Lynne Rienner, 1993), 125–49, here 129.

27. Max Huber, 'Völkerrechtliche Grundsätze, Aufgaben und Probleme des Roten Kreuzes', in *Schweizer Jahrbuch für internationales Recht* 1944, 11–57, 13.

28. Huber, 'Völkerrechtliche Grundsätze', 16.

29. Birgitt Morgenbrod and Stephanie Merkenich, *Das Deutsche Rote Kreuz unter der NS-Diktatur 1933–1945* (Paderborn: Schöningh, 2008), 375.

30. Jean-Claude Favez, *Warum schwieg das Rote Kreuz? Eine internationale Organisation und das Dritte Reich* (Munich: Deutscher Taschenbuchverlag, 1994), 40 ff.

31. Forsythe, *Humanitarians*, 39. Marcel Junod, *Warrior without Weapons* (Geneva: ICRC, 1982).

32. Eros Francescangeli, 'La Croce rossa italiana nella guerra civile spagnola attraverso I documenti conservati nel suo Archivio storico', in *Giornale di storia contemporanea,* A10, number 1 (2007), 42—51, here 45, Mario Mariani, *La Croce Rossa Italiana. L'eopopea di una grande instituzione* (Milan: Mondadori 2006), 157 ff.

33. See Rainer Baudendistel, *Between Bombs and Good Intentions: The Red Cross and the Italo-Ethiopian War, 1935—1936* (New York: Berghahn, 2006). See also Aram Mattioli, *Experimentierfeld der Gewalt: Der Abessinienkrieg und seine internationale Bedeutung 1935—1941* (Zurich: Orell Füssli Verlag, 2005). Bahru Zewde, *A History of Modern Ethiopia 1855—1991* (Addis Ababa: Addis Ababa University Press, 2007). Richard Pankhurst, *The Ethiopians* (Oxford: Blackwell Publishers, 1998). Michael Burleigh, *Moral Combat: Good and Evil in World War II* (New York: Harper Perennial 2012), 8 ff. See also Gerald Steinacher (ed.), *Tra Duce, Führer e Negus: l'Alto Adige e la guerra d'Abissinia 1935—1941* (Trento: Temi, 2008).

34. Michael Barnett, *Empire of Humanity: A History of Humanitarianism* (Ithaca: Cornell University Press, 2011), 93.

35. See Favez, *Red Cross and the Holocaust*, 21; Timothy Snyder, *Bloodlands: Europe between Hitler and Stalin* (New York: Basic Books, 2010); David P. Forsythe, *Human Rights in International Relations* (Cambridge: Cambridge University Press, 2012), 22.

CHAPTER 2

1. 'Rüstung und Rotes Kreuz', *Bilanz* 5/89, 193 ff. See also Cornelia Rauh-Kühne, 'Schweizer Eigeninteressen im Vordergrund: Die Schweizer Aluminiumindustrie im Zweiten Weltkrieg', *Neue Zürcher Zeitung* [website], (21 March 2002). <http://www.nzz.ch/aktuell/startseite/article813UL-1.379421> (accessed 29 May 2014).

2. Jean-Claude Favez, *The Red Cross and the Holocaust* (Cambridge: Cambridge UP, 1999), 283 f. Yves Sandoz, 'Max Huber and the Red Cross', *The European Journal of International Law* 18.1 (2007): 171—97.

3. Vogelsanger, *Max Huber*, 173: 'In seinem Dasein bedeutete der Antritt des neuen Amtes den endgültigen Durchbruch zur Caritas'.

4. Max Huber, Der barmherzige Samariter: Betrachtungen über Evangelium und Rotkreuzarbeit (Zurich: Schulthess & Co., 1943). English translation with a foreword by William Temple (the late archbishop of Canterbury) and an introduction by Adolf Keller: *The Good Samaritan. Reflections on the Gospel and Work in the Red Cross* (London: Victor Gollancz, 1945).

5. Eugen Th. Rimli (ed.), *Das Buch vom Roten Kreuz: Das Rote Kreuz von den Anfängen bis heute* (Zurich: Fraumünster Editions, 1944), 11, 13 f.

6. Peter Vogelsanger, *Max Huber: Recht, Politik, Humanität aus Glauben* (Frauenfeld and Stuttgart: Verlag Huber, 1967), 177. See also Max Huber, 'Völkerrechtliche

Grundsätze, Aufgaben und Probleme des Roten Kreuzes', in *Schweizer Jahrbuch für internationales Recht* 1944, 11–57, 49.

7. Paul Ruegger in the foreword to Max Huber, *Denkwürdigkeiten 1907–1924: Mit Einleitung und Anmerkungen* (Zurich: Orell Füssli, 1974), 7: 'den hohen geistigen Führer der Rotkreuzbewegung in schwerster Zeit'.

8. Favez, *Red Cross and the Holocaust*, 21, 283 f. Paul Stauffer, '*Sechs furchtbare Jahre . . .*' *Auf den Spuren Carl J. Burckhardts durch den Zweiten Weltkrieg* (Zurich: Verlag Neue Zürcher Zeitung, 1998), 17 ff.

9. See Gerald Steinacher, *Hakenkreuz und Rotes Kreuz: Eine humanitäre Organisation zwischen Holocaust und Flüchtlingsproblematik* (Innsbruck: Studienverlag, 2013), 25 ff. See Favez, *Red Cross and the Holocaust*, 14, 28.

10. See David P. Forsythe, *Humanitarian Politics: The International Committee of the Red Cross* (Baltimore: Johns Hopkins University Press, 1977).

11. See Stauffer, '*Sechs furchtbare Jahre . . .*'. See also Steinacher, *Hakenkreuz und Rotes Kreuz*, 91 ff.

12. Stauffer, '*Sechs furchtbare Jahre . . .*', 9.

13. Stauffer, '*Sechs furchtbare Jahre . . .*', 11.

14. Carl J. Burckhardt, *Richelieu: Der Aufstieg zur Macht* (Munich: Verlag Georg D. W. Callwey 1941) (Erstauflage 1935 Callway in Munich), here 536.

15. Stauffer, '*Sechs furchtbare Jahre . . .*', 366.

16. Paul Stauffer, 'Grandsigneuraler "Anti-Intellektueller": Carl J. Burckhardt in den Fährnissen des totalitären Zeitalters', in Aram Mattioli (ed.), *Intellektuelle von rechts: Ideologie und Politik in der Schweiz 1918–1939* (Zurich: Orell Fuessli, 1995), 113–34, here 114.

17. Carl J. Burckhardt, 'Entdeckung des Unerwarteten', in Carl J. Burckhardt et al. (eds.), *Geschichte zwischen Gestern und Morgen*, Munich: neue edition List Verlag 1974), 7–21, 15 f.

18. Stauffer, 'Grandsigneuraler "Anti-Intellektueller"', 124 and 120 f.

19. Stefan Schomann, *Im Zeichen der Menschlichkeit: Geschichte und Gegenwart des Deutschen Roten Kreuzes* (Munich: Deutsche Verlags-Anstalt, 2013), 216–17.

20. Burckhardt to Hitler, 23 May 1936, ACICR, Detenus politiques en Allemagne CR 110/4—3.01. [73]. YV M.75.

21. Quoted in Paul Stauffer, *Zwischen Hoffmannsthal und Hitler: Carl J. Burckhardt, Facetten einer aussergewöhnlichen Existenz* (Zurich: Neue Zürcher Zeitung, 1991), 209: 'der Mann ware irgendwo einmal brauchbar. Schade, dass wir solche Diplomaten nicht haben'. See also Steinacher, *Hakenkreuz und Rotes Kreuz*, 28 ff.

22. Stauffer, '*Sechs furchtbare Jahre . . .*', 355: '*es gibt einen bestimmten Aspekt des Judentums den ein gesundes Volk bekämpfen muss*'.

23. According to Stauffer this passus was later withdrawn after intervention of the editor/publishing house. Stauffer, '*Sechs furchtbare Jahre . . .*', 355. 'dass die Juden in der ganzen Welt dem Faschismus, dessen Wesen ihnen ursprünglich nicht durchaus artfremd gewesen war, nun einen Krieg auf Leben und Tod erklären mussten, ja, dass sie, um einer völlig unleidlichen Lage zu entgehen, den Ausbruch des Zweiten Weltkrieges herbeiwünschten.'

24. George L. Mosse, *Toward the Final Solution: A History of European Racism* (New York: H. Fertig 1978). For Switzerland, see Aram Mattioli (ed.), *Antisemitismus in der Schweiz 1848–1960* (Zurich: Orell Füssli Verlag, 1998).

25. Edgar Bonjour, 'Paul Ruegger, der grand old man der Schweizer Diplomatie', *Basler Zeitung* 13 August 1977, Newspaper collection, Biographische Sammlung Ruegger, AfZG Zurich.

26. Maglione had served as Nuncio to Switzerland from September 1, 1920 to June 23, 1926 at the embassy of the Vatican in Bern, Switzerland, the appointment having been made by Pope Benedict XV. Stefan Glur, *Vom besten Pferd im Stall zur persona non grata: Paul Ruegger als Schweizer Gesandter in Rom 1936–1942* (Bern: Lang, 2005), 100. See also Moorehead, *Dunant's Dream*, 560.

27. Glur, *Vom besten Pferd*, 17. The Presidency of the International Committee of the Red Cross, in *Revue International de la Croix-Rouge et Bulletin des Sociétés de la Croix-Rouge*, Supplement, 2 (February 1948): 58–60.

28. Glur, *Vom besten Pferd*, 171 ff. and 182. Georg Kreis, 'Am Posten im faschistischen Italien', *Neue Zürcher Zeitung* [website], (21 January 2006). <http://www.nzz.ch/aktuell/startseite/articleDGHT3-1.5226> (accessed 25 May 2014).

29. Dominique-D. Junod, *The Imperiled Red Cross* (London: Kegan Paul, 1995), 42.

30. Stephan Winkler, *Die Schweiz und das geteilte Italien: Bilaterale Beziehungen in einer Umbruchsphase 1943–1945* (Basel: Helbing and Lichtenhahn, 1992), 55 ff. Glur, *Vom besten Pferd*, 257. Caroline Moorehead, *Dunant's Dream: War, Switzerland and the History of the Red Cross* (London: Carroll & Graf, 1998), 550.

31. James Crossland, *Britain and the International Committee of the Red Cross 1939–1945* (New York: Palgrave Macmillan 2014), 202.

32. Neville Wylie, *Britain, Switzerland and the Second World War* (Oxford: Oxford University Press, 2003), 329.

33. Winkler, *Die Schweiz und das geteilte Italien*, 20.

34. Glur, *Vom besten Pferd*, 134.

35. Luc van Dongen, *La Suisse face à la seconde guerre mondiale 1945–1948: Émergence et construction d'une mémoire publique*, 2nd edn (Geneva: Les Bastions, 1998), 22 ff.

36. Neville Wylie, 'Switzerland: A Neutral of Distinction?', in Neville Wylie (ed.), *European Neutrals and Non-Belligerents During the Second World War* (Cambridge: Cambridge University Press, 2002) 331–54, here 346–7.

37. Schlussbericht der Unabhängigen Expertenkommission Schweiz—Zweiter Weltkrieg (UEK), *Die Schweiz, der Nationalsozialismus und der Zweite Weltkrieg: Schlussbericht* (Zurich: Pendo Verlag, 2002), 109 ff. Somewhat ironically, in Evian only the dictator of the Dominican Republic Rafael Trujillo Molina was willing to offer a larger number of European Jews refuge. See Marion A. Kaplan, *Dominican Haven: The Jewish Refugee Settlement in Sosúa 1940–1945* (New York: Museum of Jewish Heritage, 2008).

38. Yehuda Bauer, *A History of the Holocaust*, rev. edn (New York: Franklin Watts, 2001), 141.

39. Deborah E. Lipstadt, 'America and the Holocaust', *Modern Judaism, A Review of Developments in Modern Jewish Studies* 10.3 (1990): 283–96, here 284. See also

Theodore S. Hamerow, *Why We Watched: Europe, America, and the Holocaust* (London: W.W. Norton Company, 2008), David S. Wyman, *The Abandonment of the Jews: America and the Holocaust 1941–1945* (New York: Pantheon Books, 1984), Richard Breitman and Allan J. Lichtman, *FDR and the Jews* (Cambridge, MA: Belknap Press, 2013), Bernard Wasserstein, *Britain and the Jews of Europe 1939–1945* (London: Clarendon Press, 1979).

40. Georg Kreis, 'Swiss Refugee Policy, 1933–1945', in Georg Kreis (ed.), *Switzerland and the Second World War* (London: Frank Cass, 2000), 103–31. See Unabhängige Expertenkommission Schweiz (UEK),—Zweiter Weltkrieg, *Die Schweiz und Flüchtlinge zur Zeit des Nationalsozialismus* (Bern: Eidgenössische Drucksachen- und Materialzentrale, 1999). See also Carl Ludwig, *Die Flüchtlingspolitik der Schweiz in den Jahren 1933 bis 1955: Bericht an den Bundesrat zuhanden der eidgenössischen Räte* Beilage zum Bundesblatt (Bern: n.p., 1957).

41. Stefan Mächler, *Hilfe und Ohnmacht. Der Schweizerische Israelitische Gemeindebund und die nationalsozialistische Verfolgung 1933–1945* (Zurich: Chronos 2005), 41.

42. Schlussbericht der Unabhängigen Expertenkommission Schweiz—Zweiter Weltkrieg (UEK), *Die Schweiz, der Nationalsozialismus und der Zweite Weltkrieg*, 113: 'unerwünschte Elemente (Juden, politische Extremisten, Spionageverdächtige) [von der Schweiz] fernzuhalten'.

43. The exact number for people rejected is difficult to calculate, because only a limited number of people denied safety were registered by the Swiss authorities and not all records survived. See UEK Bergier Commission final report page 117, See also Heinz Roschewski, 'Heinrich Rothmund in seinen persönlichen Akten. Zur Frage des Antisemitismus in der Schweizer Flüchtlingspolitik 1933–1945', *Studien und Quellen*, 22 (1996): 107–36, 108.

44. Jean-Claude Favez, *Warum schwieg das Rote Kreuz? Eine internationale Organisation und das Dritte Reich* (Munich: Deutscher Taschenbuchverlag, 1994), 91 f.

45. Unabhängige Expertenkommission Schweiz—Zweiter Weltkrieg(UEK), *Die Schweiz und Flüchtlinge zur Zeit des Nationalsozialismus*, 78.

46. Stefan Mächler, 'Kampf gegen das Chaos—die antisemitische Bevölkerungspolitik der eidgenössischen Fremdenpolizei und Polizeiabteilung 1917–1954', in Aram Mattioli (ed.), *Antisemitismus in der Schweiz 1848–1960* (Zurich: Orell Füssli Verlag, 1998), 357–421. Ludwig, *Flüchtlingspolitik,* 52 ff.

47. Mächler, *Hilfe und Ohnmacht*, 182.

48. Gerhart M. Riegner, 'Vorbeugender Antisemitismus', in Madeleine Dreyfus and Jürg Fischer, *Manifest vom 21. Januar 1997. Geschichtsbilder und Antisemitismus in der Schweiz*, 49–56, 52.

49. 'Man liess die Juden nicht an die zentralen Stellen der Schweizer Politik, der Schweizer Presse, der Schweizer Wirtschaft herein, dann brauchte man sie nachher auch nicht aus diesen Stellen rauszuschmeissen.' Gerhart M. Riegner, 'Vorbeugender Antisemitismus', in Madeleine Dreyfus and Jürg Fischer (eds.), *Manifest vom 21. Januar 1997. Geschichtsbilder und Antisemitismus in der Schweiz* 49–56, here 50.

50. Quoted in Rings, *Schweiz im Krieg*, 325. See also Heinz Roschewski, 'Heinrich Rothmund in seinen persönlichen Akten. Zur Frage des Antisemitismus in der Schweizer Flüchtlingspolitik 1933-1945',*Studien und Quellen*, 22 (1996): 107–36.

51. Schlussbericht der Unabhängigen Expertenkommission Schweiz—Zweiter Weltkrieg (UEK), *Die Schweiz, der Nationalsozialismus und der Zweite Weltkrieg*, 111:'*Unsere Agentur ist nicht dazu da, dass es den Juden gut geht*'.

52. Monika Imboden and Brigitte Lustenberger, 'Die Flüchtlingspolitik der Schweiz in den Jahren 1933 bis 1945', in Carsten Göhrke and Werner G. Zimmermann (eds.), '*Zuflucht Schweiz': Der Umgang mit Asylproblemen im 19. und 20. Jahrhundert* (Zurich: Chronos, 1994), 257–308, here 273:'*Die Einführung des "J"-Stempels, initiiert durch die Schweiz, ist einer der grössten Schandflecke der eidgenössischen Flüchtlingspolitik*'.

53. *Final Report of the Independent Commission of Experts Switzerland—Second World War*, 109.

54. *Final Report of the Independent Commission of Experts Switzerland*, 114.

55. DDS, vol. 14, no. 237, Appendix p. 777 (original French). Note of de Haller to Pilet-Golaz, 23 September 1942. *Final Report of the Independent Commission of Experts Switzerland,* 172.

56. Forsythe, *Humanitarians,* 187. Thanks to David Forsythe for additional information on this point.

57. De Haller to Royall Tyler, United Nations Geneva, June 20, 1945, BAR E2001 (E)-1-155, dodos.ch/2182 See also *Abschlussbericht Unabhängige Expertenkommission Schweiz,* 169.

58. Werner Rings, *Schweiz im Krieg 1933–1945, Ein Bericht* (Zurich: Chronos, 1997), 309–14.

59. Robert Nicole, 'Bericht über die Schweizer Ärztemission nach Finnland', in Reinhold Busch (ed.), *Die Schweiz, die Nazis und die erste Ärztemission an die Ostfront* (Berlin Verlag Frank Wünsche, 2002).

60. Rings, *Schweiz im Krieg 1933–1945*, 310.

61. Gerhart M. Riegner, *Never Despair: Sixty Years in the Service of the Jewish People and the Cause of Human Rights* (Chicago: Ivan R. Dee, 2006), 47.

62. There were however some private initiatives by leftist circles in Switzerland. Swiss doctors, organised in the 'Centrale Sanitaire Suisse-Schweizerische Ärzte und Sanitätshilfe', organised help for refugees of the Spanish Civil War and sent small medical teams to aid Tito's communist partisans in Yugoslavia in 1944–5. Centrale Sanitaire Suisse (ed.), *Bericht über die Arbeit der Centrale Sanitaire Suisse in den Jahren 1937 bis 1945* (Zurich: CSS, 1945).

63. van Dongen, *La Suisse face à la seconde guerre mondiale*, 151.

64. Jonathan Petropoulos, *The Faustian Bargain. The Art World in Nazi Germany* (Oxford: Oxford University Press, 2000), 70.

65. Forsythe, *The Humanitarians*, 48.

66. Forsythe, *Humanitarians,* 48.

67. Bergier Commission final report, 116. See also Herbert R. Reginbogin, *Faces of Neutrality: A Comparative Analysis of the Neutrality of Switzerland and Other Neutral Nations during WWII* (Berlin: LIT Verlag, 2009) 21.

68. Imboden and Lustenberger, 'Die Flüchtlingspolitik der Schweiz', 296. For an overview on Switzerland and WWII see Marc Perrenoud, 'La Suisse, les Suisses, la neutralité et le IIIe Reich (1941-1945)' in *Revue d'Histoire de la Shoah*, 203 (October 2015) : 51–86.

69. Letter Friedrich K. to the ICRC in Geneva, 30 July 1933, ACICR, Detenus politiques en Allemagne CR 110/4—3.01 [4992].YV M.75.

70. Favez, *Red Cross and the Holocaust*, 17.

71. 'Copie' written notes, signed Huber, 1 September 1933, ACICR, CR 110/4-3. 01.YV M.75.

72. Letter by president of Swedish Red Cross Prince Carl to German Red Cross president, 11 August 1933, ACICR, CR 110/4-3.01,YV M.75.

73. German Red Cross presidency answers to Swedish Red Cross president Prince Carl, 5 October 1933, signed von Winterfeldt-Menkin, ACICR, CR 110/4-3.01, YV, M.75.

74. Herzog von Sachsen-Coburg und Gotha an Max Huber, 12 September 1935, ACICR, CR 110/4—3.01,YV M.75.

75. Deutsches Rote Kreuz Hauptverwaltung to Sidney Brown from the ICRC, 11 September 1935 (*Vertraulich!*), ACICR, CR 110/4—3.01.YV M.75.

76. Commission des Détenus Politiques, Séance du 10 septembre 1935, ACICR, CR 110—2.02.

77. 'Vom nationalsozialistischen Standpunkt aus betrachet steht der politische Verbrecher auf der gleichen Stufe wie der kriminelle Verbrecher; dies geht auch aus der neuen Strafgesetzgebung hervor.' 'Heil Hitler!' Reinhard Heydrich, Preussische Geheime Staatspolizei to the Chief of staff of the Duke of Coburg (German Red Cross), 13 February 1936, ACICR, CR 110/4—3.01.YV M.75.

78. His Nazi Party membership was publicly denied. Given the archival evidence it is somewhat surprising that he was able to keep his Nazi Party membership hidden until recently. According to the Nazi Party membership files in the National Archives, he had joined the Nazi Party in 1933. RG 242 BDC, NSDAP Ortsgruppenkartei A 3340, MFOK—H012, Hartmann, Walther Georg, born 17 July 1892, membership number: 2673264, joined the party May 1 1933. 'Beruf: Schriftsteller, Wohnung: DRK Praesidium Ettal Nuernberg Oberbayern'. NARA, BDC Series 3002 NSDAP Census Berlin July 1939, roll number A–3340 PC–1–034. Parteistatistische Erhebung 1939: Personalien und NSDAP-Mitgliedschaft 1 May 1933, listed as member of 'NS-Volkswohnfahrt, NS-Reichsluftschutzbund and Reichskulturkammer'. Hartmann is listed as 'Politischer Leiter', 'angeschlossene Vereine, Rotes Kreuz—führend tätig'. RG 242 BDC, Reichskulturkammer Generalkartei A3339–RKK–X035 Hartmann, Walther Georg 'Abteilungsleiter'. It is not clear whether this is just a file card or an actual membership listing. In the party census of 1939, however, he is listed

as member of the Reichskulturkammer. Special Thanks to Jan Lambertz for helping me with this research.

79. In the personnel list of the DRK in 1940, Hartmann is also mentioned as a Nazi Party member. See also Schomann, *Im Zeichen der Menschlichkeit*, 267, 217 f.

80. Birgitt Morgenbrod and Stephanie Merkenich, *Das Deutsche Rote Kreuz unter der NS-Diktatur 1933–1945* (Paderborn: Schöningh, 2008). Dieter Riesenberger, *Das Deutsche Rote Kreuz: Eine Geschichte 1864–1990* (Paderborn: Schöningh Verlag, 2002), 354 ff. Bernd Biege, *Helfer unter Hitler: Das Rote Kreuz im Dritten Reich* (Reinbek: Kindler, 2000), 10. Markus Wicke, *SS und DRK Das Präsidium des Deutschen Roten Kreuzes im nationalsozialistischen Herrschaftssystem 1937–1945* (Potsdam:Vicia, 2002). Schomann, *Im Zeichen der Menschlichkeit*, 267 f.

81. 'Durch das Reichsgesetz vom 9.12.1937 ueber das DRK wurde die Organisation vollkommen neu als einheitl.[...] Rechtskörperschaft unter Schirmherrschaft Adolf Hitlers gebildet.' [...] [...] 'je nach den Anforderungen von Reich, Partei u. Wehrmacht.' *Meyers Lexikon*, Achte Auflage, Bibliographisches Institut Leipzig 1942, 598.

82. Wendy Lower, *Hitler's Furies: German Women in the Nazi Killing Fields* (Boston: Houghton Mifflin Harcourt, 2013), 45.

83. Letter to Sally Meyer, 13 September 1933 signed Sidney H. Brown. Secretary of the ICRC, ACICR, CR 110/4—3.01.YV M.75.

84. Favez, *Red Cross and the Holocaust*, 56 f.

85. Christopher R. Browning and Jürgen Matthäus, *The Origins of the Final Solution: The Evolution of Nazi Jewish Policy, September 1939–March 1942* (Lincoln: University of Nebraska Press, 2004), 195.

86. Favez, *Red Cross and the Holocaust*, 57.

87. 'Helfen als Kunst des Möglichen, Ein Vortrag von Prof. Max Huber über das Internationale Komitee vom Roten Kreuz', *Neue Zürcher Zeitung*, 25 January 1944. Archiv für Sozialgeschichte Zürich, Mappe 49.5 ZA 1 'Internationales Komitee vom Roten Kreuz (IKRK)'.

88. Monty Penkower, 'The World Jewish Congress Confronts the International Red Cross During the Holocaust', in Jeffrey S. Gurock (ed.), *America, American Jews and the Holocaust*, vol. 7 of American Jewish History (New York: Routledge,1998), 377–404, here 379.

89. Mark Roseman, *The Villa, The Lake, The Meeting: Wannsee and the Final Solution* (London: Penguin Press 2002).

90. See Alan Steinweis, *Kristallnacht 1938* (Cambridge, MA: Harvard University Press, 2009).

91. Aktennotiz Riegner, 17 November 1942, Archives of the World Jewish Congress, AfZG Zurich, NL Stauffer 14 (V), 31.1.3 Ar WJC. Schlussbericht der Unabhängigen Expertenkommission Schweiz—Zweiter Weltkrieg (UEK), *Die Schweiz, der Nationalsozialismus und der Zweite Weltkrieg, Die Schweiz, der Nationalsozialismus und der Zweite Weltkrieg*, 122. Riegner, *Never Despair*, 48 f. Favez, *Red Cross and the Holocaust*, 39, 277.

92. Favez, *Red Cross and the Holocaust*, 6 and 293 f.
93. Ibid., 38 ff. Richard Breitman, *Official Secrets: What the Nazis Planned, What the British and Americans Knew* (New York: Hill & Wang, 1998), 173. Unabhängige Expertenkommission Schweiz (UEK),—Zweiter Weltkrieg, *Die Schweiz und Flüchtlinge*, 101.
94. Favez, *Red Cross and the Holocaust*, 87.
95. Huber, *Das Internationale Komitee vom Roten Kreuz*, 7: 'einer internationalen, von nationalen Interessen völlig freien Institution'.
96. Forsythe, *Humanitarians*, 2.
97. NL Burckhardt UB Basel Burckhardt to Rothmund, 23 January 1946. BI 46 i Dossier 9, Heinrich Rothmund: 'der einzigen Institution, durch welche die Schweiz bisweilen etwas wie eine Grossmachtstellung ausübte, die einzige, auf die die Schweiz in ihrer Not jetzt sich einigermassen berufen konnte'.
98. Swiss commission of experts—Bergier report final report 132 f.
99. Unabhängige Expertenkommission Schweiz—Zweiter Weltkrieg (Independent Commission of Experts Switzerland—Second World War) (ed.), *Switzerland, National Socialism and the Second World War*. Final Report (Zurich: Pendo Verlag, 2002), 132 f.
100. See Neville Wylie, *Barbed Wire Diplomacy: Britain, Germany, and the Politics of Prisoners of War, 1939–1945* (Oxford: Oxford University Press, 2010).
101. Favez, *Red Cross and the Holocaust*, 66. See also Wylie, *Barbed Wire Diplomacy*, 155 ff. See also Isabelle Vonèche Cardia, *Neutralité et Engagement : Les Relations entre le Comité International de la Croix-Rouge (CICR) et le Gouvernement Suisse, 1938–1945* (Lausanne: Société d'histoire de la Suisse romande, 2012), 143 ff. Isabelle Vonèche Cardia, 'Les raisons du silence du Comité International de la Croix-Rouge (CICR) face aux déportations', in *Revue d'Histoire de la Shoah*, 203 (October 2015) : 87–122. S. P. MacKenzie, 'The Shackling Crisis: A Case Study in the Dynamics of Prisoner-of-War Diplomacy in the Second World War', *The International History Review* 17 (1995): 78–98; revised version published as: 'Krieger in Ketten: Eine Fallstudie über die Dynamik der Kriegsgefangenpolitik', in Günter Bischof and Rüdiger Overmans (eds.), *Kriegsgefangenschaft im Zweiten Weltkrieg: Eine vergleichende Perspektive* (Ternitz [Austria]: Gerhard Höller, 1998), 45–68.
102. Favez, *Red Cross and the Holocaust*, 66. The shackling crisis is also prominently discussed in the Festschrift for Burckhardt in occasion of his 70th birthday. See Hermann Rinn und Max Rychner (eds.), *Dauer im Wandel. Festschrift zum 70. Geburtstag von Carl J. Burckhardt* (Munich: Verlag Georg D. W. Callwey), 196. On pages 9–21 Burckhardt's closest aid writes about the shackling crisis and how Burckhardt and the ICRC avoided a major meltdown of the Geneva Convention.
103. Aktennotiz Riegner, 17 November 1942, Archives of the World Jewish Congress, AfZG Zurich, NL Stauffer 14 (V), 31.1.3 Ar WJC.
104. Favez, *Red Cross and the Holocaust*, 88.
105. Riegner, *Never Despair*, 48 f., here 49.

106. Isabelle Vonèche Cardia, 'Les raisons du silence du Comité International de la Croix-Rouge (CICR) face aux déportations', *Revue d'Histoire de la Shoah*, 203 (October 2015): 87–122.

107. Memo from the American consul Paul C. Squire, about his interview with Dr Carl J. Burckhardt, 7 November 1942, quoted in Jean-Claude Favez, *The Red Cross and the Holocaust* (Cambridge: Cambridge University Press, 1999), 293 f.

108. Forsythe, *Humanitarians*, 49.

109. Moorehead, *Dunant's Dream*, 706.

110. Sandoz, 'Max Huber and the Red Cross', 193.

111. [Burckhardt] to Nationalrat Dr A. Oeri in Bern, 11 December 1942, AfZG Zurich, NL Stauffer 14 (V), 3.1.1.2 Ar IKRK.

112. Jean Pictet, *The Fundamental Principles of the Red Cross Proclaimed by the Twentieth International Conference of the Red Cross, Vienna, 1965: Commentary* (Geneva: Henry Dunant Institute, 1979), 6.

113. Caroline Moorehead, *Dunant's Dream. War, Switzerland and the History of the Red Cross* (New York: Carroll and Graf Publishers, 1998), 545.

114. [Burckhardt] to Nationalrat Dr A. Oeri in Bern, 11 December 1942, AfZG Zurich, NL Stauffer 14 (V), 3.1.1.2 Ar IKRK.

115. Max Huber, *Völkerrechtliche Grundsätze: Aufgaben und Probleme des Roten Kreuzes* (Zurich: Polygraphischer Verlag A.G, 1944), 337.

116. Favez, *Red Cross and the Holocaust*, 282.

117. 'Humanitarianism: Does Help Hurt?', *Economist*, 10 September 1998, 6.

118. Moorehead, *Dunant's Dream*, xxxi.

119. Remembering the Shoah: The ICRC and the international community's efforts in responding to genocide, 28 April 2015, Speech by ICRC president Peter Maurer, <https://www.icrc.org/en/document/remembering-shoah-icrc-and-international-communitys-efforts-responding-genocide-and>.

CHAPTER 3

1. See Meir Dworzecki, 'The International Red Cross and its Policy vis-à-vis the Jews in the Ghettos and Concentration Camps in Nazi-occupied Europe', in Israel Gutman et al. (eds.), *Rescue Attempts during the Holocaust: Proceedings of the Second Yad Vashem International Historical Conference, Jerusalem, April 8–11, 1974* (Jerusalem: Yad Vashem, 1977), 71–110.

2. Note from ICRC, director Prisoners of War and Civilian Internees Committee for Mr James, American Red Cross, Washington, DC, 7 May 1943 (Confidential), NARA, RG 200, American National Red Cross, Box 1018, Folder 619.2 Camps—Europe, General.

3. Crossland, *Britain and the International Committee of the Red Cross*, 115 f.

4. 'Aktennotiz über eine Unterredung mit Prof. Carl Burckhardt vom Internationalen Roten Kreuz vom 18. Mai 1943', signed Riegner, 19 May 1943. AfZG Zurich, NL Stauffer 14 (V), 31.1.3 Ar WJC.

5. Before the Nazi takeover of Austria in 1938, he was a prominent Austrian diplomat who had served in the Austrian embassy in Berlin. After the annexation of Austria by Nazi Germany in 1938, he was out of a job and ultimately started to work for the ICRC. After his service in the ranks of the ICRC, he returned in the diplomatic service of the Austrian Republic, from 1946 to 1955 as diplomat in Rome and later Austrian ambassador at the Vatican. See Rudolf Agstner et al. (eds.), *Österreichs Diplomaten zwischen Kaiser und Kreisky: Biografisches Handbuch der Diplomaten des Höheren Auswärtigen Dienstes 1918–1959* (Vienna: DÖW, 2009), 415–17. Favez, *Red Cross and the Holocaust,* 287 f. For Schwarzenberg see also Colienne Meran, Marysia Miller-Aichholz, Erkinger Schwarzenberg (ed.) *Johannes E. Schwarzenberg, Erinnerungen und Gedanken eines Diplomaten im Zeitenwandel 1903–1978* (Vienna: Böhlau 2013) in particular the contribution by Oliver Rathkolb, 'Johannes Schwarzenberg – Eine Persönlichkeit der Zeitgeschichte im 20. Jahrhundert', 251–61.

6. François Bugnion, *The International Committee of the Red Cross and the Protection of War Victims* (Geneva: International Committee of the Red Cross/Oxford: Macmillan Education, 2003), 208.

7. Suzanne Ferrière to Kullmann, 16 February 1943, G59/6—169, Archives du Comité international de la Croix-Rouge, ACICR G 59/6—170, Microfilm reel number 9, USHMM-19.045 M. Receipt for medication to Commission Mixte de Secours de International Red Cross Geneva from the ghetto Theresienstadt 'Jüdische Selbstverwaltung Theresienstadt 30. November 1943, Betrifft: Medikamentensendung laut Zuschrift vom 30.9.1943, Dr Paul Israel Eppstein, Dr Benjamin Israel Murmelstein.' CZA A320\25-150.

8. '*Die Versorgung mit Lebensmitteln wie auch Medikamenten in den fast ausschliesslich dem Arbeitseinsatz dienenden jüdischen Lagern im Osten wird als vollkommen ausreichend bezeichnet, so dass Sendungen dorthin grundsätzlich als nicht notwendig angesehen werden.*' Quoted in Favez, *Warum schwieg das Rote Kreuz?* 250. Letter Hartmann to Burckhardt, 5 June 1943, ACICR G 59/2.

9. *Report of the Joint Relief Commission of the International Red Cross 1941–1946* (Geneva: International Red Cross Committee; League of Red Cross Societies 1948), 12.

10. Forsythe, *Humanitarians,* 44. Christian Gerlach, *Extremely Violent Societies: Mass Violence in the Twentieth-Century World* (Cambridge: Cambridge University Press, 2010), 240. William N. Medlicott, *The Economic Blockade* (London: H. M. Stationery Office, 1952–1959).

11. The Jewish communities in Palestine (Yishuv) donated money for an estimated 100.000 food parcels delivered through the Red Cross. See Dina Porat, *The Blue and the Yellow Stars of David: The Zionist Leadership in Palestine and the Holocaust, 1939–1945* (Cambridge, MA: Harvard University Press 1990), pp. 126–9.

12. Favez, *The Red Cross and the Holocaust,* 98.

13. Ibid., 279.

14. Letter of J. E. Schwarzenberg to Adolf Keller from the 'Europäische Zentralstelle für kirchliche Hilfsaktionen', Geneva, 20 March 1945. Archives du Comité

international de la Croix-Rouge, ACICR G 59/[0] 1.03, Microfilm reel number 1, USHMM, RG—19.045 M.

15. Siordet, *Inter Arma Caritas*, 1947, 77.

16. Hanna Zweig-Strauss, *Saly Mayer, 1882–1950: Ein Retter jüdischen Lebens während des Holocaust* (Cologne: Böhlau, 2007). Thanks to Claus W. Hirsch for recommending this book about Mayer's background.

17. For the history of the JDC, see Yehuda Bauer, *My Brother's Keeper: A History of the American Jewish Joint Distribution Committee 1929–1939* (Philadelphia: Jewish Publication Society of America, 1974), and Yehuda Bauer, *American Jewry and the Holocaust: The American Jewish Joint Distribution Committee 1939–1945* (Detroit: Wayne State University Press, 1981).

18. 'Note für Herrn Dr. Bachmann (evtl. für Herrn Burckhardt)' by Schwarzenberg, 26 July 1944: '*erfahrener und diskreter Freund des Hauses*'. Archives du Comité international de la Croix-Rouge, ACICR G59/[0]-1.06, microfilm reel 1, USHMM, RG—19.045 M.

19. Ibid.

20. Wyman, *Abandonment of the Jews*, 209 ff. Breitman, *Official Secrets*. Breitman and Lichtman, *FDR and the Jews*. For knowledge about the Holocaust and late rescue efforts, see also Samuel Moyn, *The Last Utopia: Human Rights in History* (Cambridge, MA: Belknap Press, 2010), 14 ff.

21. Other reasons existed for the creation of the WRB; 1944 was an election year, and Jewish voters were of particular interest to Roosevelt.

22. Breitman, *Official Secrets*, 192.

23. Executive Office of the President, War Refugee Board, Washington, DC, 12 September 1945, Letter from William O'Dwyer, executive director, to the JDC in New York, JDC Archives New York, 1945/54, Reel 193, Folder 1710.

24. Stauffer, '*Sechs furchtbare Jahre…* ', 328.

25. JDC Archives New York, Saly Mayer Collection 3/2/2/23b. On 12 March 1943 Max Huber wrote to Saly Mayer, president of the Association of Jewish Communities in Switzerland.

26. Suzanne Ferriere to Kullmann, 16 February 1943, G59/6—169, Archives du Comité international de la Croix-Rouge, ACICR G 59/6—170, Microfilm reel number 9, USHMM-19.045 M.

27. Extrait PV 36 du Bureau, séance du 3 novembre 1943 Bureau, 12 December 1943, ACICR, G3 carton 30, Yad Vashem RG-M 75.2.YV.ID3724108.

28. Leland Harrison forwards a message from the WRB to Max Huber, January 29, 1944, Archives du Comité international de la Croix-Rouge, ACICR G596—170, Microfilm reel number 9, USHMM-19.045 M.

29. JDC Archives New York, SM3/2/2/23b. Daniel J. Reagan to Max Huber, Geneva, 11 February 1944.

30. Letter Daniel J. Reagan from the US Legation in Bern to president Max Huber, 11 February 1944, Archives du Comité international de la Croix-Rouge, ACICR G59/6—170, Microfilm reel number 9, USHMM-19.045 M. See also

JDC Archives New York, SM3/2/2/23b. Daniel J. Reagan to Max Huber, Geneva, 11 February 1944.

31. JDC Archives New York, Saly Mayer Collection 3/2/2/23b, Daniel J. Reagan, commercial attaché, US legation in Bern contacts Saly Mayer on 11 February 1944.

32. JDC Archives New York, Saly Mayer Collection, Roll 8, Folder 23. '100,000 Dollars 300,000 Frs from Joint', meeting notes, 'Schwarzenberg quote' [1944].

33. JDC Archives New York, Saly Mayer Collection, 3/2/2/23b, Saly Mayer to Max Huber, 16 February 1944.

34. Zweig-Strauss, *Saly Mayer*, 167.

35. Schwarzenberg to Daniel J. Reagan, commercial attaché, US legation in Bern, 13 March 1944. Papers of the War Refugee Board (Microfilm Publication Bethesda, MD: University Publications of America, 2002). Microfilm LM0306, Reel 20, Folder 16, frames 631–632, USHMM.

36. AMRC, national headquarters, memo, Henry W. Dunning, May 6, 1944, NARA, RG 200, Box 1018, Folder 619.2 'Camps – Europe, General'. handwritten note: 'Mr. Allen – information. Probably not much that we can do. MP'

37. Francis B. James AMRC Special Representative to R. Gallopin Director Relief Prisoners of War ICRC Geneva, February 7, 1944. NARA, RG 200, Box 1018, Folder 619.2 'Camps – Europe, General'.

38. AMRC, national headquarters, memo, Henry W. Dunning, May 6, 1944, NARA, RG 200, Box 1018, Folder 619.2 'Camps – Europe, General'. handwritten note: 'Mr. Allen – information. Probably not much that we can do. MP'.

39. Sten Söderberg, *Svenska Röda Korset, 1856–1965: de första 100 åren* (Stockholm: AB Svensk Litteratur, 1965), 297.

40. Bugnion, *International Committee of the Red Cross*, 239.

41. Jewish activists were very sceptical about the ICRC report from the very beginning. In a telegram from [Dr Fred Ullmann? in Geneva] to Ernest Frischer, a Jewish member of the Czechoslovak State Council in London was informed about the Theresienstadt visit of the ICRC: 'Dieser Bericht der hier beim Internationalen Roten Kreuz geheimgehalten wird, scheint die Lage viel zu günstig zu beurteilen und muss mit grösster Vorsicht aufgenommen werden.' Telegram from [Fred Ullmann?] for Ernest Frischer in London, 25 July 1944, CZA A320\25-143. Ernest Frischer wrote to ICRC official J. Celleriere in London on 17 February 1945: 'It is now clear to me that the sole aim of the Germans, by inviting in summer 1944 representatives of the International and Danish Red Cross to Terezin, was to deceive the world through their testimony. These two delegates were allowed to come and see conditions in Terezin, which in fact, were quite tolerable. They were assured by the Germans that Terezin was not a transitional camp for further deportation and that the inmates would remain there. No sooner had the delegates left Terezin, the Germans commenced with the deportations.' Ernest Frischer to J. Celleriere ICRC London, 17 February 1945, CZA A320\25-16.

42. Steven Spielberg Film and Video Archive, USHMM, <http://www.ushmm.org/online/film/display/detail.php?file_num=5278> (accessed 14 July 2015).

43. Cesarani, *Becoming Eichmann,* 196 f. A report about tjis visit was also shared with the Intergovernmental Committee for Refugees, see J. Schwarzenberg ICRC to G. Kullmann, Haut Commissariat pour les refugies, London, 'Concerns: visite du camp de Theresienstadt par les Delegues du Comité International de la Croix-Rouge.' May 4, 1945, Archives du Comité international de la Croix-Rouge, ACICR G 59, G59/6—169. Microfilm reel 9, USHMM-19.045 M.

44. Wyman, *Abandonment of the Jews,* 238.

45. Reginbogin, *Faces of Neutrality,* 135 ff. See Paul A. Levine, *From Indifference to Activism: Swedish Diplomacy and the Holocaust 1938–1944* (Uppsala: Gotab, 1996), 68 ff. Paul A. Levine, 'Swedish Neutrality during the Second World War: Tactical Success or Moral Compromise?', in Wylie (ed.), *European Neutrals and Non-Belligerents,* 304–30, here 319. Rudolf L. Bindschedler et al. (eds.), *Schwedische und Schweizerische Neutralität im Zweiten Weltkrieg* (Basel: Helbing and Lichtenhahn, 1985).

46. Paul Levine, *From Indifference to Activism: Swedish Diplomacy and the Holocaust; 1938–1944* (Uppsala: Uppsala University Press, 1996), 69.

47. Ibid., 69. W. Churchill, cited in Liefland, 'They must get in before the end; *Churchill och Sverige 1944 och 1945'* in Utrikespolitik och historia, Eds. Mats Bergquist et al., Stockholm: Militärhistoriska förlaget 1987. Thanks to Michael Dick for pointing me to this quote.

48. Martin Gabriel Jürg, *The American Conception of Neutrality after 1941* (London: Macmillan, 1988), 49–50.

49. Ibid., 52.

50. Ibid., 50.

51. van Dongen, *La Suisse face a la seconde guerre mondiale,* 46.

52. Ibid., 39.

53. Stamm, *Der 'grosse Stucki',* 277.

54. For Sweden see Steven Koblik, *The Stones Cry Out: Sweden's Response to the Persecution of the Jews, 1933–1945* (New York: Holocaust Library, 1988).

55. Burleigh, *Moral Combat,* 467. Leni Yahil, 'The uniqueness of the rescue of Danish Jewry', in *Rescue Attempts during the Holocaust. Proceedings of the Second Yad Vashem International Historical Conference—April 1974* (Jerusalem: Yad Vashem, 1977), 617–25.

56. Levine, *From Indifference to Activism,* 72.

57. Konrad Stamm, *Der 'grosse Stucki'. Eine schweizerische Karriere von weltmännischem Format. Minister Walter Stucki (1888–1963)* (Zurich: Verlag Neue Zürcher Zeitung 2013), 275.

58. Jörg Kistler, 'Das Politische Konzept der Schweizerischen Nachkriegshilfe in den Jahren 1943–1948' (Ph.D. dissertation, University of Bern, 1980), 214.

59. 'Protokoll einer Besprechung über die Flüchtlingsfrage am 29 Oktober 1943 im Sitzungszimmer des Bundesrates', Bundesarchiv Bern E 2001 (D) 1968/74, 13, meeting on 29 October 1943.

60. See Arieh Ben-Tov, *Facing the Holocaust in Budapest: The International Committee of the Red Cross and the Jews in Hungary, 1943–1945* (Geneva: Springer, 1988). See also Deborah S. Cornelius, *Hungary in World War II: Caught in the Cauldron* (New York: Fordham University Press, 2011), 277 ff.

61. Braham, *The Politics of Genocide,* 1298.

62. Wyman, *Abandonment of the Jews,* 236.

63. Executive Office of the President, War Refugee Board, Washington, DC, November 1944, 'German Extermination Camps—Auschwitz and Birkenau', JDC Archives New York, 1945/54 Reel 193, Folder AR 45/54–2050, attached report 'The Extermination Camps of Auschwitz (Oswiecim) and Birkenau in Upper Slesia'. See also Favez, *Red Cross and the Holocaust,* 44 f.

64. Wyman, *Abandonment of the Jews,* 237.

65. Breitman, *Official Secrets,* 198; Levine, *From Indifference to Activism,* 70 ff.

66. Quoted in Levine, *Raoul Wallenberg in Budapest,* 145.

67. Handler, *A Man for All Connections,* 7 ff. Randolph L. Braham, *The Politics of Genocide: The Holocaust in Hungary,* vol. 2 (New York: Columbia University Press, 1994), 1085 ff.

68. For Wallenberg and protective passports, see Cornelius, *Hungary in World War II,* 341 f.

69. Archives du Comité international de la Croix-Rouge, ACICR G 59 [0] 1.01, Folder 'Kullmann (finanzielle Hilfe via schwedischen Vertreter in Budapest) 10 Oct. 1944–22 Nov. 1944'. 'Mitteilung 10.10.1944 (vertraulich)'. Microfilm reel 1, USHMM, RG-19.045 M.

70. Wyman, *Abandonment of the Jews,* 240–3; Ben-Tov, *Facing the Holocaust,* 294, 388; Paul A. Levine, *Raoul Wallenberg in Budapest: Myth, History and Holocaust* (London: Vallentine Mitchell, 2010). See Andrew Handler, *A Man for All Connections: Raoul Wallenberg and the Hungarian State Apparatus 1944–1945* (Westport, CT: Praeger, 1996), 7 ff.

71. Report of the War Refugee Board for Week of 15–20 May 1944 by Executive Director J.W. Pehle. Papers of the War Refugee Board (Bethesda, MD: University Publications of America, 2002). Microfilm LM0305, Reel 26, Folder 1, frames 46–58, USHMM.

72. Favez, *Red Cross and the Holocaust,* 249.

73. Siordet, *Inter Arma Caritas,* 1947, 76.

74. Alex Kershaw, *The Envoy: The Epic Rescue of the Last Jews in Europe in the Desperate Closing Months of World War II* (Philadelphia: Da Capo, 2010), 157.

75. Braham, *Politics of Genocide,* 1090.

76. Ben-Tov, *Facing the Holocaust,* 183.

77. Ibid., 184.

78. Wyman, *Abandonment of the Jews,* 238.

79. David Kranzler, *The Man Who Stopped the Trains to Auschwitz: George Mantello, El Salvador, and Switzerland's Finest Hour* (Syracuse: Syracuse University Press, 2000), 166.

80. Letter Pilet-Golaz to Minister Jaeger in Budapest 7 July 1944, Diplomatische Dokumente der Schweiz dodis.ch 11974 Swiss Federal Archives E 4800 (A) 1967/111/330.

81. Folder 'Verkehr mit deutschen Behörden 18.8.1944-19.12.1944'. Handwritten copy of a letter to German Minister Berber, 14 August 1944: '*Bitte helfen Sie uns mit Nachdruck in der ungarischen Sache. Sie ist von allergrösster aussenpolitischer Bedeutung...* *Ein Deutscher der heute seinen Namen mit einer solchen Rettung verbindet, erwirbt sich ein ganz besonderes Verdienst*'. Archives du Comité international de la Croix-Rouge, ACICR G 59/[0]–1.04, microfilm reel 1, USHMM, RG–19.045 M.

82. 'Helfen als Kunst des Möglichen: Ein Vortrag von Prof. Max Huber über das Internationale Komitee vom Roten Kreuz', *Neue Zürcher Zeitung*, 25 January 1944. Archiv für Sozialgeschichte Zürich, Mappe 49.5, ZA 1 'Internationales Komitee vom Roten Kreuz' (IKRK): [*Die*] '*humanitäre Tätigkeit darf nicht durch Gedanken an möglichen Prestigegewinn unseres Landes für die Nachkriegszeit um ihre Lauterkeit gebracht werden*'.

83. Huber, *Das Internationale Komitee vom Roten Kreuz*, 17.

84. NL Burckhardt UB Basel B II 46 i, Dossier 3, Martin Bodmer. Schreiben Burckhardt an Martin Bodmer 3 November 1947, 'Persönlich und Vertraulich'.

85. Letter with official government letterhead by Eduard de Haller Delegate of the Swiss government for aid and relief assistance to Burckhardt 'dear friend' (Personelle et confidentielle), 3 August 1944. Archives du Comité international de la Croix-Rouge, ACICR G 59/[0]–1.05, microfilm reel 1, USHMM, RG–19.045 M.

86. Schomann, *Im Zeichen der Menschlichkeit*, 263–4: '*Es muss vermieden werden, dass eine andere Organisation dem Komitee zuvorkommt*'.

87. Ambassador Ruegger to Burckhardt, 16 September 1944, IfZG Zurich, NL Ruegger 23.9.1 'Carl Jacob Burckhardt, president of the ICRC, July 1944–July 1946'.

88. Harrison, US legation in Bern, to Secretary of State, Washington, DC, 13 July 1944. Papers of the War Refugee Board (Bethesda, MD: University Publications of America, 2002). Microfilm LM0306, Reel 6, Folder 5, frames 469–471, USHMM. See also McClelland to WRB Washington, DC, 4 July 1944. War Refugee Board Papers, Box 70, Folder 10, FDRL. Thanks to Rebecca Erbelding, USHMM, for sharing this document with me.

89. Harrison, US legation in Bern, to WRB, Washington, DC, 29 July 1944. War Refugee Board Papers, Box 66, Folder 6, General Correspondence McClelland, FDRL. Thanks to Rebecca Erbelding, USHMM, for sharing this document with me.

90. Aktennotiz zu der am 21. Juli 1944 mit Herrn Professor Burckhardt stattgehabten Unterredung. Geneva 21 July 1944 (Confidential), signed Mathieu Muller, Agudas Jisroel Weltorganisation (World Organization for orthodox Jews), Yad Vashem Archives M.20, Archives of A. Silberschein, Geneva (Relico), ID 3687094, Document # 110–112.

91. Letter to Saly Mayer from [Agudas Jisroel Weltorganisation Genf], 7 August 1944, Yad Vashem Archives M.20, ID 3687094, Archives of A. Silberschein, Geneva (Relico), Document # 107 and 108. Relico was an Aid Committee for the Jewish populations in European war zones founded in 1939 by Dr Abraham Silberschein in Geneva.

92. NL Ruegger 23.9.1 IfZG Zurich, letter of Carl Jacob Burckhardt to Paul Ruegger, 7 August 1944, page 2: 'Juden in Ungarn'.

93. Ibid.

94. Invitation to various Jewish organizations to meet in Geneva on August 10, signed Carl J. Burckhardt, August 8, 1944, Archives du Comité international de la Croix-Rouge, ACICR G G59/7/00—171, Microfilm reel 9, USHMM-19.045 M.

95. Knuchel to Burckhardt 18 September 1944, Archives du Comité international de la Croix-Rouge, ACICR G59/7/00—171, Microfilm reel 9, USHMM-19.045 M.

96. 'Abschliessend erklärt Prof. Huber, das IRK werde sein Möglichstes leisten, um der leidenden Menschheit zu helfen.' Aktennotiz zu der am 10. August 1944 unter dem Vorsitz der Herren Prof. Max Huber und Prof. C. J. Burckhardt stattgefundenen Orientierungssitzung, 15 August 1944 Yad Vashem Archives M.20, Archives of A. Silberschein, Geneva (Relico), ID 3687094, Document # 113–116.

97. Max Huber, Völkerrechtliche Grundsätze, Aufgaben und Probleme des Roten Kreuzes, Schweizer Jahrbuch für internationales Recht 1944, 11–57, 36.

98. 'Millionen unserer Glaubensbrüder sind der Ausrottung zum Opfer gefallen, und unsere Gemeinschaft ist in Europa in noch nie dagewesener Weise dezimiert worden.' Rabbinerverband der Schweiz, 15 August 1944 to the ICRC Geneva, Archives du Comité international de la Croix-Rouge, ACICR G59/7/00—171, Microfilm reel 9, USHMM-19.045 M.

99. J. W. Pehle, executive director of the WRB, to Nahum Goldmann, WJC, New York, 9 August 1944. Papers of the War Refugee Board (Bethesda, MD: University Publications of America, 2002). Microfilm LM0306, Reel 6, Folder 5, frames 455–56, USHMM.

100. Barnett and Weiss, Humanitarianism, 37.

101. Stauffer, 'Sechs furchtbare Jahre...', 344.

102. 'Wir sind kein Weltgericht, wir helfen einzelnen. Wir benutzen die Presse nicht für moralische Proteste [...]'. 'Protokoll der Informationssitzung über die Judenauswanderung aus Ungarn', 10 August 1944. Archives du Comité international de la Croix-Rouge, ACICR G59/7/00—171, Microfilm reel number 9, USHMM-19.045 M.

103. Archives du Comité international de la Croix-Rouge, ACICR G59/7/00—171, 'Protokoll der Informationssitzung über die Judenauswanderung aus Ungarn vom 10. August 1944' Microfilm reel number 9, USHMM-19.045 M.

104. Cornelius, Hungary in World War II, 334 ff.

105. Kershaw, The Envoy, 138.

106. Ronald Florence, Emissary of the Doomed: Bargaining for Lives in the Holocaust (New York: Viking, 2010), 268 ff.

107. Braham, *The Politics of Genocide*, 253, Wyman, *Abandonment of the Jews*, 393, 240–3.

108. In 1948 the Hungarian government even thanked Swiss Consul Charles Lutz for his work in favour of victims of Nazi persecution during the German occupation of Budapest. See Hungarian Legation in Bern to Swiss State Department in Bern, 10 August 1948, Diplomatische Dokumente der Schweiz dodis.ch 14297, Swiss Federal Archives E 2500(-)1982/120/60.

109. Thomas Streissguth, *Raoul Wallenberg, Swedish Diplomat and Humanitarian* (New York: Saddleback Educational, 2001), 87 ff. Wyman, *Abandonment of the Jews*, 243; Cornelius, *Hungary in World War II*, 359 f., 469; Levine, *Raoul Wallenberg in Budapest*, 372 ff.; Moshe Bejski, 'The "Righteous among the Nations" and Their Part in the Rescue of Jews', in Gutman et al. (eds.), *Rescue Attempts during the Holocaust*, 627–47.

110. Wallenberg had close connections with Ivar Olsen who was the War Refugee Board representative in Sweden. Olsen also worked for the US-wartime secret service. There is, however, no evidence to this day that Wallenberg was a spy; see Levine, *Wallenberg in Budapest*, 372 ff.

111. Visit to Switzerland Mr Carter's report. Meeting with Bachmann ICRC, 7 March 1945. Abschrift. 6.1.1/82509756/ITS Digital Archive, Bad Arolsen.

112. Favez, *Red Cross and the Holocaust*, 250.

113. Telegram, US representative in Budapest to Secretary of State and seemingly forwarded to the US legation in Bern, 13 May 1945 (SECRET), NARA, RG 59, Entry D–File 1945–1949, Box 4082, 800.142/5–1445.

114. Schoenfeld, Budapest, via army, to Secretary of State (Secret), 26 November 1945, NARA, RG 59, 800.142/11-2645, Box 4082. Embassy Budapest to Secretary of State (Secret), 17 April 1946, NARA, RG 59, 800.142/4-1746, Box 4082. Ben-Tov, *Facing the Holocaust*, 378.

115. Stefano Picciaredda, *Diplomazia umanitaria: La Croce Rossa nella Seconda Guerra Mondiale* (Bologna: Il Mulino, 2003), 231. Even the remaining Swiss diplomats in Berlin were 'escorted' to Moscow and released only days later. See Widmer, *Minister Hans Frölicher*, 95.

116. Report of the War Refugee Board for Week of 15–20 May 1944 by Executive Director J. W. Pehle. Papers of the War Refugee Board (Bethesda, MD: University Publications of America, 2002). Microfilm LM0305, Reel 26, Folder 1, frames 46–58, USHMM.

117. Yehuda Bauer, *Jews for Sale? Nazi–Jewish Negotiations, 1933–1945* (New Haven: Yale University Press, 1994), 245.

118. Ralph Hewins, *Count Folke Bernadotte: His Life and Work* (Minneapolis: T. S. Denison, 1950), 31–51. Frithiof Olof Dahlby, *Folke Bernadotte. Ett minnesalbum. Utgivet till förmån för och under medverkan av Svenska Scoutrådet och Svenska Röda Korset* (Stockholm: Norstedt 1948).

119. Wallenberg and Bernadotte got to know each other at the 1933 world's fair in Chicago. The young Wallenberg was very much impressed by Bernadotte, his

senior by seventeen years, as illustrated in a letter to his mother dated 27 June 1933. Raoul Wallenberg, *Letters and Dispatches 1924–1944* (New York: Arcade, 1995), 90.

120. Caroline Moorehead, *Dunant's Dream. War, Switzerland and the History of the Red Cross* (New York: Carroll and Graf Publishers INC 1998), 546. Best, *War and Law*, 86.

121. Stauffer, *'Sechs furchtbare Jahre...'*, 342.

122. Ibid., 344.

123. JDC Archives New York, Geneva Office, AR 45/54, 1815, War Refugee Board, Washington, DC, Office of the Executive Director, 8 December 1944. See also Bauer, *Jews for sale*, 199.

124. Bauer, *Jews for Sale*, Yehuda Bauer, 'Die Verhandlungen zur Rettung der Juden 1944/45', *Vierteljahshefte für Zeitgeschichte* 25.2 (April 1977); Bauer, *American Jewry and the Holocaust*; Wyman, *Abandonment of the Jews*, 248–51; Peter Longerich, *Heinrich Himmler: A Life* (Oxford: Oxford University Press, 2011), 708 f., 724 ff.; Anna Porter, *Kasztner's Train The True Story of an Unknown Hero of the Holocaust* (New York: Walker and Company, 2007).

125. JDC Archives New York, Saly Mayer Collection, 2/1/3/15, Mayer's notes about a meeting with McClelland and M.W. [identity unknown] on 7 February 1945.

126. NL Burckhardt, UB Basel 3 B II 46 b, Burckhardt to Himmler, 19 February 1945.

127. JDC Archives New York, Saly Mayer Collection, Roll 7, Folder 15, Notes in Saly Mayer collection about negotiations with Himmler.

128. 'Secretary of State Stettinius to the Chargé in Switzerland (Huddle), 9 January 1945', Franklin D. Roosevelt Presidential Library, Archives (FDRL), Records of the War Refugee Board, Box 30, Folder 2 of 2 'Situation in Germany and German-controlled-territory'.

129. Burckhardt to Stucki in Paris Stucki, 17 February 1945, Quoted in Stamm, *Der Grosse Stucki*, 295 f. 'Auch über die Judenfrage muss gesprochen werden.' See letter Burckhardt to Stucki, 19 February 1945, NL Burckhardt, UB Basel B II 46 h Dossier 1.

130. NL Burckhardt, UB Basel B II 46 h Dossier 1, Burckhardt to Max Petitpierre 17 March 1945.

131. Handwritten letter Burckhardt to Ruegger, 20 March 1945. AfZG NL Paul Ruegger, 23.9.1 'Correspondence Carl Jacob Burckhardt, president of the ICRC, July 1944–July 1946': *Für die Zukunft des CICR habe ich grosse Bedenken'*.

132. Ben-Tov, *Facing the Holocaust*, 378.

133. 'Telephongespräch zwischen Herrn Dr. Bachmann und Herrn Dr. Riegner', Geneva, 13 February 1945. Archives du Comité international de la Croix-Rouge, ACICR G 59 [0] 1.02, microfilm reel 1, USHMM, RG-19.045 M.

134. Note pour Monsieur Gallopin signed R.M. Frick Cramer copie a M. Burckhardt, 28 February 1945. IfZG Zurich, NL Stauffer 14 (V), 3.1.1.2 Ar IKRK, Verhandlungen mit Kaltenbrunner.

135. 'Dementi - Die Mission Prof. Burckhardts in Deutschland' NZZ, 15 March 1945. NL Stauffer 14 (V), 3.1.1.2 Ar IKRK, Verhandlungen mit Kaltenbrunner.
136. Handwritten letter, Burckhardt to Ruegger, 20 March 1945. AfZG NL Paul Ruegger, 23.9.1. 'Correspondence Carl Jacob Burckhardt, president of the ICRC, July 1944–July 1946'.
137. JDC Archives New York, G 45–54 2/2/6/ORG.118, Daily News Bulletin Issued by the Jewish Telegraphic Agency LTD, London, Vol. 26, No. 59 Friday, 9 March 1945.
138. 'Burckhardt sees Hitler: Red Cross Head Reported Pleading for Allied "Hostages",' New York Times, 15 March 1945.
139. Longerich, Heinrich Himmler, 724. See Ian Kershaw, The End: The Defiance and Destruction of Hitler's Germany, 1944–45 (New York: Penguin Press, 2011), 336 f.
140. 'Besprechungen mit Obergruppenführer Dr. Kaltenbrunner vom 13. März 1945 betr. Heimschaffung und Behandlung der in Deutschland festgehaltenen Häftlinge (Wirtshaus an der Strasse Feldkirch-Innsbruck).' 19 March 1945 (Vertraulich) NL Stauffer, AfZG Zurich, NL Stauffer 14 (V), 3.1.1.2 Ar IKRK, Verhandlungen mit Kaltenbrunner.
141. JDC Archives New York, Saly Mayer Collection, Roll 8, Folder 21, Letter Roswell McClelland to General O'Dwyer, 6 April 1945.
142. Leni Yahil, The Holocaust: The Fate of the European Jewry (New York: Oxford University Press, 1990), 650.
143. 'Besprechungen mit Obergruppenführer Kaltenbrunner am 24. April in Innsbruck' 14 May 1945. NL Stauffer 14 (V), 3.1.1.2 Ar IKRK, Verhandlungen mit Kaltenbrunner.
144. Sune Persson, Rettung im letzten Augenblick: Folke Bernadotte und die Befreiung Tausender KZ-Häftlinge durch die Aktion 'Weisse Busse' (Berlin: Landt, 2011). Sune Persson, Escape from the Third Reich. The Harrowing True Story of the Largest Rescue Effort Inside Nazi Germany (New York: Skyhorse Publishing, 2009).
145. Sune Persson, 'Folke Bernadotte and the White Buses', in David Cesarani and Paul A. Levine, 'Bystanders' to the Holocaust: A-Re-evaluation (London: Frank Cass 2002), 237–68. See also Oliver von Wrochem u.a. (ed.), Skandinavien im Zweiten Weltkrieg und die Rettungsaktion Weisse Busse. Ereignisse und Erinnerung (Berlin: Metropol 2012); Ingrid Lomfors, Blind fläck: Minne och glömska kring svenska Röda korsets hjälpinsats i Nazityskland 1945 (Stockholm: Bokförlag Atlantis 2005).
146. Count Folke Bernadotte, The Curtain Falls: The Last Days of the Third Reich (New York: A. Knopf, 1945), 80.
147. Robert Gerwarth, Hitler's Hangman: The Life of Heydrich (New Haven, CT: Yale University Press, 2011), xiv, 106.
148. Burckhardt to Ruegger, 20 March 1945, AfZ, NL Ruegger, 23.9.1, 'Correspondence Carl Jacob Burckhardt, president of the ICRC, July 1944–July 1946. Official letter Burckhardt to Ruegger, 11 May 1945, AfZG NL Paul Ruegger, 23.9.1, 'Correspondence Carl Jacob Burckhardt, president of the ICRC, July 1944–July 1946'.

149. Burckhardt to Charles de Watteville, copy in Ruegger's archive, 18 February 1945, AfZ, NL Ruegger, 23.9.1 Korrespondenz Burckhardt: '*Brief "über all das, was wir für die Juden getan haben…" Lieber Freund –…was nun die Hilfe für die Juden, als Ganzes gesehen betrifft, so haben wir im ungarischen Sektor wahre Wunder gemacht, 80% Leben gerettet, im Laufe einer angeordneten Ausrottungskampagne! Dafür könnten uns die Leute dankbar sein. Ich frage mich, ob ihre [der Juden] Verstimmung, von der Sie schreiben, nicht teilweise auf gewisse Anstrengungen der Liga zurückgehen.… Das ist ein rechter Privatbrief, wie man ihn am Sonntag morgen schreibt. Verbrennen Sie ihn*'.

150. See also an earlier letter to Ruegger: Burckhardt to Ruegger, 2 February 1945, AfZ, NL Ruegger, 23.9.1 Korrespondenz Burckhardt.

151. Here Burckhardt failed to mention that the character and function of the concentration camps changed drastically over time. In 1934 the system of concentration camps was mostly used to terrorize political opponents of the Nazi regime.

152. Ruegger to Burckhardt, 21 June 1945, AfZ, NL Ruegger, Korrespondenz Burckhardt.

153. Report by Haefliger, May 24, 1945, ACICR G 44/13-18. Haefliger drove to nearby American forces and lead them to the concentration camp, in order to prevent any possible last minute atrocities by the SS guards. For his unauthorised initiative he fell into disgrace with the ICRC in Geneva and left Switzerland for Vienna. It was only in 1990 that Haefliger was officially rehabilitated by ICRC president Cornelio Sommaruga.

154. Favez, *The Red Cross and the Holocaust,* 268.

155. For further reading see Bugnion, *The International Committee of the Red Cross,* Moorehead, *Dunant's Dream,* Arieh J. Kochavi, *Confronting Captivity: Britain and the United States and their POWs in Nazi Germany* (Chapel Hill: University of North Carolina Press, 2005) and Foster Rhea Dulles, *The American Red Cross: A History* (New York: Harper and Brothers, 1950).

156. Favez, *The Red Cross and the Holocaust,* 46.

157. Arieh J. Kochavi, *Confronting Captivity: Britain and the United States and their POWs in Nazi Germany* (Chapel Hill: University of North Carolina Press, 2005), 2 ff.

158. 'Defend Treatment of War Prisoners: 2 Witnesses Tell House Body That Observance of Geneva Rules Beat Nazi Propaganda,' *New York Times,* 1 May 1945, 9.

159. Bass, *Stay the Hand of Vengeance,* 178.

160. 'Yanks Bare Prison Horror; "Ghosts" Fight Over Food', NYT April 4, 1945, page 1.

161. Visit to Switzerland Mr Carter's report. Meeting with Bachmann ICRC, March 7, 1945. Abschrift. 6.1.1/82509754/ITS Digital Archive, Bad Arolsen.

162. 'Reich's Cruelty to US Captives Denounced by Stimson, Stettinius. They Lay It to "Fanatical" Continuance of "Hopeless War" and Say Perpetrators of "Atrocities" Will Be Punished', NYT April 13, 1945, page 13.

163. 'Defend Treatment of War Prisoners. 2 Witnesses Tell House Body That Observance of Geneva Rules Beat Nazi Propaganda', NYT May 1, 1945, p. 9.

164. '99% of US Captives in Reich Survived, Red Cross Reports', NYT June 2, 1945, p. 8.

165. Annual Report for the Year Ending June 30, 1945, The American National Red Cross, Washington, DC, 122.

166. 'Yad Vashem honors American GI who told Nazis "We are all Jews"', in *The Jerusalem Post*, 3 December 2015.

167. Burleigh, *Moral Combat*, 385.

168. Annual Report for the Year Ending June 30, 1945, The American National Red Cross, Washington, DC, 124.

169. Timothy Snyder, *Bloodlands: Europe between Hitler and Stalin* (New York: Basic Books, 2010), x f.

170. Best, *War and Law*, 151.

CHAPTER 4

1. George C. Cheever, field representative of Civilian War Relief, to Norman Hackney, field supervisor, American Red Cross Heaquarters, Third US Army, 14 April 1945. For this and other documents about special relief efforts for Buchenwald of the American Red Cross, see NARA, RG 200, Records of the American Red Cross 1935–1941, Box 1018, Folder 619.2 'Camps Europe, Germany Buchenwald'.

2. Letter Hartmann to Mister James, American Red Cross Headquarters, 12 June 1945. Attached memorandum dated 4 June 1945 titled 'Concerning the Reorganisation of the Red Cross in Germany', NARA, RG 200 (AMRC), Box 1018, Folder 619.2/02 'German Red Cross'.

3. 'The International Red Cross Was Silent' by S. Z. Kantor, in *Jewish Frontier* May 1945, 17–20, 20.

4. ICRC delegate J. Friedrich to Bachmann and Max Huber, 'Betrifft; Allgemeine Situation in Deutschland' 15 June 1945, Archives du Comité international de la Croix-Rouge, ACICR G 59/6—167.06, Microfilm reel number 9, USHMM-19.045 M.

5. ICRC delegate J. Friedrich to Bachmann and Max Huber, 'Betrifft; Allgemeine Situation in Deutschland' 15 June 1945, Archives du Comité international de la Croix-Rouge, ACICR G 59/6—167.06, Microfilm reel number 9, USHMM-19.045 M.

6. Max Huber to Secretary of State James Byrnes about the organisation and activities of the Red Cross in Germany, 23 August 1945, NARA, RG 59, 800.142/9-2045, Box 4082. The ICRC badly wanted to learn the US government's position. At the same time, the American Red Cross representative in Geneva forwarded information about the German Red Cross to his Washington

headquarters, which was forwarded to Albert Clattenburg's division in the State Department. This information included the fact that Hartmann had initially been arrested by Allied troops, but was then allowed to carry on certain Red Cross work on a local level. See reports by Walther Georg Hartmann to League of Red Cross Societies, NARA, RG 59, box 4082, 800.142/7-1945 CS/LE.

7. The American National Red Cross, *Annual Report for the Year Ending June 30, 1945* (Washington, DC: American Red Cross Society, 1946), 129.

8. Maurice Bourquin, 'The Red Cross and Treaty Protection of Civilians in Wartime', *Revue International de la Croix-Rouge et Bulletin des Sociétés de la Croix-Rouge 1*, Supplement (January 1948): 11–20, here 18.

9. 'In einem aussichtslosen Krieg gegen eine Welt wurden Menschen ohne Zahl, an den Fronten, hinter den Fronten, in den Städten, im flachen Land, durch alle verfügbaren Arten der Explosionskraft zerstört oder ganz einfach zusammengetrieben und vergast.' Carl J. Burckhardt, 'Entdeckung des Unerwarteten', in Carl J. Burckhardt et al. (eds)., *Geschichte zwischen Gestern und Morgen*, Munich: neue edition List Verlag 1974, 7–21, 15.

10. James Crossland, *Britain and the International Committee of the Red Cross, 1939–1945* (New York: Palgrave Macmillan, 2014), 200.

11. Max Huber Ethos, internationales, in Karl Strupp/Hans-Jürgen Schlochauer, *Wörterbuch des Völkerrechts*, vol. 1 (Berlin: de Gruyter, 1960), 445–8, 446.

12. Moorehead, *Dunant's Dream*, 544.

13. Ibid.

14. Isabelle Vonèche Cardia, 'Les raisons du silence du Comité International de la Croix-Rouge (CICR) face aux déportations', in *Revue d'Histoire de la Shoah*, 203 (October 2015) : 87–122, 87 f.

15. See S. Z. Kantor collection, Acc. 1997.A.0360, carton 1, USHMM. Kantor had contacts with Rabbi Wise in New York, a possible link between him and Riegner. Kantor's 28-page manuscript 'Internees, Deportees and Hostages' deals mostly with the Geneva Conventions, humanitarian law and the work of the ICRC regarding civilians. On July 28, 1943 he wrote to Secretary of State Cordell Hull and stressed possible ways for a humanitarian intervention by the ICRC. In October 1943 and March 1944 Kantor wrote to Norman H. Davis, Chairman of the American Red Cross and forwarded this manuscript alongside with his proposals: 'I should like to draw attention to the fact that in all cases, in which there is no possibility of diplomatic intervention by a protecting Power, only the International Red Cross Committee [...] can approach the Axis, and satellite governments or the respective national Red Cross Societies.' Kantor to Davis, 6 March 1944.

16. S. Z. Kantor, 'The International Red Cross Was Silent', *Jewish Frontier* (May 1945): 17–20, 17.

17. Ibid., 17.

18. Ibid., 19.

19. Ibid., 19.

20. ICRC delegation in Washington to ICRC in Geneva, Sujet: Press attacks on policies of the ICRC, signed Charles Huber, 15 May 1945, See also Note no. 1809, Note pour la Délégation du CICR a Washington 3 July 1945, Concerne: attaques de presse. ACICR, G 59/4-1.01, Microfilm 7, USHMM.

21. Quoted in Schomann, *Im Zeichen der Menschlichkeit,* 263–4: '*Ihr Einfluss ist gross in den angelsächsischen Ländern*'.

22. Riegner to Huber, 25 July 1946, Central Zionist Archives, Jerusalem, C3\501-6t.

23. Report on the Work of the Preliminary Conference of the National Red Cross Societies Geneva 26 July–3 August 1946, CZA, Jerusalem, C3\1884\2-1t. At the 1947 meeting of humanitarian agencies held in preparation for a conference to revise the Geneva Conventions, Riegner spoke in the name of the murdered Jews of Europe and for all the other civilian victims of the recent war. See Penkower, 'World Jewish Congress', 396 f.

24. Riegner, *Never Despair,* 143.

25. Junod, *Imperiled Red Cross,* 24 ff.

26. Forsythe, *Humanitarians,* 52.

27. Geoffrey Best, *War and Law since 1945* (Oxford: Clarendon, OR New York: Oxford University Press, 1994), 91. Bugnion, *International Committee of the Red Cross,* 979.

28. O'Connor's title as head of the AMRC changed over time: In 1946 honorary president was the US president, Chairman was O'Connor. Through later reform O'Connor was named president of the American Red Cross and the US president named honorary Chairman.

29. George Korson, *At His Side: The Story of the American Red Cross Overseas in World War II* (New York: Coward-McCann, 1945), x ff.

30. His private correspondence suggests O'Connor's network included many prominent people from the lawyer establishment in New York, some prominently FDR associates among them. O'Connor had a personal connection to James Aloysius 'Jim' Farley one of the first Irish-Catholic politicians in the US, who played a major role in high politics. Farley served under FDR as postmaster general and in later years chairman of the board of Coca-Cola. Another democratic politician and FDR confident in O'Connor's circle appears to have been Thomas J. Walsh, of Irish-Catholic descendent as well. Dartmouth College Library, Basil O'Connor papers, correspondence dating from 1946 to 1949, Box 4.

31. Victor Cohn, *Four Billion Dimes* (Minneapolis: 1955; reprint of article series).

32. Breitman, *FDR and the Jews,* 23.

33. Timothy Takaro, 'The Man in the Middle' in *Dartmouth Medicine* (Autumn 2004): 52–7.

34. Louis Finkelstein (ed.), *Thirteen Americans: Their Spiritual Autobiographies,* Institute for Religious and Social Science, 1953, 'Basil O' Connor' 219–30, 220. 'Christians and Jews honor O'Connor', Pittsburg Press, 10 January 1946, 22.

35. O'Connor ultimately received many honors for his work including the Lasker Scientific Award (then considered to be a kind of 'American Nobel' prize).

Alden Whitman, 'Basil O'Connor, Polio Crusader, Dies', in *New York Times*, 10 March 1972, 40. See also Finkelstein (ed.), *Thirteen Americans,* 219–30, 229.

36. Charles Hurd, *The Compact History of the American Red Cross* (New York: Hawthorn Books, 1959), 251.

37. Ibid., 233.

38. See Julia F. Irwin, *Making the World Safe. The American Red Cross and a Nation's Humanitarian Awakening* (New York: Oxford University Press, 2013).

39. Quoted in ibid., 207.

40. Ibid., 208.

41. Annual Report for the year ending June 30 1947, The American National Red Cross Washington, DC, 120.

42. Best, *War and Law,* 82.

43. B. de Rougé, secretary general of the League of Red Cross Societies, Geneva, to Basil O'Connor, chairman of the League of Red Cross Societies and president of the American Red Cross, Washington, DC, 27 January 1948, NARA, RG 200 (AMRC), Box 118, Folder 041, League of RC Societies General Correspondence.

44. Best, *War and Law,* 82.

45. Burckhardt to de Haller, 28 October 1946 (confidential and personal), Nachlass Burckhardt UB Basel, B II 46 I, Nr. 14.

46. 'Die Commission Mixte ist und bleibt eine heute von Amerika abhängige Unternehmung'. Burckhardt to Rothmund, 23 January 1946 (confidential and personal), NL Burckhardt UB Basel, B I 46 i, Dossier 9, Heinrich Rothmund.

47. *Report of the Joint Relief Commission of the International Red Cross 1941–1946* (Geneva: International Red Cross Committee and League of Red Cross Societies, 1948), 445, 448.

48. Burckhardt to Dr Robert Böhringer 3 October 1947, Nachlass Burckhardt UB Basel, B II 46 i, Dossier 15 Nr. 7.

49. UB Basel, NL 110, B I c 5, 4: Letter from Carl J. Burckhardt to Paul Ruegger, 10 July 1946.

50. 'O'Connor Demands A "Free" Red Cross. Warns World League Meeting in England of Political Control – Russians to Attend', NYT July 9, 1946, p. 2.

51. 'Standing Committee of the International Red Cross. Minutes of the Meetings of the Special Committee to Study Ways and Means of Reinforcing the Action of the International Committee of the Red Cross, Paris, 26 and 27 November 1946', NARA, RG 200 (AMRC), Box 103, Folder 041 'International Red Cross, Special Commission to Study Ways and Means of Reinforcing the Efficacy of the Work of the ICRC'.

52. Ralph Hewins, *Count Folke Bernadotte, His Life and Work* (Minneapolis: T.S. Denison and Company, 1950), 185 f.

53. Ibid., 185 f.

54. 'Financing Commission, Meeting of 11 April 1949', NARA, RG 200, American National Red Cross, Box 103, Folder 041, ICRC—Commission for the Financing of the ICRC—Established August 1946.

55. François Bugnion, The *International Committee of the Red Cross and the Protection of War Victims* (Geneva: International Committee of the Red Cross; Oxford: Macmillan Education, 2003), 980.

56. Ibid., 980.

57. W. W. Jefferson, Director International Cooperation, to Mr Nicholson, AMRC National Headquarters, 4 April 1946. NARA, RG 200 AMRC, Box 114, Folder 041 'International Red Cross, Preliminary Conference of Red Cross Societies, Geneva, 26 July –3 August 1946. Preparation for 17th International Conference August 1948'.

58. Letter de Rouge, League of Red Cross Societies, to James T. Nicholson, American Red Cross, 'My dear Nick', 27 December 1947, NARA, RG 200 AMRC, Box 118, Folder 041, 'League of RC Societies General Correspondence'.

59. 'Standing Committee of the International Red Cross. Minutes of the Meetings of the Special Committee to Study Ways and Means of Reinforcing the Action of the International Committee of the Red Cross, Paris, 26 and 27 November 1946', NARA, RG 200 (AMRC), Box 103, Folder 041, 'International Red Cross, Special Commission to Study Ways and Means of Reinforcing the Efficacy of the Work of the ICRC'.

60. Standing Committee of the International Red Cross. Minutes of the Meetings of the Special Committee to study Ways and Means of reinforcing the Action of the International Committee of the Red Cross, Paris, 26 and 27 November 1946 NARA, RG 200 (AMRC), Box 103, Folder 041 'International Red Cross, Special Commission to Study ways and Means of reinforcing the Efficacy of the work of the ICRC', page 32.

61. Report Albert E. Clattenburg to Secretary of State, 26 August 1947, NARA, RG 59, 514.2 Geneva/8-2647, Box 2387. See also Best, *War and Law* 151 f.

62. See International Committee of the Red Cross, *Report on the Work of the Conference of Government Experts for the Study of the Conventions for the Protection of War Victims (Geneva, April 14–26, 1947)* (Geneva: n.p., 1947). See also 'Red Cross Delegates return from Geneva', NYT, May 20, 1947, p. 22. Best, *War and Law*, 152.

63. Best, *War and Law*, 85.

64. August R. Lindt, *Die Schweiz, das Stachelschwein: Erinnerungen* (Bern: Zytglogge, 1992), 174.

65. Aktennotiz, Probleme mit den verschiedenen osteuropäischen Staaten. 30 October 1946, Diplomatische Dokumente der Schweiz, dodis.ch1905, Swiss Federal Archives E 2001(E)-/1/1.

66. Bugnion, *The International Committee of the Red Cross*, 989 f.

67. Joerg Kistler, 'Das Politische Konzept der Schweizerischen Nachkriegshilfe in den Jahren 1943–1948', Diss., University of Bern, 1980, 215.

68. Rothmund to Ruegger, 14 May 1947, AfZ, NL Ruegger, Dossiers 23.9.6–23.11.1: 'Inzwischen war auch das Verhältnis der Schweiz zu Sowjetrussland zu einer außergewöhnlich heiklen und schwierigen politischen Frage für die Schweiz

geworden, sodass auch aus diesem Grunde mir wieder die Hände gebunden waren. Eine Arbeit für das Komitee von der Schweiz aus im Balkan z.B. über die sich Kullmann, wohl als leisen Köder, mir gegenüber im November 1944 einmal geäußert hatte, war vollständig ausgeschlossen'.

69. 'Report on European Regional Conference, League of Red Cross Societies, Belgrade,Yugoslavia', 22 October 1947. Mr Philip E. Ryan, Director International Activities. Melvin A. Glasser signed. NARA, RG 200 (AMRC), Box 124, Folder 0.41, RC Conference Belgrade.

70. Best, *War and Law*, 85.

71. Léon Nicole, 'Croix Rouge', *Voix Ouvrière* (6 August 1946), Schweizerisches Sozialarchiv, Zurich, Folder 49.5 ZA 1 'Internationales Komitee vom Roten Kreuz' (IKRK).

72. Catherine Rey-Schyrr, *De Yalta à Dien Bien Phu. Historie du Comité international de la Croix-Rouge, 1945–1955* (Geneva: CICR et Georg Editeur, 2007), 193 ff.

73. Tommaso Giglio, 'Passaporto per SS e collaborazionisti. Casa di Riposo "Cardinal Boetto"', *L'Unità* (29 January 1947), 1.

74. 'L'activité hitlerienne en Suisse', *Voix Ouvrière* (4 February 1947), 6. 'Le SS J. Chatrousse est arrêté à Genès', *Ce Soir* 23/24 March 1947.

75. Note du CICR, William H. Michel, Attention de M. de Traz, Concerne: Délivrance en Italie des documents 10.100 bis, 25 March 1947, ACICR, G 68/00/Ti.

76. 'L'activité hitlerienne en Suisse', *Voix Ouvrière* (4 February 1947), 6.

77. Department of State, Llewellyn E. Thompson, Chief Division of Eastern European Affairs, to Swiss ambassador Karl Bruggmann, 9 December 1946, English translation of the original article in Russian by N. Polyanov, 'Activity of Geneva Committee of the Red Cross', *Trud*, 1 December 1946, NARA, RG 59, D–File 1945–1949, Box 4082, 800.142/12–946.

78. Ibid.

79. For a collection of this press coverage see Schweizerisches Sozialarchiv, Zurich, Folder 49.5 ZA 1 'Internationales Komitee vom Roten Kreuz (IKRK)': 'Widerlegte Angriffe auf das Internationale Rote Kreuz', *Neue Zürcher Zeitung*, 2 May 1944, Blatt 6, 'Das Rote Kreuz: Dr. Piderman antwortet dem Roten Kreuz', *Vorwärts*, 30 March 1946, Léon Nicole, 'Croix Rouge', *Voix Ouvrière*, 6 August 1946, 'Das Rote Kreuz: Dr. Piderman antwortet dem Roten Kreuz', *Vorwärts*, Fortsetzung 1 April 1946. On Guido Piderman and his work for Soviet POWs in Finland, see also the letter Le Chef de la Division des Affaires etrangeres du Département politique, P. Bonna, au Ministre de Suisse a Stockholm, P. Dinichert, 28 December 1942, Schweizerisches Bundesarchiv, Diplomatische Dokument der Schweiz, Band 14, Dokumentennummer 286, 28 December 1942, Seite 950–51, ref. no. 60 006 571, E 2011 (D) 2/177.

80. 'Um das "internationale Komitee vom Roten Kreuz!" Eine notwendige Klarstellung', *Die Tat*, 30 October 1946, Schweizerisches Sozialarchiv, Zurich, Folder 49.5 ZA 1 'Internationales Komitee vom Roten Kreuz" (IKRK)':

'Abermals, wenn wir die Wochenpresse richtig lesen, klappt es nicht in Genf, wieder bekommt das alte Komitee eines ausgewischt, und diesmal heftig... Nicht eigentlich verbrecherisch sei jedoch der Ursprung dieser verwerflichen Handlungen, sondern eher verminderter Zurechnungsfähigkeit infolge Altersschwäche zuzuschreiben'.

81. Forsythe, *Humanitarians*, 53.

82. Moscow to State Department, 20 July 1948 (Restricted), NARA, RG 59, 800.142/7-2048, Box 4083.

83. 'Ein Angriff auf das Rote Kreuz', *Neue Zürcher Zeitung*, 19 August 1946, Schweizerisches Sozialarchiv, Zurich, Folder 49.5 ZA 1 'Internationales Komitee vom Roten Kreuz (IKRK)'.

84. 'Widerlegte Angriffe auf das Internationale Rote Kreuz', *Neue Zürcher Zeitung*, May 2, 1944, Blatt 6, Schweizerisches Sozialarchiv, Zurich, Folder 49.5 ZA 1 'Internationale Komitee vom Roten Kreuz (IKRK)'.

85. 'L'activité du CICR en faveur des civils détenus dans les camps de concentration en Allemagne (1939-1945)', *Revue Internationale de la Croix Rouge*, March 1946, first and second part (Documents). Comité international de la Croix-Rouge, *L'activité du CICR en faveur des civils détenus dans les camps de concentration en Allemagne (1939–1945)* (Geneva: Comité international de la Croix-Rouge, 1947). (first edition 1946). See Maurice Bourquin, 'The Red Cross and Treaty Protection of Civilians in Wartime', *Revue International de la Croix-Rouge et Bulletin des Sociétés de la Croix-Rouge, Supplement* 1 (January 1948): 11–20. *Report of the Joint Relief Commission of the International Red Cross 1941–1946* (Geneva: International Red Cross Committee and League of Red Cross Societies, 1948). Geneva got a further much-needed public relations boost with the publication of a book in 1951 by the former ICRC delegate Marcel Junod about his experiences during the Spanish Civil War and Italy's invasion of Ethiopia. The book was widely read and very successful, and the foreword by Max Huber provided a space in which to publicize the virtues of the Red Cross: Marcel Junod, *Warrior without Weapons* (New York: Macmillan, 1951), 15.

86. International Committee of the Red Cross, *Report of the International Committee of the Red Cross on Its Activities during the Second World War (1 September 1939–30 June 1947):* XVIIth International Red Cross Conference, Stockholm, August 1948, 3 volumes (Geneva: ICRC, 1948). Comité international de la Croix-Rouge. *Rapport du CICR sur son activité pendant la Seconde Guerre mondiale: XVIème Conférence internationale de la Croix-Rouge, Stockholm, août 1948*, 3 volumes (Geneva: mpr. du Journal de Genève, 1948).

87. Frédéric Siordet, *Inter Arma Caritas: The Work of the International Committee of the Red Cross during the Second World War* (Geneva: International Committee of the Red Cross, 1947). A second English edition was published in 1973. Frédéric Siordet was well chosen. An expert in international law, the lawyer had during the 1930s and 1940s worked at the Swiss legation in France. After 1943 he often worked for the ICRC as well. From 1951 to 1979, he was a member of the

ICRC Assembly and vice-president. He helped with the revision of the proposed Geneva Convention and in 1952 represented the ICRC at the international conference of the Red Cross in Toronto. Melchior Borsinger, 'Tribute to Frederic Siordet', *International Review of the Red Cross* 280 (January/February 1991): 34–6, here 35.

88. Siordet, *Inter Arma Caritas*, 100 f.

89. Siordet, *Inter Arma Caritas*, 108.

90. Siordet, *Inter Arma Caritas*, 7.

91. Rothmund to Burckhardt, 17 January 1946, NL Burckhardt UB Basel, B I 46 i, Dossier 9, Heinrich Rothmund: 'Denn wenn das Rote Kreuz nicht einsieht, dass es nicht liquidieren, sondern im schlimmsten Fall bloss sich umbringen lassen darf, so sollte man ihm nicht noch geringe Mittel geben, um sich eine zeitlang über Wasser halten zu können. Aber der Bundesrat sollte einsehen, dass sich für die Schweiz noch einmal eine Gelegenheit zeigt, ihre Position zu retten. Anstatt sich von allen Seiten anöden zu lassen, dies und jenes sei falsch gemacht worden oder die Schweiz sei überhaupt verdächtig den Nazis geholfen zu haben'.

92. Rothmund chief of police to ICRC president Burckhardt 'Sehr vereehrter Herr Präsident and Minister' February 22, 1945, Archives du Comité international de la Croix-Rouge, ACICR G59/6—167.01, Microfilm reel number 9, USHMM-19.045 M.

93. Report of US ambassador in Bern, Leland Harrison, to Secretary of State about Huber's retirement, 17 February 1947 (RESTRICTED), 'Subject: Reaction of Swiss Socialist and Communist Press to the Retirement of Professor Max Huber, President of the International Committee of the Red Cross', NARA, RG 59, Entry D–File 1945–1949, Box 4082, 800.142/2–1747.

94. 'Subject: Reaction of Swiss Socialist and Communist Press to the Retirement of Professor Max Huber, President of the International Committee of the Red Cross'. [State Department, US Embassy Bern], Restricted, no. 14811, Bern, 17 February 1947. NARA, RG 200 (AMRC), Box 104, Folder 0.41, International Red Cross Committee Personnel.

95. James T. Nicholson to Chairman, Executive Vice Chairman, AMRC, 21 March 1947, attached report from the State Department, [State Department, US Embassy Bern] Restricted no. 14811, Bern, 17 February 1947. NARA, RG 200 (AMRC), Box 104, Folder 0.41, International Red Cross Committee Personnel.

96. Burckhardt to Rothmund, 23 January 1946 (confidential and personal), NL Burckhardt UB Basel, B I 46 i, Dossier 9, Heinrich Rothmund.

97. Hans Wolf de Salis, ICRC Rome, to Burckhardt, 23 January 1948, NL Burckhardt Basel, B II 46 k.

98. Burckhardt to Ruegger, 7 August 1944, AfZ, NL Ruegger, 23.9.1, Correspondence of Carl Jacob Burckhardt ICRC President July 1944–July 1946.

99. Report of the meeting of 23 October 1947 in Bern between Huber, Bodmer, van Berchem, and de Haller concerning the presidency of the International Committee of the Red Cross (SFPD 2800–1967/61). See Junod, *Imperiled Red Cross*, 38.

100. A Monsieur le conseiller fédéral Petitpierre—Note pour les réunions des Commissions parlementaires des Affaires étrangères, 12 September 1947, signed de Haller, Dodis.ch 1712, Swiss Federal Archives E 2001(E)-/1/136.

101. A Monsieur le conseiller fédéral Petitpierre—Note pour les réunions des Commissions parlementaires des Affaires étrangères, 12 September 1947, Dodis.ch 1712, Swiss Federal Archives E 2001(E)-/1/136.

102. Letter from Ruegger to Petitpierre, New Delhi, 27 December 1947 (AFPD, 2800–1967/69). Junod, *Imperiled Red Cross*, 39 f.

103. Martin Bodmer to Burckhardt ('Lieber Carl'), 10 October 1947 (Confidential!), Nachlass Burckhardt UB Basel, B II 46 I, N. 12 Dossier 10, Max Wolf. 'kritischen Frühjahrsmonate des Jahres 1948 (in welchen die Existenz auch unseres Landes auf dem Spiele stehen kann) auf meinem jetzigen Posten aushalte'.

104. Letter Burckhardt to Max Huber, 19 October 1947, NL Burckhardt UB Basel, B II 46 i, Dossier 10, Max Wolf.

105. Letter Burckhardt to Martin Bodmer 3 November 1947 (Personal and Confidential), Nachlass Burckhardt UB Basel B II 46 i, Dossier 3, Martin Bodmer. 'Die jetzigen Probleme, Komitee—Nationale Gesellschaften—Liga kommen mir, a distance, im Verhältnis zu dem—hic et nunc—der wirklichen Pflichten, so ephemer vor'.

106. Letter Burckhardt to Martin Bodmer 3 November 1947 (Personal and Confidential), Nachlass Burckhardt UB Basel, B II 46 i, Dossier 3, Martin Bodmer.

107. In December 1945 Burckhardt favored initially his confident Hans Bachmann for a leadership position in the ICRC. Bachmann was a strong personality who gets things done according to Burckhardt. Burckhardt Legation Paris to Max Huber Präsident ad interim des Internationalen Komitees vom Roten Kreuz, Genf, 29 December 1945 IFZG Zurich NL Stauffer 12 (V), NL CJB.

108. Letter Martin Bodmer, vice president of the ICRC to Basil O'Connor, AMRC, Washington, DC, 20 February 1948, NARA, RG 200 (AMRC), Box 104, Folder 0.41 'International Red Cross Committee Personnel': 'our President en conge, M. Carl J. Burckhardt, has been unable to meet our wishes that he should return to Geneva in the near future. He cannot at the present time relinquish his functions as Swiss Minister in Paris'.

109. Extract Journal de Genève 10 February 1948. Letter B. de Rouge to James T Nicholson, executive vice president of the American National Red Cross, Washington, DC, 10 February 1948, NARA, RG 200 (AMRC), Box 104, Folder 0.41, International Red Cross Committee Personnel.

110. Bericht Nr. 4, Swiss Legation London, Ruegger to Petitpierre, 8 April 1948, Archiv für Zeitgeschichte, Zurich, NL Paul Ruegger 23.8.1, Bericht Nr. 4 vom 8.4.1948.

111. Petitpierre to Ruegger Telegramm [April 1948]. AfZG Zurich, NL Ruegger, 23.8.1: 'Beglückwünsche Sie zum Entschluss im Interesse unseres Landes

bedauere aber gleichzeitig lebhaft auf Ihre gegenwärtige Mitarbeit Verzicht leisten zu müssen stop Hoffe weiterhin auf Ihre wertvolle Mitarbeit für uns stop Erledigung schwelender Fragen nach Ihrer Rückkehr stop beste Wünsche. Petitpierre'.

112. Letter Ruegger to Eden, 8 April 1948, Archiv für Zeitgeschichte, Zurich, NL Ruegger 23.8.3, Abschiedskorrespondenz, February–April 1948 (et al. with Anthony Eden).

113. Mission Paul Rueggers to Moscow, November 1950, Institut für Zeitgeschichte, Zurich NL Ruegger, 28.3.6.

114. David P. Forsythe and Barbara Ann J. Rieffer-Flanagan, *The International Committee of the Red Cross: A Neutral Humanitarian Actor* (New York: Routledge, 2007), 17.

115. Burckhardt to Rothmund, 23 January 1946 (Confidential and Personal), NL Burckhardt UB Basel, B I 46 i, Dossier 9, Heinrich Rothmund.

116. Finanzielle Bedürfnisse des IKRK. Japanische und deutsche Zuschüsse. Notwendigkeit neuer Einlagen des Bundes, Eduard de Haller, 18 October 1945, Dodis.ch 1713. Swiss Federal Archives Bern, E 6100(A)-/24/2173.

117. Burckhardt to Rothmund, 23 January 1946 (Confidential and Personal), NL Burckhardt UB Basel, B I 46 i, Dossier 9, Heinrich Rothmund: 'der Bundesrat hat dem Komitee 5 Millionen vorgestreckt. Diese 5 Millionen sind nicht dazu da, um eine grossangelegte Hilfsaktion aufzubauen, sondern nur, um diesem Komitee die Liquidation in anständiger Form und das Durchführen der noch verbleibendenen Aufgaben zu ermöglichen'.

118. Rothmund to Burckhardt, 17 January 1946, NL Burckhardt UB Basel, B I 46 i Dossier 9, Heinrich Rothmund: 'Denn wenn das Rote Kreuz nicht einsieht, dass es nicht liquidieren, sondern im schlimmsten Fall bloss sich umbringen lassen darf, so sollte man ihm nicht noch geringe Mittel geben, um sich eine zeitlang über Wasser halten zu können. Aber der Bundesrat sollte einsehen, dass sich für die Schweiz noch einmal eine Gelegenheit zeigt, ihre Position zu retten. Anstatt sich von allen Seiten anöden zu lassen, dies und jenes sei falsch gemacht worden oder die Schweiz sei überhaupt verdächtig den Nazis geholfen zu haben'.

119. Deutsche Vermögenswerte in der Schweiz und damit zusammenhängende Fragen. Verhandlungen mit den Alliierten, Politische Department Antrag vom 4. März 1946, Vertraulich, March 8, 1946, dodis 68, Schweizerische Bundesarchiv Bern E 1004.1(-)1000/9/467.

120. Konferenz betreffend Verwendung blockierter deutscher und japanischer Fonds für das Internationale Komitee vom Roten Kreuz, Protokoll der Sitzung vom 14. September 1946 in Bern, Bernerhof, 18 September 1946. Diplomatische Dokumente der Schweiz dodis.ch 1999, Swiss Federal Archives E 2001–03(-)-/7/12.

121. Bericht von Oberstleutnant Bracher über den Besuch von Winston Churchill in der Schweiz 23. August–20. September 1946. 18 October 1946, Diplomatische

Dokumente der Schweiz, dodis.ch 2184, Federal Archives of Switzerland E 2800(-)1990/106/18.

122. Marco Wyss, *Arms Transfers, Neutrality and Britain's Role in the Cold War. Anglo-Swiss Relations 1945–1958* (Leiden and Boston: Brill 2013), 53.

123. Négociations de Washington, Positionspapier Max Petitpierre, 19 February 1946, Diplomatische Dokumente der Schweiz Dodis.ch 63, Swiss Federal Archives Bern E 2800(-)1990/106/2.

124. Konferenz der Finanz- und Wirtschaftsdelegation des Bundesrates vom 7. Februar 1946, Traktandum: Deutsche Vermögenswerte in der Schweiz; Vorbereitung der Verhandlungen in Washington, dodis 65 E 2801(-)1968/84/29. Linus von Castelmur, *Schweizerisch-Alliierte Finanzbeziehungen im Übergang vom Zweiten Weltkrieg zum Kalten Krieg. Die deutschen Guthaben in der Schweiz zwischen Zwangsliquidierung und Freigabe (1945–1952)* (Zurich: Chronos 1992), 91.

125. The estimates by Washington of these transactions was based largely on the stolen Belgian gold reserve and essentially ignored other cases, such as looted Dutch National Bank gold. Schlussbericht der Unabhängigen Expertenkommission Schweiz—Zweiter Weltkrieg, Vermögensrechtliche Aspekte der Nachkriegszeit, 444, 445.

126. Van Dongen, *La Suisse face à la seconde guerre mondiale*, 39.

127. Schlussbericht der Unabhängigen Expertenkommission Schweiz—Zweiter Weltkrieg, Vermögensrechtliche Aspekte der Nachkriegszeit, 444, 445.

128. Négociations de Washington, Positionspapier Max Petitpierre, 19 February 1946, DiplomatischeDokument der SchweizDodis.ch 63, Swiss Federal Archives Bern E 2800(-)1990/106/2.

129. 'Herr Minister H. Froehlicher wünscht, dass die deutschen Fonds für die deutsche Interessensvertretung in der Schweiz reserviert bleiben. Die Tätigkeit des IKRK liegt auch im Interesse der Schweiz. Aus diesem Grunde sollten die vom Roten Kreuz benötigten Mittel von der Schweiz bereitgestellt (...) werden.' Konferenz betreffend Verwendung blockierter deutscher und japanischer Fonds für das Internationale Komitee vom Roten Kreuz, Protokoll der Sitzungvom 14. September 1946 in Bern, Bernerhof, 18 September 1946. Diplomatische Dokumente der Schweiz dodis.ch 1999, Swiss Federal Archives E 2001–03(-)-/7/12.

130. Konferenz betreffend Verwendung blockierter deutscher und japanischer Fonds für das Internationale Komitee vom Roten Kreuz, Protokoll der Sitzungvom 14. September 1946 in Bern, Bernerhof, 18 September 1946. Diplomatische Dokumente der Schweiz dodis.ch 1999, Swiss Federal Archives E 2001–03(-)-/7/12.

131. ICRC Delegation to the US, Memorandum for the War Department, Issue of German and Japanese funds forwarded by Clattenburg, 14 March 1946, NARA, RG 59, FW 800.142/3-1446, Box 4082.

132. But the ICRC continued to fight and in response hired some powerful American lawyers. After long legal battles the US government gave finally in.

The ultimate decision was now with the Swiss government, which ruled in favor of the ICRC. The money was secretly transferred to the ICRC in 1949. Japans motivations behind this donation at the moment of surrender still remain somewhat unclear. 'Wartime Red Cross donation secretly made in '49', *Japan Times*, 17 August 2001.

CHAPTER 5

1. 'Das Internationale Komitee vom Roten Kreuz', *Neue Zürcher Zeitung*, 10 September 1945, Archiv für Sozialgeschichte Zürich, Mappe 49.5 ZA 1 'Internationales Komitee vom Roten Kreuz (IKRK)'.
2. In French, the phrase is '*l'esprit humanitaire triomphant*'. Van Dongen, *La Suisse face à la seconde guerre mondiale*, 92.
3. In French, the phrase is 'le mythe d'une Suisse essentiellement vertueuse et courageuse'. Van Dongen, *La Suisse face à la seconde guerre mondiale*, 92.
4. Jean Ziegler, *Die Schweiz, das Gold und die Toten* (Munich: C. Bertelsmann, 1997), 293.
5. Independent Commission of Experts Switzerland—Second World War) (ed.), *Switzerland, National Socialism and the Second World War*, Final Report, 498 f.
6. Van Dongen, *La Suisse face à la seconde guerre mondiale*, 54ff.
7. 'Geschichtsfälschungen sind zur Aufgabe schlechter Journalistik und schlechter Politik geworden'. Max Wolf on Walter Bringolf, 31 July 1947, 'Lieber Herr Bringolf', References to article in *Vorwärts* from 18 July 1947. NL Burckhardt UB Basel B II 46 i Dossier Max Wolf Nr. 18.
8. Quoted in Stauffer, 'Grandseigneuraler "Anti-Intellektueller": Carl J. Burckhardt in den Fährnissen des totalitären Zeitalters', in Aram Mattioli (ed.), *Intellektuelle von rechts: Ideologie und Politik in der Schweiz 1918–1939* (Zurich: Orell Fuessli, 1995), 113–34, here 124.
9. Paul Stauffer, *Zwischen Hofmannsthal und Hitler: Carl J. Burckhardt, Facetten einer aussergewöhnlichen Existenz* (Zurich: Neue Zürcher Zeitung, 1991), 170 ff.
10. Stauffer, *Zwischen Hofmannsthal und Hitler*, 237.
11. See Herbert S. Levine, 'The Mediator: Carl J. Burckhardt's Efforts to Avert a Second World War', *Journal of Modern History* 45.3 (September 1973): 439–55.
12. James Crossland, *Britain and the International Committee of the Red Cross 1939–1945* (New York: Palgrave Macmillan, 2014), 138 f.
13. Stauffer, '*Sechs furchtbare Jahre…*', 155.
14. Ibid., 140.
15. See Wolfgang Graf Vitzthum, 'Bürgschaft für das geheime Deutschland: Zu Widerstandstat und Staatsverständnis der Brüder Stauffenberg', in Hans-Günter Richardi and Gerald Steinacher (eds.), *Für Freiheit und Recht in Europa: Der 20. Juli 1944 und der Widerstand gegen das NS-Regime in Deutschland, Österreich und Südtirol* (Innsbruck: Studienverlag, 2009), 130–51.
16. Neville Wylie, *Britain, Switzerland and the Second World War* (Oxford: Oxford University Press, 2003), 295. See also Rainer F. Schmidt, *Rudolf Hess, 'Botengang*

eines Toren'? Der Flug nach Grossbritannien vom 10. Mai 1941 (Dusseldorf: Econ, 1997), 165 ff.

17. Stauffer, *'Sechs furchtbare Jahre…'*, 198. James Crossland, 'A Man of Peaceable Intent: Burckhardt, the British and Red Cross Neutrality during the Second World War', *Historical Research* 84.223 (2011): 165–82, here 182.

18. 'Professor Burckhardt's Visit', *Manchester Guardian*, 13 November 1941, 4.

19. Carl Jacob Burckhardt to William Matheson. UB Basel Mscr. G IV 60. Burckhardt to Matheson, 27 April 1941: 'Seit dem Jahre 35 in welchem ich durch das Rote Kreuz gezwungen war, politische Aufgaben zu übernehmen, die mich dann in die schwere Danziger Krisis und nun in diese tägliche Tretmühle führten, ja, seit 35 musste ich all meinen geplanten und begonnenen Arbeiten zurückstellen'. While in London, Burckhardt wrote to Matheson on 30 January 1942: ' Ich habe wie ich vor drei Wochen aus London nach fast 3monatlichen Abwesenheit zurückkehrte im internationalen Roten Kreuz 320 und beim mir zuhause 170 Privatbriefe vorgefunden. Ich habe bis zu 14 Stunden im R. K. zu arbeiten, …. 6 Stunden Vorlesungen in der Woche zu halten. … Mit dem Roten Kreuz beschäftige ich mich seit dem 15. September 1939 tagtäglich'.

20. Due to his involvement in the attempt to kill Hitler on July 20, 1944, Hassell was arrested by the Gestapo and executed soon after. Gregor Schoellgen, *Ulrich von Hassell 1881–1944: Ein Konservativer in der Opposition* (Munich: CH Beck, 1990), 124, 136.

21. Crossland, 'Man of Peaceable Intent', 165–82.

22. Joachim C. Fest, *Hitler* (New York: Harvest HBJ Book, 1992), 646.

23. Gerhard L. Weinberg, *A World at Arms. A Global History of World War II* (Cambridge: Cambridge University Press: 2005 edition), 237 f.

24. Klemens von Klemperer, *German Resistance against Hitler: The Search for Allies Abroad, 1938–1945* (Oxford: Clarendon Press, 1992), 35.

25. Schmidt, *Rudolf Hess*, 163.

26. Paul Stauffer, 'Rudolf Hess und die Schutzmacht Schweiz 1941–1945', *Schweizerische Zeitschrift für Geschichte* 37 (1987): 260–84, here 281 f. See also Stauffer, *'Sechs furchtbare Jahre…'*, 150 ff.

27. Stauffer, *'Sechs furchtbare Jahre…'*, 153.

28. Archiv für Zeitgeschichte, NL Paul Ruegger 27.2, 'Vermittlung des Schweizer Botschafters im Fall Rudolf Hess 1946–1985', Letter from Hess to Ruegger, 2 November 1944.

29. In this context, see also the exchange of letters between Ruegger and British Brigadier Dr John R. Rees, a wartime and civilian psychiatrist, who was one of the physicians charged with caring for Hess. Rees was working on the case from a medico-legal angle and planned to write a book about it. See Archiv für Zeitgeschichte, NL Paul Ruegger 27.2, 'Vermittlung des Schweizer Botschafters im Fall Rudolf Hess 1946–1985'. See Stauffer, 'Rudolf Hess und die Schutzmacht Schweiz', 260–84. Paul Ruegger reported to Rees about his meeting with Hess in December 1944 in Wales and his impression about the man's sickness. When

in 1945 Rees declared Hess fit to stand trial in Nuremberg, the political pressure to do so must have been enormous; however, when his book came out in 1947, he stated a very different point of view on Hess: 'It is certainly not possible to maintain that all his abnormalities have been simulated willfully... The main probable diagnosis would appear to be paranoid schizophrenia'. John R. Rees (ed.), *The Case of Rudolf Hess: A Problem in Diagnosis and Forensic Psychiatry* (London: W. Heinemann, 1947), xiii.

30. Stauffer, 'Rudolf Hess und die Schutzmacht Schweiz', 282 ff.

31. Neal H. Petersen (ed.), *From Hitler's Doorstep: The Wartime Intelligence Reports of Allen Dulles, 1942–1945* (University Park: Pennsylvania State University Press, 1996), 162–3.

32. Peter Black, *Ernst Kaltenbrunner: Ideological Soldier of the Third Reich* (Princeton: Princeton University Press, 1984), 256.

33. Gary Jonathan Bass, *Stay the Hand of Vengeance: The Politics of War Crimes Tribunals* (Princeton: Princeton University Press, 2002), 11.

34. Richard Breitman, *Official Secrets: What the Nazis Planned, What the British and Americans Knew* (New York: Hill and Wang, 1998), 213.

35. Martha Minow, *Between Vengeance and Forgiveness: Facing History after Genocide and Mass Violence* (Boston: Beacon Press, 1998), 26.

36. Arieh J. Kochavi, *Prelude to Nuremberg: Allied War Crimes Policy and the Question of Punishment* (Chapel Hill: University of North Carolina Press, 1998), 238. George Ginsburgs and Vladimir Nikolaevich Kudriavtsev (eds.), *The Nuremberg Trial and International Law*, Law in Eastern Europe 42 (Dordrecht: Kluwer Academic Publishers, 1990).

37. 'The Kharkov Trial', *The Spectator*, 23 December 1943, 1.

38. Simpson, *Splendid Blond Beast*, 144.

39. Ibid., 246.

40. Ibid., 160.

41. N. Polyanov, 'Activity of Geneva Committee of Red Cross', *Trud*, 1 December 1946. NARA, RG 59, D-File 1945–49, Box 4082, 800.142/12-946. Translation attached to a letter from State Department DC to Swiss Minister Charles Bruggmann, 9 December 1946.

42. 'Die Frage der "Kriegsverbrecher": Moskauer Polemik gegen das Internationale Komitee vom Roten Kreuz', *Neue Zürcher Zeitung*, 20 May 1944, Blatt 1, Schweizerisches Sozialarchiv, Zurich, Folder 49.5 ZA 1 'Internationales Komitee vom Roten Kreuz (IKRK)'.

43. 'Die Frage der "Kriegsverbrecher": Moskauer Polemik gegen das Internationale Komitee vom Roten Kreuz', *Neue Zürcher Zeitung*, 20 May 1944, Blatt 1, Schweizerisches Sozialarchiv, Zurich, Folder 49.5 ZA 1 'Internationales Komitee vom Roten Kreuz (IKRK)'.

44. 'Colonel Rosenthau, einer der amerikanischen Bonzen des Nürnberger-Prozesses hat einer schweizerischen Parteigrösse in London in Gegenwart Laskis gesagt: "20 Millionen Deutsche müssen sterben". Wenn das Internationale Komitee vom Roten Kreuz somit auf diesem Gebiete etwas machen will, so

muss es den Mut haben, die soeben angedeuteten Kräfte in die Schranken zu fordern. Ich gehe mit Ihnen völlig einig: diesen Mut sollte es haben'. Burckhardt to Rothmund, 23 January 1946. 'Persönlich und Vertraulich' UB Basel, NL Burckhardt, B I 46 i Dossier 9, Heinrich Rothmund.

45. Stauffer, *'Sechs furchtbare Jahre...'*, 513, 484.

46. Ibid., 488.

47. Burleigh, *Moral Combat*, 544.

48. Stauffer, *'Sechs furchtbare Jahre...'*, 484.

49. Archiv für Zeitgeschichte, NL Paul Ruegger 27.3 'Korrespondenz Wolf Rüdiger Hess–Paul Ruegger 1984/1985'; copy of the report by Paul Ruegger 'Das Urteil in Nuernberg', 3 October 1946, to Bundesrat member Max Petitpierre.

50. Archiv für Zeitgeschichte, NL Paul Ruegger 27.3 'Korrespondenz Wolf Rüdiger Hess–Paul Ruegger 1984/1985'; copy of the report by Paul Ruegger 'Das Urteil in Nuernberg', 3 October 1946, to Bundesrat Max Petitpierre.

51. Archiv für Zeitgeschichte, NL Paul Ruegger 27.3 'Korrespondenz Wolf Rüdiger Hess–Paul Ruegger 1984/1985'; copy of the report by Paul 'Das Urteil in Nuernberg', 3 October 1946, to Bundesrat member Max Petitpierre. Page 4 reads in part: 'Zu wiederholen ist indessen, dass niemand im Ernst die Notwendigkeit einer Repression der im Nürnberger Prozess erhärteten Massendelikte leugnet'.

52. Archiv für Zeitgeschichte, NL Paul Ruegger 27.3 'Korrespondenz Wolf Rüdiger Hess–Paul Ruegger 1984/1985; copy of the report by Paul Ruegger 'Das Urteil in Nuernberg', 3 October 1946, to Bundesrat member Max Petitpierre. Page 4 reads in part: 'Höchstens wird die—theoretische—Wünschbarkeit einer Ausweitung des begonnenen Rechtsweges angedeutet und—im Hinblick auf die Massendeportationen aus Polen, den baltischen Staaten z.T. dem Balkan— darauf angespielt, dass im arktischen Zirkel sich noch heute ein furchtbares menschliches Drama zu entfalten scheint'.

53. Kochavi, *Prelude to Nuremberg*, 183 ff.

54. Paul Ruegger from London to Swiss Foreign Office and Swiss Federal Police authorities in Bern, 22 May 1946, page 3. Bundesarchiv Bern E4260 (...) 1974/34, 135, N 44/Kriegsverbrecher.

55. Michael Ignatieff, *The Warrior's Honor: Ethnic War and the Modern Conscience* (New York: Metropolitan Books, 1998), 139.

56. Geoffrey Best, *War and Law since 1945* (Oxford: Oxford University Press, 1994), 160.

57. Eva Wortel, 'Humanitarians and Their Moral Stance in War: The Underlying Values', *International Review of the Red Cross* 91.876 (December 2009): 779–801, here 780.

58. S. Z. Kantor, 'The International Red Cross Was Silent', *Jewish Frontier* (May 1945): 17–20, 20.

59. David P. Forsythe, 'Humanitarian Protection: The International Committee of the Red Cross and the United Nations High Commissioner for Refugees', *International Review of the Red Cross* 83.843 (September 2001): 675–97, here 687.

60. Stauffer, 'Sechs fuchtbare Jahre . . .', 351.

61. Burckhardt to Huber, 27 February 1946. UB Basel Nachlass Burckhardt, BII 46 h Dossier 2, 3 Teil 1. The Papal Nuncio alluded here was probably Msgr. Philippe Bernardini in Bern.

62. 'Kaltenbrunner verlangt drei Schweizer Zeugen', *Basler Nachrichten*, 5 March 1946, 2.

63. Huber to Burckhardt, 15 March 1946. UB Basel Nachlass Burckhardt, BII 46 h Dossier 2, 3 Teil 1.

64. Burckhardt to Huber, 18 March 1946. UB Basel Nachlass Burckhardt, BII 46 h Dossier 2, 3 Teil 1.

65. CJB to Max Huber, 18 March 1946. UB Basel NL Burckhardt, B II 46h, Dossier 2, 3 Teil 1.

66. CJB to Max Huber, 18 March 1946. UB Basel NL Burckhardt, B II 46h, Dossier 2, 3 Teil 1. 'Ich habe den Reichskanzler während des Zweiten Weltkriegs nie gesehen'.

67. 'Kaltenbrunner sagte:. . . das ist der grösste Unsinn, man sollte alle Juden entlassen. Das ist meine persönliche Ansicht'. Burckhardt to Bachmann, 9 April 1946, UB Basel. NL Burckhardt, B II 46h, Dossier 2, 3 Teil 2. 'Ich bekam im Verlaufe des Gesprächs in der Tat den Eindruck, Dr. Kaltenbrunner sei es daran gelegen dass den Anträgen des I.K. Folge geleistet werde und er erkläre sich bereit sie bei den entscheidenden Stellen in Berlin zu befürworten, wobei er sagte dass neben dem Reichsführer für alle zwischenstaatlichen Vereinbarungen Herr von Ribbentrop kompetent sei'. Attached to Burckhardt's letter to Bachmann is a typewritten draft memo date 9 April 1946 with numerous deletions, corrections, and notes probably by Carl Jacob Burckhardt.

68. Ernst Haiger et al., *Albrecht Haushofer* (Munich: Langewiese-Brandt, 2002). For his mind-set and biography see also Albrecht Haushofer, *Moabiter Sonette*, Berlin Lothar Blanvalet 1946 (a selection of poems written in prison by Haushofer and posthumously published).

69. Emphasis in the original: Max Huber, *Principles and Foundations of the Work of the International Committee of the Red Cross: 1939–46* (Geneva: International Committee of the Red Cross, 1946), 19.

70. Stauffer, 'Sechs furchtbare Jahre . . .', 184: 'Wie man heute weiss, hat Burckhardt der Maxime des Rotkreuz-Apolitismus vorwiegend verbal gehuldigt'.

71. James Crossland, 'Man of Peaceable Intent', 165.

72. James Crossland, *Britain and the International Committee of the Red Cross 1939–1945* (New York: Palgrave Macmillan, 2014), 141.

73. Eckart Conze, Norbert Frei, Peter Hayes, and Moshe Zimmermann (eds.) *Das Amt und die Vergangenheit: Deutsche Diplomaten im Dritten Reich und in der Bundesrepublik* (Munich: Karl Blessing Verlag, 2010), 375 ff.

74. Marianne von Weizsäcker to Burckhardt, 25 September 1953. UB Basel Nachlass Burckhardt B II 46 a Dossier 2, 3 'Bank Safe Original Dokumente'. See also

Herbert S. Levine, *Hitler's Free City: A History of the Nazi Party in Danzig, 1925–1939* (Chicago: University of Chicago Press, 1973), 142 ff.

75. Weizsäcker to Burckhardt, 7 September 1939. UB Basel Nachlass Burckhardt B II 46a, Dossier 2, 3 'Bank Safe Original Dokumente'.

76. 'Ich war für den Frieden, ganz gleichgültig auf welcher Basis, und ich bezweifle, dass ein Mensch von Herz und Verstand anders denken konnte'. Ernst von Weizsäcker, *Erinnerungen,* ed. Richard von Weizsäcker (Munich: Paul List, 1950), 267.

77. Conze et al. (eds.), *Das Amt und die Vergangenheit,* 388.

78. Klemens von Klemperer, *German Resistance against Hitler: The Search for Allies Abroad, 1938–1945* (Oxford: Clarendon Press, 1992), 26. See also Ulrich Völklein, *Die Weizsäckers: Macht und Moral—Porträt einer deutschen Familie* (Munich: Droemer 2004), 205.

79. Weizsäcker, *Erinnerungen.*

80. Crossland, 'Man of Peaceable Intent', 169. Leonidas Hill, 'Three Crises, 1938–39', *Journal of Contemporary History* 3.1 (January 1968): 113–44. See also Thomas W. Maulucci, 'German Diplomats and the Myth of the Two Foreign Offices', in David A. Messenger and Katrin Paehler, *A Nazi Past. Recasting German Identity in Postwar Europe* (Lexington: University Press of Kentucky, 2015), 139–67.

81. NARA, RG 242, BDC, NSDAP Zentralkartei, Roll T087, Ernst von Weizsäcker, Mitgl.-Nr. 4814617. According to BDC-records it would appear that his wife Marianne had joined the Nazi Party in 1936, two years before her husband. Marianne Freifrau von Weizsäcker, born 8 August 1889, Mitgliedsnummer 3762854, NARA, RG 242 BDC, NSDAP-Ortsgruppe, Roll Y059. For Weizsäcker's version of his SS and Nazi membership, see his memoirs, *Erinnerungen,* 152.

82. NARA, RG 242, BDC, SS officers, Roll 234B, 621 ff. Ernst von Weizsäcker, born 25 May 1882. In German, the text of his 1938 résumé reads: 'Im Sommer 1933 nach der Machtergreifung wurde ich als Gesandter in die Schweiz versetzt. Vom Sommer 1936 bis Frühjahr 1937 leitete ich kommissarisch die Politische Abteilung des Auswärtigen Amts. Vom Mai 1937 bis zum März 1938 war ich Direktor der Politischen Abteilung; Anfang April wurde ich zum Staatssekretär des Auswärtigen Amtes ernannt'. Weizsäcker received his SS Totenkopfring and SS Ehrendegen; in 1942 he was promoted to the honorary rank of SS Brigadeführer.

83. NARA, RG 242, BDC, SS officers, Roll 234B, 621 ff. Ernst von Weizsäcker, born 25 May 1882. When he joined the SS, documents in his file seem to indicate that he promised 'verspreche, die [Nazi-]Bewegung mit allen Kräften zu fördern'.

84. Hans Froelicher, Notiz für Herrn Minister Zehnder, 23 December 1947, Diplomatische Dokumente der Schweiz dodis.ch 4841, Swiss Federal Archives E 2001(E)1967/113/533.

85. Notice à l'intention de Monsieur le Conseiller fédéral Petitpierre, 2 October 1947, Diplomatische Dokumente der Schweiz, www.dodis.ch DoDis-4422, Schweizerisches Bundesarchiv, Bern (CH-BAR) E 2802(-)1967/78/6.

86. Stauffer, '*Sechs furchtbare Jahre . . .*', 483.

87. Ibid., 166. On Burckhardt as a witness and source see also the article by Georg Kreis, 'C.J. Burckhardt – die Anatomie eines grossen Arrangements', in *Basler Zeitung*, 24 April 1992.

88. Defense Exhibit Index US vs. Weizsaecker, et al. Tribunal IV, Case 11, NARA, RG 238, War Crimes Records Collection, United States of America v. Ernst von Weizsaecker et al., M897, Roll 1, page 233. The exhibit index also states that Objection sustained 27 July 1948 and Objection Sustained 15 September 1948.

89. Swiss Minsister, Swiss Legation in Paris, Affidavit by Carl J. Burckhardt, Minister of Switzerland to France, signed Burckhardt, 5 October 1948, NARA, RG 238, War Crimes Records Collection, United States of America v. Ernst von Weizsaecker et al., M897, Roll 119.

90. 'Passages concerning Weizsaecker Nr 169 c', authenticated 16 February 1948, NARA, RG 238, War Crimes Records Collection, United States of America v. Ernst von Weizsaecker et al., M897, Roll 119. The exhibit index also states that an objection was sustained on 27 July 1948 and another objection was sustained on 15 September 1948.

91. In German, the phrase is 'unausstehlichen Amerikaner'. See Stauffer, '*Sechs furchtbare Jahre...*', 166.

92. Burckhardt, *Meine Danziger Mission*, 181 f.

93. Marianne von Weizsäcker to Burckhardt, 25 September 1953. UB Basel Nachlass Burckhardt B II 46 a Dossier 2, 3 'Bank Safe Original Dokumente'.

94. Eidesstattliche Erklärung Max Huber, Zurich 20 March 1948, NARA, RG 238, War Crimes Records Collection, United States of America v. Ernst von Weizsaecker et al., M897, Roll 119.

95. Eidesstattliche Erklärung Walther G. Hartmann, February 11, 1948. NARA, RG 238, War Crimes Records Collection, United States of America v. Ernst von Weizsaecker et al., M897, Roll 119.

96. Schwarzenberg in his memories see Colienne Meran, Marysia Miller-Aichholz, Erkinger Schwarzenberg (ed.) *Johannes E. Schwarzenberg, Erinnerungen und Gedanken eines Diplomaten im Zeitenwandel 1903–1978* (Vienna: Böhlau, 2013), 199.

97. Eidesstattliche Versicherung Karl Wolff, December 12, 1947, NARA, RG 238, War Crimes Records Collection, United States of America v. Ernst von Weizsaecker et al., M897, Roll 118. Not surprisingly people like Wolff used these despositions to put themselves in the best possible light with the Americans.

98. For the impact on humanitarian law and human rights see Best, *War and Law*, 210.

99. Telford Taylor, *Guilt, Responsibility, and the Third Reich* (Cambridge: W. Heffer and Sons, Ltd, 1970), 5.

100. Letter from David Bruce to Matthew Connelly, 5 August 1949, accompanied by a letter from Carl J. Burckhardt and Max Huber to Harry S. Truman, Zurich, 30 July 1949, Official File Truman Papers, Harry S. Truman Presidential Museum and Library.

101. Katrin Paehler, 'Auditioning for Postwar: Walter Schellenberg, the Allies, and Attempts to Fashion a Usable Past', in David A. Messenger, Katrin Paehler, *A Nazi Past. Recasting German Identity in Postwar Europe* (Lexington: University Press of Kentucky, 2015), 29–56.

102. Quoted in Paehler, *Auditioning for Postwar*, 46.

103. 'Die Verteidiger der Unschuld' AZ 4/22/1949. 'Etter, Will und Weizsäcker. Vom Nürnberger Prozess', *Volksstimme*, 9/1/1948.

104. Philipp Etter to Dr Adolf Keller in Geneva about Ernst von Weizsäcker, Letterhead 'Bundespräsident der Schweizerischen Eidgenossenschaft', Bern, 11 December 1947. Schweizerisches Bundesarchiv J2.181/1987/52/3127, Verurteilung Ernst von Weizsäckers im 13. Nürnberger Kriegsverbrecher-Prozess. See also Letter Etter to Keller, NARA, RG 238, War Crimes Records Collection, United States of America v. Ernst von Weizsaecker et al., M897, Roll 118.

105. Valentin Gitermann, 'Ein aufrichtiger Freund der Schweiz', *Volksrecht. Sozialdemokratisches Tagblatt* 8/18/1948 (frontpage).

106. 'Es ist eine Schande für unser Land, dass für einen Mitschuldigen der Hitler-Barbarei, für einen Mitschuldigen am grauenhaften Leid und Elend, das der Krieg über die Menschheit brachte, ein Bundesrat und diverse Korpskommandanten als Entlastungszeugen auftreten!' 'Merkwürdige Eidgenossen', A.Z. 8/5/1948.

107. See Folder with press clippings at the Swiss Federal Archives J2.181/1987/52/3127 Verurteilung Ernst von Weizsäcker im 13. Nürnberger Kriegsverbrecher-Prozess.

108. 'Die Urteilsverkündung in Nürnberg. Mitschuld Weizsäckers an der Ermordung der Juden.', NZZ 4/13/1949. 'Sieben Jahre Gefängnis für Weizsäcker. Das Urteil im Wilhelmstrasse-Prozess', Die Tat 4/15/1949.

109. Kochavi, *Prelude to Nuremberg*, ch. 5.

110. 'Der Prozess gegen die Wilhelmstrasse'. NZZ, 10/17/1948.

111. N. Polyanov, 'Activity of Geneva Committee of Red Cross', *Trud,* 1 December 1946, NARA, RG 59, D-File 1945–49, Box 4082, 800.142/12–946. Translation attached to a letter from State Department DC to Swiss Minister Charles Bruggmann, 9 December 1946.

112. N. Polyanov, 'Activity of Geneva Committee of Red Cross', *Trud* 1 December 1946, NARA, RG 59, D-File 1945–49, Box 4082, 800.142/12–946. Translation attached to a letter from State Department DC to Swiss Minister Charles Bruggmann, 9 December 1946.

113. Stauffer, 'Rudolf Hess und die Schutzmacht Schweiz', 260–84, here 278.

114. British ambassador Duff Cooper in Paris to Burckhardt, 9 March 1946 (Personal!), UB Basel Nachlass Burckhardt B II 46 a Dossier 2, 3 Bank Safe Original Dokumente.

115. Van Dongen, *La Suisse face à la seconde guerre mondiale*, 47.

116. Stauffer, '*Sechs furchtbare Jahre . . .*', 150–6.

117. Levine, *Hitler's Free City*, 143.

118. Treasury Chambers London to Burckhardt, 25 September 1953, UB Basel Nachlass Burckhardt B II 46 a Dossier 2, 3 Bank Safe Original Dokumente.

119. See letter of Ernst von Weizsäcker, 7 September 1939, reprinted in Burckhardt, *Meine Danziger Mission*, 358.

120. Adolf Frisé, *Carl. J. Burckhardt: Im Dienste der Humanität* (St. Gallen: Pflugverlag, 1950).

CHAPTER 6

1. 'Die Diplomatie der Menschlichkeit hat Grosses erreicht: Das Internationale Rote Kreuz am Kriegsende', NZZ, 25 August 1945, Archiv für Sozialgeschichte Zürich, folder 49.5 ZA 1, 'Internationales Komitee vom Roten Kreuz' (IKRK).

2. *Inter Arma Caritas*, 1947, 115 ff. 'Army will study prisons in France. Reich captives' plight likened to that of Dachau victims – Many to be returned', *New York Times*, 15 October 1945, p. 7. See also Fabien Théofilakis, *Les prisonniers de guerre allemands: France, 1944–1949* (Paris: Fayard, 2014).

3. Junod, *Imperiled Red Cross*, 21.

4. *Inter Arma Caritas*, 1947, 117.

5. *Inter Arma Caritas*, 1947, 118.

6. James Crossland, *Britain and the International Committee of the Red Cross 1939–1945* (New York: Palgrave Macmillan, 2014), 189.

7. German original: 'für alles was Sie in den schweren Jahren geleistet haben'; AfZG Zurich, Ruegger Nachlass, Dossiers 28.2.10.5, letter, Adenauer to Ruegger, 15 August 1955.

8. NARA, RG 200, Records of the American Red Cross, 1935–1941, folder 619.2.02 Memorandum, Max Huber, ICRC, 'Relief activity of the International Committee of the Red Cross for Camps and D.P.s of the United Nations in Germany', Geneva, 30 August 1945.

9. Huber to Byrnes, Memorandum of the ICRC in favour of ex-POWs and DPs of the United Nations still in Germany, 30 August 1945, through ICRC delegation, Washington, DC, 27 September 1945, NARA RG 59, 800.142/9-2745, box 4082.

10. Department of State Memorandum, signed Albert E. Clattenburg, 3 October 1945, forwarded to War Department, NARA, RG 59, 800.142/Geneva 10-345, box 4082.

11. Department of State Memorandum, signed Albert E. Clattenburg, 5 October 1945, forwarded to War Department, NARA, RG 59, 800.142/Geneva 10-345, box 4082.

12. Françoise Krill, 'The ICRC's policy on refugees and internally displaced civilians', *International Review of the Red Cross,* September 2001, vol. 83, no. 843, 607–27.

13. Office of Military Government for Germany (US), Internal Affairs and Communication Division, APO 742, 27 February 1947, Subject: ICRC and Its Relationship to USFET and Military Government, Dwight P. Griswold, Director, NARA, RG 200, AMRC, box 103, folder 41.

14. Barnett, *Empire of Humanity*, 111–12. 'The International Refugee Organization', *Yearbook of the United Nations, 1947–1948,* 955.

15. Tony Kushner and Katharine Knox, *Refugees in an Age of Genocide. Global, National and Local Perspectives during the Twentieth Century* (London: Frank Cass, 1999), 217.

16. The International Tracing Service, headquartered in the town of Bad Arolsen in the US occupation zone of Germany, also worked within the framework of the IRO. 'The International Refugee Organization', *Yearbook of the United Nations 1947–1948,* 958.

17. Cohen, *In War's Wake*, 38.

18. Frank T. Cleverley, American Red Cross, to William H. McCahon, acting assistant chief of the Division of Protective Services Department of State, 30 December 1947. NARA, RG 59, box 4082, 800.142/12-3047.

19. War Department, Lt. Col. Ray J. Laux, Civil Affairs Division, 26 February 1948 to State Department, Protective Services, NARA, RG 59, 800.142/2-2648, box 4083.

20. 'Das Internationale Rote Kreuz am Kriegsende', NZZ, 25 August 1945, Archiv für Sozialgeschichte Zürich, Folder 49.5 ZA 1 'Internationales Komitee vom Roten Kreuz' (IKRK).

21. See Keith Lowe, *Savage Continent: Europe in the Aftermath of World War II* (New York: Picador St. Martin's Press 2012), 125 ff.

22. Buruma, *Year Zero*, 79.

23. Marrus, *The Unwanted*, 325.

24. Robert G. Moeller, 'Germans as Victims? Thoughts on a Post-Cold War History of World War II's Legacies', *History & Memory* 17, nos. 1/2 (2005): 151.

25. R. M. Douglas, *Orderly and Humane: The Expulsion of the Germans after the Second World War* (New Haven: Yale University Press, 2012).

26. Douglas, *Orderly and Humane*, 1. See Rey-Schyrr, *De Yalta à Dien Bien Phu* ('Les personnes déplacées et les réfugiés',) 178.

27. Former Secretary of State Madeleine Albright has noted the quandary of collective punishment: 'Legal philosophers have long debated whether it is better to have a system in which some who are innocent are punished along with the guilty or one in which the innocent are held harmless but some who are guilty escape.' Madeleine Albright, *Prague Winter: A Personal Story of Remembrance and War, 1937–1948* (New York: Harper Perennial, 2012), 339.

28. An estimated four million expellees lived in the German Democratic Republic (East Germany).

29. United States Office Preparatory Commission International Refugee Organization, Washington, DC, 30 June 1948 'Summary of Provisions of the Displaced Persons Act of 1948 . . . and Definitions of Eligibility under the IRO Constitution', NARA, RG 59, Entry 1419, IRO and DP Commission, box 21, folder 'PCIRO Monthly Digest 1947–49'.

30. Barnett, *Empire of Humanity*, 112.

31. Rey-Schyrr, *De Yalta à Dien Bien Phu*, 175 ff. Klaus Eisterer, *Französische Besatzungspolitik; Tirol und Vorarlberg 1945/46* (Innsbruck: Haymon, 1990), 77 ff.

32. Douglas, *Orderly and Humane,* 286.

33. *Inter Arma Caritas,* 1947, 118. *Report of the International Committee of the Red Cross on Its Activities during the Second World War* (1 September 1939–30 June 1947) Volume 1, General Activities, Geneva, May 1948, 672.

34. An example for attempting to gain some support for Germans is this report: 'Die Not der aus den Ostgebieten ausgewiesenen Deutschen' Vereinigte Hilfswerk vom Internationalen Roten Kreuz, IKRK and Liga, Geneva, November 1945, CZA L17\1797. This memoranda talks about the news reports about the desperate situations of the German expellees from the former East provinces, but also about the consequences for Germany to loose such waste territories and its food production. The report has the cover sheet with the letterhead in German of the Joint Relief Commission of the International Red Cross (League and ICRC). The report has no author, but it seems to be compiled by the German Red Cross, possibly even by Hartmann.

35. Anne-Laure Sans, 'Aussi Humainement que Possible'. Le Comité International de la Croix-Rouge et l'expulsion des minorités allemandes dà Europe de L'Est 1945–1950 (Pologne—Tchécoslovaquie), Ph.D. thesis, Université de Genève (Geneva, 2003).

36. Douglas, *Orderly and Humane,* 235.

37. Quoted in Douglas, *Orderly and Humane,* 150.

38. Douglas, *Orderly and Humane,* 153.

39. Carl Jacob Burckhardt, Legation de Suisse a Paris, to IRC Committee member Jacques Cheneviere, 30 October 1945. Archives du Comité international de la Croix-Rouge, ACICR G 59/6—170, USHMM RG-19.045M, reel 9.

40. Burckhardt to Rothmund, 23 January 1946, NL Burckhardt, UB Basel, B I 46 i Dossier 9, Heinrich Rothmund.

41. Burckhardt to Max Huber, president ad interim of the ICRC, 29 December 1945 AfZG Zurich, NL Stauffer 12 (V), NL CJB.

42. Burckhardt to Max Huber, president ad interim of the ICRC, 29 December 1945 AfZG Zurich, NL Stauffer 12 (V), NL CJB.

43. Douglas, *Orderly and Humane,* 296.

44. Douglas, *Orderly and Humane,* 296.

45. Burckhardt to Rothmund Paris, 23 January 1946. NL Burckhardt, UB Basel, B I 46 i Dossier 9, Heinrich Rothmund.

46. Burckhardt to Rothmund, January 23, 1946, NL Burckhardt, UB Basel, B I 46 i Dossier 9, Heinrich Rothmund. 'Wie ich höre, ist der Aufruf des Komitees in Amerika sehr übel aufgenommen worden'.

47. 'Ich habe mit den Amerikanern in jedem Zusammenhange die Erfahrung gemacht, dass sie einen nur respektieren, wenn man ihrer oft erpresserischen Kälte mit Kälte entgegentritt'. Burckhardt to Max Huber, President ad interim of the ICRC, December 29, 1945 AfZG Zurich NL Stauffer 12 (V), NL CJB.

48. See Joerg Kistler, *Das Politische Konzept der Schweizerischen Nachkriegshilfe in den Jahren 1943–1948*, University of Bern, Ph.D., 1980.

49. Burckhardt to Rothmund, 23 January 1946 (personal and confidential), NL Burckhardt, UB Basel, B I 46 i Dossier 9, Heinrich Rothmund.

50. Heinrich Rothmund to Burckhardt, 17 January 1946, NL Burckhardt, UB Basel, B I 46 i Dossier 9, Heinrich Rothmund. 'Im Osten und in Deutschland müssen wir mitansehen, dass diesen Winter über noch Millionen von Menschen sterben…Es ist nicht unverständlich, dass die Völker, die unter den organisierten Scheusslichkeiten der Nazis am meisten gelitten haben, heute noch Mühe haben einzusehen, dass das was heute dem deutschen Volk geschieht, letzten Endes auf alle zurückfällt und dass im Interesse aller jede aus Rache entstandene Vergeltung unterbleiben sollte. Das heisst, dass es heute noch nicht angeht, alle technischen Möglichkeiten der Hilfeleistung auszuschöpfen, weil die Bereitschaft dazu noch weitherum fehlt'.

51. Burckhardt to Rothmund, 23 January 1946 (personal and confidential), NL Burckhardt, UB Basel, B I 46 i Dossier 9, Heinrich Rothmund. 'Organisierte Scheusslichkeiten sind nicht nur eine Spezialität der Nazis, sondern eine Spezialität unserer Generation überhaupt'. See Auch Stauffer, *Sechs furchtbare Jahre*, 355.

52. Stauffer, *Sechs furchtbare Jahre*, 355.

53. Burckhardt to Rothmund, 23 January 1946 (personal and confidential), NL Burckhardt, UB Basel, B I 46 i Dossier 9, Heinrich Rothmund. 'Dass heute Millionen Menschen im Osten und in Deutschland sterben, das ist von einer ganz ausschlaggebenden Gruppe, die heute in der Welt an der Macht ist, bewusst gewollt, und ist nicht nur das, was man mit dem Begriff "Schicksal" bezeichnen mag. Das Schicksal hätte auch anders sein können'. See also Stauffer, *Sechs furchtbare Jahre*, 355.

54. Burckhardt to Rothmund, 23 January 1946 (personal and confidential), NL Burckhardt, UB Basel, B I 46 i Dossier 9, Heinrich Rothmund. 'Colonel Rosenthau, einer der amerikanischen Bonzen des Nürnberger-Prozesses hat einer schweizerischen Parteigrösse in London in Gegenwart Laskis gesagt: "20 Millionen Deutsche müssen sterben." Wenn das Internationale Komitee vom Roten Kreuz somit auf diesem Gebiete etwas machen will, so muss es den Mut haben, die soeben angedeuteten Kräfte in die Schranken zu fordern. Ich gehe mit Ihnen völlig einig: diesen Mut sollte es haben'.

55. Rothmund to Burckhardt, 17 January 1946, NL Burckhardt, UB Basel, B I 46 i Dossier 9, Heinrich Rothmund.

56. Rothmund to Ruegger, 14 May 1947, AfZ, NL Ruegger, Dossiers 23.9.6–23.11.1.

57. Rothmund to Ruegger, 3 December 1944, AfZ, NL Ruegger, Dossiers 23.9.6–23.11.1. 'In St. Gallen habe ich mich mit Herrn Saly Mayer verabredet. Ich möchte auch noch wissen, wie es von jüdischer Seite tönt. Es könnte nämlich auch heissen: "Jetzt wird der Bock zum Gärntner gemacht."'

58. A few years later, in 1947 and now with a couple years of experience as an IGCR delegate, Rothmund wrote to Ruegger detailing his thoughts about which Jews should be allowed to remain in Switzerland and which should be forced to leave: 'Of course I agree that Switzerland will keep the old people and the one who are sick...Concerning all the others, in my opinion, only a few hundred, especially outstanding and important personalities can stay. But then no more. The rest must be redirected elsewhere as intended. If we fail to do so, the slightest weakening of the economic situation will inevitably cause antisemitism.' Rothmund to Ruegger, 14 May 1947, AfZ, NL Ruegger, Dossiers 23.9.6–23.11.1.

59. Cf. Arieh J. Kochavi, *Prelude to Nuremberg: Allied War Crimes Policy and the Question of Punishment* (Chapel Hill: University of North Carolina Press, 1998), 57. Cf. Phayer, *Pius XII*, 267–8; Steinacher, *Nazis on the Run,* 11.

60. Kochavi, *Confronting Captivity*, 255 ff.

61. See Harald Stadler, Martin Kofler, and Karl C. Berger (eds.), *Flucht in die Hoffnungslosigkeit. Die Kosaken in Osttirol* (Innsbruck: Studienverlag, 2005). See also Martin Kofler, *Osttirol im Dritten Reich 1938–1945* (Innsbruck: Studienverlag, 1996), 231 ff. See Stefan Karner and Othmar Pickl (eds.), *Die Rote Armee in der Steiermark: Sowjetische Besatzung 1945* (Graz: Leykam, 2008).

62. Jim Sanders, Mark Sauter and R. Cort Kirkwood, *Soldiers of Misfortune: Washington's Secret Betrayal of American POWs in the Soviet Union* (Washington, DC: National Press Books, 1992), 85.

63. Nikolai Tolstoy, *Victims of Yalta* (London: Hodder and Stoughton, 1977), 176 ff.

64. Marrus, *The Unwanted,* 317.

65. Rashke, *Useful Enemies*, 297.

66. Cohen, *In War's Wake*, 9.

67. Cohen, *In War's Wake*, 9.

68. Cohen, *In War's Wake*, 30.

69. Holborn, *International Refugee Organization*, 31.

70. Holborn, *International Refugee Organization*, 33.

71. Arthur Rucker, 'The Work of the International Refugee Organization', *International Affairs* (Royal Institute of International Affairs) 25/1 (January 1949): 66–73.

72. Christopher Simpson, *Blowback: America's Recruitment of Nazis and Its Effects on the Cold War* (New York: Weidenfeld and Nicolson 1988), 138 ff. Richard Breitman et al., *US Intelligence and the Nazis* (New York: Cambridge UP, 2005).

73. Intergovernmental Committee on Refugees, 24 June 1947, Morton W. Royse, Memorandum for Mr Byington, US Embassy, 'Subject: Persons liable to forcible repatriation, reference to your telegram (SECRET) NARA, RG 84, US Embassy Italy, Rome, Classified General Records, 1947, box 20, Entry 2780, folder 848 'Inter-governmental Committee on Refugees'. See also Michael Phayer, 'Discussion Session Six: Pius XII—Post-war Assistance to Fleeing Nazis and Policies on Hidden Jewish Children', in David Bankier, Dan Michman, and Iael

Midam-Orvieto, eds., *Pius XII and the Holocaust, Current State of Research* (Jerusalem: Yad Vashem/Shlomo Press, 2012), 193.

74. 'Extension of activities of the Intergovernmental Committee on Refugees', 30 July 1946, signed Herbert Emerson, USHMM, RG-43.048M, IRO, carton 62, reel 5.

75. Catherine Rey-Schyrr, *De Yalta à Dien Bien Phu: Historie du Comité international de la Croix-Rouge, 1945–1955* (Genève: CICR et Georg Editeur, 2007), 183 ff.

76. J. Friedrich, delegate of the ICRC to Prof. Max Huber and M. Bachmann, 'Betrifft; Allgemeine Situation in Deutschland' signed, 15 June 1945, Archives du Comité international de la Croix-Rouge, ACICR G 59/6—167.06, USHMM, RG-19.045 M, reel 9.

77. Lithuanians in a camp in Linz (Upper Austria) asked the ICRC for protection in order to stay in Austria and not being deported to their now Soviet controlled homeland. Neniskis Peter, Sekretär des ehemaligen Litauischen Verbandes e.V. an das Intern. Rote Kreuz Linz/Donau, 'Betr,: Litauische Kriegsflüchtlinge im Gebiet Oberösterreich', 19 June 1945. See also Hungarian Committee Salzburg to ICRC delegation, 29 June 1945, Archives du Comité international de la Croix-Rouge, ACICR G 59/6—167.06, USHMM, RG-19.045 M, reel 9.

78. Aide Committee of the Baltic Republics Estonia, Latvia, Lithuania, in Leipzig, 5 June 1945 signed Dipl. Ing. A. Dancauskis director Archives du Comité international de la Croix-Rouge, ACICR G 59, G59/6—167.06, USHMM RG-19.045 M, reel 9.

79. Meeting, Hotel de la Metropole in Geneva, 9 January 1945, present were among others Carl J. Burckhardt and Dr Marti Delegate of the ICRC, ACICR, G59/6—167.05, USHMM, RG-19.045 M, reel 9.

80. 'Le plus grand nombre des refugiés qui s'adressent au Comité international de la Croix Rouge sont des personnes originaires de territoires de l'Est et qui, pour des raisons *diverses* [handwritten addition] que nous ne pouvons apprécier, supposent qu'elles ne peuvent actuellement regagner leur patrie sans que leur sécurité personnelle soit mise en danger'. Max Huber to Sir Herbert Emerson, 21 August 1945, ICRC Archives, Archives Generales, B G 68/00. See also Huber to Herbert W. Emerson, Director, Intergovernmental Committee on Refugees London, August 21, 1945. Archives du Comité international de la Croix-Rouge, ACICR G59/6—169, USHMM, RG-19.045 M, reel 9.

81. Proces-Verbal de la séance da 22 August 1945 entre MM Kullmann, Rothmund, president Huber and P. Kuhne 'Concerne: Aide aux refugies se trouvent dans les territoires d'Allemagne occupies par les Allies occidenteux' Archives du Comité international de la Croix-Rouge, ACICR G 59/6—170, USHMM, RG-19.045 M, reel 9.

82. Jacques Chenevière vice-president ICRC to Burckhardt November 9, 1945, 'Mission de M. de Bondeli a Londres 30 mai 1947, 5.5.1947–9.6.1947', Intergovernmental Committee on Refugees London to President of the ICRC, 5 May 1947 Archives du Comité international de la Croix-Rouge, ACICRG 59/6—169, USHMM, RG-19.045 M, reel 9.

83. 'Travel Documents' in *Report of the International Committee of the Red Cross on Its Activities during the Second World War* (1 September 1939–30 June 1947) Volume 1, General Activities, Geneva, May 1948, 671.

84. 'Session Pleniere du Comite Intergouvernemental pour les refugies' 20 November 1945, Archives du Comité international de la Croix-Rouge, ACICR G 59/6—167.01, USHMM, RG-19.045 M, reel 9.

85. Note pour la delegation du CICR a Berlin, a l'attention de Monsieur Lindt, 18 February 1946. Archives du Comité international de la Croix-Rouge, ACICR G 59/6—169, USHMM, RG-19.045 M, reel 9.

86. Max Huber to Eleanor Roosevelt, Member of the United States Delegation to the United Nations Organization, 14 February 1946. Archives du Comité international de la Croix-Rouge, ACICR G59/6—169, USHMM, RG-19.045 M, reel 9.

87. '*Report of the International Committee of the Red Cross on Its Activities during the Second World War* (1 September 1939–30 June 1947), volume 1, General Activities, Geneva, May 1948, 672.

88. Note a la Delegation du CICR a Francfort, signed P. Kuhne, 16 December 1946, Archives du Comité international de la Croix-Rouge, ACICR G59/6—169, Microfilm reel number 9, USHMM-19.045 M.

89. 'Refugees and Stateless Persons', in *Report of the International Committee of the Red Cross on Its Activities during the Second World War* (1 September 1939–30 June 1947), volume 1, General Activities, Geneva, May 1948, 665.

90. Ibid., 666.

91. Ibid., 664.

92. Ibid., 666–7.

93. Richard J. Evans, 'Nazis on the Run by Gerald Steinacher – Review,'. *The Guardian*, 24 June 2011.

94. Intergovernmental Committee on Refugees, 24 June 1947, Morton W. Royse, Memorandum for Mr Byington, US Embassy, 'Subject: Persons liable to forcible repatriation, reference to your telegram' (secret). NARA, RG 84, US Embassy Italy, Rome, Classified General Records, 1947, box 20, Entry 2780, folder 848: 'Inter-governmental Committee on Refugees'.

95. Cohen, *In War's Wake*, 46.

96. Rey-Schyrr, *De Yalta à Dien Bien Phu*, 177.

97. US embassy in Moscow to the State Department, Washington, DC, and the embassy in Vienna, Berlin, and Rome, signed Durbrow, 12 June 1947 (Secret), NARA, RG 84, Rome embassy, box 20, folder 848, 'Displaced Persons'.

98. Cohen, *In War's Wake*, 48 f.

99. NARA, RG 59, Entry 1419, box 21, IRO and DP Commission, IRO subject file 1946–1952, folder 'Adherence Switzerland'.

100. See Richard Rashke, *Useful Enemies: John Demjanjuk and America's Open-Door Policy for Nazi War Criminals* (Harrison, NY: Delphinium, 2013), 23. Cohen, *In War's Wake*, 49.

101. United States Office Preparatory Commission International Refugee Organization, Washington, DC, 30 June 1948, 'Summary of Provisions of the Displaced Persons Act of 1948 . . . and definitions of eligibility under the IRO constitution', NARA, RG 59, Entry 1419, IRO and DP Commission, box 21, folder 'PCIRO Monthly Digest 1947–49'. Displaced Persons Act, 25 June 1948, 80th session of the US Congress.

102. Rashke, *Useful Enemies*, 3.

103. IRO file on Iwan Demjanjuk, born 3 April 1920, case 805.783, IRO form dated 29 March 1948. USHMM archive, ITS digital collection.

104. Rashke, *Useful Enemies*, xiv.

105. USHMM, ITS Collection Data Base Central Name Index, Michael Seifert, document I.d. 37517457.

106. In 2008 Seifert was extradited from Canada to Italy and sentenced to a life-long prison sentence, which ended with his death in 2010. See Mimmo Franzinelli, *Le stragi nascoste: L'armadio della vergogna, impunità e rimozione dei crimini di guerra nazifascisti 1943–2001* (Milan: Mondadori, 2003). See Franco Giustolisi, *L'Armadio della vergogna* (Rome: Beat, 2011). See Giorgio Mezzalira and Carlo Romeo (eds.), *'Mischa' l'aguzzino del lager di Bolzano: Dalle carte al processo a Michael Seifert* (Bolzano: Circolo Culturale ANPI, 2002).

107. Quoted in Cohen, *In War's Wake*, 49.

108. Cohen, *In War's Wake*, 49.

109. Cohen, *In War's Wake*, 99.

110. John Lewis Gaddis, *The United States and the Origins of the Cold War, 1941–1947* (New York: Columbia University Press, 2000). See also Les K. Adler and Thomas G. Paterson, 'Red Fascism: The Merger of Nazi Germany and Soviet Russia in the American Image of Totalitarianism, 1930's–1950's', *American Historical Review*, vol. 75 (April 1970), 1046–64. See Michael Phayer, *Pius XII, the Holocaust, and the Cold War* (Bloomington: Indiana University Press, 2008) For Austria, see James Jay Carafano, *Waltzing into the Cold War. The Struggle for Occupied Austria* (College Station: Texas A and M University Press, 2002). Thanks to Guenter Bischof for his advice and suggestions to this crucial question.

111. Cohen, *In War's Wake*, 35.

112. Burckhardt to Martin Bodmer, 3 November 1947, 'Persönlich und Vertraulich', Nachlass Burckhardt, UB Basel B II 46 i, Dossier 3.

113. 'The International Refugee Organization', *United Nations Yearbook 1947–1948* (New York: United Nations, 1948), 959.

114. USHMM, ITS, IRO file on Andrej B. ITS-No. B-1961.

115. 'Humanität ohne Grenzen', Biege, *Helfer unter Hitler*, 181.

116. David P. Forsythe, 'Humanitarian Protection: The International Committee of the Red Cross and the United Nations High Commissioner for Refugees', *International Review of the Red Cross* 83 (2001): 683, 684.

117. See Catherine Rey-Schyrr, *De Yalta à Dien Bien Phu*, 175–99, esp. 178.

CHAPTER 7

1. Herbert H. Lehman, director general UNRRA, to Sir Herbert W. Emerson, director IGCR in London, 10 December 1943, attached resolution number 5 and 10 defining different duties of the two organizations. ACICR, G 59/6—168, reel 9, USHMM.

2. 'The International Refugee Organization', *Yearbook of the United Nations 1947–48*, 963.

3. United States Office Preparatory Commission International Refugee Organization, Washington, DC, 14 May 1948, 'Legal and other protection of refugees', NARA, RG 59, Entry 1419, IRO and DP Commission, Box 21, Folder 'PCIRO Monthly Digest 1947-49'.

4. The International Refugee Organization, *Operational Manual*, Revised, No. 0591, Published 1 May 1951, p. 7 ff. 'Resettlement'. NARA, RG 59, Entry 1419, Box 20, IRO and DP commission, Folder 'Operational Manual'.

5. Letter from Madame E. de Ribaupierre, ICRC Geneva, Division for Prisoners of War and Civilian Internees 1949, ACICR, Archives Générales, G. 68, Titres de voyage, Italie 1949/50, box 955, folder 'Circulaire Fr. 30 c'.

6. Mark Wyman, *DPs: Europe's Displaced Persons 1945–51* (Ithaca: Cornell University Press, 1998), 183.

7. United Nations, Economic and Social Council, London, 6 May 1946. Special Committee for Refugees and Displaced Persons, Fact-finding sub-committee, Summary record of the Fourth Meeting, held on 7 April 1946, London, page 4 NARA, RG 59, Box 25, Entry 1419, International Refugee Organization (IRO) and DP Commission, Folder 'Special Committee on Refugees and Displaced Persons – Sub-Committee Fact-finding'.

8. Gerard Daniel Cohen, *In War's Wake: Europe's Displaced Persons in the Postwar Order* (New York: Oxford University Press, 2013), 43.

9. Cohen, *In War's Wake*, 37 f.

10. Louise Holborn, The *International Refugee Organization. a Specialized Agency of the United Nations: Its History and Work, 1946–1952* (London: Oxford University Press, 1956), 44.

11. United Nations, Economic and Social Council, London, 13 May 1946. Special Committee for Refugees and Displaced Persons, Fact-finding sub-committee, NARA, RG 59, Box 25, Entry 1419, International Refugee Organization (IRO) and DP Commission, Folder 'Special Committee on Refugees and Displaced Persons – Sub-Committee Fact-finding'.

12. United Nations, Economic and Social Council, London, 6 May 1946. Special Committee for Refugees and Displaced Persons, Fact-finding sub-committee, Summary record of the Fourth Meeting, held on 7 April 1946, London, p. 9, NARA, RG 59, Box 25, Entry 1419, International Refugee Organization (IRO) and DP Commission, Folder 'Special Committee on Refugees and Displaced Persons – Sub-Committee Fact-finding'.

13. United Nations, Economic and Social Council, London, 6 May 1946. Special Committee for Refugees and Displaced Persons, Fact-finding sub-committee, Summary record of the Fourth Meeting, held on 7 April 1946, London, p. 18, NARA, RG 59, Box 25, Entry 1419, International Refugee Organization (IRO) and DP Commission, Folder 'Special Committee on Refugees and Displaced Persons – Sub-Committee Fact-finding'.

14. Cohen, *In War's Wake*, 35.

15. Cohen, *In War's Wake*, 37.

16. 'The International Refugee Organization', *Yearbook of the United Nations 1947–48*, 963.

17. Cohen, *In War's Wake*, 39.

18. Angelika Königseder and Juliane Wetzel, *Lebensmut im Wartesaal: Die jüdischen DPs (Displaced Persons) im Nachkriegsdeutschland* (Frankfurt a. M.: Fischer Verlag, 2004), 25.

19. Holborn, *International Refugee Organization*, 50.

20. Gerald Steinacher, *Nazis on the Run: How Hitler's Henchmen Fled Justice* (Oxford: Oxford University Press, 2011), 5.

21. Holborn, *International Refugee Organization*, 208.

22. Mark Aarons and John Loftus, *Unholy Trinity: The Vatican, The Nazis, and The Swiss Banks* (New York: St. Martin's, 1998), 194 ff. Christopher Hale, *Hitler's Foreign Executioners: Europe's Dirty Secret* (Stroud, Gloucestershire: The History Press, 2011), 379 ff.

23. Cohen, *In War's Wake*, 45.

24. Cohen, *In War's Wake*, 44.

25. See ITS Digital Archives Bad Arolsen Record Group 3.1.1.2 e.g. 'Permanent Screening Board' September 13, 1946, 'Subject: People screened and found not eligible for Displaced Persons' UNRRA Team 120, ITS Digital Archive Bad Arolsen 3.1.1.2/82024676.

26. PCRO, Decision of Review Board, No. Geneva 14560. 17 November 1949, 3.2.1.5/81277482/ITS Digital Archive, Bad Arolsen.

27. See ITS Digital Archives Bad Arolsen, see Record Group 3.2.1.5 e.g. IRO, Decision of the Review Board, No. Geneva 3308, 24 May 1949, ITS Archives Bad Arolsen, 3.2.1.5/81256248 and 81282730.

28. See ITS Digital Archives Bad Arolsen, see Record Group 3.2.1.5/81282730/ITS Digital Archive, Bad Arolsen.

29. Chris Cottrell, 'Germany: Ex-Nazi with Link to Auschwitz Is Arrested', *New York Times*, 6 May 2013. 'Hans Lipschis—"Ich war nur Koch in Auschwitz"' *Die Welt*, 21 April 2013.

30. Liste SS Zentralverwaltung Stand: 1.1.1945, Rottenführer Hans Lipschis born 7 November 1919. NARA, RG 242, BDC, SS Lists 6291, Roll A0018. See also list 5768 on Roll A0017.

31. Application for German citizenship (*Einbürgerungsantrag*) filed by Hans Lipschis, 16 August 1941. As additional proof of his ethnic German background, Lipschis

listed his membership in the Cultural Association for Germans in Lithuania (*Kulturverband der Deutschen Litauens*). The copy of Hans Lipschis' proof of citizenship (*Abschrift der Einbürgerungs-Urkunde*) is dated 27 February 1943, NARA, RG 242, BDC, EWZ, Baltic Anträge, Roll E010, p. 1576 ff.

32. USHMM, Archives of the International Tracing Service Bad Arolsen ITS, IRO-file on Lipsys Antanas, born 7 November 1919, ITS-Nr.: L–6197, Data basis USHMM.

33. Rochelle G. Saidel, *The Outraged Conscience: Seekers of Justice for Nazi War Criminals in America* (New York: State University of New York, 1984), 6.

34. See Catherine Rey-Schyrr ('Les personnes déplacées et les réfugiés'. *De Yalta à Dien Bien Phu. Historie du Comité international de la Croix-Rouge, 1945–1955* (Geneva: CICR and Georg Editeur, 2007), 175–99, here 178.

35. Michel Veuthey, 'Assessing Humanitarian Law', in *Humanitarianism across Borders: Sustaining Civilians in Times of War*, ed. Thomas G. Weiss and Larry Minear (Boulder, CO: Lynne Rienner, 1993), 125–49, here 129.

36. Max Huber to Sir Herbert Emerson, 21 August 1945, ACICR, Archives Generales, B G 68/00.

37. Letter from Madame E. de Ribaupierre, ICRC Geneva, Division for Prisoners of War and Civilian Internees 1949, ACICR, Archives Générales, G. 68, Titres de voyage, Italie 1949–50, box 955, folder 'Circulaire Fr. 30 c'.

38. 'Refugees and Stateless Persons', *Report of the International Committee of the Red Cross on its Activities during the Second World War (September 1, 1939–June 30, 1947)*, vol. 1, General Activities (Geneva: May 1948), 663–7, here 664.

39. 'Travel Documents', *Report of the International Committee of the Red Cross on its Activities during the Second World War (September 1, 1939–June 30, 1947)*, Volume 1, General Activities (Geneva: May 1948), 669–72, here 669.

40. Letter from R. Gallopin, Director–Delegate, ICRC, to Leland Harrison American Legation in Bern, 3 September 1947 (TOP SECRET) and enclosure ICRC Geneva, 'Note regarding travel document of the International Committee of the Red Cross', 22. July 1947, translation (TOP SECRET), NARA, RG 59, D File 1945–49, Box 4082, 800.142/9–1247.

41. ICRC Geneva, 'Note regarding travel document of the International Committee of the Red Cross', 22 July 1947, translation (TOP SECRET), NARA, RG 59, D File 1945–49, Box 4082, 800.142/9–1247.

42. 'Das Internationale Rote Kreuz am Kriegsende', *Neue Zürcher Zeitung*, 25 August 1945, Archiv für Sozialgeschichte, Zürich, Folder 49.5 ZA 1 'Internationales Komitee vom Roten Kreuz (IKRK)'.

43. Michael R. Marrus, *The Unwanted: European Refugees in the Twentieth Century* (Oxford: Oxford University Press, 1985), 95. Michael N. Barnett, *Empire of Humanity: A History of Humanitarianism* (Ithaca: Cornell University Press, 2013), 88–9. Unabhängige Expertenkommission Schweiz–Zweiter Weltkrieg, *Die Schweiz und Flüchtlinge zur Zeit des Nationalsozialismus* (Bern: Unabhängige Expertenkommission Schweiz, Zweiter Weltkrieg, 1999), 36 ff.

44. John Torpey, *The Invention of the Passport: Surveillance, Citizenship, and the State* (Cambridge: Cambridge University Press, 2000), 129. For the history of passports, see also Jane Caplan and John Torpey, *Documenting Individual Identity: The Development of State Practices in the Modern World* (Princeton: Princeton University Press, 2001).

45. Torpey, *Invention of the Passport*, 129.

46. Rey-Schyrr, *De Yalta à Dien Bien Phu*, 190.

47. 'Etablissement par le CICR de certificate de voyage', 1 September 1944. ICRC Archives Geneva, Archives Generales, Archives, B G 68/00/Ti.

48. Hansjakob Stehle, 'Pässe vom Papst? Aus neu entdeckten Dokumenten: Warum alle Wege der Ex-Nazis nach Südamerika über Rom führen', *Die Zeit*, 4 May 1984, 9–12, here 10: 'ganz ungewöhnliches Reisedokument'.

49. 'Travel Documents', *Report of the International Committee of the Red Cross of the Red Cross Activities during the Second World War (September 1, 1939–June 30, 1947)*, vol. 1, General Activities (Geneva: May 1948), 669–72, here 669.

50. Gerald Steinacher, *Nazis on the Run: How Hitler's Henchmen Fled Justice* (Oxford: Oxford University Press, 2011) 56. See also Henri Coursier, 'Aid to Refugees', *International Review of the Red Cross* (June 1961): 123–32, here 130.

51. Office of the United Nations High Commissioner for Refugees, *The Red Cross and the Refugees* Geneva: United Nations High Commissioner for Refugees, 1963), 9.

52. Wyman, *DPs: Europe's Displaced Persons*, 36.

53. Office of the United Nations High Commissioner for Refugees, *Red Cross and the Refugees*, 6.

54. Stehle, 'Pässe vom Papst', 10. Jean-Claude Favez, *The Red Cross and the Holocaust* (Cambridge: Cambridge University Press, 1999), 2, 287 f.

55. Burckhardt to Watteville[?], 18 February 1945, AfZ, NL Ruegger, 23.9.1 Korrespondenz Burckhardt: 'Schwarzenberg ist vielleicht nicht der geeignete Mann. Er ist nicht der Chef der Abteilung die sich mit den Deportierten befasst, der Chef ist Roger Gallopin. Schwarzenberg hat gute altösterreichiche Beamten qualitäten, aber er hat keinen "esprit de corps" er lädt alle Verantwortung immer auf Vorgesetzte und Mitarbeiter ab, er redet viel herum, dramatisiert, schimpft über die Schweiz'.

56. Letter from Madame E. De Ribaupierre, ICRC Geneva, Division for prisoners of war and civilian internees, 1949, ACICR, Archives Generales, G. 68, Titres de voyage, Italie 1949–1950, box 955, folder 'Circulaire Fr. 30 c.'.

57. E. de Ribaupierre, 'Le Comitè international de la Croix-Rouge et le probléme des Réfugiés', *Revue International de la Croix Rouge*, 1950, 332–47.

58. Elisabeth de Ribaupierre, 'Le Comitè international de la Croix-Rouge et le probléme des Réfugiés', *Revue International de la Croix'Rouge* (1950): 332–47, here 334.

59. Dupuis in Gitta Sereny, *Into That Darkness: From Mercy Killing to Mass Murder* (London: Andre Deutsch 1974), 317.

60. Jean Pictet, *The Fundamental Principles of the Red Cross proclaimed by the Twentieth International Conference of the Red Cross, Vienna, 1965, Commentary* (Geneva: Henry Dunant Institute, 1979), 50.

61. ICRC delegation in Rome to ICRC headquarters in Geneva, 29 September 1945, ICRC Geneva, Archive, Archives Générales, G. 68, Titres de voyage 1945–93, TVCR 1994.060, folder 00639.

62. Blanco travel document of the ICRC, enclosure no. 7 to dispatch No. 15447, 12 September 1947 (TOP SECRET) from American Legation in Bern, Switzerland, stamp Legation of the United States of America, 5 Sept. 1947 Bern, Specimen, NARA, RG 59, Decimal File 1945–49. Box 4082, 800.142/9-947.

63. 'Aid to Refugees', *International Review of the Red Cross* (June 1961): 130. Ribaupierre, 'Le Comitè international de la Croix-Rouge et le problème des Rèfugiès', 334.

64. 'Travel Documents', 670.

65. Report Vincent La Vista, 'Subject: Illegal Emigration Movements in and through Italy', Appendix B, page 10, report attached to letter from State Department, Washington, DC, to Ambassador Leland Harrison, Bern, 11 July 1947, NARA, RG 84, Austria, Political Advisor (Top Secret), General Records 1945–1955, Entry 2057, Box 2, Folder 1947, 130.9-820.02, Appendix E, page 5.

66. Sereny, *Into That Darkness*, 317.

67. Vincent La Vista Report.

68. Vincent La Vista Report.

69. Ribaupierre, 'Le Comitè international de la Croix-Rouge et le probléme des Réfugiés', 334: '*Le CICR affirme de cette manière sa neutralité çe document ets remis aussi bien à un réfugié de l'Est européen privé de sa nationalité qui ne veut pas renter dans son pays d'origine mais bien émigrer outre-mer, qu'à un ressortissant du même pays incarcèrè en Espagne, par exemple, qui manifeste le désir de renter dans sa patrie'.*

70. Yehuda Bauer, *Out of the Ashes: The Impact of American Jews on Post-Holocaust European Jewry* (Oxford: Pergamon Press, 1989).

71. 'Telephon conversations' [12 July 1946]. JDC Archives, Saly Mayer Collection, Roll 3, Folder 10: '*Dr. J. Loewenherz, hat[beim] Amerikanische[n] Konsulat die Affidavits eingereicht, wo man ihn aufmerksam machte, dass er mit den jetzt besitzenden Rot-Kreuz-Pässen kein Visum erhalten könne, sondern nur mit einem Identitätsausweis von Bern. Was er machen soll'?*

72. One of those cases was in Innsbruck, Austria, in 1947, where fifteen people applied for ICRC travel documents for their emigration to Venezuela. The group became stranded in Paris and was arrested by the French police because they were without transit visas. Jacques Oettinger to Irwin Rosen, 'Innsbruck incident', 26 February 1947, JDC Archives NY, G45–54/4/20/4/AU.256.

73. Application for an ICRC travel document for Jacob S., born 21 December 1889, ICRC Genoa, 27 June 1949. ICRC archives Geneva, application number 100.526. See also Anna Pizzuti, *Vite di carta. Storie di ebrei stranieri internati dal fascismo* (Rome: Donzelli, 2010). See also the database and website *Foreign*

Jews Interned in Italy during the War <http://www.annapizzuti.it/> accessed 20 February 2015.

74. Ribaupierre, 'Le Comitè international de la Croix-Rouge et le probléme des Réfugiés', 335. See also Christiane Uhlig and Unabhängigen Expertenkommission Schweiz—Zweiter Weltkrieg, *Tarnung, Transfer, Transit: Die Schweiz als Drehscheibe verdeckter deutscher Operationen (1938–1952)* (Zurich: Chronos, 2001), 190.

75. Rey-Schyrr, *De Yalta à Dien Bien Phu*, 194.

76. Ribaupierre, 'Le Comitè international de la Croix-Rouge et le probléme des Réfugiés', 335.

77. O. Lampanen, ICRC delegation in Rome, to ICRC Headquarters in Geneva, 29 September 1945, ICRC, Geneva, Archive/Agence, Titres de Voyage, 1945–93, TVCR 1994.060, folder 00639.

78. Hans W. de Salis, ICRC Rome, to the director of ICRC Milan, Samuel Girod, 29 January 1947, ICRC Geneva, Archive/Agence, Titres de Voyage, 1945–93, TVCR 1994.060, folder 00642 'Milan'. See also Steinacher, *Nazis on the Run*, 62.

79. Steinacher, *Nazis on the Run*, 73–4.

80. Ribaupierre, 'Le Comité international de la Croix-Rouge et le probléme des Réfugiés', 335.

81. Elias Juan Agusti, consulate general of the Republic of Argentina in Genoa, to the ICRC delegate in Genoa, Leo Biaggi de Blasys, 24 August 1948, ACICR Archives Générales, G. 68, Titres de Voyage, box 954, Italie 1944–1948, folder 'Titres de voyage: Italie'.

82. Letter from ICRC delegate in Genoa, Leo Biaggi de Blasys, to the ICRC in Geneva, 3 September 1948, ACICR Archives Générales, G. 68, Titres de Voyage, box 954, Italie 1944–48, folder 'Titres de voyage: Italie'.

83. In January 1947, the US consul in Vienna, Laurence C. Frank, wrote to the Secretary of State Washington 'Indiscrimate Issuing and Use of Identity Documents of the International Red Cross' (TOP SECRET), 'Summary of Information', 16 December 1946, NARA, RG 84, Foreign Service Posts, Austria, Polit. Advisor, Top Secret General Records 1947–1949, Entry 2057, Box 2.

84. 'Travel Documents', 670.

85. 'Travel Documents', 670.

86. Steinacher, *Nazis on the Run*, 73.

87. Titres de voyage, note pour le Dr Rothmund, 2 June 1945, ACICR G59/6—167.01, reel 9, USHMM.

88. Quoted in Uhlig and Unabhängigen Expertenkommission Schweiz—Zweiter Weltkrieg, *Tarnung, Transfer, Transit*, 194: '*weil wir unter Umständen einmal in einem Einzelfall ein gewisses Interesse haben, dass das CICR einen Ausweis ausstellt, und nicht die Polizeiabteilung*'. See BAR, E 4260 (C) 1974/34, vol. 194, Schürch to Rothmund, 'Travel Papers of the Red Cross, Visit of Herr Kühne', 17 February 1948. See Guy Walters, *Hunting Evil: The Nazi War Criminals Who Escaped and the Quest to Bring Them to Justice* (New York: Broadway Books, 2009), 112 ff. For Rothmund's role, see Uki Goñi, *The Real Odessa* (London: Granta, 2002), 152 ff.

89. Schürch to Rothmund, 'Travel Papers of the Red Cross, Visit of Herr Kühne', 17 February 1948, BAR, E 4260 (C) 1974/34, vol. 194.

90. Steinacher, *Nazis on the Run*, 13.

91. Steinacher, *Nazis on the Run*, 63.

92. Holborn, *International Refugee Organization,* 324.

93. 'Concerns: ICRC Travel Document', D.[avid] de Traz to Sir Herbert Emerson, 15 April 1946, ACICR G 59/6—169, reel 9, USHMM.

94. Mission a Londres, conference du Comité intergouvernemental pour les refugies concernant l'adoption d'un document de voyage pour les refugies, signed D.[avid] de Traz, 18 October 1946. Folder Comité Intergouvernemental pour les refugies, Mission de M. de Traz a Londres 4–16 octobre 1946, ACICR G59/6—167.03, reel 9, USHMM.

95. Mission a Londres, Participation du ICRC au fonds de réparations, signed D.[avid] de Traz, 18 October 1946. Folder Comité Intergouvernemental pour les refugies, Mission de M. de Traz a Londres 4–16 octobre 1946, ACICR G59/6—167.03, reel 9, USHMM.

96. Letter D. de Traz to W. Beckelmann, Assistant Director Intergovernmental Committee for Refugees London, 20 November 1946, ACICR, G59/6—169, reel 9 USHMM.

97. Letter D. de Traz to W. Beckelmann, Assistant Director Intergovernmental Committee for Refugees London, 20 November 1946, ACICR, G59/6—169, reel 9 USHMM.

98. JDC Archives New York, AR 45/54, Reel 156, Folder 1664, letter dated 10 May 1950, P. Kuhne, deputy chief of the Executive Division of the ICRC to US Jewish Joint Distribution Committee, New York, attached appeal signed by ICRC President Paul Ruegger and Honorary President Max Huber (Geneva, 1 May 1950), original in French, ICRC 'Réfugiés et apatrides'.

99. Torpey, *Invention of the Passport,* 144. See also Office of the United Nations High Commissioner for Refugees, *Red Cross and the Refugees*, 10.

100. Torpey, *Invention of the Passport,* 144. See also Daniel-Erasmus Khan, *Das Rote Kreuz: Geschichte einer humanitären Weltbewegung* (Munich: Beck 2013).

101. Steinacher, *Nazis on the Run*, 63.

102. Uhlig and Unabhängigen Expertenkommission Schweiz—Zweiter Weltkrieg, *Tarnung, Transfer, Transit*, 189.

103. 'Gau Tirol–Vorarlberg: Hauptmann Herbert Bauer mit dem Eichenlaub ausgezeichnet', *Bozner Tagblatt*, 3 November 1944, 3: '*Als Junge gehörte er in der Verbotszeit der Hitler-Jugend an und war wegen seines tätigen Einsatzes für die nationalsozialistische Bewegung schweren Verfolgungen und Massregelungen ausgesetzt*'.

104. NARA, RG 242, formerly BDC, NSDAP–Ortsgruppenkartei, Roll A0090, Herbert Bauer, born 16 April 1919, number 6329975. Steinacher, *Nazis on the Run*, 30, 98 ff.

105. 'Gau Tirol–Vorarlberg: Hauptmann Herbert Bauer mit dem Eichenlaub ausgezeichnet', 3: '*der hervorragend bewährte Offizier, dessen Wagemut und Tapferkeit nach Ablauf kurzer Zeit neuerdings die Anerkennung des Führers gefunden hat*'.

106. See Gerald Steinacher, '"A Man with a Wide Horizon": The Postwar Professional Journey of SS Officer Karl Nicolussi-Leck', in David A. Messenger and Katrin Paehler (eds.), *A Nazi Past: Recasting German Identity in Postwar Europe* (Lexington: University of Kentucky Press, 2015), 225–48.

107. Application for a Red Cross travel document for Herbert Bauer, born 16 April 1919, ICRC Rome, 7 April 1948, ICRC Archives in Geneva, Titres de voyage, application no. 74.969. See Steinacher, *Nazis on the Run*, 98 ff. See Walters, *Hunting Evil*, 250.

108. Application for a Red Cross travel document for Hubert Karl Freisleben, ICRC Rome, 28 August 1947, Letter of the Vatican Commission for Refugees (PCA) to the ICRC in Rome, 27 August 1947. ICRC Archive in Geneva, 'Titres de Voyage CICR 1945–1993', application no. 62,175.

109. In the SS officers file, he is identified as Dr Hubert von Freisleben, born 20 September 1913, SS no. 304.163, NARA, RG 242, formerly BDC, SS officers roll SSO–220.

110. Hermann Duxneuner, born 4 July 1909. His 1939 résumé reads, in part: '*Nach dem Umsturz trat ich in das Wirtschaftsamt ein und führe dort die Arisierungen im Gau Tirol*'. NARA, RG 242, BDC, RuSHA—SS officers, Roll B0067.

111. Wolfgang Meixner, ' "Arisierung": Die "Entjudung" der Wirtschaft im Gau Tirol–Vorarlberg,' *Tirol und Vorarlberg in der NS-Zeit* (Innsbruck: StudienVerlag, 2002), 319–40. For Austrian Nazis in Argentina, see also Edith Blaschitz, 'Austrian National Socialists: The Route to Argentina', in Oliver Rathkolb (ed.), *Revisiting the National Socialist Legacy: Coming to Terms with Forced Labor, Expropriation, Compensation and Restitution* (Innsbruck: Studienverlag, 2002), 226–40. See also Gerald Steinacher, 'The Cape of Last Hope: The Post-war Flight of Nazi War Criminals through Italy/South Tyrol to South America', in Klaus Eisterer and Günter Bischof (eds.), T*ransatlantic Relations: Austria and Latin America in the 19th and 20th Century* Transatlantica 1 (Innsbruck: Studienverlag, 2006), 203–24.

112. Steinacher, *Nazis on the Run*, 66 ff. Application for Red Cross travel document for Hermann Duxneuner, born 4 July 1909, ICRC Rome, 20 December 1946, application no. 36.075. Attached is a letter of recommendation from the Vatican Commission for Refugees (PCA) dated 19 January 1948.

113. Steinacher, *Nazis on the Run,* 66 ff. SS file Kurt Baum, born 3 November 1918, NARA, RG 242, formerly BDC, SS enlisted men, Roll A054. Application for travel document for Kurt Baum, born 3 November 1918, 20 December 1946, ICRC Verona, ICRC Geneva, Archives, Titres de voyage, number 36074.

114. Goñi, *Real Odessa*, 260.

115. Henry Friedlander, *Origins of Nazi Genocide: From Euthanasia to the Final Solution* (Chapel Hill: University of North Carolina Press, 1997), 134 f. See also Gerald L. Posner and John Ware, *Mengele: The Complete Story* (New York: Cooper Square Press, 2000).

116. Application for a Red Cross travel document for Helmut Gregor, ICRC in Genoa, 16 May 1949, ACICR, Titres de voyage, application no. 100.501.

117. Eichmann himself provided some clues about the role of Catholic priests and the Red Cross in his escape, see Hannah Arendt, *Eichmann in Jerusalem: A Report on the Banality of Evil* (New York: Viking Press, 1963), 215.

118. For Alvensleben's wartime crimes, see Christopher R. Browning and Jürgen Matthäus, *Origins of the Final Solution* (Lincoln: University of Nebraska Press, 2004), 31, 32, 73.

119. See Christian Jansen and Arno Weckbecker, *Der 'Volksdeutsche Selbstschutz' in Polen 1939/40*, Schriftenreihe der Vierteljahreshefte für Zeitgeschichte 64 (Munich: R. Oldenbourg, 1992).

120. Stangneth, *Eichmann vor Jerusalem*, 372 f. Andreas Schulz and Günter Wegmann, *Die Generale der Waffen-SS und der Polizei: Die militärischen Werdegänge der Generale, sowie der Ärzte, Veterinäre, Intendanten, Richter und Ministerialbeamten im Generalsrang*, vol. 1 (Bissendorf: Biblio Verlag, 2003), see Alvensleben, 16–21.

121. Steinacher, *Nazis on the Run*, 50 ff. and *Hakenkreuz und Rotes Kreuz: Eine humanitäre Organisation zwischen Holocaust und Flüchtlingsproblematik* (Innsbruck: Studienverlag, 2013), 140 f. See also Stangneth, *Eichmann vor Jerusalem*, 377 ff.

122. See Steinacher, *Nazis on the Run*.

123. Ribaupierre, 'Le Comitè international de la Croix-Rouge et le probléme des Réfugiés', 335.

124. See Federica Bertagna and Matteo Sanfilippo, 'Per una prospettiva comparata dell'emigrazione nazi- fascista dopo la seconda guerra mondiale', *Studi Emigrazione/Migration Studies* 41/155 (2004), 527–53. See also See Matteo Sanfilippo, 'Fuga di nazisti o migrazioni? A proposito di un libro di Gerald Steinacher', *Studi Emigrazione* 46/173 (2009), 196–204. Matteo Sanfilippo, Archival Evidence on Postwar Italy as a Transit Point for Central and Eastern European Migrants, in Rathkolb (ed.), *Revisiting the National Socialist Legacy*, 241–58.

125. See Goñi, *Real Odessa*; Stangneth, *Eichmann vor Jerusalem*, Steinacher, *Nazis on the Run*; Walters, *Hunting Evil*; Aarons and Loftus, *Unholy Trinity*; Michael Phayer, *Pius XII, the Holocaust, and the Cold War* (Bloomington: Indiana University Press, 2007) and Simpson, *Blowback*.

126. Goñi, *Real Odessa*, 323.

127. Volker Koop, *Hitler's fünfte Kolonne: Die Auslands-Organisation der NSDAP* (Berlin Be.bra, 2009), 260.

128. Holger Meding, *Flucht vor Nürnberg? Deutsche und österreichische Einwanderung in Argentinien 1945–1955* (Cologne: Böhlau, 1992), 134.

129. See Bertagna and Sanfilippo, 'Per una prospettiva comparata dell'emigrazione nazi- fascista', 532.

130. Aarons and Loftus, *Unholy Trinity*, 87. See also Alexander Korb, *Im Schatten des Weltkriegs: Massengewalt der Ustasa gegen Serben, Juden und Roma in Kroatien 1941–1945* (Hamburg: Hamburger Edition, 2013). See also Andrea Casazza, *La fuga dei nazisti* (Genoa: Il melangolo, 2007), 59 ff. and Daniel Stahl, *Nazi-Jagd: Südamerikas Diktaturen und die Ahndung von NS-Verbrechen* (Göttingen:

Wallstein, 2013.), 77 ff. and 352 ff. Documents at the ICRC archives set the number of ICRC travel papers issued for Croatians in Italy at closer to 20,000. See Krunoslav Draganović and Juraj Magjerec, La Confraternita dei Croati di San Girolamo, Roma, 132 Via Tomacelli, to the president of the ICRC Geneva, Paul Ruegger, 7 June 1950, ICRC Archive in Geneva, Archives Generales, G. 68, Titres de voyage, Italie 1949–50, box 955, folder 'Titres de voyage: Italie'.

131. Rey-Schyrr, *De Yalta à Dien Bien Phu*, 175–99.
132. Uhlig and Unabhängigen Expertenkommission Schweiz—Zweiter Weltkrieg, 'Reisepapieren an mehrere belastete Deutsche', *Tarnung, Transfer, Transit*, 189–96, here 196.
133. See Daniel Palmieri and Irene Herrmann, ' "Refugees on the Run": ICRC Travel Documents in the Aftermath of the Second World War', *Contemporanea: rivista di storia dell'800 e del'900*, 16/1 (January–March 2013), 91–109, here 104. Palmieri and Herrmann list a number of 13 'war criminals who obtained the ICRC travel document'.
134. Bernd Biege, *Helfer unter Hitler: das Rote Kreuz im Dritten Reich* (Reinbek: Kindler, 2000), 183: '*nur die Spitze eines (auch heute noch weitgehend unerforschten) Eisbergs dar*'.
135. Steinacher, *Nazis on the Run*, 186.
136. Richard L. Rashke, *Useful Enemies: John Demjanjuk and America's Open-Door Policy for Nazi War Criminals* (Harrison: Delphinium, 2013), 23.
137. Pascal Hollenstein, 'Das Rote Kreuz verhalf Tausenden Nazis zur Flucht: Neue Forschungsresultate zeigen das Mass der Fluchthilfe auf', *Neue Zürcher Zeitung*, 7 September 2008, Archiv für Sozialgeschichte Zürich, Mappe 49.5 ZA 1 'Internationales Komitee vom Roten Kreuz (IKRK)'. Philip Kerr, 'Telling Stories We Need to Hear', *The Wall Street Journal*, 25 June 2011. David Cesarani, '*Nazis on the Run: How Hitler's Henchmen Fled Justice*', *New Statesman*, 22 June 2011. Richard J. Evans, '*Nazis on the Run* by Gerald Steinacher—Review'. 'This level-headed book details who helped the Nazis flee Germany, and why' (*The Guardian* [24 June 2011]). Robert Gerwarth, 'Wish You Were Here: The Church, the Red Cross and the Nazis', *The Irish Times*, 9 July 2011.

CHAPTER 8

1. NARA, Department of State RG 59, Biographic Register 1946–1952, box 11, *Register of the Department of State 1948* (Washington, DC: United States Government Printing Office, 1948), 161.
2. Max Paul Friedman, *Nazis and Good Neighbors: The United States Campaign Against the Germans of Latin America in World War II* (Cambridge: Cambridge University Press 2005), 146, 192, 221–2. See also Harvey Sturm, 'Jewish Internees in the American South 1942-1945', in *American Jewish Archives* 1990: 27–48; on Clattenburg, see 41 ff.

3. Breitman, *Official Secrets*. Breitman and Lichtman, *FDR and the Jews*. Wyman, *Abandonment of the Jews*, 209 ff.

4. US ambassador Leland Harrison to the Secretary of State, Washington, DC, May 18, 1945 (Secret), NARA, RG 59, box 4082, 800.142/5-1845.

5. State Department, Special Projects Division (SPD), 28 September 1945, NARA, RG 59, box 4082, 800.142/9-2845.

6. Byrnes to Huber, 19 October 1945, NARA, RG 59, box 4082, 800.142/9-2845. The Secretary of State ordered that the letter of thanks should be delivered personally to Huber by a high-ranking official of the US embassy in Bern. Leland Harrison confirmed that this was done as ordered by the State Department; he wrote a personal cover letter of thanks to Huber and also shared his regrets that he could not deliver the letter from Byrnes personally.

7. Max Huber to Secretary of State James Byrnes, 12 March 1946, NARA, RG 59, box 2386, 514.2 Geneva/3-1246.

8. 'Gerade für das Internationale Komitee ist es wichtig, das Recht und die tatsächliche Möglichkeit rechtsschöpferischer Initiative zu besitzen.' Max Huber, *Das Internationale Komitee vom Roten Kreuz, seine Aufgabe, seine Schwierigkeiten und Möglichkeiten, Vortrag gehalten am 24. Januar 1944 auf Einladung der Studentenschaften beider Zürcher Hochschulen im Auditorium Maximum der Eidgenössischen Technischen Hochschule von Prof. Max Huber, Honorarprofessor der Universität Zürich. Präsident des Internationalen Komitees vom Roten Kreuz* (Zurich: Polygraphischer Verlag A.G. 1944), 32.

9. Albert E. Clattenburg, Department of State SPD, letter to Mr Russell, 8 October 1945, NARA, RG 59, box 2386, FW 514.2 Geneva/9-545.

10. The following message transmitted at request of Basil O'Connor Chairman AMRC, Message for the Secretary of State, 18 July 1945 (Restricted), NARA, RG 59, box 4082, 800.142/7-1845.

11. Albert E. Clattenburg, Department of State SPD, 19 December 1945, NARA, RG 59, box 2386, 514.2 Geneva/12-1945.

12. Cable from Albert E. Clattenburg, March 1947, NARA, RG 59, box 2386, 514.2 Geneva/3-2-1247.

13. 'Report on meeting of Government experts called at Geneva, 14 April 1947 by International Red Cross Committee.' Part 6. Conference Arrangements, NARA, RG 59, box 2387514.2 Geneva/8-2647.

14. Albert E. Clattenburg to the Secretary of State, Report of the American delegation to Geneva, 14 to 26 April 1947, 26 August 1947, NARA, RG 59, box 2387, 514.2 Geneva/8-2647.

15. Albert E. Clattenburg to the Secretary of State, additional letter dated 26 August 1947 (SECRET), NARA, RG 59, box 2387, 514.2 Geneva/8-2647.

16. Clattenburg, Chairman of the United States Delegation, to the Secretary of State, August 26, 1947 (SECRET), RG 59 Department of State 1945–49, box 2387, 514.2/Geneva 8-2647.

17. Report Albert E. Clattenburg to the Secretary of State, 26 August 1947 (SECRET) NARA, RG 59, box 2387, 514.2 Geneva/8-2647, Appendix A to

confidential report. Confidential Incoming telegram from American Consulate at Geneva, Switzerland, 28 April 1947.

18. Report Clattenburg Secretary of State, 26 August 1947, p. 11, NARA, RG 59, box 2387, 514.2 Geneva/8-2647.

19. Report Albert E. Clattenburg to the Secretary of State, 26 August 1947 (SECRET), NARA, RG 59, box 2387, 514.2 Geneva/8-2647, Appendix D to confidential report, 13–14.

20. Report Albert E. Clattenburg to the Secretary of State, 26 August 1947, NARA, RG 59, box 2387, 514.2 Geneva/8-2647. See also Best, *War and Law*, 151.

21. Embassy of France, Washington, DC to State Department, 2 July 1947, NARA RG 59 Department of State 1945–49, box 2386, 514.2 Geneva/7-247.

22. AIDE-Memoire, Department of State, 4 August 1947, 'reference is made to the Swiss aid memoire Mr Bisang of the Swiss legation left with Clattenburg on July 10', RG 59, Department of State 1945–49, box 2386, 514.2/Geneva 7-847.

23. Legation of Switzerland, Washington, DC, AIDE-Memoire, 8 July 1947, Reference: The diplomatic conference to be called for the adoption of the draft conventions agreed upon at the International Red Cross Committee Meeting Geneva, 14–26 April 1947, NARA, RG 59, box 2386, 514.2 Geneva/7-847.

24. Letter of Basil O'Connor to Secretary of State George C. Marshall, 24 June 1947, NARA, RG 59, box 2386, 514.2 Geneva/6-2447.

25. Harold W. Starr from the American National Red Cross to Clattenburg, 19 June 1947, NARA, RG 59, box 2386, 514.2 Geneva/6-1947.

26. Assistant Secretary for the Secretary of State to Basil O'Connor, signed John E. Peurifoy July 7, 1947, NARA, RG 59, box 2386, Geneva 514.2/6-2447.

27. Outgoing Telegram, Department of State, Washington (Confidential), May 17, 1948 to US embassy London signed Marshall, RG 59, box 2390, 514.2 Stockholm/5-1748.

28. American Embassy London to the Secretary of State, May 4, 1948, Subject: Revision of Geneva Prisoners of War Convention and Other Humanitarian Conventions (Confidential): signed George Tait, American Consul General, RG 59, box 2390, 514.2 Stockholm/5-448.

29. Foreign Office to Eldred Kuppinger, US Embassy London, May 3, 1948 (Confidential) signed J. W. O. Davidson, 514.2 Stockholm/5-448.

30. Bernadotte, *Instead of Arms*, 148.

31. Max Huber to Albert E. Clattenburg, 24 June 1947, NARA, RG 59, box 4082, 800.142/6-2447 CS/T.

32. American Consul General in Vienna, Laurence C. Frank, to the Secretary of State, Washington, DC, 20 January 1947, Subject: 'Indiscriminate Issuing and Use of Identity Documents of the International Red Cross' (Top Secret), NARA, RG 84, Foreign Service Posts, Austria, Polit. Advisor, Top Secret General Records 1947–1949, Entry 2057, box 2, folder 1947, 130.9-820.02.

33. Laurence C. Frank, to the Secretary of State, Washington, DC, January 20, 1947, 'Summary of Information', 16 December 1946, NARA, RG 84, Austria, Polit.

Advisor, Top Secret General Records 1947–1949, Entry 2057, box 2, folder 1947, 130.9-820.02.

34. American Legation in Vienna and US Embassy in Rome, 10 April 1947 (Top Secret), NARA, RG 84, Foreign Service Posts, Austria, Polit. Advisor, Top Secret General Records 1947–1949, Entry 2057, box 2, folder 1947, 130.9-820.02.

35. Report Vincent La Vista, 'Subject: Illegal Emigration Movements in and through Italy', 15 May 1947, Appendix B, page 10, report attached to letter from State Department, Washington, DC, to Ambassador Leland Harrison, Bern, 11 July 1947, NARA, RG 84, Austria, Political Advisor (Top Secret), General Records 1945–1955, Entry 2057, box 2, folder 1947, 130.9-820.02.

36. Steinacher, *Nazis on the Run*, 71.

37. Office Memorandum, United States Government, State Department, 20 June 1947, Albert E. Clattenburg to Robinson (Top Secret), NARA, RG 59, dec. file 1945–1949, box 4082, 800.142/5-1547.

38. 'Red Cross Delegates Return from Geneva', *New York Times*, 20 May 1947, 22.

39. John M. Cabot, American Legation Belgrade, Yugoslavia, to Albert E. Clattenburg (Personal and Confidential), 19 May 1947, NARA, RG 59, box 2386, 514.2 Geneva/5-1947.

40. American embassy, Belgrade, to the Secretary of State, 8 February 1946 (Secret), NARA, RG 59, box 4082, 800.142/2-846.

41. ICRC Archives, A PV, Bureau, minutes of meeting of 13th March 1947 at 9.30, no. 204, 1997 ff., ACICR Archives, Bureau Séance du jeudi, 13 mars 1947 (Confidential).

42. Schürch to Rothmund, 'Travel papers of the Red Cross, Visit of Herr Kühne', 17 February 1948, BAR, E 4260 (C) 1974/34, vol. 194.

43. Leland Harrison, Bern, to the Secretary of State, 9 September 1947 (Secret), NARA, RG 59, 800.142/9-947, box 4082.

44. 'During the next two years it is the hope of the United States Government that progress may be made towards the adaption of new Conventions covering the rights of individual victims of war, whatever civilians, prisoners of war or sick and wounded. The United States Government has been glad to collaborate with the International Red Cross Committee to this end and hopes to continue that collaboration to its successful termination. The United States Government cannot avoid pointing out that a situation such as you have been directed to bring to the attention of responsible officials of the International Red Cross may arouse suspicion and distrust in various quarters and it advances this reason, as well as its knowledge that the International Red Cross Committee wishes to keep its reputation unsullied, as grounds for immediate and drastic action' State Department, Washington, DC, Signed by an official "for the Secretary of State", to Ambassador Leland Harrison, Bern, 11 July 1947 (Top Secret), NARA, RG 59, dec. file 1945–1949, box 4082, 800.142/5-1547.

45. Ibid.

46. Memorandum, to Karl L. Rankin, Counsellor of Legation, Vienna, 4 August 1947 (Top Secret), NARA, RG 84, Foreign Service Posts, Austria, Polit. Advisor, Top Secret General Records 1947–1949, Entry 2057, box 2. On antisemitism among US State Department officials, see Richard Breitman and Allan J. Lichtman, *FDR and the Jews* (Cambridge, MA: Belknap Press of Harvard University Press, 2013).

47. US ambassador Leland Harrison, Bern, to the Secretary of State, Washington, DC, 12 September 1947, Subject: 'Conference with ICRC Officials regarding Documentation Matters in Italy' (Top Secret), NARA, RG 59, dec. file 1945–1949, box 4082, 800.142/9-1247. See Telegram Leland Harrison, Bern, to the Secretary of State, 9 September 1947 (Secret), NARA, RG 59, dec. file 1945–1949, box 4082, 800.142/9-547.

48. Department of State Incoming Telegram (Top Secret), 1 October 1947, Rome to Department of State, signed Dunn, NARA, RG 59, dec. file 1945–49, box 4082, 800.142/10-147.

49. US ambassador Leland Harrison, Bern, to the Secretary of State, Washington, DC, Subject: 'Conference with ICRC Officials regarding Documentation Matters in Italy' (Top Secret), 12 September 1947, NARA, RG 59, dec. file 1945–1949, box 4082, 800.142/9-1247.

50. ICRC delegation in Rome, signed H. W. de Salis, to Mr Gallopin at the ICRC in Geneva, 8 September 1947, ACICR, Archives Generales, G 68/Titres de voyage: Italie.

51. US Ambassador Leland Harrison, Bern, to the Secretary of State, Washington, DC, 12 September 1947, Subject: 'Conference with ICRC Officials regarding Documentation Matters in Italy' (Top Secret), NARA, RG 59, dec. file 1945–1949, box 4082, 800.142/9-1247. A specimen of the ICRC travel document was attached to Harrison's report. Blanco travel document of the ICRC—Enclosure no. 7 to dispatch No. 15447, 12 September 1947 (Top Secret) from American Legation, Bern, Switzerland, stamp Legation of the United States of America, 5 September 1947 Bern, Specimen, NARA, RG 59, dec. file 1945–1949, box 4082, 800.142/9-947.

52. 'Red Cross Sessions Will Open in Geneva', *New York Times*, 20 April 1949, 10.

53. Roger Gallopin to US ambassador Leland Harrison, Bern, 3 September 1947, (Top Secret), NARA, RG 59, dec. file 1945–1949, box 4082, 800.142/9-1247.

54. ICRC Geneva, 'Note regarding Travel Document of the International Committee of the Red Cross', 22 July 1947, translation, (Top Secret), NARA, RG 59, dec. file 1945–1949, box 4082, 800.142/9-1247.

55. Department of State, Washington, DC, to US embassy, Rome, 25 September 1947, (Secret), NARA, RG 59, dec. file 1945–1949, box 4082, 800.142/9-547.

56. US ambassador Leland Harrison, Bern, to the Secretary of State, Washington, DC, 13 October 1947, Subject: 'Conference with ICRC Official regarding Documentation Matters in Italy' (Top Secret), NARA, RG 59, dec. file 1945–49, box 4082, 800.142/5-1547.

57. US ambassador Leland Harrison, Bern, to the Secretary of State, Washington, DC, 13 October 1947, Subject: 'Conference with ICRC Official regarding Documentation Matters in Italy' (Top Secret), NARA, RG 59, dec. file 1945–49, box 4082, 800.142/5-1547.

58. US ambassador Leland Harrison, Bern, to the Secretary of State, Washington, DC, 13 October 1947, Subject: 'Conference with ICRC Official regarding Documentation Matters in Italy' (Top Secret), NARA, RG 59, dec. file 1945–49, box 4082, 800.142/5-1547.

59. George L. Brandt to Albert E. Clattenburg, 19 January 1946, NARA, RG 59, box 2386, 514.2-Geneva/1-2946 CS/W.

60. George L. Brandt to Department of State, 18 February 1948 (Confidential), NARA, RG 59, box 4083, 800.142/2-1848.

61. From *Risorgimento* (6 February 1948), weak translation from Italian in original State Department document. George L. Brandt to Department of State, 18 February 1948 (Confidential), NARA, RG 59, box 4083, 800.142/2-1848.

62. Department of State, Report Maurice A. Altaffer, American Consul General, American Consulate, Bremen, to the Secretary of State, 13 January 1949, Subject: 'Recrudescence of Secret Activities of German Rightist Groups; Underground Route Established by Them via Tirol and Italy to Argentine; Encouragement Given Them by Peron Government', (Secret), RG 59, decimal file 1945–1949, box 6744, 862.20235/1-1349.

63. Department of State, Report Maurice A. Altaffer, American Consul General, American Consulate, Bremen, to the Secretary of State, 13 January 1949, Subject: 'Recrudescence of Secret Activities of German Rightist Groups; Underground Route Established by Them via Tirol and Italy to Argentine; Encouragement Given Them by Peron Government', (Secret), RG 59, dec. file 1945–1949, box 6744, 862.20235/1-1349.

64. Department of State program visit of Paul Ruegger, 28 June 1948, NARA, RG 59, 800.142/6-2848, box 4083.

65. Memo from E. de Ribaupierre to ICRC president Ruegger, 28 August 1950, ACICR Archives Generales, G. 68, Titres de voyage, Italie 1949–50, box 955, folder 'titres de voyage: Italie'. See also Steinacher, *Nazis on the Run*, 74.

66. Steinacher, *Hakenkreuz und Rotes Kreuz*, 149.

67. Letter from Hans Wolf de Salis, ICRC delegation in Rome, to Carl Jacob Burckhardt, 23 January 1948, UB Basel, NL Burckhardt, B II 46 K: 'Die Arbeit ist gar zu dringend, denn die Gefahr in der einige Tausend der hiesigen Flüchtlinge schweben wird täglich bedrohlicher, so dass man alles dransetzen muss, sie fortzuschaffen, was jetzt auch in größerem Massstabe gelingt. Ich glaube, Ihre Intervention zu Gunsten der Römerdelegation hat doch geholfen: vorhanden sind wir noch da, wenn auch offiziell nur auf kürzeste Frist verlängert (während inoffiziell ich höre, es würde uns genügend Zeit geboten, um die Arbeit gut zu Ende zu führen)'.

68. Steinacher, *Nazis on the Run*, 83. See E. de Ribaupierre to Umberto Vaccari, AGIUS in Rome, 15 March 1951, ACICR, Archive/Agence, Titres de voyage, 1945–93, TVCR 1994.060, folder 00639.

69. Christiane Uhlig et al., *Tarnung, Transfer, Transit. Die Schweiz als Drehscheibe verdeckter deutscher Operationen (1938–1952)*, ed. Unabhängigen Expertenkommission Schweiz—Zweiter Weltkrieg (Zurich: Chronos, 2001), 191.

70. In addition to the ICRC's involvement in Nazis escape from justice, State Department officials also worried about the possibility that ICRC delegates could be linked to Nazi underground movement. In most cases, the Americans' suspicions and the resulting rumours were without foundation. See Steinacher, *Nazis on the Run,* 167–8. See François Bugnion, 'L'action du CICR pendant la Seconde Guerre mondiale. Le CICR infiltré par les Nazis?', *Revue internationale de la Croix-Rouge,* 821 (September–October 1996): 606–11. Report of the OSS to X-2 Washington, DC, 15 May 1944, Subject: 'IRC Report', (Secret), NARA, RG 226, OSS, Entry 210, box 381, folder 3. Department of State, Incoming Telegram (Confidential), 9 September 1947, US ambassador Leland Harrison, Bern, to State Department, NARA, RG 59, dec. file 1945–1949, box 4082, 800.142/9-947, US embassy, Berlin, to the Secretary of State, Washington, DC, 1 October 1947, (Confidential) NARA, RG 59, dec. file 1945–1949, box 4082, 800.142/10-147, Department of State, Incoming Telegram, (Confidential), US ambassador Leland Harrison, Bern, to the Secretary of State, Washington, DC, 23 September 1947, NARA, RG 59, dec. file 1945–1949, box 4082, 800.142/9-2347. Department of State, Incoming telegram from Leland Harrison, Bern, to the Secretary of State, Washington, DC, 23 September 1947, NARA, RG 59, dec. file 1945–1949, box 4082, 800.142/9-2347.

CHAPTER 9

1. Folke Bernadotte to the Secretary of State, XVIIth International Red Cross Conference Stockholm, November 1947, received 23 December 1947, with references to the letter from July 1947. NARA, RG 59, box 2390, 514.2 Stockholm/12-2347.

2. Albert E. Clattenburg, additional letter to the Secretary of State, 26 August 1947, NARA, RG 59, box 2387, 514.2 Geneva/8-2647.

3. Department of State Protective Services Division, meeting 15 April 1948, RG 59, box 2390, 514.2 Stockholm/4-1548.

4. US Embassy in Madrid to the Secretary of State, 2 July 1948 (Confidential), 'Subject: Participation of Spain in International Red Cross Conference to be held at Stockholm in August 1948,' NARA, RG 59, box 2390, 514.2 Stockholm/7-248.

5. Maurice Bourquin, 'The Red Cross and Treaty Protection of Civilians in Wartime', *Revue internationale de la Croix-Rouge*, Supplement 1 (Jan. 1948): 20. Bourquin was a Belgian jurist and professor of law at the University of Geneva and had extensive diplomatic experience. He led the Belgian delegation at the 1949 Geneva Conference for the reform of the conventions. Antonio Cassese, *Five Masters of International Law* (Oxford: Hart, 2011), 62n26.

6. Draft telegram to 'Generalissimo Stalin' 31 March 1948, signed ICRC Vice-presidents Gloor and Bodmer, Archiv für Zeitgeschichte Zurich, NL Paul Ruegger 28.3.1.1 'Vorbereitungen zu einer IKRK-Mission nach Russland und einem Treffen mit Joseph Stalin: Korrespondenz März 1948 und Expose [1948]' In 1950 Ruegger finally made it to Moscow to talk with the president of the Soviet Red Cross and Red Crescent, see NL Paul Ruegger 28.3.6.1.

7. Office Memorandum United States Government, 7 July 1948, Subject: Approval of proposed US delegation to the 17th International Red Cross conference, Stockholm, Sweden, August 20–30, 1948. NARA, RG 59, box 2390, 514.2 Stockholm/7-748.

8. Ibid.

9. The Secretary of State to Basil O'Connor, Chairman, Delegation of the United States to the Seventeenth International Red Cross Conference, Stockholm, Sweden, 9 August 1948 (Restricted) NARA, RG 59, box 2390, 514.2 Stockholm/8-948.

10. It is also important to note that even though humanitarian law and human rights law are closely linked, they are different concepts. Humanitarian law, codified in the Geneva Conventions, aims to protect the lives, health, and human dignity of individuals at times of war. Human rights law is broader in that it applies at all times, both in war and in peace with some limitations in war time.

11. James T. Nicholson, vice president, American Red Cross Headquarters in Washington, DC, to Maj. G. J. George, Aide to the Secretary of Defense, Pentagon, 2 January 1951, George C. Marshall Foundation Archives, George Marshall Papers, B181, F4.

12. Report de Haller 'Rapports entre le Comité international et la Croix-Rouge américaine.' Visit of M. Gallopin, Geneva on 6 December 1947, dated 10 December 1947. Schweizerisches Bundesarchiv, E 2001 (E), 1968/75, vol. 2, folder Croix-Rouge américaine 1946/48, B. 55.21.AM.

13. Department of State, Memorandum of Conversation, 'Subject: American Attitude toward the International Red Cross', 6 January 1948, NARA, RG 59, box 4083, 800.142/1-648.

14. Nouveau téléphone de la Légation des Etats Unis 11 June 1948. Schweizerisches Bundesarchiv, E 2001 (E), 1968/75, vol. 2, folder Croix-Rouge américaine 1946/48, B. 55.21.AM.

15. Archiv für Zeitgeschichte Zurich, NL Ruegger, dossiers 28.3.2.1 Amerikareise Paul Ruegger, June 1948. It is not clear if this speech was ever delivered on the radio, but it indicates the strategies contemplated for winning over US public support for the ICRC cause.

16. Memoranda to Pres. Truman consigned on 28 June 1948, Archiv für Zeitgeschichte, Zurich, NL Ruegger, dossiers 28.3.2.1.

17. PRO, Foreign Office 369/3969 Memorandum 'Gift of 10,000,000 Swiss francs by the Jap Empress to the International Red Cross Society' Davidson, 7 August 1948.

18. Letter Ruegger to Secretary of State George C. Marshall, 13 July 1948, Archiv für Zeitgeschichte, Zurich, NL Ruegger, dossiers 28.3.2.1.

19. 'Palestine Groups Aided By Red Cross. Jews and Arabs Cooperating With International Agency Its Head Declares Here', *New York Times*, 20 June 1948, p. 52.

20. See Junod, *Imperiled Red Cross*.

21. Archives du Comite international de la Croix-Rouge, ACICR G59/5—166/02, folder 'Activités des délégués du CICR en faveur des émigrants de l'Exodus'. 'Report on the work of the Delegates of the International Committee of the Red Cross in behalf of the Emigrants of the "Exodus"' [September 1947], Cover letter, Ribaupierre to British Consulate Geneva, 28 October 1947, ACICR G59/5—166.04, USHMM-19.045 M, reel 9.

22. For Department of State, Division of Protective Services from Bern, 28 May 1948 (confidential), NARA, RG 59, file 800.142/5-2848.

23. Letter, Eleanor Roosevelt to George C. Marshall, 27 April 1951, George C. Marshall Foundation, Archives, George Marshall Papers, B182, F24.

24. See Max Huber, 'The Principles of the Red Cross', in *Foreign Affairs* July 1948. The article drew heavily on Huber's 1946 book on the principles and foundations of the ICRC's impartiality. See also Junod, *Imperiled Red Cross*, 226.

25. National Archives of the UK (PRO), Foreign Office 369/3969, Letter Ruegger to Bevin, 24 July 1948. Memorandum attached.

26. PRO, Foreign Office 369/3969 'Record of Conversation between M. Zehnder, the Political director of the Swiss Foreign Office, and Mr. Makins', Geneva, 2 August 1948.

27. PRO, Foreign Office 369/3969, Memorandum Davidson, Foreign Office, 9 August 1948.

28. PRO, Foreign Office 369/3969, Memorandum Davidson, Foreign Office, 9 August 1948.

29. PRO, Foreign Office 369/3969, Folder notes 'Swiss Government's concern at the Swedish proposal that the International Red Cross Committee should be internationalized.'

30. PRO, Foreign Office 369/3969, Telegram from FO to Stockholm, 23 August 1948 (Important, Restricted).

31. 'Preliminary Draft Report of the Special Commission to Study Ways and Means to Reinforce the Efficacy of the Work of the ICRC', 26 June 1948, NARA, RG 200 (AMRC), box 103, folder 041 'International Red Cross, Special Commission to Study Ways and Means of Reinforcing the Efficacy of the Work of the ICRC'.

32. Letter of invitation by Folke Bernadotte, chairman of the Standing Commission of the International Red Cross Conference, Commission Permanente de la Conference international de la Croix Rouge Geneva, to Basil O'Connor, chairman of the American Red Cross, June 1947. NARA 200, AMRC, box 106, folder 041, 17th IRC Conference, 1948, Agenda Correspondence.

33. Swedish National Archives (RA), 730236 Svenska Röda Korset, F2, 4 (1948) "Svenska Röda Korsets rapport inför konferensen."

34. Ralph Hewins, *Count Folke Bernadotte, His Life and work* (Minneapolis: T.S. Denison and Company, 1950), 195. The Swedish media covered the conference widely, see e.g. *Svenska Dagbladet* 8/21/1948, front page 'International Red Cross Conference opened at the Opera House with over 60 delegations attending.' It is also interesting to note that in the days prior to the conference, Swedish editions of the book by Marcel Junod (*Warrior without Weapons*) as well as Max Huber's book (*The Good Samaritan* with a foreword by Bernadotte!) were promoted with inserts in this newspaper.

35. 'Reflections on the Stockholm meeting, received 25 January 1949, by Mrs. Joe Hume Gardner, national administrator, Volunteer Services' to AMRC Washington, NARA, RG 200, AMRC, box 109, folder 041, 17th ICRC Conference 1948, Reports, General. See also NARA, RG 200 Records of the American National Red Cross 1947–1964, box 826, folder 494.1, ARC 1304, 'Report of the American National Red Cross prepared for the XVII. Int. Red Cross Conference, Stockholm, 20–30 August 1948'. Leaflet printed in 100.000 copies to get the message about the work and purpose about the Red Cross to the US Red Cross family.

36. 'Reflections on the Stockholm meeting, received 25 January 1949, by Mrs. Joe Hume Gardner, national administrator, Volunteer Services' to AMRC Washington, NARA, RG 200, AMRC, box 109, folder 041, 17th ICRC conference 1948, Reports, General.

37. Hewins, *Count Folke Bernadotte*, 196.

38. *Seventeenth International Red Cross Conference Report* (Stockholm: n.p., August 1948), 25. *Library of Congress*<http://www.loc.gov/rr/frd/Military_Law/pdf/RC_XVIIth-RC-Conference.pdf> (accessed 14 September 2015).

39. Best, *War and Law*, 86.

40. *Seventeenth International Red Cross Conference Report.*

41. 'Report on the XVIIth International Red Cross Conference, Stockholm, Sweden, August 1948' by Basil O'Connor, president of the American National Red Cross, NARA, RG 200, AMRC, box 827, folder 494, Arc 1305.

42. Best, *War and Law*, 86–7.

43. *Seventeenth International Red Cross Conference Report.*

44. *Seventeenth International Red Cross Conference Report.* Basil O'Connor had little doubt about why the Soviets boycotted Stockholm: because of the presence of delegates from Fascist Spain and the Soviet grievances against the ICRC for not helping Soviet POWs. 'Report on the XVIIth International Red Cross Conference, Stockholm, Sweden, August 1948' by Basil O'Connor, president of the American National Red Cross. NARA, RG 200, American National Red Cross, box 827, folder 494, Arc 1305.

45. XVIIth International Red Cross Conference (Confidential) Melvin A. Glasser, secretary of the American Red Cross delegation, to Mr Caile Galub, 21 August 1948, box 109, folder 041, 17th ICRC Conference 1948, Reports, General.

46. Hewins, *Count Folke Bernadotte*, 184.

47. Ibid., 188.

48. Frank T. Cleverley, American Red Cross HQ in Washington, DC, 15 December 1948 to Publications Control Committee, NARA, RG 200 Records of the American National Red Cross 1947–1964, Box 826, Folder 494.1, ARC 1304, 'Report of the American National Red Cross prepared for the XVII. Int. Red Cross Conference, Stockholm, 20–30 August 1948'.

49. 'Report on the XVIIth International Red Cross Conference, Stockholm, Sweden, August 1948' by Basil O'Connor, president of the American National Red Cross, NARA, RG 200, American National Red Cross, box 827, folder 494, Arc 1305.

50. Ibid.

51. 'Reflections on the Stockholm meeting, received 25 January 1949, by Mrs. Joe Hume Gardner. national administrator, Volunteer Services' to AMRC Washington, NARA, RG 200, AMRC, box 109, folder 041, 17th ICRC conference 1948, Reports, General.

52. Ted Schwarz, *Walking with the Damned* (New York: Paragon House, 1992), 306. Donald Macintyre, 'Israel's Forgotten Hero: The Assassination of Count Bernadotte – and the Death of Peace', in *The Independent*, London 18 September 2008. William Henry Chamberlin, 'Bones of Contention' in the *Wall Street Journal*, 22 September 1948, 6.

53. See *Svenska Dagbladet*, 18 September 1948, 6 and *Svenska Dagbladet*, 19 September 1948, 6.

54. Sune O. Persson, *Mediation and Assassination: Count Bernadotte's Mission to Palestine* (London: Ithaca Press, 1979), 4–5. Folke Bernadotte, *Till Jerusalem. Med en epilog av generalmajor Åge Lundström* (Stockholm: Norstedt 1950). After her husband's death Estelle Bernadotte (Manville) would be very active in UN, Red Cross matters and the Girl Scouts movement in Sweden. See also UCLA Library Special Collections, Ralph J. Bunche collection. Ralph J. Bunche was Bernadotte's successor as UN envoy in Palestine/Israel and corresponded with Estelle after the assassination of Folke Bernadotte. See also Elad Ben-Dror, *Ralph Bunche and the Arab-Israeli Conflict: Mediation and the UN, 1947–1949* (London and New York: Routledge 2016).

55. Kati Marton, *A Death in Jerusalem* (New York: Pantheon Books, 1994), 260.

56. Junod, *Imperiled Red Cross*, 231.

57. Junod, *Imperiled Red Cross*, 291.

58. American Red Cross, National Headquarters, Washington, DC, 24 June 1948, 'Subject: Visit of President Ruegger, President of the International Committee of the Red Cross'. NARA, RG 200 American National Red Cross, box 103, folder 041, International Committee of the Red Cross—Visits (Paul Ruegger).

59. Forsythe, *Humanitarians*, 55.

60. Bernadotte, *Instead of Arms* 149.

61. The US State Department concluded about French intentions: 'It is not impossible that one of those conditions may be their desire to see the International Committee of the Red Cross, whose action has given rise to reservations on the

part of the USS.R. eliminated from active participation in the work of the Conference' French embassy, Washington, DC, to State Department, 19 January 1949, NARA, RG 59, box 2388, 514.2 Geneva/1-1949.

62. French Embassy, Washington, DC, to State Department, 19 January 1949, NARA, RG 59, box 2388, 514.2 Geneva/1-1949.

63. British Embassy, Washington, DC, to State Department, 14 March 1949, NARA, RG 59, box 2388, 514.2 Geneva/3-1449.

64. Department of State, incoming telegram from Bern to Secretary of State, 7 April 1949, NARA, RG 59, box 4083, 800.142/4-749.

65. State Department Memorandum from Western, 22 April 1949 (Confidential), NARA, RG 59, box 2388, FW 514.2 Geneva/4-1949 CS/MD.

66. State Department to Harrison, 6 May 1949 (Urgent, Secret), NARA, RG 59, box 2388, 514.2 Geneva/5-649.

67. Best, *War and Law*, 110.

68. Harrison to State Department, 7 May 1949 (Urgent, Secret), NARA, RG 59, box 2388, 514.2 Geneva/5-749.

69. From Moscow to Secretary of State, press articles in *Pravda*, 13 May 1949, NARA, RG 59, box 2388, 811.20200 (D)/5-1349.

70. James Crossland, *Britain and the International Committee of the Red Cross 1939–1945* (New York: Palgrave Macmillan, 2014).

71. US Embassy Lisbon to Secretary of State, Report Clattenburg, Subject: International Red Cross Conference in Stockholm, Achievements and Shortcomings, 15 September 1948, (Restricted) NARA, RG 59, box 2390, 514.2 Stockholm/9-1548.

72. Embassy of the United States of America, Lisbon, report Clattenburg 'Subject: International Red Cross Conference at Stockholm: Part Played by the International Red Cross Committee', 15 September 1948 (Confidential) NARA, RG 59, box 2390, 514.2 Stockholm 9-1548.

73. Clattenburg to Secretary of State, Subject: International Red Cross Conference at Stockholm—Report titled 'The United States Government and the International Red Cross Conference', 10 September 1948 (Confidential) NARA, RG 59, box 2390, 514.2 Stockholm/9-1048, Report, p. 3–4.

74. Clattenburg to Secretary of State, Subject: International Red Cross Conference at Stockholm—Report titled 'The United States Government and the International Red Cross Conference', 10 September 1948 (Confidential), NARA, RG 59, box 2390, 514.2 Stockholm/9-1048.

75. American embassy London to State Department 'Subject: Revision of Geneva Prisoners of war Convention and Other Humanitarian Conventions', 19 April 1948 attached memoranda Foreign Office, 'Memoranda. Work by Prisoners of War', 19 April 1948, NARA, RG 59, box 2386, 514.2A12/4-1948.

76. Embassy of the United States, Lisbon, to the Secretary of State, Subject: International Red Cross Conference Stockholm, Attitude of British Government toward Draft Convention for Protection of Civilians (TOP SECRET), 15 September 1948, NARA, RG 59, box 2390, 514.2 Stockholm/9-1548.

77. US Embassy Lisbon to the Secretary of State, Clattenburg report, Subject: International Red Cross Conference in Stockholm, Achievements and Shortcomings, 15 September 1948, NARA, RG 59, box 2390, 514.2 Stockholm/9-1548.

78. State Department to AMRC, 26 October 1948, NARA, RG 59, box 2388, 514.2 Geneva/10-2648.

79. Best, *War and Law,* 115.

80. 82nd Congress, 1st Session, Senate, Message from the President of the United States, transmitting copies of the Geneva Conventions of 12 August 1949, for the protection of war victims, which were signed on behalf of the United States and a number of other states, April 26, 1951 (included letter from Dean Acheson to the US President, 25 April 1951).

81. *Geneva Convention Relative to the Protection of Civilian Persons in Time of War of August 12, 1949, Geneva Conventions of 12 August 1949, for the Protection of War Victims,* Department of the Army (Washington, DC: US Government Printing Office, 1950), 173–5.

82. Article 87, *Geneva Convention Relative to the Protection of Civilian Persons in Time of War of August 12, 1949.*

83. Best, *War and Law,* 135.

84. Ibid., 180.

85. Ibid., 165–6.

86. Ibid., 138.

87. For the ICRC working group on war crimes headed by Max Huber, see Best, *War and Law,* 160–1.

88. Department of the Army Pamphlet no. 20–150, *Geneva Conventions of 12 August 1949, for the Protection of War Victims,* Department of the [US] Army, October 1950. Department of State Publication 3938 (Washington, DC: US Government Printing Office, 1950), 12, 14.

89. Vincent is referring to State Department telegram no. 1667 of 2 December 1949.

90. John Carter Vincent, American Minister in Bern, to the Secretary of State, on the signing of Geneva Convention for the Protection of War Victims, December 21, 1949 (Restricted) NARA, RG 59, box 2389, 514.2 Geneva/12-2149.

91. Ibid.

92. Ibid.

93. For more information on the legal and technical aspects of the Geneva Conventions, see the website of the ICRC in Geneva 'Treaties and State Parties to such treaties' <https://www.icrc.org/applic/ihl/ihl.nsf/vwTreaties1949.xsp> (accessed December 1, 2015).

94. From Bern to the Secretary of State, Restricted 2#1938, 23 December 1949. NARA, RG 59, box 2389, 514.2 Geneva/12-2349.

95. Best, *War and Law,* 110, 166.

96. '29 Nations Sign Red Cross Pacts. Revised Geneva Conventions Concern Civilians in War as Well as Combatants', *New York Times,* 9 December 1949, 5.

97. Moorehead, *Dunant's Dream*, 559.

98. ICRC President Paul Ruegger to General Marshall, 21 December 1950, The George C. Marshall Foundation, Archives, George Marshall Papers, B181, F4.

99. Foster Rhea Dulles, *The American Red Cross: A History* (New York: Harper, 1950), 527.

100. Michael Ignatieff (ed.), *Human Rights as Politics and Idolatry* (Princeton: Princeton University Press, 2001), 5.

101. Forsythe, *Humanitarians*, 55.

102. Best, *War and Law*, 210.

103. The 'Geneva Refugee Convention' of 1951 and its 1967 protocol, which is still in effect today, was also a result of the DP-crisis of the postwar years. Refugee rights were part of the human rights achievements in those years, but already shaped by the Cold War as well. See Cohen, *In War's Wake*, 11.

104. See Forsythe, *Humanitarians*, 57–8.

105. Paul Ruegger to 'Lieber Herr Generaldirektor' (Dear Mr General-Director) [possibly Arnold Bloch, director of the Aluminium–Industrie–Aktiengesellschaft, Lausanne], 23 July 1950, Archiv für Zeitgeschichte, Ruegger Nachlass 28.2.9.1, correspondence from the spring of 1948 to mid-August 1955.

106. 'Zum Wechsel in der Leitung des IKRK', *Neue Zürcher Zeitung*, 9 February 1955, evening ed., p. 1, Archiv für Zeitgeschichte Zurich, Nachlass Ruegger, Dossiers 28.2.94–28.2.10.4: 'Nur verhältnismässig wenige sind in der Lage, zu erkennen, welche gewaltige Arbeit Ruegger in dieser Zeit geleistet und welche aussergewöhnlichen Verdienste er sich um diese Institution erworben hat. Er hat sein Amt in der für das Internationale Komitee stets schwierigen und undankbaren Nachkriegszeit übernommen'.

107. Hans Haug, *Rotes Kreuz: Werden, Gestalt, Wirken* (Bern: Huber, 1966), 82.

CONCLUSION

1. Favez referred to this as an 'humanitäre Aufholjagd'; *Don Suisse*, 335.

2. Best, *War and Law*, 151–2.

3. Civilian protection was not the main focus of the UDHR, which is focused heavily on political rights.

4. Forsythe, *Humanitarians*, 58.

5. Sven Nordlund, 'The war is over – Now you can go home!' Jewish Refugees and the Swedish Labour Market in the Shadow of the Holocaust', in *'Bystanders' to the Holocaust: A Re-evaluation*, ed. David Cesarani and Paul A. Levine (London: Frank Cass, 2002), 173.

6. Alvin H. Rosenfeld, *The End of the Holocaust* (Bloomington: Indiana University Press, 2011), 52 ff., here 80.

7. Moorehead, *Dunant's Dream*, 452–3; Favez, *The Red Cross and the Holocaust*, 250.

8. Stuart E. Eizenstat, *Imperfect Justice: Looted assets, slave labor, and the unfinished business of World War II* (New York: PublicAffairs, 2003), 184.

9. 'Humanitarianism. Does help hurt?', *Economist*, 10 September 1998, p. 6.
10. Hans Magnus Enzensberger (ed.), *Krieger ohne Waffen, Das Internationale Komitee vom Roten Kreuz* (Frankfurt a. M.: Eichborn, 2001), p. 8.
11. Elie Wiesel quoted in Thomas Maissen: 'Aktivdienst, Wirtschaftsbeziehungen, Holocaust. Etappen der schweizerischen Erinnerungskultur nach 1945', in *Kriegserfahrung und nationale Identität in Europa nach 1945. Erinnerung, Säuberungsprozesse und nationales Gedächtnis*, ed. Kerstin von Lingen (Paderborn: Schöningh 2009), 242.
12. Heiner Lichtenstein, *Angepasst und treu ergeben. Das Rote Kreuz im 'Dritten Reich'* (Cologne: Bund, 1988), 10. 'Schutz von Massenmördern vor ihrer Bestrafung durch organisierte Fluchthilfe nach Übersee' als die 'schwere Sünden des Internationalen Roten Kreuzes' [...].
13. 'Moralisches Scheitern', in Tagesanzeiger Nr. 127, 3 June 1995, Archiv für Sozialgeschichte Zürich, Mappe 49.5 ZA 1 'Internationales Komitee vom Roten Kreuz' (IKRK). 'Das IKRK von heute kann nur die Unterlassungen und möglichen Irrtümer der Vergangenheit bedauern.'
14. Riccardo Orizio 'Così la Croce Rossa salvó i nazisti. L'organizzazione ora ammette: per ingenuità aiutammo Mengele, Priebke e Eichmann. Aperti gli archivi storici. Ma noi non conoscevamo la vera identità di chi voleva fuggire', in *Corriere della Sera*, 19 June 1998, 11.
15. '"Moral Failure" on Holocaust', *Los Angeles Times*, 8 October 1997.
16. Moorehead, *Dunant's Dream*, 563.
17. Clár Ní Chonghaile, 'Impunity in Conflict has Cast a Dark Shadow over Aid Work in 2015', *The Guardian* (US ed.), 28 December 2015.

Selected Bibliography

ARCHIVAL SOURCES AND ABBREVIATIONS

ACICR	Archives of the International Committee of the Red Cross, Geneva
AJDC	Archives of the American Jewish Joint Distribution Committee, New York
AfSG	Archiv für Sozialgeschichte, Zurich
AfZG	Archiv für Zeitgeschichte, Zurich
BAR	Schweizerisches Bundesarchiv, Bern
CZA	Central Zionist Archives, Jerusalem
Dartmouth	Dartmouth College Library
dodis	Diplomatische Dokumente der Schweiz
FDRL	Franklin D. Roosevelt Presidential Library and Museum, NY
GMF	The George C. Marshall Foundation, Lexington, Virginia
ITS	International Tracing Service Archives, Bad Arolsen, Germany
LOC	Library of Congress, Washington, DC
NARA	U.S. National Archives and Record Administration, College Park, MD
PRO	National Archives of the UK, Kew, England
RA	Swedish National Archives (Riksarkivet)
StaBS	State Archives of the Canton Basel–Stadt
SNB	Schweizer Nationalbibliothek, Bern
Truman Library	Harry S. Truman Presidential Museum & Library, Independence, MO
UB Basel	Universitätsbibliothek, Basel, Switzerland
UCLA	University of California, Special Collections Library
USHMM	United States Holocaust Memorial Museum, Archives and Library
YV	Yad Vashem Archives: International Institute for Holocaust Research, Yad Vashem/Jerusalem

SELECTED SECONDARY SOURCES (LIST MOST OFTEN CITED AND USED
PUBLICATIONS; FOR A COMPLETE LIST SEE THE ENDNOTES)

Barnett, Michael. *Empire of Humanity: A History of Humanitarianism.* Ithaca, NY: Cornell University Press, 2011.

Barnett, Michael and Thomas G. Weiss, eds. *Humanitarianism in Question: Politics, Power, Ethics.* Ithaca, NY and London: Cornell University Press, 2008.

Bass, Gary Jonathan. *Stay the Hand of Vengeance: The Politics of War Crimes Tribunals.* Princeton, NJ: Princeton, NJ University Press, 2002.

Baudendistel, Rainer. *Between Bombs and Good Intentions: The Red Cross and the Italo-Ethiopian War, 1935–1936.* New York: Berghahn Books, 2006.

Bauer, Yehuda. *Jews for Sale? Nazi–Jewish Negotiations, 1933–1945.* New Haven, CT: Yale University Press, 1994.

Ben-Tov, Arieh. *Facing the Holocaust in Budapest: The International Committee of the Red Cross and the Jews in Hungary, 1943–1945.* Dordrecht: Brill Academic Publishers, 1988.

Bernadotte, Folke. *Instead of Arms: Autobiographical Notes.* New York: Bonniers 1948.

Best, Geoffrey. *War and Law since 1945.* Oxford: Oxford University Press, 1994.

Biege, Bernd. *Helfer unter Hitler. Das Rote Kreuz im Dritten Reich.* Reinbek bei Hamburg: Kindler, 2000.

Braham, Randolph L. *The Politics of Genocide: The Holocaust in Hungary,* vol. 2. New York: Columbia University Press, 1994.

Breitman, Richard. *Official Secrets: What the Nazis Planned, What the British and Americans Knew.* New York: Hill and Wang, 1998.

Breitman, Richard and Norman J. W. Goda. *Hitler's Shadow: Nazi War Criminals, U.S. Intelligence and the Cold War.* Washington, DC: National Archives, 2010.

Breitman, Richard, Norman J. W. Goda, Timothy Naftali, and Robert Wolfe. *U.S. Intelligence and the Nazis.* Cambridge: Cambridge University Press, 2005.

Breitman, Richard and Allan J. Lichtman. *FDR and the Jews.* Cambridge, MA: Belknap Press, 2013.

Bugnion, François. *The International Committee of the Red Cross and the Protection of War Victims.* Geneva: International Committee of the Red Cross/Oxford: Macmillan Education, 2003.

Burleigh, Michael. *Moral Combat: A History of World War II.* Harper Collins Publishers, New York, 2011.

Cardia Vonèche, Isabelle. *Neutralité et Engagement: Les Relations entre le Comité International de la Croix-Rouge (CICR) et le Gouvernement Suisse, 1938–1945.* Lausanne: Société d'histoire de la Suisse romande, 2012.

Cohen, Gerard Daniel. *In War's Wake: Europe's Displaced Persons in the Postwar Order.* New York: Oxford University Press, 2013.

Conze, Eckart, Norbert Frei, Peter Hayes, and Moshe Zimmermann (eds.). *Das Amt und die Vergangenheit: Deutsche Diplomaten im Dritten Reich und in der Bundesrepublik.* Munich: Karl Blessing Verlag, 2010.

Crossland, James. *Britain and the International Committee of the Red Cross 1939–1945*. New York: Palgrave Macmillan, 2014.

Douglas, R. M. *Orderly and Humane: The Expulsion of the Germans after the Second World War*. New Haven, CT: Yale University Press, 2012.

Favez, Jean-Claude. *Warum schwieg das Rote Kreuz? Eine internationale Organisation und das Dritte Reich*. Munich: Deutscher Taschenbuchverlag, 1994.

Favez, Jean-Claude. *The Red Cross and the Holocaust*. Cambridge: Cambridge University Press, 1999.

Forsythe, David P. *The Humanitarians: The International Committee of the Red Cross*. Cambridge: Cambridge University Press, 2005.

Forsythe, David P. *Human Rights in International Relations*. 2nd edition. Cambridge: Cambridge University Press, 2006.

Foucault, Michel. *Discipline and Punish: The Birth of the Prison*. New York: Pantheon, 1977.

Goñi, Uki. *The Real Odessa: How Perón Brought the Nazi War Criminals to Argentina*. London: Granta, 2002.

Hale, Christopher. *Hitler's Foreign Executioners: Europe's Dirty Secret*. Stroud: The History Press, 2011.

Hewins, Ralph. *Count Folke Bernadotte, His Life and Work*. Minneapolis: T.S. Denison and Company, 1950.

Holborn, Louise. The *International Refugee Organization. a Specialized Agency of the United Nations: Its History and Work, 1946–1952*. London: Oxford University Press, 1956.

Hurd, Charles. *The Compact History of the American Red Cross*. New York: Hawthorn Books, 1959.

Ignatieff, Michael. *The Warrior's Honor: Ethnic War and the Modern Conscience*. New York Metropolitan Books, 1998.

Independent Commission of Experts Switzerland—Second World War) (ed.), *Switzerland, National Socialism and the Second World War*. Final Report. Zurich: Pendo Verlag, 2002.

Irwin, Julia F. *Making the World Safe. The American Red Cross and a Nation's Humanitarian Awakening*. New York: Oxford University Press, 2013.

Junod, Dominique-D. *The Imperiled Red Cross and the Palestine-Eretz-Yisrael Conflict, 1945–1952: The Influence of Institutional Concerns on a Humanitarian Operation*. London: Kegan Paul, 1995.

Jürg, Martin Gabriel. *The American Conception of Neutrality after 1941*. London: Macmillan, 1988.

Kershaw, Alex. *The Envoy: The Epic Rescue of the Last Jews in Europe in the Desperate Closing Months of World War II*. Philadelphia: Da Capo, 2010.

Kochavi, Arieh J. *Prelude to Nuremberg: Allied War Crimes Policy and the Question of Punishment*. Chapel Hill: University of North Carolina Press, 1998.

Kochavi, Arieh J. *Confronting Captivity: Britain and the United States and their POWs in Nazi Germany*. Chapel Hill: University of North Carolina Press, 2005.

König, Mario. *Die Schweiz, der Nationalsozialismus und der Zweite Weltkrieg.* Zurich: Pendo Verlag GmbH, 2002.

Kreis, Georg (ed.). *Switzerland and the Second World War.* London: Frank Cass, 2000.

Levine, Paul A. *From Indifference to Activism: Swedish Diplomacy and the Holocaust 1938–1944.* Uppsala: Gotab, 1996.

Lichtenstein, Heiner. *Angepaßt und treu ergeben: Das Rote Kreuz im 'Dritten Reich.'* Cologne: Bund-Verlag, 1988.

Longerich, Peter. *Heinrich Himmler: A Life.* Oxford: Oxford University Press, 2011.

Ludwig, Carl. *Die Flüchtlingspolitik der Schweiz in den Jahren 1933 bis 1955: Bericht an den Bundesrat zuhanden der eidgenössischen Räte* Beilage zum Bundesblatt. Bern: n.p., 1957.

Mächler, Stefan. *Hilfe und Ohnmacht. Der Schweizerische Israelitische Gemeindebund und die nationalsozialistische Verfolgung 1933–1945.* Zurich: Chronos 2005.

Marrus, Michael R. *The Unwanted: European Refugees in the Twentieth Century.* Oxford: Oxford University Press, 1985.

Mattioli, Aram (ed.). *Intellektuelle von rechts: Ideologie und Politik in der Schweiz 1918–1939* Zurich: Orell Fuessli, 1995.

Minear, Larry. *The Humanitarian Enterprise: Dilemmas and Discoveries.* Bloomfield, CT: Kumarian Press, 2002.

Moorehead, Caroline. *Dunant's Dream: War, Switzerland, and the History of the Red Cross.* New York: Harper Collins, 1999.

Morgenbrod, Brigitt, and Stephanie Merkenich. *Das Deutsche Rote Kreuz unter der NS-Diktatur 1933–1945. Mit einem Geleitwort von Rudolf Seiters und einem Vorwort von Hans Mommsen.* Paderborn u.a.: Ferdinand Schöningh, 2008.

Moyn, Samuel. *The Last Utopia. Human Rights in History.* Cambridge, MA: Belknap Press of Harvard University Press, 2010.

Persson, Sune. *Escape from the Third Reich. The Harrowing True Story of the Largest Rescue Effort Inside Nazi Germany.* New York: Skyhorse Publishing 2009.

Phayer, Michael. *Pius XII, the Holocaust, and the Cold War.* Bloomington: Indiana University Press, 2007.

Pictet, Jean. *The Fundamental Principles of the Red Cross Proclaimed by the Twentieth International Conference of the Red Cross, Vienna, 1965: Commentary.* Geneva: Henry Dunant Institute, 1979.

Rashke, Richard. *Useful Enemies: John Demjanjuk and America's Open-Door Policy for Nazi War Criminals.* Harrison, NY: Delphinium, 2013.

Reginbogin, Herbert R. *Faces of Neutrality: A Comparative Analysis of the Neutrality of Switzerland and Other Neutral Nations during WWII.* Berlin: LIT Verlag, 2009.

Rey-Schyrr, Catherine. *De Yalta à Dien Bien Phu. Historie du Comité international de la Croix-Rouge, 1945–1955.* Geneva, CICR et Georg Editeur, 2007.

Riegner, Gerhart M. *Never Despair: Sixty Years in the Service of the Jewish People and the Cause of Human Rights.* Chicago: Ivan R. Dee, 2006.

Riesenberger, Dieter. *Das Deutsche Rote Kreuz. Eine Geschichte 1864–1990.* Munich: Ferdinand Schöningh, 2002.

Rings, Werner. *Schweiz im Krieg 1933–1945, Ein Bericht.* Zurich: Chronos, 1997.

Schomann, Stefan. *Im Zeichen der Menschlichkeit: Geschichte und Gegenwart des Deutschen Roten Kreuzes.* Munich: Deutsche Verlags-Anstalt, 2013.

Sereny, Gitta. *Into That Darkness: From Mercy Killing to Mass Murder.* London: André Deutsch 1974.

Simpson, Christopher. *Blowback: America's Recruitment of Nazis and Its Effects on the Cold War.* New York: Weidenfeld and Nicolson, 1988.

Siordet, Frederic. *Inter Arma Caritas: The Work of the International Committee of the Red Cross during the Second World War.* Geneva: International Committee of the Red Cross, 1947.

Stamm, Konrad. *Der 'grosse Stucki'. Eine schweizerische Karriere von weltmännischem Format. Minister Walter Stucki (1888–1963).* Zurich: Verlag Neue Zürcher Zeitung, 2013.

Stauffer, Paul. *Zwischen Hoffmannsthal und Hitler, Carl J. Burkhardt.—einer aussergewöhnlichen Existenz.* Zurich: Verlag Neue Zürcher Zeitung, 1991.

Stauffer, Paul. *'Sechs furchtbare Jahre…' Auf den Spuren Carl J. Burckhardts durch den Zweiten Weltkrieg.* Zurich: Verlag Neue Zürcher Zeitung, 1998.

Steinacher, Gerald. *Nazis on the Run: How Hitler's Henchmen Fled Justice.* Oxford: Oxford University Press, 2011.

Steinacher, Gerald (ed.). *Tra Duce, Führer e Negus: l'Alto Adige e la guerra d'Abissinia 1935–1941.* Trento: Temi, 2008.

Steinacher, Gerald. *'Als der gute Samariter die Schweiz retten sollte:* Das Rote Kreuz im Dienst der geistigen Landesverteidigung', in Peter Meilaender and Hans Rindisbacher (eds.), *Das Kalb vor der Gotthardpost: Swiss Culture, History, and Politics in the Work of Peter von Matt.* Bern: Peter Lang, 2016 (forthcoming).

Steinacher, Gerald. 'The Red Cross and the Holocaust: 1942 as a Turning Point for the Humanitarians?', in Dan Michman, Dina Porat et al. (eds.), *The End of 1942—A Turning Point in World War II?* Jerusalem: Yad Vashem 2016 (forthcoming).

Torpey, John. *The Invention of the Passport: Surveillance, Citizenship, and the State.* Cambridge: Cambridge University Press, 2000.

Unabhängige Expertenkommission Schweiz (UEK),—Zweiter Weltkrieg, *Die Schweiz und Flüchtlinge zur Zeit des Nationalsozialismus.* Bern: Eidgenössische Drucksachen- und Materialzentrale, 1999.

van Dongen, Luc. *La Suisse face à la seconde guerre mondiale 1945–1948: Émergence et construction d'une mémoire publique.* 2nd ed. Geneva: Les Bastions, 1998.

von Klemperer, Klemens. *German Resistance against Hitler: The Search for Allies Abroad, 1938–1945.* Oxford: Clarendon Press, 1992.

von Lingen, Kerstin. *SS und Secret Service: 'Verschwörung des Schweigens': Der Fall Karl Wolff.* Paderborn: Schöningh, 2010.

Wallenberg, Raoul. *Letters and Dispatches 1924–1944.* New York: Arcade, 1995.

Wasserstein, Bernard. *Britain and the Jews of Europe 1939–1945.* London: Clarendon Press, 1979.

Wylie, Neville. *Britain, Switzerland and the Second World War*. Oxford: Oxford University Press, 2003.

Wylie, Neville. *Barbed Wire Diplomacy: Britain, Germany, and the Politics of Prisoners of War, 1939–1945*. Oxford: Oxford University Press, 2010.

Wylie, Neville (ed.). *European Neutrals and Non-Belligerents During the Second World War*. Cambridge: Cambridge University Press, Reissue, 2014.

Wyman, David S. *The Abandonment of the Jews: America and the Holocaust 1941–1945*. New York: Pantheon Books, 1984.

Wyman, Mark. *DPs: Europe's Displaced Persons*. Ithaca, NY: Cornell University Press, 1998.

Zweig-Strauss, Hanna. *Saly Mayer, 1882–1950: Ein Retter jüdischen Lebens während des Holocaust*. Cologne: Böhlau, 2007.

Index of Names